A HISTORY OF IRELAND *in* INTERNATIONAL RELATIONS

A HISTORY
OF IRELAND *in*
INTERNATIONAL
RELATIONS

OWEN McGEE

IRISH ACADEMIC PRESS

First published in 2020 by
Irish Academic Press
10 George's Street
Newbridge
Co. Kildare
Ireland
www.iap.ie

9781788551137 (Paper)
9781788551144 (Kindle)
9781788551151 (Epub)
9781788551168 (PDF)

British Library Cataloguing in Publication Data
An entry can be found on request

Library of Congress Cataloging in Publication Data
An entry can be found on request

All images courtesy of Wikimedia Commons, except Frank Aiken at the
UN, courtesy of UN Photo/MB.

Typeset in Minion Pro 11.5/14.5 pt

Cover front: detail from J.M. Morton, *The New Ireland* (London, 1938).

For Ailis

Contents

Introduction

Has Ireland a Significant International Story to Tell?

The writing of international history always has an economic focus, even within strategic studies.[1] Within this 'macro-economic' field, if the resources of all nations theoretically count, the politics of small nations usually figure only when they are deemed significant within the world of international finance.[2] Reflecting this, most studies of Ireland on the world stage do not precede the country's embrace of the Eurozone. Thereafter, the Irish experience was often treated as a case study of modernisation.[3] Degrees of influence within international relations have often been equated with an ability to determine 'whose story wins'.[4] As small nations rarely figure prominently in international relations, their stories are even less likely to do so. This can produce defensive reactions. Some nineteenth-century Irish writers attributed the absence of studies of Ireland on the world stage to the fact that 'our souls were not confined to the pages of a cheque-book' and the Irish public's belief that 'we have not been exclusively created for the worship of the golden calf'.[5] More recently, Irish foreign ministers have claimed a century of continuity in the Irish state's sense of values.[6] However, the fact that the first Irish policy document on foreign affairs dates only from the time of the country's entry into the European Union indicates the relevance of the aforementioned scholarly consensus regarding the writing of international history.[7]

Up until at least the 1970s, knowledge of international affairs in Ireland was reputedly confined to 'a small circle of cognoscenti'.[8] This consisted mostly of diplomats who kept a very low profile, did not author books and believed that public discussion of Ireland's role in international relations was best avoided, even in the country's national parliament, because the geopolitical realities governing the Irish state were matters that 'few Irish policymakers outside the military and diplomatic nexus understood'.[9] In a curious parallel with the former eastern bloc, Irish state archives only began to be fully opened during the 1990s.[10] Ireland may not have been worshipping the golden calf, but its inhabitants could have been forgiven if they wondered why their government was so secretive. Nevertheless, certain realities were self-evident. Ireland did not receive a state visit from any country until the 1960s; an event that is still in the living memory of much of its population.[11] Reflecting this, during the storied political career of Éamon de Valera (1882–1975), Ireland went from a position of having no recognised ambassadors to a grand total of fourteen ambassadors, but this was still less than a quarter of the diplomatic representation of the smallest of mainland European states. Only in the last couple of decades has Ireland developed a diplomatic corps of a size comparable to that of a small European nation and, in turn, started to embrace a truly broad range of international concerns.[12] What value, therefore, lies in a strictly chronological and historical study of the evolution of Ireland's international profile?

Historians have a natural tendency to be preoccupied with the notion of roots and branches, even if they are not necessarily believers in the idea of canonical texts whose influence is felt throughout all ages.[13] In the United States, for instance, this has been reflected by a deep preoccupation with the vision of the state's founding fathers and the degree to which it either remains relevant or was ever truly coherent in the first place.[14] Few have doubted A.J.P. Taylor's belief that Britain's quintessential role in international relations was rooted in the geopolitics underpinning the Congress of Vienna (1815).[15] Nevertheless, practitioners of international history in Britain have often deemed it more important to look as far back as early-modern reformations or even to medieval statecraft.[16] There are, of course, other examples. Not all contemporary theorists on international relations who speculate on the economic rise of Asia are blind to the fact that the history of Japan or India, let alone China, did not begin with the bombing of Hiroshima or the creation of Pakistan.[17] Likewise, human rights theorists with a legal background understand that such ideas did not begin with the

United Nations. Rather, theories of natural law and natural rights can be traced back to classical antiquity, while some have even suggested that the birth of a quintessentially modern notion of human rights, with a particular emphasis on racial equality, began with Catholic missionaries in early-modern South America.[18] Norman Davies' students of history in the College of Europe's headquarters in Bruges and Warsaw have been keen to argue that the existence of centuries of writings on the idea of a European civilisation indicates that the Anglo-American, or 'cold war', consensus regarding an inherent geopolitical and ideological balance of power within Europe was largely artificial.[19] Clearly, as Zara Steiner has pointed out, there are many different vantage points and approaches that can be adopted in the writing of international history.[20]

This study does not attempt to present Ireland's story as having been pivotal in international relations. However, it does attempt to counterbalance the frequently insular narratives of the Republic of Ireland and Northern Ireland by placing them in the context of a broader narrative on international history. Irish studies of international affairs and the early years of the Irish state receive much attention. However, the pages of *International Organization* and various European or UN policy documents are treated as no less important. Although it is a work of political history rather than a theoretical or macro-economic study, this book hopes to answer the call of the late Garret FitzGerald for the international economic context behind Irish political history to be fully integrated into the narrative of both the Irish state and its international relations.[21] To the best of the author's knowledge, ideological shortcuts have been avoided while attempting this.

After the establishment of Ireland's International Financial Services Centre in 1987, debates on Ireland's relationship with Europe became more vibrant and occasionally took a polemical turn.[22] The post-1945 European integration project was closely related to developments in the world of international finance. Ireland's initial reaction to this trend was fear of being drawn into foreign wars. This book suggests, however, that the European project was certainly of note from its inception for its evidently genuine commitment to embracing equally the concerns of both small and large nations in order to facilitate peace.[23] For this very reason, Ireland's international profile as a small nation has become tied into the greater European question of whether or not economics and questions of education can become the future determinant of the international order more so than military stratagem.[24] In the light of this trend, some have asked whether or not there is room for the Irish state or, indeed, Europe to remould international debates through the exercise a degree of 'smart power' in international relations.[25] If no conclusive answer can be offered to that question, this idea nevertheless mirrors very traditional Irish debates on questions such as pacifism, anti-belligerence and military neutrality.[26] It also reflects broader trends in works of international relations theory, such as the relationship between economic change and human rights.[27] This study surveys a wide selection of national and international literature on such themes to clarify when or where these debates have met and, in particular, how the Irish experience fits within the broader story of historical developments in international relations. In short, does Ireland have a significant international story to tell in the light of its own historical experience? It is hoped that readers of this book may find some original answers to that question or else discover grounds for drawing their own original conclusions.

Endnotes

1 Zara Steiner, 'On writing international history', *International affairs, vol. 73 no. 3: globalisation and international relations* (Jul. 1997), 531.

2 Paul Kennedy, *The rise and fall of the great powers: economic change and military conflict from 1500 to 2000* (New York and London, 1988).

3 William Crotty, D.E. Schmitt (eds), *Ireland on the world stage* (New York, 2002); Ben Tonra, *Global citizen and European republic: Irish foreign policy in transition* (Manchester, 2006); B. Tonra, M. Kennedy, J. Doyle, N. Dorr (eds), *Irish foreign policy* (Dublin, 2012).

4 Joseph Nye, 'The information revolution and soft power', *Current history*, vol. 113 (2014), 19–22.

5 Owen McGee (ed.), *Eugene Davis' souvenirs of Irish footprints over Europe* (1889, 2nd ed., Dublin, 2006), 179–80.

6 Charles Flanagan, 'Identity and values in Irish foreign policy', *Irish studies in international affairs* (2016), 1–5.

7 Department of foreign affairs, *Challenges and opportunities abroad: white paper on foreign policy* (Dublin, 1996).

8 E.M. Browne, 'Ireland in the EEC', *The world today*, vol. 31 no. 10 (Oct. 1975), 424–32.

9 Michael Kennedy, 'Irish foreign policy 1919–1973', in Thomas Bartlett (ed.), *Cambridge history of Ireland*, vol. 4 (Cambridge, 2017), 604–5, ft. 4 (quote).

10 Ciaran Brady (ed.), *Interpreting Irish history* (Dublin, 1994), 151–3.

11   Government of Ireland, *A memory of John Fitzgerald Kennedy: visit to Ireland, 26–29 June 1963* (Dublin, 1964).

12   Department of foreign affairs and trade, *The global island: Ireland's foreign policy for a changing world* (Dublin, 2015).

13   Martin Puchner, *The written world: how literature shapes history* (New York, 2017).

14   Joyce Appleby, *Liberalism and republicanism in the historical imagination* (New York, 1992).

15   A.J.P. Taylor, *Europe: grandeur and decline* (London, 1967).

16   Brendan Simms, *Britain's Europe: a thousand years of conflict and cooperation* (London, 2016).

17   Richard Storry, *A history of modern Japan* (London, 1982).

18   Brian Tierney, *The idea of natural rights* (New York, 1997); F.A.M. von Geusau, *Neither justice nor order: reflections on the state of the law of nations* (Tilburg, 2014), chapter 4.

19   Norman Davies, *Europe: a history* (Oxford, 1996); F.A.M. von Geusau, *Cultural diplomacy: waging war by other means?* (Tilburg, 2009).

20   Zara Steiner, 'On writing international history', *International affairs, vol. 73 no. 3: globalisation and international relations* (Jul. 1997), 531–46.

21   Garret FitzGerald, *Reflections on the Irish state* (Dublin, 2003), ix.

22   John Cooney, Tony McGarry, *Ireland and Europe in times of world change: Humbert International School chronicle and directory 1987–2002* (Ballina, 2002).

23   B.A. McKenzie, 'The European Youth Campaign in Ireland: neutrality, Americanisation and the cold war 1950 to 1959', *Diplomatic history*, vol. 40 no. 3 (2016), 421–44.

24   Frans Alting von Geusau, *European unification into the twenty-first century* (Tilburg, 2012); *International organization: transnational relations and world politics,* vol. 25 no. 3 (summer 1971).

25   Mark Leonard, J. Pisani-Ferry, E. Ribokova, J. Sharipo, G. Wolff, 'Security Europe's economic sovereignty', *Survival*, vol. 61 no. 5 (2019), 75–98.

26   M. Kennedy, D. McMahon (eds) *Obligations and responsibilities: Ireland and the United Nations* (Dublin, 2005).

27   *International organization: the global partnership: international agencies and economic development*, vol. 22 no.1 (winter 1968); *International organization: international institutions and environmental crisis*, vol. 26 no. 2 (spring 1972); Ian Clark, *Globalization and international relations theory* (Oxford, 1999); Paul Collier, *Wars, guns and votes: democracy in dangerous places* (London, 2005).

1

Ireland's Place in World History: From the Fianna to the First World War

If ancient Greece and Rome were the cradle of European civilisation, for much of history Ireland existed independently from this idea of civilisation. German scholars of the Celtic west of Europe have suggested that the Irish were 'the most important and influential of the Celtic peoples', but Celtic culture was driven forcibly from the European continent by the Roman Empire.[1] The Irish produced one of the earliest forms of written language and received Christianity early, but rather than diocesan churches they promoted monastic orders whose illuminated manuscripts were noteworthy for developing a uniquely Celtic artistic imagery. Irish monks also served as missionaries abroad, including in central Europe. Nevertheless, a defining trait of Irish society was its ambivalent attitude to the sea. Although the Irish were self-consciously islanders, they were not a great seafaring people and most always chose to live inland. Irish explorations of the Atlantic and the North Sea were not unknown, but were limited because of the harshness of the climate on the Atlantic coastline. Here circular stone forts had existed since the earliest times, but they were seemingly designed to guard against attacks by land rather than invasions by sea.[2]

Despite a broadly similar culture across the island, scholars have often considered that a greater degree of political unity existed between Ulster, in the north of Ireland, and Scotland than between various parts of the island of Ireland itself.[3] Before and after the arrival of Christianity, northern Irish kings resided near the northeast coast of

Ireland, which is only a short distance from the west coast of Scotland.[4] Law tracts in the Irish language (Gaeilge) show that their yearly dues, unlike that of all other Irish kingdoms, included ships.[5] Both medieval Irish wonder voyage literature and the earliest Irish heroic sagas of the Fianna emanated from this region. Irish voyage literature involved the discovery of fantasy islands with magical qualities. Although similar metaphors existed in ancient Greek literatures, Irish belief systems were noticeably different. Befitting the status of the Irish as northern Europeans, a spiritual notion of otherworldly ghosts rather than a Mediterranean belief in underworld demons was paramount.[6] Meanwhile, the geopolitics of this literature was rooted in northern Irish familiarity with the numerous islands off the western coast of Scotland: 'Dáil Éireann', the title of the modern Irish parliamentary assembly, is itself a name derived from ancient Irish kingdoms, including Ulster kingdoms that encompassed western Scottish isles.[7] From the sixth until the sixteenth century, a northern O'Neill dynasty, with roots in the west of Ireland, frequently claimed to be the legitimate rulers of the whole of Ireland. The fact that the Christian church established its ecclesiastical capital (Armagh) within the O'Neill kingdom probably bolstered their purely secular claim to rule, but it was rarely, if ever, recognised.[8]

The western Scottish isles were considered to be a homogenous Kingdom of the Isles during the short-lived North Sea Empire of King Cnut, an eleventh-century Danish king who also conquered England and whose daughter married the Holy Roman Emperor. Cnut's equating secular rulers' powerlessness before God with their inability to command the seas may have reflected the influence of an Irish Christian culture in which sea voyages were often considered to serve 'a penitential function'.[9] Despite centuries of raids by sea, Scandinavian culture never became a dominant force in Ireland. On the east coast, the future capital of Dublin minted coinage for Cnut and became a trading centre with a focus on Wales and northern England. In the early eleventh century, forces led by Brian Bóruma (Boru), a southern Irish king who hoped to receive recognition as king of all Ireland, defeated Danish-backed forces in this region, but Irish society remained very poorly equipped to deal with invasions by sea.[10] As a result, native Irish kings were completely unable to deal with a Norman invasion by sea in the late twelfth century, which also introduced to Ireland the practice of feudalism. This was a Latin legal system under which land was assigned to individuals purely on the basis of royal decrees. For four centuries, this new, centralised legal and political order would coexist alongside a native Irish society characterised by local dynastic kingdoms.

The Normans created new, fortified town walls and castles to subjugate local populations while also encouraging native Irish chieftains to act as mercenaries in Anglo-Scottish wars.[11] Through such military expeditions, the Irish learnt new methods of horsemanship, archery and shipbuilding, while fortified stone dwellings, akin to tower homes rather than castles, became more common. Ulster soldiers who fought as part of Edward I's invasion of western Scotland (1296–1304) were able to re-establish themselves as local Scottish lords, in the process making the west coast of Scotland and the Kingdom of the Isles nominally safe for the Norman kings of England while also being considered an acceptable arrangement by opposing Scottish kings.[12] This allowed many Irish chieftains to occupy a secure middle ground in Norman society that seemed to guarantee political stability. As a result, many reacted unfavourably when Donal O'Neill, calling himself 'King of Ulster and, by hereditary right, true heir of the whole of Ireland', supported the Scottish Bruce dynasty when it defied secular and clerical rulers by launching a major, albeit unsuccessful, invasion of Ireland (1315–18). This campaign claimed that the Irish and Scottish nations were one, that both aspired that 'God willing, our nation may be restored to her former liberty', while O'Neill would defend his actions by sending a remonstrance to Pope John XXII, in which he accused the Normans of England of inherent treachery and argued that it was the Irish alone who had 'eminently endowed the Irish church'.[13]

A desire to emphasise an inheritance to rule that predated Norman times surfaced across Irish-speaking society during the fourteenth century, including in Scotland and the Kingdom of the Isles, which retained its own coronation rites, bishop and legal system, including a record-keeper and weights-and-measures officer.[14] Gaelic chieftains also expected none but their own family members to hold high ecclesiastical office. This was a cause of tension because in the eyes of the diocesan church, which was urban and Latin speaking, Gaeilge speakers' sense of values was less Christian than the new Norman settlers.[15] Particularly in the northern half of the country, Irish society was predominantly rural, nomadic and caste-based, and dealt not in currency but exclusively in goods and even (in the post-Viking age) people.[16] It has been suggested that the closest international parallel with Irish society at this time can actually be found in Japan, where a similar bardic, as well as military-chieftain, culture existed, and 'constant feuding between the clans ... was not the ideal circumstance for traders and merchants'.[17]

Although Irish music and culture partly became a tool of Christian expression, reputedly at English insistence, churchmen condemned the arts of poetry and music that, in Irish society, were not used for mere artistic or entertainment purposes. Instead, they were used to celebrate the status of an Irish bardic tradition as the supposed custodian of literally *all* values, learning and sense of history, dating back to the earliest times.[18] A native style of music, played on bagpipes or the wire-strung harp, existed to accompany such recitations, but this musical art form was 'not merely not European' but was 'quite remote from it', being 'closer to some forms of Oriental music', practiced from the Middle to Far East, in its combined use of grace notes, improvisation and historical storytelling.[19] Irish culture became self-referential and historicist to a high degree because of the absence of an Irish-speaking population abroad with which to engage in cultural exchanges, except in Scotland. Critically, however, this link with Scotland began to decline during the later fourteenth century. Continental political ties developed among the Scottish nobility through their intermarriage with the French during the Anglo-French wars of the fourteenth and fifteenth centuries, but no corresponding development took place within Ireland. Instead, intermarriage between Irish and old Norman families created a greater degree of insularity within Irish society, as did a growing religious use, by the fifteenth century, of Irish rather than Latin as the language of communication.[20]

The Irish adapted to urban, or Latin, culture better in the southern half of the island. By the fourteenth century, Gaeilge-speaking Irish noble families acted alongside the Normans as traders in several port towns along the southern coastline of Ireland. Reflecting Anglo-Norman ties with Calais and the European lowlands, these Irish families traded materials and foodstuffs, such as hides and fish, with Belgium, France and Spain and, soon thereafter, also made inroads via Bristol into business life in Wales and England. The English Crown, however, viewed the Irish as inherently disloyal, as well as inhabitants of a different domain, and so responded with discriminatory legislation.[21] Under the Statute of Kilkenny, written in French during 1366 (English would not become the language of England until the fifteenth century), the King's subjects were forbidden to trade or intermarry with the Irish, to use the Irish language or to recognise Irish law. Contact with Irish musicians, poets and singers – each of whom occupied royal court status within Gaeilge-speaking Irish society – were also forbidden 'in view of the danger of espionage'.[22] On the whole, however, trade and commerce served to strengthen Anglo-Irish links because the overseas trade of Dublin in particular was confined to the Irish Sea, involved more imports than exports and attempted to regulate other urban trade within Ireland.[23]

The pivotal role of bankers and a mercantile–military elite in fifteenth-century Europe impacted on Ireland during the dynasty of the Tudors, a family of Welsh origins that put an end to Norman rule in England in 1485 and allowed private commercial enterprise to become a feature of government.[24] The Tudors reinvented Anglo-Irish relations by refusing to recognise the historic Kingdom of the Isles and making parliamentary government (which had hitherto met rarely in either England or Ireland) an instrument of English power by ruling that all Irish parliaments must be perpetually subordinate to the English parliament. The motive of the Tudor policy of 'leaving the great Irish families undisturbed as long as they acknowledged the royal authority in church and state' (a policy often termed 'surrender and re-grant') was primarily financial, but it served to undermine Gaelic Irish society quickly, most notably in Ulster.[25] Amidst opposition, some of the northern O'Neills accepted Tudor titles and developed a familiarity with London court society primarily because the traditional O'Neill claim to kingship was not only in the process of being outlawed but also faced a new military opposition from loyal Scottish lords.[26] This soon created an Irish determination to look to the European continent for alternative allies. The emergence of Scottish dynastic ties to England and France coincided with the creation of Scottish cities and universities during the fifteenth century, but attempts to found a university in Ireland, during 1320 and 1464, had failed, while Irish students were often not welcome in England.[27] The exclusion of Ireland from the continental intellectual renaissance marked primarily by the late medieval creation of the university had caused Ireland to become something of an educational backwater for the first time.[28]

During the later sixteenth century, Elizabeth I's programme of dissolving Irish monasteries coincided with the state execution of all clergymen who refused to accept the English Crown as the religious head of Christendom. It also led to the creation of the first Irish university, Trinity College in Dublin, nominally as a Protestant theological college. As a response, Catholic religious orders founded the first of many Irish Colleges on the European continent. The first was created in Spain, where trading links had long existed between Gaelic Irish chieftains near the west and southwest coasts of Ireland and regions such as Galicia. In common with Irish trade with Bordeaux, the Spanish lowlands, Brittany and Italy, these trade links were now purposively curtailed by legislation.[29] There was no Irish support for the attempted Spanish invasion of England in 1588. Some Irish nobles, however, had sent family members to Spanish Flanders to acquire more modern military expertise. In the 1590s, Ulster chieftains made the unusual move of considering pledging their allegiance to the Spanish Hapsburg dynasty, in an attempt to acquire Spanish assistance, whilst endeavouring to appeal to a distinct sense of Irish nationality based on Catholicism. They mounted a resistance to English rule that, in the wake of a couple of military victories, seemed likely to stimulate a nationwide rebellion, but this endeavour was defeated in 1602 in the wake of a very small Spanish invasion attempt on the southern coast of Ireland.[30] Meanwhile, on a national level, the formation of over a dozen Irish Colleges on the European continent, located in Spain, Portugal, Belgium, France, Italy and even Prague, was of limited significance because they were designed primarily for the training of priests. Although no longer complete unknowns in European court society, Irishmen were generally viewed in Europe only as a potential source of additional manpower, be it for political intrigues on the continent itself or against England, rather than as representatives of a distinct nation in international relations.[31] This was because the Irish parliament served little purpose other than to make requests for English subsidies to sustain an insolvent Irish administration that was nevertheless able to facilitate extensive exchequer returns to London, based upon rents, customs and taxes, that helped to ensure that 'Irish money balanced the royal books' of England.[32]

The increasingly confessional nature of European states did not reflect the origins, nature and purpose of contemporary wars in Europe where the balance of power was considered to rest with the outcomes of Atlantic trade wars that were fought between the Spanish, French, Dutch and English. The Dutch played the most pivotal role because their bankers were the most adept financiers of both wars and state debts. Dutch tradesmen would succeed in getting appointed as mayors of major Irish towns such as Dublin, Drogheda and Limerick several times over the course of the seventeenth century.[33] The status of the Netherlands as the cockpit of Europe was reflected by its desire to maintain its competitive advantage in the world of trade and its consequent authorship of the rules of international relations. Hugo Grotius defined the bases of international law as resting equally upon a recognition of the sovereignty of nation-states and their right to free trade on the ocean. An alternative method the Dutch employed to maintain their advantage, however, was to sustain their army through hiring soldiers from within other states' jurisdiction.[34] Irish expatriate soldiers, most notably Owen Roe O'Neill, attained senior military rank in the Netherlands, albeit in the Spanish Netherlands. Here O'Neill would suggest during the 1620s that an effort should be made to establish an Irish republic despite the fact that the only republic in Europe at the time was Spain's enemy, the United Provinces of the Netherlands (established 1581), the sovereignty of which would not be recognised by Spain until the Westphalia settlement of 1648.[35]

The primary objective of the Tudor and Stuart dynasties in Britain was maximising the power of the English navy through financial speculation in colonial plantation schemes, beginning in Ireland and subsequently in North America. After initial Tudor plantations in the eastern Irish province of Leinster and the southern Irish province of Munster, upon the accession of the Stuarts a major plantation scheme was launched in Ulster. As this was launched at the same time as the first English plantation scheme in America, it effectively introduced a new dynamic into the framing of Irish political developments: namely, the development of an Atlantic economy. In the opinion of Sir Walter Raleigh (1554–1618), this was based upon one simple principle: 'whosoever commands the sea, commands the trade; whosoever commands the trade commands the riches of the world and consequently the world itself.[36] London and lowland Scottish investors profited greatly from the plantation of Ulster (purchasing, for instance, the entire townland of Derry), which had much of the best quality land in Ireland. A perpetual sense of insecurity would exist among these planters, however, because the manner in which courts arranged the dispossession of land from its prior legal owners was frequently illegal.[37] Among the profiteers was Sir Arthur Chichester, 'the landless second son of a minor Devonshire gentleman', who suddenly became exclusive owner of all commercial shipping and fishing rights in Ulster as well as one of the largest landed estates in either Britain or Ireland. Regarding this development, historian Sean Connolly has noted that

> All this is, at first sight, little short of piracy, yet public policy [supported by the Privy Council of Scotland] also played a part in the transactions ... The two enterprises were in fact complimentary. Gaelic Ulster and Gaelic Scotland represented a single ungovernable hinterland. The passage back and forth across the narrow waters of the North Channel of mercenary fighters had long sustained the rebelliousness of one [Ulster] and the militarised disorder of the other [Scotland]. Plantation in Ulster, along with continued efforts to discipline the clan chiefs of the Highlands and Islands, would fracture this zone ... removing a major threat to the security of all three British kingdoms ... [and] transformed irreversibly the face of what had previously been the last stronghold of Gaelic Ireland.[38]

Being urban recipients of state aid, many of these planters were of note for introducing more commercial practices into Irish agriculture. Meanwhile, during the 1630s, Sir Thomas Wentworth, a new English appointee to lead the Irish administration, attained a complete monopoly of all Irish trade in Virginia tobacco.[39] Maryland, the second such American colony, was supposed to be filled exclusively with unwanted Catholic subjects. Controversially, however, rather than encouraging his unwanted (Irish) Catholic subjects to become planters, Wentworth allowed them to join in their thousands the Spanish army in Flanders in an effort to improve Anglo-Spanish relations. This proved to be a major setback to Anglo-Dutch relations. In turn, it created controversy over the specific manner in which Charles I was financing the Royal Navy, causing a civil war to break out in England in which Wentworth became the first political casualty.[40] Just prior to his death, Wentworth had extended the operations of the English admiralty to Ireland in an effort to suppress piracy and enhance English security while he also disbanded the Irish parliament.[41] Irish Catholics from the south of Ireland reacted by creating an alternative form of political assembly known as the Irish Confederation. Meanwhile, Owen Roe O'Neill, who had received the military services of those who had left for Spanish Flanders, returned to Ireland to lead an undisciplined rebel force in Ulster. Both of these groups claimed to support the Stuart king and did not seek any foreign intervention, but the Irish Confederation would be offered, not by its own request, the services of a papal nuncio who was expected to act in a purely advisory capacity on church–state relations.[42]

The Irish Confederation dissolved voluntarily on receiving promises from English royalists that its demand for national political rights for Ireland, including a separate Irish admiralty as well as full liberties for Irish Catholics, would be met.[43] These promises were made shortly before the king's trial and execution in 1649, however, and so they would soon be broken. O'Neill, who was looked upon by many Irish speakers in Ulster as a potential Irish king, died suddenly later the same year not long after he signed a truce with an English parliamentarian force that had come to Ireland with Oliver Cromwell.[44] Cromwell's reputation in Ireland would be shaped primarily by his decision to ignore the truce that was signed with O'Neill as soon as the latter died. Thereafter, Cromwell hunted down all alleged Irish rebels and introduced land laws that denied all Catholics the right to own land. During Cromwell's Irish campaigns of the 1650s, up to 30 per cent of the Irish population would be lost due to warfare, plague or exodus.[45] Meanwhile, after being 'all things to all men' for the duration of the English civil war, the southern Irish royalist James Butler intrigued for the underground court of Charles II on the European continent, looking for French and Spanish support against Cromwell, before the restoration of the Stuart monarchy in 1660 made this unnecessary. Thereafter, as a reward, Butler was granted land and a university chancellorship in England; was promoted from a marquis to the Duke of Ormond; and, as a long-term leader of an Irish administration, controversially maintained all Cromwell's discriminatory legislation. Ormond could also be said to have laid the basis for the future integration of Ireland into the British Empire by arranging that virtually all appointees to lead the Irish administration would henceforth be drawn from the ranks of career diplomats in the English foreign office which, upon the Act of Union with Scotland in 1707, essentially became a British foreign office.[46] In the words of Sir William Temple, who was England's diplomat at the Hague at the same time as he directed government policy regarding Ireland, the sole purpose of the Irish administration was to provide security for ever-growing English investments and plantation schemes in Ireland, to be overseen by English appointees who would 'own and support upon all occasions that which is truly a loyal English protestant interest'.[47] This policy was upheld by all eighteenth-century Irish parliaments, each of which upheld Cromwellian land settlements that denied Catholics the right to exercise political power and in the process created a strongly colonial mindset among a new ruling class.[48]

Over the course of the eighteenth century, Dublin became a hub for financial activity, including the creation of new banks and a national canal network. Plans were also implemented to make Dublin a more elegant city with fine parks and buildings to house a governmental administration and parliament.[49] However, although Ireland was nominally a distinct kingdom, it was governed in the manner of a colony where the first priority was to create a mercantile system to serve greater British economic interests, thereby ensuring that any expansion in overseas trade that operated via Ireland did not enhance the profile of the country in any way.[50] Ireland's absence of valuable natural resources, excepting wood and peat, had made overseas trade essential to its prosperity. Nevertheless, the British aristocracy usually considered the most prominent Irish landowners, even Ormond, to be poor country squires because they were literally just one step away from bankruptcy.[51] Meanwhile, the wealth and political influence of new Irish parliamentary leaders, who built stately homes in Ireland, was purposively made dependent on receiving their education and 'marrying well' in England, the latter feat being something that frequently served as a ticket to inheriting family seats in both the British and Irish parliaments.[52] Against this political backdrop, occasional stirrings of a colonial or cultural nationalism in eighteenth-century Irish writings were of comparatively little significance.

Jonathan Swift, a Dublin-born Protestant clergyman and pamphleteer of English parentage, called on the British Royal Navy to conquer the Spanish Indies rather than waste English money on land wars in Europe.[53] George Berkeley, a philosophical Irish Protestant bishop of English parentage, celebrated the importance of the new Bank of England to all such enterprises. By helping to enhance the performance of British government stock on the Amsterdam stock exchange, it had created a strong Anglo-Dutch banking nexus and stimulated public finance schemes in England that satisfied commercial interests in both the imperial parliament and the London stock exchange that it was in their best interests to allow the British state a degree of perpetual credit that no other European state, most notably France, could match.[54] Both Swift and Berkeley were personal investors in the London South Sea Company, a state-backed private enterprise intended to secure a monopoly over (hitherto Spanish-controlled) South American trade. Thereafter, many Irish individuals would benefit financially from opportunities presented by the British Empire, including emigrating to British North America and the Caribbean, although this generally served only to sever any loyalty, or connection, they had to a specifically Irish polity.[55] Mirroring this development, some Catholic exiles from Ireland became either diplomats or knighted military officers in Spain, Austria, Prussia and even Russia, but in the process they ceased to have any connection with their birthplace and would never return to Ireland.[56] This reflected the fact that Ireland, or Irish families, had never become a distinct player in the dynastic order of early-modern Europe.

The Williamite Wars (1689–91) that deposed the brief rule of James II (1685–9), a Catholic Stuart monarch, were fought largely on Irish soil. In strengthening Anglo-Dutch ties, they paved the way for Protestant families from Saxony in Germany to inherit the British throne and also stimulated much European interest, albeit primarily on a financial level only. James II had granted some Irish ships the right to trade directly with the Canary Islands, a Spanish archipelago off the coast of Morocco that was noted for its sugar trade, a wine trade with England, as well as being a basis for Spanish–American trade.[57] Anglo-Dutch competition would effectively counteract this trend. Meanwhile, direct Irish imports from the American colonies had always been outlawed in order to give English tobacco and sugar companies a complete monopoly over the Irish market. The export of Irish foodstuffs to the American colonies had been encouraged, however, and this helped to facilitate the commercial development of Cork city and Galway town on the south and west coast of Ireland respectively. Cork and Galway merchants who were Catholics soon had to flee the country, however, because of their legal inability to own property. Combined with the legal bans on their holding parliamentary, civil or military office, this meant that it was very difficult for them to continue in business.[58] During the early eighteenth century, some Irish Catholic exiles had associated themselves briefly with the Jacobite court in exile in France but, unlike some Scottish Jacobites of Ulster descent,[59] they were evidently unwilling to conspire against England. Reflecting this trend, by the 1760s a movement had developed within Ireland that sought only to restore Catholics' rights to sit in the Irish parliament.[60] Meanwhile, a group of Irish Catholic merchants in Bordeaux who traded with Cork merchants and the French East India Company began acting as informal intermediaries in Anglo-French and even Anglo-American diplomatic relations.[61]

Upon visiting Dublin in 1771, Benjamin Franklin thought that the Irish parliament could potentially be an ally of the American colonies in seeking independence from Britain. Once America began to struggle free, Franklin also believed that a direct trade agreement could be reached between the United States and Ireland by means of a formal commercial treaty. The first American consular office established in Ireland would report in 1790 that 'no country in Europe contains more real friends to America … who rejoice more in her rising prospects' than Ireland.[62] The Irish parliament of the day, however, was never the potential friend to America that Franklin believed. Simon Harcourt, a former British ambassador to Paris and the English lord lieutenant of Ireland, had persuaded the Irish parliament to send 4,000 troops to put down the American struggle for independence and also to raise an Irish volunteer force to defend the English colony in Ireland in these soldiers' absence. Thereafter, William Eden, a member of the British imperial board of trade who had attempted to outfox the Americans, decided upon being appointed leader of the Irish administration to remove the restrictions on direct trade between Ireland and the colonies solely in an effort to defeat the French naval blockade of supplies to the British troops.[63] Once it became clear that this strategy had failed and it had lost its American colonies, the British imperial parliament passed three acts to set down rules for the Irish administration. The supremacy of the British Privy Council in all legal matters was reaffirmed. Although it was stated that the British parliament did not legislate directly for Ireland, it was ruled that the Irish parliament must enact any legislation relating to overseas trade that had been adopted in the imperial parliament.[64]

Some absentee landowners in Ireland were in favour of abolishing the Irish parliament altogether, considering it irrelevant compared to the ever-growing economic needs of the empire. Through espousing such politics, some Irishmen such as George Macartney became governors of the British West Indies, Ireland, the East India Company and the Cape of Good Hope, as well as a British ambassador to China.[65] Similar motives inspired William Eden's move, as a British Privy Councillor and vice-treasurer for Ireland, in creating a Bank of Ireland in 1783. Although nominally a national bank, it was actually a sister bank to the Bank of England and was governed by a former British diplomat. He had been able to establish his own bank in Ireland upon marrying the daughter of a wealthy London banker and buying a sugar plantation in the British West Indies.[66] Henceforth, plantation owners in Dublin as well as in the rising new northern town of Belfast were able to manage their West Indies plantations from afar and, in turn, use this wealth to create in their hometowns new chambers of commerce that had a decidedly imperial focus.[67] Meanwhile, Britain's response to Catholic petitions to have their liberties restored was to allow them to serve in the British army and to permit some to vote whilst still denying them a right to sit in parliament. Purposively, a state-funded Catholic seminary college was created at Maynooth in order to make the historic Irish Colleges on the European continent redundant while a Jesuit college was established at Stonyhurst, England to serve as a launching pad for wealthy Irish Catholics to enter the British diplomatic service.[68]

A group of republican clubs known as the Society of United Irishmen had called for the reform of the Irish parliament to make it a representative national assembly that would include Irishmen of all religious denominations. This demand, however, came from outside the Irish parliament, mostly from journalists, minor merchants and some volunteers. Ultimately, the potential impact of the United Irishmen initiative was neutralised by the lack of any effective platform after the disbandment of the Catholic petition movement and the outlawing of volunteering. A wealthy Londoner who had experience of British diplomatic work suggested to the United Irishmen that they cultivate links with revolutionary France. This same man, however, had also been the leader of the University of Cambridge branch of the freemasons, a fraternity that was an instrument of the British Empire's military networks and foreign policy intrigues.[69] Thereafter, the United Irish movement became an underground movement that involved British intelligence operatives whose sole purpose was to manipulate Irish political circumstances in order to bring about an Act of Union between Britain and Ireland.[70] As a result, the United Irish leaders, perhaps mostly notably Lord Edward FitzGerald, a great admirer of the United States who renounced his aristocratic title upon befriending Thomas Paine in Paris,[71] effectively became the victims of a conspiracy. Although not an admirer of the United States, Theobald Wolfe Tone would later be described by many as a founder of Irish nationalism. In his writings, he espoused the novel idea of an Irish parliament being a neutral in Britain's wars whilst also acting as an eloquent United Irish advocate for Catholic liberties. However, Tone's subsequent career, upon being persuaded to join the French army and promote two minor French invasion attempts of Ireland, was an unmitigated disaster that can best be described as a mere footnote to the French revolutionary wars.[72]

The chief architect of the Act of Union between Britain and Ireland in 1800 was Robert Stewart, a Dublin Presbyterian who converted to Anglicanism at Cambridge University so that he could intermarry with the British aristocracy, acquire the new title of Viscount Castlereagh and inherit family seats in both the British and Irish parliaments. Castlereagh would become famous internationally for organising a diplomatic alliance with Prussia and Russia to defeat Napoleonic France and subsequently chairing the Congress of Vienna (1814–15) to redraw the map of Europe. In Ireland, however, he was widely denounced for provoking and suppressing (in a very draconian fashion) an ill-advised rebellion in the summer of 1798 and subsequently bribing MPs into accepting his union proposals.[73] Meanwhile, expatriated Irishmen had little bearing on either the revolutionary wars or Castlereagh's attempts to contain them. The loyalty of a century-old Irish brigade in the French army to the Bourbon dynasty had led to its disbandment in 1792. Reflecting Robert Emmet's brief attempt to organise another Irish rebellion that year, a Napoleonic Irish Legion was formed in 1803 that carried on its flag an image of a crownless harp and the inscription 'L'independence d'Irlande', but this legion would not survive the restoration of Bourbon monarchical rule in 1815.[74] Among those United Irishmen who survived the British intelligence war with France were some who found a better life in the United States. This included a future American consul to France as well as men who, upon entering academic or professional life in America, formed pioneering (and non-denominational) Irish American voluntary organisations that championed the cause of full political liberties for Catholics not only in America but also in Britain and Ireland.[75]

During Castlereagh's term as foreign secretary (1812–20), British governments under Prime Minister Lord Liverpool broke promises made to Irish politicians at the time of the Act of Union that Ireland would retain a distinct exchequer. Lord Liverpool abolished all Irish customs houses, in the process making all Irish ports mere extensions of that of the city of Liverpool, where new shipping companies now carried all trade to and from Ireland and all customs were collected. This engendered Dublin's dramatic economic decline and also quickly put an end to Cork, Limerick and Galway's status as Atlantic ports.[76] Traditional Irish links with the European continent also declined rapidly. Some interest in French soldiering would remain in Ireland up until the 1870s, when there were Irish celebrations of the choice of Marshal Patrice de MacMahon as the first president of the Third Republic. However, like the Franco-Irish composer Augusta Holmes' miliantly nationalist symphonic piece *Irlande* (1882), this was essentially an echo of purely historical cultural links.[77]

Over the course of the nineteenth century, use of the Irish language declined from approximately half to just 5 per cent of the Irish population. Celebrated Irish painters and English-language writers in London purposively adopted the role of representatives of a historic culture that could be romanticised only because it was now past.[78] Notoriously, in the recent past, Scottish writer James MacPherson had made the ancient Irish Fianna sagas the basis of his own original English-language verse that was translated into several European languages and was celebrated by artists and politicians in both Europe and America. However, when it was discovered that he had misrepresented his own original writings as being direct translations from an ancient text by a non-existent Scottish Gaelic poet 'Ossian' (a name derived from the legendary Irish Fianna, or 'Fenian', Oisín), many people abroad assumed thereafter that the notion that an Irish culture and language had ever existed, let alone thrived, was purely a fiction.[79] 'Ossianic' societies soon acquired British royal patronage, while Charles Villiers Stanford, a Dublin-born founder of the music school of the University of Cambridge, composed a *Lament for the Sons of Ossian* to equate all Irish nationalists with being ignorant believers in a historical fiction. This prompted W.B. Yeats, an Irish cultural nationalist poet, to purposively entitle his first collection *The Wanderings of Oisin*.[80] These debates about Irish life altered around the end of the nineteenth century. The Catholic Church, which had been legalised within the United Kingdom in 1850, encouraged an Irish language revival as part of a cultural nationalist movement that essentially defined itself against two notions of an Anglophone world. First, it labelled the equation of modernity with secularism as an Anglophone delusion. Second, it labelled cosmopolitan cultures and commercialism as an anti-intellectual force. If Britain had been, in Napoleon Bonaparte's words, a 'nation of shopkeepers', Irish cultural nationalists were now encouraged to believe that Ireland's destiny was to be a nation of schoolteachers.[81]

****

To enable British industrialisation, Ireland's role in the nineteenth-century United Kingdom economy was to be a provider of agricultural produce and additional labour. A process of involuntary emigration coincided with a traumatic Great Famine (1845–51) that cost a million lives and led a further million to attempt to emigrate.[82] The British government's response was controversial because it refused to interfere with the continued exportation of Irish food. It also ordered that the starving should be made to do more manual labour in order to be deserving of receiving charitable assistance.[83] A precedent was also set. Britain refused to allow poverty relief aid from outside legal jurisdictions to reach Ireland, and this would become a source of controversy later that century when, during a period of mass evictions and fears of renewed famine in Ireland, recipients of American aid were prosecuted.[84] Assisted emigration schemes to the British colonies continued unabated. American opposition to state-aid for denominational education encouraged the Catholic Church to promote this trend because religious education could receive more overt political backing in the British colonies, including Canada.[85] This indirectly affected the experience of Irish emigrants to America. As a result of emigration, more Irish-born soldiers fought in the American civil war (1861–5) than in any other war in modern times,[86] but the Catholic Church's ongoing resistance to state-education programmes meant that the experience of Irish migrants to America continued to be characterised by a sense of social insecurity or isolation.[87]

A contrary trend stemmed from the British government's expulsion from Ireland of nationalist rebels who had attempted to emulate the 1848 revolutions in Europe. Realising that the American government 'hailed the European revolutions of 1848 as extensions of their own',[88] these expatriate Irishmen enthusiastically embraced an American republican patriotism by combining anti-British expressions of American foreign policy with fierce critiques of British rule in Ireland.[89] The United States itself 'remained properly cautious … in terms of promoting republican principles abroad' because direct intervention could promote harmful retaliation. During the 1850s, American expansionist ambitions to fulfil their nation's 'manifest destiny' (a term coined by John O'Sullivan, an influential American diplomat of Irish descent) found an alternative outlet in filibuster campaigns, which were privately organised military expeditions in foreign territories that enjoyed unofficial state backing. This development originated with America's desire to capitalise upon the chaotic situation facing many European colonies in Latin America, not least through utilising secret freemason networks.[90] Previously, Irish adventurers like Daniel Florence O'Leary acquired fame in South American campaigns led by Simon Bolivar and made this a prelude to entering the British diplomatic service.[91] Now, however, Irish filibusters were inclined to offer their services to the American government instead. The creation of the American Fenian Brotherhood among Irish emigrants, several of whom were veterans of previous filibuster campaigns (American or otherwise),[92] was a direct manifestation of this trend.[93] At their public national conventions, the American Fenians, while calling for an independent Ireland, expressed their total identification with the American principle that only republican governments effectively championed liberty.[94]

Junior American consuls, first created in Ireland during 1790, remained in place under the Union and continued to report on trading possibilities. American ships had traded directly with a dozen different Irish port towns, but by the 1830s this situation had changed to being just an occasional importer of Ulster linens via Liverpool.[95] The Americans responded by introducing a direct trading line with Galway town, which was deemed to be without rival as an Irish port and was expected in New York to become 'one of the most flourishing cities in Ireland'. Between 1858 and 1863, sixteen American steamers operated direct trade between Galway and New York before a combination of competition from a new British government-backed enterprise in Liverpool and the oubreak of the American civil war led to their sudden demise.[96] Irish nationalist journalists from Galway and the west of Ireland thereafter left for the United States, where they formed what were effectively 'pro-Irish' American newspapers that the British government frequently seized whenever they were imported into Ireland because of their critiques of British foreign policy.[97]

This tradition of Fenian journalism embodied a paradox. American foreign policy *was* based on drawing a stark contrast between American republican liberties and the supposedly morally corrupt values of European monarchical governments, including an allegedly arrogant British government. To a significant extent, however, this American national identity was only an expression of a fear that the European powers (with which the United States still did most of its trade) might use their influence on any of the American continents in order to destroy the young American republic.[98] Boosting overseas trade and an expansionist impulse were always the central dynamics of American foreign policy.[99] Against this backdrop, 'most Americans sympathised with Irish nationalism, but not to the point of sparking a crisis with Britain'.[100] The radical American republican Charles Sumner, a one-time chairman of the US Foreign Relations Committee, developed an informal association at this time with a circle of professional revolutionaries, Irish or otherwise. Anglo-American tensions would remain for so long as Sumner was in office, not least because one of Sumner's ideas (rooted in his past experience of the annexation of Alaska) was that the United States should be granted Canadian territory as reparation for Britain's allegedly hostile actions during the US civil war.[101] This was an idea that some American Fenian filibusters echoed.[102] Canadian raids, however, also involved key British intelligence operatives,[103] effectively making the Canadian 'Fenian' raids a mere episode to embarrass those Americans who had spoken about annexing Canada. For Britain, this event was seen to have permanently neutralised the Fenian threat. It also served to make the Fenians, at best, a mere embarrassing footnote in the future writing of American history.[104] After denouncing the Canadian raids and castigating all secret society conspiracies for being 'at once the terror and the offspring of the sway of tyrants',[105] John Savage, the president of the American Fenian Brotherhood, worked with the conservative American Republican presidents Andrew Johnson and Ulysses Grant in securing an amnesty for all Fenian prisoners, in turn giving birth to an internal legal debate on American citizenship and naturalisation laws.[106] American-Irish Fenians, who had always promoted a tradition of American state-militia service, also worked within the Grand Army of the Republic Association in an effort to heal US civil war divisions.[107] Ignoring Catholic condemnations of their politics,[108] many distanced themselves from immigrant politics, represented not least by the Democratic Party's infamous Tammany Hall machine in New York,[109] and embraced the perhaps more conservative Republican Party,[110] including John Devoy, a journalist and recent political exile from Ireland who also attempted to cultivate a rapport with politicians in Ireland from his New York base.

Devoy was exiled from Ireland because he was a leading member of a nationalist–revolutionary secret society known as the Irish Republican Brotherhood (IRB). This had used Fenian fund-collection channels in the United States to establish the *Irish People*, a shortlived Dublin journal (1863–5). In its take on international relations, the *Irish People* was less a champion of American republican values than it was an advocate of the Eurocentric idea that Ireland, like Poland (which had just witnessed a failed uprising), was indisputedly one of the suppressed nationalities of Europe.[111] Although the IRB was supposed to have an oath-bound discipline, its leaders and members were politically talented individuals rather than soldiers. As a result, a misconception about the IRB existed among those American militia soldiers who had joined the American Fenian Brotherhood.[112] A proclamation by Irish republican rebels during 1867 was inspired by French republican adventurers who had served under infamous continental revolutionary Giuseppe Garibaldi and mistakenly believed that a UK-wide potential for a republican revolution existed.[113] 'Fenianism' was practically negated as an aspect of Anglo-American tensions during 1872, but a tradition of vocally pro-Irish Congressmen and newspaper editors in America developed thereafter. This provided the inspiration for men like John Devoy to attempt to initiate cross-Atlantic political communications. Uniquely and controversially, however, Devoy also saw this as a means to revive the IRB.[114]

American influence on Ireland grew more significant after Ulysses Grant, accompanied by the US minister to France and the 'ever brash' foreign affairs staff of the *New York Herald*, visited Ireland in early 1879 upon being granted the freedom of Dublin.[115] Devoy, one of several Fenians who worked for the *New York Herald*, also came to Ireland to secretly reorganise the IRB, which he publicly called upon to 'come out of the rat holes of conspiracy' and form a new Irish nationalist party at Westminster with American financial support.[116] This was a prelude to a US tour by Irish politician Charles Stewart Parnell, who was able to address the American House of Representatives about Ireland, thanks mostly to William Carroll, a Donegal-born American freemason and Republican Party activist who claimed to be a descendant of Charles Carroll, a governor of Maryland of Irish descent who had been the sole Catholic signatory to the American Declaration of Independence in 1776.[117] Through the freemasons, Carroll had become the leader of the American Clan na Gael, a secret society that was designed to replace the Fenian Brotherhood, which soon disbanded, and which Devoy soon remodelled upon less masonic lines.[118] An end result of this 'new departure' was to make the idea of fund collection in America by means of Irish relief organisations an acceptable notion to many Irish politicians. The British government was very opposed to this development, however, because it considered that it amounted to illegal attempts to collect funds abroad for either party political or seditious purposes (the IRB reached a peak in terms of its resources during the period 1879–84).[119] For this reason, many Irish politicians were arrested and the freedom of the Irish press was often curtailed throughout the 1880s.[120] A British secret service even promoted bogus dynamiting conspiracies in Paris, New York, Philadelphia and Chicago with two goals in mind: first, to convince American and French intelligence services of their need to cooperate more with the British; and, second, to justify mass arrests in Ireland on the grounds that all Irish nationalists supposedly possessed the same financiers as these largely fictitious American and Parisian 'dynamitards'.[121] While this devious propaganda was ultimately countered by Irish politicians at its root during 1889,[122] it served to discredit Irish nationalism in both America and France.[123] Reflecting this, although James Blaine, an Anglophobe US Secretary of State, appointed Irish republican rebel Patrick Egan to an American diplomatic office,[124] circumstantial evidence that some US citizens of Irish birth had irresponsibly become involved in 'dynamitard' conspiracies led Blaine to accept at face value British propaganda that portrayed Irish nationalist activists of the day as 'the scum of Europe'.[125]

After the UK franchise was extended to include half of adult males in 1884, Irish nationalists perpetually won the vast majority of the Irish seats at Westminster. To defuse this situation and to stem the decline of the landed aristocracy's political power in Ireland, British Prime Minister W.E. Gladstone decided to promote the idea of establishing a devolved parliamentary assembly in Ireland that would be without fiscal autonomies.[126] Parnell's acceptance of this idea helped to take the steam out of the idea of establishing an independent Irish republic, be it American-inspired or otherwise. Gladstone's idea was also actively promoted by new Irish organisations that were founded with the Catholic Church's patronage within British colonies such as Canada and Australia.[127] By the 1890s, American sympathisers with Ireland, such as Eugene Kelly (manager of the Emigrants Savings Bank in New York) and some leaders of America's new Catholic universities, had also accepted this trend while also encouraging the Irish community in America to adopt Catholic moral perspectives on various social and political issues, including American foreign policy regarding the Philippines and

Cuba.[128] Against this backdrop, the existence of marginal Irish filibuster, or war correspondent, intrigues during the Anglo-Boer War (1899–1902) were essentially a last hurrah for defunct practices.[129] Irregularities in international affairs that had grown immediately before, during and after the US civil war had been eclipsed by new intergovernmental organisations that had started to become effective. These included the International Telegraph (later Telecommunications) Union (1865), the Universal Postal Union (1874), the Hague Conference on Private International Law (1893) and the Permanent Court of Arbitration (1899), which would virtually become a global body in the wake of the second Hague Convention of 1907. Present at the latter convention was a representative of a new Irish political party, Sinn Féin, which called for all Irish political representatives to abstain from the British imperial parliament and make a unilateral stand for Irish independence.[130] This idea had first been championed many years before by Daniel O'Connell, an Irish advocate for Catholic liberties and eloquent critic of the international slave trade who had acquired Europe-wide fame as a political liberal during the 1830s and 1840s.[131]

In its initial conception, Sinn Féin had an essentially Eurocentric worldview. Arthur Griffith, a humble Dublin printer who had formerly intrigued in South Africa, maintained that a combination of Britain's 'financial plunder of Ireland' and 'the custom house interdict upon direct trade between Ireland and the [European] continent' was preventing Irish nationalists from acquiring an international audience.[132] During 1904, at a time when Hungary was launching the most expensive parliamentary building in Europe, Griffith pointed to the dual monarchy compromise that Hungary had reached with Austria in 1866 as providing a potential parallel for Ireland.[133] As Hungary had no distinct defence or foreign affairs ministries, this was a rather poor suggestion. Griffith soon modified his idea, however, by proposing instead within his *Sinn Féin Policy* (1906) that Ireland should send its own consular representatives abroad with a view to establishing an independent Irish voice in international relations. Although Griffith emphasised that 'the policy of Sinn Féin proposes ... to bring Ireland out of the corner and make her assert her existence in the world', his citation of Argentina and Holland as 'friendly nations' essentially reflected the fact that he was over-preoccupied with the impact that the British financial world

was having upon Ireland.[134] The broader European trend of growing
appreciation for all things American had a relatively limited impact on
Sinn Féin, even though it did attempt to promote some new (American-
inspired) Irish co-operative banks and had pointed approvingly to the
claim of Michael Davitt, the author of *The Fall of Feudalism in Ireland*
(New York, 1903) and an Irish spokesman on the Russian question, that
the vote of pro-Irish congressmen in America would have far greater
consequences for the future of international relations than the vote of
Irish politicians at Westminster.[135]

✳✳✳✳✳✳✳✳✳✳✳✳✳✳✳✳✳✳✳✳✳✳✳✳✳✳✳✳✳✳✳✳✳✳✳✳

By the turn of the twentieth century, Ireland occupied a very paradoxical
position. The cultural Gaelic League had become the principal forum
for Irish nationalism despite the fact that Ireland was, for all intents
and purposes, an English-speaking nation. On an ideological level, its
nationalist politicians saw hope in the rise of the democratic republic of
the United States. They also valued the existence of Irish communities
abroad and were disinclined to entirely disavow the legacy of past
republican United Irish or Fenian conspiracies. Be that as it may, the
reality of Ireland's place in the Atlantic economy was governed purely
by its membership of the British Empire. Therefore, Anglo-American
relations formed an overarching context that essentially limited Irish
ambitions.

   In American politics, Irish newspaper editors in Chicago or New
York had long championed the expansion of the American navy
whilst simultaneously campaigning against the creation of any formal
arbitration treaty between the United States and Britain on the grounds
that this might force America to take part in Britain's global wars.
While this was a justifiable stance on American foreign policy, it was
combined with a more controversial propaganda against manipulative
British financial influences within America. Diplomats of the French
republic in America privately shared this preoccupation.[136] Its public
expression within the immigrant press of what was becoming known
as 'Irish America', however, led American governments to view new
publications such as Devoy's *Gaelic American* (which supported Sinn
Féin while declaring that 'Europe, not England, is the mother country

of America') as advocates of an eccentric brand of 'hyphen-American' politics that was, if anything, unpatriotic, not least because it was evidently rooted more in a cultural Anglophobia than a thorough grasp of the dynamics of the American economy.[137] Indeed, ever since the 1820s, Anglo-American tensions had been minimised by the fact that the United Kingdom had been willing to discourage European interference on the American continents in return for the United States conceding to the Royal Navy the right to be the primary policer of the seas. This understanding, although informal, allowed Anglo-American trade to both flourish and coexist. If rivalries existed, this was rooted in the expectation that, ultimately, the United States would naturally assume a monopoly over trade on all the American continents, whether through its own foreign direct investment schemes or the emergence of other republican governments (possibly even in Canada) that would reject the practice of monarchy.[138] American interest in Ireland had never really extended beyond the question of trading possibilities. As a result, by the 1910s, the United States had become interested primarily in maintaining the existing 'strong commercial relationship between the north-east of Ireland and the US'. The attitude of American consular officers within Ireland towards Irish nationalism now fitted neatly within this paradigm.[139]

In recent decades, the powerful shipbuilding industries of Liverpool and Glasgow had led to the closure of independent shipbuilding companies in the historic Irish cities of Dublin and Waterford. New shipbuilding firms had developed, however, in the rising northern Irish town of Belfast because they operated as subsidiaries of those in Liverpool and especially Glasgow. From the 1860s onwards, this turned Belfast into a thriving commercial centre. This was illustrated by the construction of numerous public buildings, including a particularly impressive City Hall to reflect London's formal recognition of Belfast as a city in 1888.[140] Nationally, Belfast was perhaps best known for producing a vocal local press that often championed a peculiar pan-Protestant reading of contemporary politics as well as international relations.[141] More significantly, however, as the home of a university since 1845, Belfast was producing significant figures that worked for the British foreign office. This included in the Far East, where Britain, like the United States, would succeed in signing a major trade treaty with

Japan in 1911.[142] At the same time, the Belfast-born diplomat James Bryce, who had previously won over American academic opinion by publishing pioneering studies of the American constitution, succeeded as the British ambassador to the United States in settling American–Canadian relations to Britain's satisfaction.[143] This arrival of a northern Irish role in British diplomacy coincided with a concerted campaign to portray all historic links between Ulster and Scotland as having been rooted purely in a common British nationalism, essentially in a desire to suppress the re-emergence of a 'Gaelic' Irish nationalism.[144]

James Bryce arranged an Anglo-American Arbitration Treaty (1911) under which any trade or related disputes between the two countries were to be sent to the Court of Arbitration in the Hague, a city located within Britain's closest financial ally, the Netherlands.[145] The US Senate, however, rejected Bryce's treaty and the *Gaelic American* declared this as a victory for 'Irish-America'. John Devoy repeated *ad nauseum* his founding editorial policy of working to ensure that 'the direction of the foreign policy of this great Republic' must never be allowed to fall into the hands of 'a clique of pro-British sycophants'.[146] The reality, however, was that Irish nationalist sympathisers in America had no access to the corridors of power. This situation in Ireland itself was not much different. Sinn Féin championed the idea of launching an Irish economic war against the British imperial treasury on the grounds that Ireland had been an almost perpetual victim of gross over-taxation,[147] but James Craig, the rising new leader of unionism in Belfast, was a wealthy businessman who both cultivated political links with London bankers and accepted fully the logic of the British imperial treasury regarding Ireland. In particular, British investments in Ireland were now negligible compared to investments in Australia and India. The wealth generated by the latter had been used by religious ministers in Ulster to establish new Irish Presbyterian theological colleges (such as Magee College in Derry), while Ireland's value as a source of revenue, providing but 4 per cent of the UK's taxation, was small enough to be comparatively insignificant.[148] Therefore, Craig and the British imperial treasury considered any injustices in the government of Ireland to be completely irrelevant compared to the much greater budgetary concerns of the empire. In an Irish electoral sense, this body of opinion was only a small minority voice, but its dominance in high politics naturally shaped the impact that the outbreak of the First World War would have upon Ireland.

Britain had anticipated the prospects of a major war with Germany as early as 1904. Although it was expected that 'at most, Ireland would be subject only to a diversionary attack', after 1905 the Royal Navy began including Ireland in a common naval defence scheme based upon the potential strategic significance of the three western Irish ports of Bearehaven (Castletownbere), Lough Swilly and Cork harbour as part of the island of Britain's 'western approaches'. This was done with an eye to the development of submarine warfare and potential attacks on trans-Atlantic shipping,[149] although the 'western approaches' concept was justified in racial as much as geopolitical terms.[150] In 1911, a treasury report claimed that Ireland was actually costing more to govern than it was contributing to national defence. Therefore, Erskine Childers of the British Foreign Office proposed that volunteer movements should be formed in Ireland to compensate for this fact until such time as the return of Ireland to the position of a contributing member of the imperial partnership was made feasible. Childers believed this could be accomplished by establishing a new colonial assembly, akin to that in Newfoundland, to govern Ireland without any cost to the imperial treasury.[151] This was a proposal that the old Irish Party at Westminster, originally founded by Parnell (who died in 1891) and now led by John Redmond, accepted. However, rather than be subjected to this situation, James Craig and Dublin-born lawyer Edward Carson called for the partition of Ireland to reflect Belfast's status as a centrally important imperial city. In support of this move, the British cabinet would soon invite Craig and Carson to serve as Treasurer and First Lord of the Admiralty respectively.[152] Meanwhile, James Bryce, on retiring as British ambassador to the United States and concentrating on diplomatic work on the European continent, would promote the idea that Ireland, like many eastern European countries, was really the home of two separate ethnicities or nationalities.[153] Prior to leaving the United States, Bryce also introduced President Taft to another Ulster-born British diplomat, Roger Casement, who would distribute his pamphlet *Ireland, Germany and the Freedom of the Seas* to all American government agencies and bodies of higher education in an attempt to convince the English-speaking world that Irish nationalism was merely a German conspiracy.[154] Casement himself would subsequently do all in his power to make his 'German Plot' conspiracy seem real.

The shocking feature of these developments to Irish nationalists was the proof they offered of their total powerlessness. Although it held the vast majority of Irish seats, the Irish Party held just an eighth of the total seats in the House of Commons and had no effective spokesman on international affairs. The idea of partitioning Ireland and establishing a powerless national assembly in Dublin was deeply unpopular in Ireland, as well as in 'Irish-America'. Britain was confident, however, that any potential American criticism could be neutered as soon as America could be persuaded to join Britain's war effort against Germany. This was because 'the day that American blood will have flowed, Irish opposition in America will become absolutely impossible'.[155] Sinn Féin had promoted a campaign of non-enlistment in the British army to weaken Britain's hold on the country ever since the *entente cordiale* between Britain and France (1904) seemed to indicate that Ireland could have no continental allies. Therefore, when a minority of Irish Volunteers opted not to enlist in the British war effort, they acquired the appropriate nickname of 'Sinn Féin volunteers'. These expressed their desire to act as a national defence force that would be neutral regarding the war, but the British government started arresting its members. Before the anti-enlistment, or Sinn Féin, volunteer movement could be completely suppressed, members of the IRB, who had infiltrated its officer corps, decided to stage a symbolic rebellion in Dublin in the name of an Irish republic. This was done in the belief that the suppression of such a rebellion would serve to revive, or boost, Irish aspirations for complete independence.[156]

The 1916 Rising, as this Easter Week rebellion would be called, took the form of an 1848-style European protest, where barricades were manned within a deposed capital city in the name of a country's right to have its own distinct political constitution. However, it was also intended to attract international attention to Ireland's desire for complete political independence. The official policy of the anti-enlistment Irish Volunteers of strict neutrality regarding the First World War was championed in small Irish publications that had been funded by the 1916 rebels, such as Arthur Griffith's *Nationality*. The latter had also argued that Ireland should seek entirely independent representation at whatever peace conference concluded the war. The British government and its supporters denied this claim of neutrality, however, by pointing to Casement's Philadelphia publication, which had been sent to all US governmental officials, and his subsequent actions in Germany. Up until the war ended in November 1918, Britain used Casement's 'German Plot' as its justification for imprisoning without trial any elected Irish politicians of professed nationalist sympathies on the grounds of their being supposedly pro-German or even paid German spies. Outrage at the extent to which the pro-enlistment Irish Party at Westminster supported this claim led to a complete swing of Irish public opinion behind the hitherto marginal Sinn Féin Party, which also attained popularity by resisting Britain's efforts to introduce wartime conscription in Ireland. The latter development also created more public sympathy for the IRB's underground efforts to keep the anti-enlistment Irish Volunteer movement in existence.[157]

Sinn Féin did not treat the international debate on the freedom of the seas until after America's entry into the First World War in April 1917. In keeping with its perpetually neutral stance, it argued that the significance of this concept to Ireland lay only in the possibility of opening up Irish ports to trade with the US after the war had ended.[158] Meanwhile, the principal policy of the revamped Sinn Féin Party was to assert that America's entry into the war should lead to the creation of a more benign and republican international order at whatever peace conference was held in the wake of the war. Indeed, a struggle for Irish independence was now launched that was based almost entirely on a claim that an American-inspired, post-war peace settlement should favour Irish claims to distinct representation at such a peace conference and, in turn, the establishment of Ireland as a distinct player in international relations alongside those new European governments that had come into existence as a result of the war, such as the republic of Finland and the kingdom of Poland.[159] Reflecting this, the challenge of securing recognition of Ireland's distinct nationality in international relations would be defined not by an attempt to fight the British army but rather by an attempt to mobilise international opinion in favour of an Irish demand for the complete evacuation of British armed forces on the grounds that British rule in Ireland had no democratic legitimacy. Ireland's republican moment had now arrived.

Endnotes

1   Doris Edel, *The Celtic West and Europe* (Dublin, 2001); Michael Richter, *Medieval Ireland* (2nd ed., Dublin, 2005), 1–2 (quote).

2   J. DeCourcy Ireland, D.C. Sheehy (eds), *Atlantic visions* (Dun Laoghaire, 1989); Michael Richter, *Medieval Ireland* (2nd ed., Dublin, 2005), 8.

3   Dáibhí Ó Cróinín, *A new history of Ireland*, vol. 1 (Oxford, 2005), 18; Brendan Smith (ed.), *Cambridge history of Ireland*, vol. 1 (Cambridge, 2018), chapter 1.

4   Dáibhí Ó Cróinín, *A new history of Ireland*, vol. 1 (Oxford, 2005), 212–15.

5   John O'Donovan (ed.) *Leabhar na gCeart or the Book of Rights* (Dublin, 1847), 141–3, 155, 157, 159, 161, 169–73.

6   Doris Edel, *The Celtic West and Europe* (Dublin, 2001), chapters 4–6.

7   Elva Johnston, 'A sailor on the seas of faith: the individual and the church in *The Voyage of Máel Dúin*', in Judith Devlin, H.B. Clarke (ed.), *European encounters* (Dublin, 2003), 239–52; F.X. Martin, F.J. Byrne (eds), *The scholar revolutionary: Eoin MacNeill* (Dublin, 1973).

8   Dáibhí Ó Cróinín, *A new history of Ireland*, vol. 1 (Oxford, 2005), 202, 210–11, 216–21; Peter Crooks (ed.), *Government, war and society in medieval Ireland* (Dublin, 2008), 321–2.

9   Doris Edel, *The Celtic West and Europe* (Dublin, 2001), 81 (quote).

10 David Dickson, *Dublin* (London, 2014), 5–10; Brendan Smith (ed.), *Cambridge history of Ireland*, vol. 1 (Cambridge, 2018), chapter 4.

11 Peter Crooks (ed.), *Government, war and society in medieval Ireland* (Dublin, 2008), 194–214. Norman coins were frequently buried alongside Gaelic heirlooms as family treasures by Gaelic chieftains of the day. A.M.P., 'Ancient cemetery in Islandmagee', *Ulster journal of archaeology*, series 1, vol. 6 (1858), 346–50.

12 Peter Crooks (ed.), *Government, war and society in medieval Ireland* (Dublin, 2008), 210; Alexander Nicolson, *History of Skye* (Glasgow, 1930), 9–12, 22–5; N.J. McKie, 'The McGhies of Balmaghie', *The Gallovidian*, vol. 7 no. 26 (summer 1905), 99–103.

13 Peter Crooks (ed.), *Government, war and society in medieval Ireland* (Dublin, 2008), 169, 173, 177–93, 194–214, 332–7.

14 G.R. Gayre, 'Some notes upon the Mackays of the Rhinns of Islay with reference to the Mackays of Kintyre, the McGhies of Galloway and the Irish MacGees' (NLI, Genealogical Office, Ms689).

15 Sean Duffy (ed.), *Atlas of Irish history* (Derbyshire, 1997), 44, 54; Brendan Smith (ed.), *Cambridge history of Ireland*, vol. 1 (Cambridge, 2018), chapter 12.

16 John O'Donovan (ed.), *Leabhar na gCeart or the Book of Rights* (Dublin, 1847), introduction, 139, 141, 143; Brendan Smith (ed.), *Cambridge history of Ireland*, vol. 1, 117.

17 Paul Kennedy, *The rise and fall of the great powers: economic change and military conflict from 1500 to 2000* (London, 1988), 17.

18 Doris Edel, *The Celtic West and Europe* (Dublin, 2001), 41, 45, 48, 72.

19 Sean O'Riada, *Our musical heritage* (Portlaoise, 1982), 20.

20 Peter Crooks (ed.), *Government, war and society in medieval Ireland* (Dublin, 2008), 313–15; Sean Duffy (ed.), *Atlas of Irish history* (Derbyshire, 1997), 44, 54.

21 Brendan Smith (ed.), *Cambridge history of Ireland*, vol. 1 (Cambridge, 2018), chapter 12; [Henry Egan Kenny], 'Trade in medieval Ireland', in Seamus McManus, *The story of the Irish race* (Connecticut, 1921), 340–5. W.R. Childs, 'Irish merchants and seamen in late medieval England', *Irish historical studies*, vol. 32 no. 25 (May 2000), 22–43.

22 Michael Richter, *Medieval Ireland* (2nd ed., Dublin, 2005), quote p. 164.

23 Colm Lennon, *Sixteenth-century Ireland* (Dublin, 1994), 36-9; David Dickson, *Dublin*, 23, 26, 52-3.

24 Paul Kennedy, *The rise and fall of the great powers: economic change and military conflict from 1500 to 2000* (London, 1988), 4-18, 21. Lawrence James, *The rise and fall of the British Empire* (London, 1995), 5.

25 Steven G. Ellis, *Ireland in the age of the Tudors 1447-1603* (London, 1998), 214, 216; Sean Connolly, *Contested island: Ireland 1460-1630* (Oxford, 2007), 93-7; Peter Crooks (ed.), *Government, war and society*, 298, 317-9.

26 Ciaran Brady, *Shane O'Neill* (Dundalk, 1997).

27 Michael Richter, *Medieval Ireland* (2nd ed., Dublin, 2005), 160, 176.

28 Doris Edel, *The Celtic West and Europe* (Dublin, 2001), 79.

29 Brendan Smith (ed.), *Cambridge history of Ireland*, vol. 1 (Cambridge, 2018), 347-52. The legislation outlawed a Spanish wine trade with Ireland and an Irish cloth trade with the continent that had operated through the ports of Bordeaux and Bruges. John Ryan S.J., *Ireland from AD800 to AD1600* (Dublin, 1934), 227-9; Colm Lennon, *Sixteenth-century Ireland* (Dublin 1994), 6, 40-2.

30 Hiram Morgan, 'Hugh O'Neill (1550-1616)' and 'Red Hugh O'Donnell (1572-1602)', *Dictionary of Irish biography* (Cambridge, 2009).

31 Mary Ann Lyons, Thomas O'Connor, *Strangers to citizens: the Irish in Europe 1600- 1800* (Dublin, 2008).

32 Raymond Gillespie, *Seventeenth-century Ireland* (Dublin, 2006), 55-60, 103-4, 124-5, 138, 273, 274 (quote).

33 M. O'Driscoll, D. Keogh, J. aan de Wiel (eds), *Ireland through European eyes* (Cork, 2013), 192.

34 Paul Kennedy, *The rise and fall of the great powers*, 78-9, 82-9.

35 Micheál Ó Siochrú, 'Owen Roe O'Neill (1580-1649)', *Dictionary of Irish biography* (Cambridge, 2009).

36 Denis O'Hearn, *The Atlantic economy: Britain, the US and Ireland* (Manchester, 2001), chapter 2 (quote p. 28).

37 Sean Connolly, *Contested island: Ireland 1460-1630* (Oxford, 2007), 302, 304.

38 Sean Connolly, *Contested island: Ireland 1460-1630* (Oxford, 2007), 289-91, 301 (quotes).

39 Raymond Gillespie, *Seventeenth-century Ireland*, 102-3, 129.

40 Lawrence James, *The rise and fall of the British empire*, 6-7, 10-11; Raymond Gillespie, *Seventeenth-century Ireland*, 123-30; Terry Clavin, 'Sir Thomas Wentworth (1593- 1641)', *Dictionary of Irish biography* (Cambridge, 2009); N.A.M. Rodger, *The safeguard of the sea: a naval history of Britain, volume one* (London, 1997), 379-94.

41 J.C. Appleby, Mary O'Dowd, 'The Irish admiralty: its organisation and development c. 1570-1640', *Irish historical studies*, vol. 24 no. 95 (May 1985), 299-326.

42 Tadhg Ó hAnnracháin, 'Gian Battista Rinnucci (1592-1653)', *Dictionary of Irish biography* (Cambridge, 2009); Jane Ohlmeyer, *Civil war and restoration in the three Stuart kingdoms: the career of Randall MacDonnell, Marquis of Antrim 1609-1683* (Cambridge, 1993).

43 J.C. Appleby, Mary O'Dowd, 'The Irish admiralty: its organisation and development c. 1570-1640', *Irish historical studies*, vol. 24 no. 95 (May 1985), 325-6.

44 Raymond Gillespie, *Seventeenth-century Ireland*, 155-8; Micheál Ó Siochrú, 'Owen Roe O'Neill (1580-1649)', *Dictionary of Irish biography* (Cambridge, 2009).

45   Jane Ohlmeyer (ed.), *Cambridge history of Ireland*, vol. 2 (Cambridge, 2018), 269.

46   Michael Perceval Maxwell, 'James Butler (1610–1688)', *Dictionary of Irish biography* (Cambridge, 2009). Early examples of British diplomats leading the Irish administration included Sir William Temple (1628–99), Sir Cyril Wyche (1632–1707) and Sir Robert Southwell (1625–1702). Later examples included William Eden (1744–1804) and Alleyne Fitzherbert (1753–1839). Entries for these men exist in *Dictionary of Irish biography*.

47   Quote from John Gibney, 'Sir William Temple (1628–99)', *Dictionary of Irish biography* (Cambridge, 2009).

48   Sean Connolly, *Religion, law and power: the making of Protestant Ireland 1660–1760* (Oxford, 1992).

49   Ian McBride, *Eighteenth century Ireland* (Dublin, 2009), 111. In the past, Irish parliaments had often met in other Leinster towns such as Drogheda, Kilkenny and Clonmel. Maurice Craig, *Dublin 1660–1860* (Dublin, 1952), 1–5, 12–15.

50   Ian McBride, *Eighteenth century Ireland* (Dublin, 2009), 10; Raymond Gillespie, *Seventeenth-century Ireland*, 248–51, 273–4.

51   NLI, Ormonde papers (additional), MSS 48,367–77.

52   David Hayton, 'James Butler (1665–1745)', *Dictionary of Irish biography* (Cambridge, 2009); C.J. Woods, 'Thomas Conolly (1738–1803)', *Dictionary of Irish biography* (Cambridge, 2009).

53   Lawrence James, *The rise and fall of the British Empire* (London, 1995), 33.

54   Paul Kennedy, *The rise and fall of the great powers: economic change and military conflict from 1500 to 2000* (London, 1988), 103–5.

55   Jane Ohlmeyer (ed.), *Cambridge history of Ireland*, vol. 2 (Cambridge, 2018), chapter 15; James Kelly (ed.), *Cambridge history of Ireland*, vol. 3 (Cambridge, 2018), chapter 23.

56   Owen McGee (ed.), *Eugene Davis' souvenirs of Irish footprints over Europe* (1889, 2nd ed., Dublin, 2006), 175–8; Jane Ohlmeyer (ed.), *Cambridge history of Ireland*, vol. 2, 403–8.

57   'Ship's pass signed by king on show', *Irish Independent*, 5 Aug. 2010.

58   Ian McBride, *Eighteenth century Ireland* (Dublin, 2009), 126–31, 196–7, 240–4.

59   Historical Manuscripts Commission, *Calendar of the Stuart Papers*, vol. 5 (London, 1912), pp. 141–2, 155, 391, 402–3, 427, 492. Copies of relevant French War Ministry papers can be found in NLI, microfilms n. 547 and n. 1944.

60   Sean Connolly, *Religion, law and power: the making of Protestant Ireland 1660–1760* (Oxford, 1992), 233–49.

61   P. Butel, L.M. Cullen (eds), *Cities and merchants: French and Irish perspectives on urban development 1500–1900* (Dublin, 1986); Turlough O'Riordan, 'Thomas Sutton (1722–1782)', *Dictionary of Irish biography* (Cambridge, 2009).

62   Bernadette Whelan, *American government in Ireland, 1790–1913: a history of the US consular service* (Manchester, 2010), 2, 87 (quote).

63   Ian McBride, *Eighteenth century Ireland* (Dublin, 2009), 110; Patrick Geoghegan, 'Simon Harcourt (1714–1777)', *Dictionary of Irish biography* (Cambridge, 2009).

64   R.D.C. Black, 'Theory and policy in Anglo-Irish trade relations 1775–1800', *Journal of the social and statistical inquiry society of Ireland*, vol. 28 (1950), 312–14.

65   Thomas Bartlett, 'George Macartney (1737–1806)', *Dictionary of Irish biography* (Cambridge, 2009).

66   Daniel Beaumont, 'William George Digges LaTouche (1747–1803)', *Dictionary of Irish biography* (Cambridge, 2009); F.S.L. Lyons (ed.), *Bank of Ireland 1783–1983* (Dublin, 1983).

67 Louis Cullen, *Princes and pirates: the Dublin Chamber of Commerce 1783–1983* (Dublin, 1983); Sean Connolly (ed.), *Belfast 400: people, place and history* (Liverpool, 2012), 22–3; Ian McBride, *Eighteenth century Ireland*, 11–12.

68 Ciaran O'Neill, 'Education, imperial careers and the Irish Catholic elite in the nineteenth century', in D. Dickson, J. Pyz, C. Shepard (eds), *Irish classrooms and British empire* (Dublin, 2012), 98–110.

69 Jessica Harland-Jacobs, *Builders of Empire: freemasons and British imperialism 1717–1927* (University of North Carolina, 2007); C.J. Woods, 'Archibald Hamilton Rowan (1751–1834)', *Dictionary of Irish biography* (Cambridge, 2009).

70 C.J. Woods, 'Leonard MacNally (1752–1820)', *Dictionary of Irish biography* (Cambridge, 2009); C.J. Woods, 'William Jackson (1737–1795)', *Dictionary of Irish biography* (Cambridge, 2009).

71 Kevin Whelan, 'Lord Edward FitzGerald (1763–98)', *Dictionary of Irish biography* (Cambridge, 2009).

72 Thomas Bartlett, 'Theobald Wolfe Tone (1763–98)', *Dictionary of Irish biography* (Cambridge, 2009).

73 Patrick Geoghegan, 'Robert Stewart (1769–1822)', *Dictionary of Irish biography* (Cambridge, 2009).

74 Marianne Elliott, *Partners in revolution: the United Irishmen and France* (Yale, 1982), 323–64.

75 Michael Funchion (ed.), *Irish American voluntary organisations* (Connecticut, 1983); Patrick Geoghegan, 'David Bailie Warden (1772–1845)', *Dictionary of Irish biography* (Cambridge, 2009).

76 Bernadette Whelan, *American government in Ireland, 1790–1913: a history of the US consular service* (Manchester, 2010), 85–95; Denis O'Hearn, 'Ireland and the Atlantic economy', in Terence McDonough (ed.), *Was Ireland a colony?: economic, politics and culture in nineteenth-century Ireland* (Dublin, 2005).

77 Owen McGee (ed.), *Eugene Davis' souvenirs of Irish footprints over Europe* (1889, 2nd ed., Dublin, 2006), 121–2, 133–6; Maria O'Brien, 'Augusta Mary Anne Holmes (1847–1903)', *Dictionary of Irish biography* (Cambridge, 2009). Holmes was the daughter of an Irish-born French military officer.

78 This dynamic particularly defined the careers of Thomas Moore and Daniel Maclise. Fintan Cullen, R.F. Foster, *'Conquering England': Ireland in Victorian London* (London, 2005), 57–9.

79 Howard Gaskill (ed.), *The reception of Ossian in Europe* (London, 2004).

80 Robert Somerville-Woodward, *The Ossianic society 1853–1863* (Dublin, 1999); W.B. Yeats, *Collected poems* (London, 1989).

81 Owen McGee (ed.), *Eugene Davis' souvenirs of Irish footprints over Europe* (1889, 2nd ed., Dublin, 2006), 179–81; Gerard Keown, *First of the small nations: the beginnings of Irish foreign policy in the interwar years 1919–1932* (Oxford, 2015), 89.

82 James Donnelly, *The great Irish potato famine* (Gloucester, 2002), chapter 7.

83 James Donnelly, *The great Irish potato famine* (Gloucester, 2002), chapter 3.

84 In 1880, at a time of about 14,000 evictions in the west of Ireland, the Irish National Land League collected about £245,000 in the United States for Irish relief aid. At the same time, a Dublin Mansion House Relief Fund collected £180,000 within the United Kingdom and the British colonies. As the former fund emanated from outside British jurisdiction, however, the Land League was declared illegal and prior recipients of its funds were imprisoned on charges of sedition. C.C. O'Brien, *Parnell*

and his party (Oxford, 1957), 134–5; T.W. Moody, *Davitt and Irish revolution* (Oxford, 1981); *Mansion House Relief Committee* (Dublin, 1881); Samuel Clark, *Social origins of the land war* (Philadelphia, 1974), 306.

85 Ciaran O'Neill, 'Education, imperial careers and the Irish Catholic elite in the nineteenth century', in D. Dickson, J. Pyz, C. Shepard (eds), *Irish classrooms and British empire* (Dublin, 2012), 108–9; Francis M. Carroll, 'Thomas D'Arcy McGee (1825–68)', *Dictionary of Irish biography* (Cambridge, 2009). On this theme, see also the *Dictionary of Irish biography* entries for John Hobart Caradoc (1799–1873) and Thomas Colley Grattan (1781–1864), and George C. Herring, *From colony to superpower: US foreign relations since 1776* (Oxford, 2008), 185–7.

86 Damian Shiels, *The Irish in the American civil war* (Dublin, 2013); Arthur Mitchell (ed.), *Fighting Irish in the American civil war and the invasion of Mexico* (North Carolina, 2017).

87 Kerby Miller, *Emigrants and exiles: Ireland and the Irish exodus to North America* (Oxford, 1985).

88 George C. Herring, *From colony to superpower: US foreign relations since 1776* (Oxford, 2008), 214.

89 See, for instance, the *Dictionary of Irish biography* entries for Thomas Devin Reilly, John Mitchel, John Savage, Joseph Brenan, Thomas Francis Meagher, Thomas D'Arcy McGee, Terence Bellew McManus, Michael Doheny, John O'Mahony, Thomas Joseph Kelly, John Devoy and John Finerty.

90 George C. Herring, *From colony to superpower: US foreign relations since 1776* (Oxford, 2008), 160, 196, 215.

91 Peter O'Leary, 'Daniel Florence O'Leary (1801–1854)', *Dictionary of Irish biography* (Cambridge, 2009). Department of foreign affairs and trade, *The Irish in Latin America* (Dublin, 2016).

92 See the *Dictionary of Irish biography* entries for James Francis Xavier O'Brien, Thomas Francis Bourke and William George Halpin.

93 George C. Herring, *From colony to superpower: US foreign relations since 1776* (Oxford, 2008), 180, 214–16.

94 William D'Arcy, *The Fenian movement in the United States* (Washington D.C., 1947). The British foreign office collected copies of these American Fenian statements for intelligence purposes. Many of these can now be found in the National Archives of Ireland in Dublin.

95 Bernadette Whelan, *American government in Ireland, 1790–1913: a history of the US consular service* (Manchester, 2010), 85, 95–7.

96 Bernadette Whelan, *American government in Ireland*, 97–9.

97 J.P. Rodechko, *Patrick Ford and his search for America* (New York, 1976); Owen McGee, 'John Finerty (1846–1908)', *Dictionary of Irish biography* (Cambridge, 2009).

98 George C. Herring, *From colony to superpower: US foreign relations since 1776* (Oxford, 2008), 96–8, 116–17, 126–9, 185–7.

99 David A. Lake, 'The state and American trade strategy in the pre-hegemonic era', *International organization: the state and American foreign economic policy*, vol. 42 no. 1 (winter 1988), 33–58.

100 George C. Herring, *From colony to superpower: US foreign relations since 1776* (Oxford, 2008), 282 (quote); David Sim, *A union forever: the Irish question and US foreign relations in the Victorian age* (New York, 2013).

101 A. Landy, 'A French adventurer and American expansionism after the civil war', *Science and society*, vol. 15 no. 4 (fall 1951), 313–33; Marta Ramon, *A provisional dictator: James Stephens and the Fenian movement* (Dublin, 2007), 205.

102 Speeches of American Fenian filibusters who were arrested in Ireland, such as John McCafferty and Thomas Francis Bourke, virtually alleged that the British foreign office had manipulated the American civil war into happening. [A.M. Sullivan], *Speeches from the dock* (Dublin, 1868). In practice, the principal American grievance with Britain was the degree to which it gave practical recognition to the Confederacy as a belligerent. Paradoxically, McCafferty himself was a former Confederate.

103 'Henri Le Caron' [Thomas Henry Beach], *Twenty-five years in the secret service* (London, 1893).

104 Leon O'Broin, *Fenian fever: an Anglo-American dilemma* (London, 1971).

105 Marta Ramon, *A provisional dictator*, quote p. 59.

106 Lucy E. Salyer, *Under the starry flag: how a band of Irish Americans joined the Fenian Brotherhood and sparked a crisis over citizenship* (Cambridge, 2018).

107 Arthur Mitchell (ed.), *Fighting Irish in the American civil war and the invasion of Mexico* (North Carolina, 2017), 238–53.

108 The text of the Vatican's official condemnation of the Fenians can be found in D'Arcy, *Fenian movement*, 329.

109 One Fenian, William Randall Roberts, did become associated with Tammany Hall and served one undistinguished term as American minister for Chile under the Democratic administration of Grover Cleveland (1884–8). Owen McGee, 'William Randall Roberts (1830–97)', *Dictionary of Irish biography* (Cambridge, 2009).

110 See the entries for John Savage, Thomas Joseph Kelly, John Finerty and Patrick Egan in the *Dictionary of Irish biography*.

111 Róisín Healy, *Poland in the Irish nationalist imagination 1772–1922: anti-colonialism within Europe* (London, 2017).

112 Owen McGee, *The IRB* (Dublin, 2005), 32–6, 62–3.

113 A. Landy, 'A French adventurer and American expansionism after the civil war', *Science and society*, vol. 15 no. 4 (fall 1951), 313–33. The text of the proclamation can be found in John Newsinger, *Fenianism in mid-Victorian Britain* (London, 1994), 54–5.

114 Owen McGee, *The IRB* (Dublin, 2005), chapters 2–4.

115 Bernadette Whelan, 'President Ulysses Grant's Irish tour, 1879', *History Ireland*, vol. 19 no. 1 (Jan.–Feb. 2011); George C. Herring, *From colony to superpower: US foreign relations since 1776* (Oxford, 2008), 265 (quote).

116 Owen McGee, *The IRB* (Dublin, 2005), 60–5.

117 Noel Kissane, *Parnell: a documentary history* (Dublin, 1991), 28–9; Owen McGee, 'William Carroll (1835–1926)', *Dictionary of Irish biography* (Cambridge, 2009). Although a Westminster MP, Parnell had an anti-British ancestor who served as an officer in the American navy during its 1812 war against Britain.

118 John Devoy, 'The story of Clan na Gael', *Gaelic American* (weekly serial, Sep. 1923–Apr. 1925).

119 Owen McGee, *The IRB* (Dublin, 2005), chapters 4–5.

120 Margaret O'Callaghan, *British high politics and a nationalist Ireland* (Cork, 1994); M.L. Legg, *Newspapers and nationalism* (Dublin, 1999), 136–8, 168–9; Owen McGee, *The IRB*, 86–7, 121–130.

121 Christy Campbell, *Fenian fire* (London, 2002); Owen McGee, *The IRB* (Dublin, 2005), chapters 4–7; British Library, Althorp Papers, Add77033, letter of E.G. Jenkinson, 3 Apr. 1884, and Add77036, letters of E.G. Jenkinson, 14 Feb. and 16 Mar. 1885.

122 T.W. Moody, 'The Times versus Parnell and Co., 1887–90', *Historical studies*, 6 (1968), 147–82.

123 Janick Julienne, 'La question Irlandaise en France de 1860 à 1890' (unpublished PhD thesis, University of Paris VII, 1997); Owen McGee, *The IRB*, 185–6.

124 Egan served as American minister to Chile (1889–93). Owen McGee, 'Patrick Egan (1841–1919)', *Dictionary of Irish biography* (Cambridge, 2009).

125 George C. Herring, *From colony to superpower: US foreign relations since 1776* (Oxford, 2008), 282 (quoting Blaine).

126 Stephen Ball (ed.), *Dublin Castle and the first home rule crisis* (Cambridge, 2008).

127 Patrick O'Farrell, *The Irish in Australia* (Kensington, 1987), chapters 5–6; Mark McGowan, *The wearing of the green: Catholics, the Irish and identity in Toronto 1887–1922* (Montreal, 1999).

128 David Noel Doyle, *Irish Americans, native rights and national empires* (Dublin, 1976); Michael Funchion (ed.), *Irish American voluntary organisations* (Connecticut, 1983), 183–9.

129 Owen McGee, *The IRB*, chapter 9.

130 The representative at the Hague conference was George Gavan Duffy, a London-Irish lawyer and Francophile Sinn Féiner. Gerard Keown, *First of the small nations: the beginnings of Irish foreign policy in the interwar years 1919–1932* (Oxford, 2015), 26.

131 Patrick Geoghegan, *Liberator: the life and death of Daniel O'Connell 1830–1847* (Dublin, 2010); Eoin MacNeill, *Daniel O'Connell and Sinn Féin* (Dublin, 1917).

132 Arthur Griffith, *How Ireland is taxed* (Dublin, 1907), 5, 8–9.

133 Arthur Griffith, *The resurrection of Hungary: a parallel for Ireland* (Dublin, 1904).

134 Arthur Griffith, *The resurrection of Hungary: a parallel for Ireland with appendices on Pitt's Policy and Sinn Féin* (3rd ed., Dublin, 1918), 162.

135 Owen McGee, *Arthur Griffith* (Dublin, 2015), 78, 129–31. A handful of Irish champions of cooperative farming and cooperative banking went on educational business tours of America during Theodore Roosevelt's term in office.

136 Jerome aan de Wiel, *The Irish factor 1899–1919: Ireland's strategic and diplomatic importance for foreign powers* (Dublin, 2008), xvii, 4.

137 Michael Doorley, *Irish-American diaspora nationalism* (Dublin, 2005); Carl Wittke, *The Irish in America* (New York, 1956), 274–6 (quote).

138 George C. Herring, *From colony to superpower*, 132–7, 142–4, 154–7, 185–7.

139 Bernadette Whelan, *American government in Ireland, 1790–1913: a history of the US consular service* (Manchester, 2010), 262 (quote), 265.

140 Sean Connolly (ed.), *Belfast 400: people, place and history* (Liverpool, 2012), 27, 31, 37, 36, 41–2.

141 L. Litvack, C. Graham (eds), *Ireland and Europe in the nineteenth century* (Dublin, 2006), 117–21.

142 Fergus Gaines, 'Sir Robert Hart (1835–1911)', *Dictionary of Irish biography* (Cambridge, 2009); Linda Lunney, 'Sir John Newell Jordan (1852–1925)', *Dictionary of Irish biography* (Cambridge, 2009).

143 James Quinn, 'James Bryce (1838–1922)', *Dictionary of Irish biography* (Cambridge, 2009).

144 G.R. Watson, *The Ulster Covenant and Scotland* (Belfast, 2012).

145 The text of the Anglo-American Arbitration Treaty can be found in *The advocate of peace*, vol. 73 no. 9 (Sep. 1911), 196–8.

146 Michael Doorley, *Irish-American diaspora nationalism* (Dublin, 2005), 28–30 (quote p. 28).

147 Owen McGee, *Arthur Griffith*, 107, 113.

148 W.E. Vaughan (ed.), *A new history of Ireland*, vol. 5 (Oxford, 1996), 791–4; W.E. Vaughan (ed.), *A new history of Ireland*, vol. 6 (Oxford, 1996), 355.

149 Jerome aan de Wiel, *The Irish factor 1899–1919: Ireland's strategic and diplomatic importance for foreign powers* (Dublin, 2008), 22; W.E. Vaughan (ed.), *A new history of Ireland*, vol. 5 (Oxford, 1996), 794 (quote). Of the £11 million spent on UK coastal defence during the 1860s, only £120,000 of this was expended in Ireland (Cork) because it was believed that any invasion attempt would be concentrated on southern England. It was also considered that Irish ports would be inconvenient bases for any enemy force to use as part of a greater attack upon Britain. The development of submarine technology altered this perspective.

150 Sir Halford Mackinder, a Glasgow Tory MP, was its effective author. For an appreciative study of his writings, see Geoffrey Sloan, 'Ireland and the geopolitics of Anglo-Irish relations', *Irish studies review*, vol. 15 no. 2 (2007), 163–79.

151 Erskine Childers, *The framework of home rule* (London, 1911), chapter 10, part 3.

152 Patrick Buckland, *James Craig* (Dublin, 1980), 36.

153 Seamus Dunn, T.G. Fraser (eds), *Europe and ethnicity: World War I and contemporary ethnic conflict* (London, 1996), chapter 10.

154 Roger Casement, *Ireland, Germany and the freedom of the seas* (Philadelphia, 1914).

155 Jerome aan de Wiel, *The Irish factor 1899–1919: Ireland's strategic and diplomatic importance for foreign powers* (Dublin, 2008), quoted 324.

156 Gabriel Doherty, Dermot Keogh (eds), *1916* (Cork, 2007).

157 NAI, Bureau of Military History papers, WS1170; Owen McGee, *Arthur Griffith*, 155–6, 161–5, 180–1.While many appeals were issued against his sentence, Casement's posthumous reputation as a hanged rebel was shaped not least by memoirs by Robert Monteith in the 1930s and the British government's offer of a return of his remains in 1965. De Valera chose to honour Casement in 1965 on the grounds of his initial work in highlighting human rights abuses in the Congo rather than his actions during the First World War. This reflected the fact that Casement's 'German Plot' had led the British government to arrest de Valera and other Sinn Féin leaders and imprison them without trial for the best part of a year on the false charge of being German agents rather than Irish nationalists. Maurice Moynihan (ed.), *Speeches and statements of Éamon de Valera 1917–1973* (Dublin, 1980), 604.

158 *Nationality*, 23 June 1917, 8 September 1917, 3 November 1917, 17 November 1917, 8 December 1917, 10 August 1918, 5 October 1918.

159 Arthur Griffith (ed.), *The Resurrection of Hungary with appendices on Pitt's policy and Sinn Féin* (3rd edition, Dublin, 1918), preface, xii.

2

A Republican Moment: Ireland's Independence Struggle in a Global Context, 1919–1922

Sinn Féin's pro-American take on international relations was intended to capitalise upon the development of a political lobby group in the United States known as the Friends of Irish Freedom. This raised the possibility of Ireland's case being presented before the US Houses of Congress.[1] The fact that the United States was the only western power to respond positively to Pope Benedict XV's call for universal peace in August 1917 also found an appreciative audience in Ireland.[2] In an address to Pope Benedict, US President Woodrow Wilson stated that the United States believed that 'peace should rest upon the rights of peoples … their equal right to freedom and security and self-government, and to participation, upon fair terms, in the economic opportunities of the world'. During its triumph in the 1918 parliamentary elections, Sinn Féin cited this remark as evidence that 'our sentiments are in keeping with the greatest organised opinion of mankind – that is, republican opinion'.[3] Neither the US president nor the Pope evidently mentioned Ireland when they met in Rome just prior to the initial meeting of Dáil Éireann.[4] Nevertheless, the members of this Irish parliamentary assembly, which was established unilaterally in the wake of the 1918 elections, adopted the stance of appealing to a universal and pacifist body of public opinion that, it was expected, was watching closely the course of Anglo-Irish relations, and to whom it was trusted that the Dáil's appointed consular representatives were making an effective case. These Dáil consuls focused particularly on the two republican powers in international relations, namely America and France. Indeed, no other countries tended to be mentioned in the Dáil's parliamentary debates.[5]

Historically, the idea that a set of egalitarian republican values existed and were likely to find support through a kind of universal brotherhood of man had been romanticised by many European artists ever since the days of Ludwig van Beethoven. On an intellectual level, however, this idea had often been associated with the cult of freemasonry.[6] In the Irish case, this had been evident in the historic examples of the United Irishmen and the Fenians once they became secret societies. By the twentieth century, however, a desire to emphasise the greater role of Catholicism in protecting religious and intellectual liberties had become an issue in Irish politics. Reflecting this, in the wake of the 1916 Rising, Sinn Féin typified freemasonry as now being on the side of perpetual warfare, military intrigues and controlled medias that were spreading falsehoods about international relations.[7] It welcomed the fact that Russia was responsible for exposing a secret Anglo-French agreement to pervert the Pope's calls for peace, and that the proposal of Alexander Kerensky for holding plebiscites on all questions of national independence 'was that substantially made by Sinn Fein'.[8] Be that as it may, Sinn Féin generally saw the entire Russian revolution as but an episode in the many military intrigues surrounding the First World War. Therefore, it drew its hope almost entirely from Woodrow Wilson's dismissal of great power, or 'balance of power', politics as a 'great game, now forever discredited'.[9] This was reflected by Sinn Féin's 1918 general election literature. This included a collection of Wilson's speeches entitled *Self-Determination and the Rights of Small Nations*; a reprint of the American Declaration of Independence alongside various historic and contemporary expressions of Ireland's desire for political independence entitled *The Case of Ireland Restated*; and a publication by a Protestant Irish Christian-democratic thinker entitled *Towards the Republic: a Study of New Ireland's Social and Political Aims*.[10] The theme of the latter publication by Aodh de Blacam was designed to reflect the fact that an American Catholic cardinal had recently noted that 'it is my impression that the strong confirmation of the Holy See of the old

American principle will give a new impetus to civil liberty the whole wide world over.'[11]

The material and economic basis of the Irish independence struggle was shaped largely by First World War circumstances. British trade between Britain and Ireland (about £100 million a year) had been greater than British trade with any independent country in the world, with the single exception of the United States, and was also greater than British trade with France and Germany combined.[12] For the duration of the war, exports from Ireland to Britain grew to the level of a positive balance of trade and this probably served to boost Sinn Féin confidence. However, German submarine warfare led the British War Office, amidst food shortages caused by decreased shipping, to make the unpopular decision that Irish food exports to Britain should now operate exclusively via Belfast.[13] This helped to sink support for the old Irish Party at Westminster, prompting some of its supporters in either academia or business to embrace Sinn Féin's re-imagining of the Atlantic economy.[14] Albeit for only a three-year period, this led to a very perceptible increase in writings on international relations within the Irish Jesuit journal *Studies*, which was published by University College Dublin (UCD).

Sinn Féin emphasised the degree to which America's entry into the war and the war itself had been economically motivated.[15] Nevertheless, the writings of Alfred Mahan, a founder of the US Naval College, were cited as providing very valuable lessons for Ireland as to why all islands and maritime nations must rely on international trade for their prosperity.[16] Unlike the British Navy League, Sinn Féin argued that there was no logical reason why the principle of the freedom of the seas should not apply to Ireland and allow for the development of its west coast ports as a home for international trade.[17] This served to revive a debate that had been silent since the 1860s regarding the potential role of the Atlantic economy in boosting Irish nationalism. Arthur Griffith suggested that the 'real test of the freedom of the seas' was the degree to which the international community allowed this to happen.[18] In this campaign, Sinn Féin found an ally in the Irish Industrial Development Association (IDA). From Cork, it claimed to have received thousands of business queries from every part of the globe, but it had hitherto been unable to respond to any of them because of the British legal restriction on separate Irish trade agreements.[19] With the support of the IDA, Henry Ford, an Irish American businessman, had long intended to establish an agricultural machinery factory in Cork as a base from which to export to a European market, but this project faced considerable British opposition.[20]

Henry Ford had been a pacifist during the First World War. In this capacity, he had promoted an American Protestant women's movement that had appealed to the Vatican for its support in creating an international pacifist movement.[21] The resulting international women's movement prompted Hanna Sheehy Skeffington to go to America to look for its support for the cause of Irish independence. It also played a part in inspiring Katherine Hughes, the founder of the Catholic women's movement in Canada (which was reputedly the world's largest lay Catholic organisation), to support the cause of Irish independence.[22] Another significant channel of pacifist support for Ireland came from Éamon de Valera's decision to look for the support of Cardinal Désiré-Joseph Mercier of Belgium, who had been the leader of a Catholic pacifist movement in Europe since 1915. Mercier would call for an independent investigation into Irish political circumstances and, in the process, attracted international support for the Irish claim that its independence struggle was a non-violent one based purely on a claim to national self-determination. As a result, G.K. Chesterton, a noted Christian humanist, became one of the very few English commentators to defy British Prime Minister David Lloyd George by expressing support for the justice of Irish nationalists' demands.[23]

This growing international association between Irish nationalism and a liberal pacifism also impacted on domestic American politics. An Irish Progressive League was created in America that championed a new anti-militarist form of labour politics radicalism that issued a direct challenge to the tradition of Irish support for socially conservative American republican patriotism, represented politically by Devoy's *Gaelic American* and the Friends of Irish Freedom.[24] This trend played a significant part in setting the tone for subsequent American debates on Ireland.[25] The most critical development in this regard, however, was that the foreign affairs committee of the US Houses of Representatives left itself open to hearing claims for Irish independence between December 1918 and September 1919. British aristocratic peers who supported

Belfast unionists deemed this to be 'intolerable gross libel' upon British statesmanship.[26] This American initiative, however, was an information gathering exercise regarding Ireland rather than an actual expression of American diplomacy. On the most critical question of the post-war peace settlement, the Irish belief that the American government and, in particular, Edward House, the key diplomatic advisor to President Wilson, would not be influenced by Britain,[27] was not well founded.[28]

The first official diplomatic exercise of the republican government of Dáil Éireann was to issue a 'message to the free nations of the world' alongside an Irish declaration of independence. In keeping with Sinn Féin propaganda ever since America's entry into the war in April 1917, this argued that 'Ireland is the gateway of the Atlantic' and that 'her independence is demanded by the Freedom of the Seas' since, geographically, Ireland was the 'point upon which great trade routes converge': 'her great harbours must be opened to all nations, instead of being the monopoly of England', and, in the process, make an independent Ireland 'a benefit and safeguard to Europe and America'.[29] America had recently announced that it intended to increase by fourfold the size of its mercantile marine. Ireland was now suggesting that altering British monopolies in international trade could be in everyone's best interests. However, the fact that Britain was essentially the prime mover in promoting the idea of creating a post-war 'League of Nations' as a forum for multilateral diplomacy played a significant part in overshadowing this Irish claim.

The Belfast-born British diplomat James Bryce, a key intermediary in Anglo-American relations, was an author of the League of Nations idea in his capacity as a member of the International Court of Justice at the Hague.[30] With an eye to Anglo-American relations, the Irish unionist leader Lord Midleton was likewise supporting the strategy of Arthur Balfour, the British foreign secretary and a long-term close personal associate who had also done much to set the tone of Anglo-Irish relations ever since the 1880s.[31] Balfour had recently sent T.P. O'Connor (a well-known and Irish-born Liverpool MP who had formerly been the chief political advisor of the late John Redmond) to America to promote its level of wartime cooperation. This was done by networking with the two key American banks that financed the Allied war effort. This included J.P. Morgan, which had been the sole agent for the British and French governments in purchasing American munitions and supplies. While O'Connor's mission was opposed both in 'Irish-America' and by Sinn Féin, a small and unsuccessful Irish League of Nations Society supported it. With the patronage of the British foreign office, this society also sought to win Irish support for the British government's right to speak on Ireland's behalf at the post-war peace conference,[32] which would be held at Versailles. With the encouragement of Edward House, Woodrow Wilson had first announced his support for the 'League of Nations' idea as part of his 'Fourteen Points for Peace' during January 1918. In doing so, he made no mention of Ireland. Sinn Féin's response was to suggest that 'diplomatic pressure, no doubt, deterred President Wilson at this stage from placing Ireland side by side with Poland', but this 'does not mean that Ireland is ruled out of the international court'. As soon as Ireland spoke out 'in definite terms for independence', it was expected that the international community would have to recognise that 'President Wilson declares that "all well defined" national aspirations must be met.'[33]

To enhance its capacity to maintain a competitive advantage over all its rivals, the British Empire purposively made all its overseas dominions representatives at the Versailles peace conference. In turn, this entitled them to both membership and voting rights in the proposed League of Nations at Geneva, which was announced as part of the final Versailles peace treaty of May 1919. As the Irish republic's consul at Paris, Sean T. O'Kelly had attempted in vain to gain admittance to Versailles. The Irish government's position with regards to the League of Nations was that it was prepared to support Irish membership of such a league if it was 'based on equality of right' with 'guarantees' that there would be no 'difference between big nations and small, between those that are powerful and those that are weak'.[34] Dublin's response to the Versailles treaty was to repudiate the UK's right to sign the agreement on behalf of Ireland and to send Éamon de Valera, as the Dáil's president, to America where he made the case that the existing covenant of the League of Nations was deeply flawed because its Article Ten meant that action on behalf of a victimised small power could only be taken if all the major powers agreed, in the process leaving unchanged the 'balance of power' diplomatic practices that had led to the First World War in the first place.[35] Typifying this as England's attempt to 'trick America', Sinn

Féin argued that 'today Ireland is doing more than all the remainder of Europe to prevent that trick succeeding' and that this reality was elevating the question of Ireland into a 'world question'.[36]

Noting that 'the domestic problems of Europe are of no consequence to the United States of America', Sinn Féin expected as early as the summer of 1918 that America would not be enthusiastic about the League of Nations idea. Reflecting this, Ireland's primary concern was simply to concentrate on the fact that 'our fellow countrymen in the states will know how to take advantage of the Irish pronouncement for independence' to ensure that 'America will understand the voice of Ireland and America will respond'.[37] The first pronouncement of US Republican Party senators on Ireland was to declare that they believed that the Dáil's representatives should have been admitted to the peace conference, but they did this only after the Versailles conference had ceased.[38] In the autumn of 1919, the Friends of Irish Freedom in America celebrated when US Republican senators rejected the idea of America joining the League of Nations. This was viewed as having undermined the possibility of an Anglo-American alliance and increased the likelihood of persuading the Republican Party to take up the cause of Irish independence as part of its election manifesto for the next US presidential election.[39] It was widely expected that the Republicans would win such an election on an isolationist foreign policy ticket. This was because Americans tended to view new institutions such as the League of Nations and the associated 'International Labour Organisation' as mere fronts for (British) imperial intrigue, as well as a means to lead America, against its own wishes, into European political entanglements. Sinn Féin was essentially correct that the United States would welcome if direct trade with Ireland could be boosted. However, America had no interest in involving itself directly in others' affairs, preferring instead to stick dogmatically to a foreign policy of '[commercial] involvement without [diplomatic] commitment'.[40] This was the Achilles heel of the Friends of Irish Freedom's campaign.

The attitude of Wilson's Democratic Party in the United States was disappointing for Ireland. A cross-party Irish delegation had attempted, in vain, to meet Wilson in Paris to offer him the freedom of Dublin. On this occasion, intimations were received from Edward House and Herbert Hoover, then the head of the American Relief Administration in Paris, that Wilson could not 'officially' take up Ireland's case. Sinn Féin read this comment mistakenly as a hint of encouragement. Wilson was actually very unhappy that the Friends of Irish Freedom had unilaterally appointed a political delegation of three prominent Democratic Party members to visit Ireland and Paris in support of the Dáil. Frank P. Walsh, a Kansas City lawyer who was formerly chairman of American Commission on Industrial Relations, led this delegation.[41] In the recent past, the Friends' treasurer Thomas Hughes Kelly, who was chairman of the New York Emigrant Savings Bank, was prevented from even landing in Ireland by the British government. According to Lord Midleton, the only reason why the British government did not issue a warrant for the arrest of Walsh was that it had decided instead to present the British government's case regarding Ireland to the American government purely as part of its negotiations for the holding of future joint Anglo-American naval conferences.[42] From Britain's point of view, the question of the freedom of the seas with regards to Ireland meant utilising the western coast of Ireland for the defence of British mercantile and military shipping alone. As acting president of the Dáil, Arthur Griffith believed that Britain's massive wartime debt to the United States should work to Ireland's advantage in presenting a different case.[43] Ireland's lack of financial clout, however, meant that it was poorly equipped to convince the Americans not to accept the Royal Navy's 'western approaches' stratagem. An additional factor that did not help the Irish case was that Wilson had been very influenced by Casement's misleading propaganda that had presented Irish nationalists as having been pro-German during the war.[44]

Dáil Éireann's economic policy was based on a desire to change banking practices in Ireland by adopting a more American-style policy of allowing extensive loans to even small businesses. This was considered as an essential first step to allow Ireland to capitalise upon various international factors. This included the capacity of many 'pre-war pastoral countries' to capitalise upon the trend of American investment in Europe to transform themselves into 'a manufacturing exporter'; the existence of 'a permanent market' on the European continent for Irish agricultural produce; and the potential, once Ireland was able to 'burst through the trade wall' of Britain, to revive various historical trade routes as well as to create entirely new ones.[45] Dáil personnel worked with the IDA and American consular services to promote direct trade between Dublin and New York, and they also worked with French consular services to initiate new direct shipping lines with Le Havre and Bordeaux.[46] These initiatives, however, involved American and French shipping lines exclusively because there was insufficient Irish risk capital to establish an Irish mercantile marine. The British government, which had already imprisoned many Sinn Féin TDs, formally outlawed Dáil Éireann in September 1919 after it began legislating on banking. Hitherto, almost half of the assets of the Irish joint stock banks and Post Office Savings Bank were held jointly as securities in London banks, and were legally tied into the operations of both the Irish Land Commission and the British government's own 'war loan fund' that had financed the First World War.[47] The Dáil issued a direct challenge to this situation in August 1919 when it launched its own National Land Bank in Dublin under the management of a former professor of economics in Toronto.[48] This bank sought to cultivate links with cooperative banks in both America and Germany and to scrap the Irish Land Commission, but the British government considered this to be an illegal initiative.

Sinn Féin's expected victory in all local government elections was intended to bring about a complete revolution in banking practices in Ireland. This was because of the willingness of all local government bodies, which swore an oath of loyalty to the Dáil as the national parliament and intended setting up their own courts, to invest their funds in the Dáil's bank to effectively transform it into a new Irish national bank. This was the essential basis of Sinn Féin's counter-state programme: enabling Irish nationalists to take administrative control of all the apparatus of government nationwide.[49] The outlawing of the Dáil, however, not only made this policy impractical but also left the Irish republican administration without a secure outlet for investing its capital other than in Dublin Corporation stock. Therefore, the administration of the Irish government outside of Dublin city became an essentially *ad hoc* process that operated without the security of having a working relationship with any bank.[50] This trend was enhanced by the fact that as soon as Sinn Féin took control of the national administration of local government during the summer of 1920, Britain sent army auxiliaries to Ireland to suppress this administration, causing fatalities in Ireland to peak thereafter.[51] This situation naturally irked Sinn Féin supporters greatly. On Griffith's insistence, the new Irish government had introduced its own oath of allegiance at the same time as it launched its own bank.[52] This initiative had the support of the vast majority of Irish elected representatives, both locally and nationally, but it was perpetually frustrated thereafter.

After direct trade between Dublin and New York was initiated, the monthly figure for Dublin's exports to America (£400,000) soon became equivalent to annual figures before the war.[53] However, this was still only 5 per cent of the amount of Irish trade with Britain. Much more American trade was operating via Belfast, while virtually no American trade was operating via Cork, Limerick or Derry. The American consular offices in Ireland fully appreciated this reality.[54] Reflecting this, President Wilson chose to close down the American government's commission on Ireland as soon as Britain formally outlawed the Dáil. The lack of international protests about the suppression of the Dáil in September 1919 practically turned Irish diplomatic representatives abroad into outlaws. As a result, de Valera could no longer address state assemblies in America, although the Friends of Irish Freedom continued to attempt to introduce him to various state governors.[55]

Harry Boland, a gregarious Dublin sportsman who had resigned as IRB president to take up a position as the Dáil's agent in America, responded by organising a well-publicised national lecture tour for de Valera.[56] However, a definite solution to the problem of being labelled an outlaw needed to be found. This focused minds upon the press. During the First World War, the *New York Times* was the only American newspaper that Britain had allowed into Ireland. This prompted Sinn Féin to typify it as the eyes and ears of the British foreign office in America. Certainly, it had long typified Ireland as 'the spoilt child of the Empire',[57] while also supporting the claim of T.P. O'Connor that Irish nationalism was neither a policy nor a coherent philosophy of self-government, but instead was a mere 'child of provocation, insult, and want of all faith in English statesmanship or English good faith'.[58] De Valera's response to the closure of the American commission on Ireland in September 1919 was to set up an Irish National Press Bureau in both Washington D.C. and New York City under Katherine Hughes. This was done with funding from Thomas Hughes Kelly and John

Castellini, a millionaire food-wholesaler from Cincinnati, Ohio, who usually funded Catholic rather than Irish causes. The official line of the Dáil's department of foreign affairs, set down by Griffith, was that the struggle for recognition of Irish independence depended entirely on direct communications with other governments: mere propaganda was insufficient, while definitions of Ireland's case with reference to the rights of other groups within the British Empire should be avoided.[59] De Valera himself, however, did not share this belief, having already directed Sean T. O'Kelly in Paris that 'in addition to using the press you should get into the closest possible contact with the South Africans, Egyptians, Indians, Australians, Canadians, New Zealanders, etc.',[60] even though the Dáil's department of foreign affairs, in keeping with its republican aspirations, neither had nor would appoint any representatives to the British dominions. This belief of de Valera's in the value of Irish propaganda within the British Empire had also been reflected by his response to an attempt to establish a support body for the Dáil in Britain. He recommended that this be done by forming an 'Irish Self-Determination League' as a purely propagandistic body that should seek to capitalise upon the fact that the term 'self-determination' was now a respectable norm in international discourse, associated with the pursuit of peace as an abstract principle.[61]

After September 1919, de Valera directed Katherine Hughes and Robert Lindsay Crawford, an Irish-born editor of the Toronto *Statesman*, to form an Irish Self-Determination League in Canada. This was supposed to work in tandem with the British organisation and to seek to establish a similar body in Australia.[62] Hughes would concentrate on this goal. By contrast, Crawford would work primarily with French-Canadian politicians in seeking to mobilise both Canadian and American sympathy for the cause of Irish independence. This initiative was supported by Judge Daniel Cohalan, who was the practical leader of the Friends of Irish Freedom in New York.[63] Although somewhat ineffective, a context to Crawford's initiative was a dynamic of cross-border Canadian–American relations, whereby American-educated Canadian politicians were more inclined to favour a distinctly North American identity as opposed to a traditional British colonial identity for Canada, which nominally had its own department of external affairs since 1909.[64]

In February 1920, de Valera shocked the Friends of Irish Freedom by suggesting to the *Westminster Gazette* that Ireland could exist within a protective British military zone in a similar manner to Cuba's relationship with the United States. The Friends of Irish Freedom not only deemed this idea to be a serious mistake but also saw it as undermining their efforts to get the US Republican Party to interest itself in the cause of Irish independence. In June 1920, Cohalan succeeded in persuading the Republican Party to issue a resolution during its Chicago national convention for selecting its next presidential candidate 'that the people of Ireland have the right to determine freely, without dictation from outside, their own government institutions and their international relations with other states and peoples'. Although the Democratic Party had already rejected the idea of introducing a pro-Irish resolution in deference to Wilson, de Valera responded to Cohalan's initiative by denouncing both Cohalan and the Friends of Irish Freedom for not also approaching the Democratic Party national convention. In doing so, de Valera bypassed entirely Cohalan's carefully cultivated American political networks and prompted the Republican Party, for fear of becoming associated with an internal Irish dispute, to drop the idea of making a pro-Irish resolution altogether. The British ambassador to the United States viewed this development as evidence of 'the immense influence Irishmen can exert on American politicians, if they proceed wisely, and how ready American politicians are to withdraw themselves from that influence if they find some honourable pretext for doing so'.[65]

Although the Republican Party rejected the candidate that Cohalan supported for the presidential election, de Valera's Cuban analogy and practical sabotage of Cohalan's tactics was the subject of much criticism even from some Catholic bishops within the Friends of Irish Freedom, who accused de Valera of a lack of judgment and a failure to understand his need for American advice on how to handle American politics. Shortly thereafter, upon the arrival in America from London of Daniel Mannix, an Irish-born Catholic archbishop of Melbourne, de Valera decided to retire from public speaking in America. He wrote to Griffith that 'the greater part of my usefulness here is over' and that he believed 'the work which is being done in Ireland towards making the government function as a *de facto* government is advancing our cause, even here, more than anything that could be done by our friends in this country'.[66] Upon de Valera's arrival in America, he had been made aware by Sir Shane Leslie and his British diplomatic friends in New York that the British government was fully confident that the Vatican was its unbending ally with regards to Ireland. To counteract this trend, de Valera had directed Sean T. O'Kelly to transfer himself from Paris to Rome, where he would eventually succeed in acquiring a papal audience during May 1920. The hardworking O'Kelly, who in the eyes of the Catholic hierarchy was a rather simple-minded or naïve individual, saw this as a triumph for the Irish republican cause, rather than what it actually achieved: a pledge of the Church's effective neutrality. This was de Valera's objective, even though this may have had very limited consequences in international relations.[67]

Writing to the IRB, which under the direction of Michael Collins (who was also the Dáil's minister for finance) did much to keep the Dáil's administration alive in an underground fashion, the old Fenian John Devoy emphasised that although 'the defeat of English intrigues in America is essential to success', 'this can only be achieved by Irishmen here working as citizens of the US, guided by men who have intimate knowledge of American affairs':

> Therefore, there should be constant consultation between you and us as to the measures that concern purely American affairs. So that your hopes may not be raised too high as to possibilities, we would remind you that our people here are less than a fifth of the total population, that scarcely more than a tenth of that fifth are directly interested in the Irish cause and that our power to influence public measures that concern Ireland depends largely on our supposed, rather than our actual, strength and on our ability to make combinations with other and friendly sections of the American people, who still require enlightenment on the Irish question.[68]

If there were some wisdom in Devoy's judgment, the Friends of Irish Freedom nevertheless declined thereafter. Cohalan blamed this entirely on de Valera, although as Cohalan (an ex-Fenian) was also fond of stating on American Republican Party platforms that Britain's wartime debt to the United States could be paid up by surrendering its control of Canada and the West Indies, Cohalan's sense of American foreign policy was seemingly about fifty years out of date.[69] In October 1920, acting on de Valera's direct orders, Harry Boland severed the secret connection that had existed between the American Clan na Gael and the IRB in Ireland on the grounds of the political influence that Cohalan wielded over the former body through Devoy.[70]

The non-inclusion of Ireland in the American presidential election campaign of the winter of 1920 was perhaps a death blow to the chances of securing international recognition for an Irish republic. Before returning to Ireland in December 1920, de Valera's final initiative in America was to direct Joseph McGarrity of Philadelphia to set up a rival organisation to the Friends of Irish Freedom. While this was entitled the 'American Association for Recognition of the Irish Republic' (AARIR), ironically, it expressed its unwillingness to deal directly with the American government. This indicated that the AARIR existed solely as a propagandist and fundraising body. Its formation coincided, however, with a fresh impulse provided to Irish propaganda in America by the existence between November 1920 and March 1921 of the congressional 'American Commission on Conditions in Ireland'. By criticising the operation of British martial law in Ireland, this body evoked a hostile reaction from Midleton, Austen Chamberlain and other British political leaders, but it created room for fund collection efforts in America for the relief of the many victims of British coercion in Ireland ever since the summer of 1920. This was done by means of a new 'American Committee for Relief in Ireland' that was led by Thomas Hughes Kelly and would send its funds to a new organisation in Dublin known as the Irish White Cross.[71] This committee succeeded in receiving subscriptions from both the east and west coasts of America, including from leaders of a new motion picture industry in California.[72]

De Valera returned to Ireland in December 1920 on the same day that Westminster passed a Government of Ireland Act, which legally established, under British law, assemblies of Northern Ireland and Southern Ireland with no powers of fiscal autonomy. Having decided to concentrate almost wholly on propaganda and fund collection efforts, de Valera attempted to link the initiative of the American Committee For Relief in Ireland with the operations of Irish self-determination leagues throughout the British Empire by making each a supporter of the 'great Christian and national work' of the Irish White Cross in offering relief to all victims of British martial law and coercion in Ireland: 'I am convinced it is a work in which Irishmen and women in every part of the world will want to take part and that the example of our friends in America will soon be followed by those in Canada, South America, Australasia, South Africa and in Britain itself.'[73]The Irish White Cross in Dublin was not formally instituted as an organisation until February 1921, around the same time as de Valera encouraged the National Land Bank to affiliate itself with the Irish Banks Standing Committee, led by the loyalist Bank of Ireland. The White Cross intentionally encompassed leaders of all religious denominations and interest groups within Irish society.[74] This was done for two reasons. First, nationally its existence illustrated the reality that it was the British government, not the Irish republican supporters of Dáil Éireann, who was adopting violent coercion in Ireland to attain its goals. Second, internationally the existence of the Irish White Cross was intended to substantiate the argument of the Irish Self-Determination Leagues that were it not for the Orange brand of freemason propaganda that the British foreign office was distributing worldwide via Reuters, the world would understand fully that the Irish demand for independence was an entirely national, democratic and economic matter, embodying no sectarian dimension. Be that as it may, this emphasis upon media work rather than appealing directly to republican governments abroad practically opened the door to an Irish acceptance of British overtures (previously rejected by Griffith, who was thereafter imprisoned) to offer Ireland the status of a British dominion. Not surprisingly, these overtures began during the summer of 1920 in the wake of the Irish failure to persuade American political parties to make the question of Irish independence a platform issue in the next US presidential election contest.[75]

Archbishop Mannix's former status as a leader of an Australian anti-conscription movement was the principal strength and weakness of the Irish Self-Determination League in Australia. Like the Canadian league but unlike the British league (which included various IRB activists),[76] this occasionally succeeded in getting either ex-government ministers or ex-cabinet members within the British dominions to chair Irish meetings.[77] This development had been made necessary in Canada because Crawford's support for supposedly pro-American (as opposed to pro-British) Canadian politicians had led to a violent backlash from the Orange Order in Canada, which adopted physical violence to prevent his Irish league from holding public meetings.[78] Meanwhile, in Australia a move had actually been made, despite opposition from some Australian labour MPs (one of whom would be expelled from the Australian parliament as a result), to label all Catholics as inherently disloyal subjects of the British Empire in order to secure the arrest of any probable sympathisers with Ireland in Australia.[79] While an Orange brand of Freemasonry certainly thrived within all the British dominions, its attacks upon the Irish Self-Determination Leagues purposively ignored the fact that the chief argument of these bodies had also been made by the Canadian and Australian prime ministers: namely, British coercion in Ireland reflected badly on all British territories and, therefore, it must be stopped for the sake of the better governance of the Empire.[80] Sir Osmond Thomas Grattan Esmonde, a new member of the Dáil's foreign affairs department, was denied entry into Australia because he refused to take an oath of allegiance to the British Crown on his arrival, while thereafter he was threatened with arrest on a charge of sedition on a visit to Vancouver. Reflecting the limits of their ambitions, the Irish Self-Determination Leagues of Australia and Canada refused to comment on Esmonde's case, however, because they feared a public backlash.[81]

From a republican point of view, the Irish diplomatic mission had faced insurmountable obstacles not only in America but also in France. Sean T. O'Kelly and George Gavan Duffy, the Irish consuls at Paris, had always arranged that their communiqués be sent to the French foreign office.[82] On the French government's orders, however, formal acknowledgement that this was taking place could not be published either in France or in Ireland.[83] In the Dáil itself, Griffith only acknowledged that the French National War Museum had requested copies of all Irish literature 'with a view to giving them a place in the Museum together with the literature issued by other countries'.[84] The intensity of French fears, or even hatred, of the Germans, which de Valera had predicted as early as April 1919 could make the Versailles settlement the basis of another war,[85] also governed French attitudes towards Ireland. The reports of the French consul in Dublin to Ariste Briand, the French foreign minister, took the form of a précis of Irish news, almost in the fashion of intelligence reports. Rather than suggesting the cultivation of diplomatic relations with Ireland, these were concerned entirely with figuring out Irish attitudes towards Franco-German relations; in short, whether the Irish were either 'pro-French' or 'pro-German'. From the contemporary French point of view, one could not be neither or both.[86]

The French press was far more interested in the Irish question in America as an aspect of Anglo-American relations and, in turn, how this might affect Franco-British relations than it was in circumstances in Ireland itself. During the spring of 1920, this began to change when Irish Catholic criticisms of a British declaration of a military curfew in Ireland (the first of many) evoked a response in Catholic France. Virtually alone amongst Parisian deputies, Marc Sangnier, who was also France's leading Christian-democratic thinker,[87] began to speak regularly in favour of complete Irish independence at public meetings. Although Sangnier's influence in France was limited somewhat by the fact that he was widely considered to be a dated politician with a pre-1914 worldview,[88] he professed to be willing, if requested by the Dáil, to either offer his pen or speak in the French National Assembly on behalf of Ireland.[89] Unlike the situation in America, there was not a noticeable Irish community in France. Nevertheless, Michael MacWhite, a Sinn Féiner and former French Foreign Legionnaire who operated a small Franco-Irish Society, served the Irish Parisian consulate well by generating publicity in the French press. The tenor of a weekly *Irish Bulletin*, which detailed all acts of British coercion and was distributed internationally in the wake of the suppression of the Dáil, would seem to have made some impression in France. Sympathetic press reporting became more common in sectional (Catholic as well as socialist) as well as provincial (agricultural as well as municipal) French newspapers.[90] However, as the Irish department of foreign affairs noted, the French national press was far more guarded because:

The fear of Germany is so great that France is very anxious not to break with England. Hence official France is not prepared to take the side of Ireland in her present struggle. The Paris press is for the most part governed in its outlook by the prevailing official viewpoint and is accordingly very guarded in its expressions on Irish questions.[91]

Considering that pro-Irish press reportage in France was 'activity which comes more properly under the head of propaganda', Duffy and O'Kelly were far from enthusiastic about this situation and so, by the summer of 1920, had already become doubtful of the continued value of the Parisian diplomatic mission. That autumn, after French press interviews were arranged with Griffith and Duffy, both men issued direct appeals to the French government to protest against Britain's treatment of Terence MacSwiney, the imprisoned mayor of Cork who, in common with many Irish political prisoners, had gone on hunger strike. In doing so, however, Duffy broke with protocol by publishing his appeal, prompting the British consulate in Paris to demand that Duffy be expelled from France immediately. As the French had to comply, Duffy relocated to Belgium. After being allowed a final sympathetic French press interview in his defence, he left for Rome, where he joined a by now ailing Sean T. O'Kelly.[92] Inspired partly by some initial Irish efforts with the Italian press, they began focusing on the idea that Ireland should present itself to Catholic Europe as a 'bulwark of religion in a godless world'.[93]

Sections of the French media were willing to question the wisdom of British plans to partition Ireland. The *Revue du Politique et Parlementaire*, a prominent French journal, deemed Westminster's Government of Ireland Act to be an unjust act that was inherently doomed to fail because it was endeavouring to create 'two Irish provinces, but no Ireland; a Quebec, or an Ontario perhaps, but no Canada'.[94] In common with most of the international press,[95] French journalists were impressed by MacSwiney's hunger-strike protest, leading to frequent critiques of British military rule in Ireland, although British protests would mean that this trend virtually ceased by the spring of 1921.[96] Being eager to negate Irish attempts to appeal to American opinion, David Lloyd George, the British prime minister, wanted to convince the international community that the Dáil and its supporters should be viewed akin to how the Confederacy was viewed by the Union during the American civil war, considering this claim to be an effective counter to de Valera's argument that the only potential parallel between contemporary Irish circumstances and American history dated from 1776.[97] London used this civil war claim to justify its stance that Irish rebels should be treated according to pre-existing law without recognising their right either to secede from the Union or to receive formal acknowledgement of their status as belligerents or political prisoners. It was clear to all observers, however, that this campaign was not working, particularly on a moral level. Due to local government elections, by the summer of 1920, Irish republican volunteers were able to supplant the authority of British police forces (many of whom voluntarily retired) as peacekeepers across most of the country, prompting Lloyd George to send army battalions of 60,000 men to Ireland to take their place. These British soldiers, however, found themselves in a situation in which they had no clearly defined responsibility other than to wield by virtue of their armed physical presence the moral authority of regular policing forces of law and order, which little to none of the general Irish populace was prepared to give them. This was reflected by the fact that as many as 100,000 unarmed men pledged to offer their services to the Irish volunteer movement in opposition to this British armed presence.[98]

In Boland's absence, Michael Collins, as acting president of the IRB (which had no more than 3,000 members), had used its secret networks in an effort to coordinate the activities of all Irish volunteer officers with the view to systemically create the basis of an Irish republican police force and army. However, the Dáil itself had no regular army. Most Irish republican volunteers performed regular civilian jobs and only about 3,000 in total had firearms. While there were several thousand volunteers in the Irish capital, the 'Acting Service Unit' in Dublin of would-be permanent Irish soldiers, who were essentially akin to mere infantrymen, amounted to just fifty men. The old revolutionary organisation of the IRB supplied this nucleus by providing a small permanent staff and an officer corps, but the directive power of its General Headquarters (GHQ) was limited because of the Dáil's restricted administrative capacity outside Dublin. The IRB, which also acted as an intelligence department for the underground Dáil, was prepared to kill a number of British intelligence agents in Dublin whenever they attempted to seize the Irish government's funds. Actual confrontations with British forces, however, was confined to the activities of a few flying columns of volunteers in Munster over whom GHQ exercised virtually no control. Particularly during the spring of 1921, some of these men attempted to resist by force the imposition of a

British military curfew in Cork. This curfew was designed to punish all sympathisers with MacSwiney's hunger strike by burning Cork city to the ground and summarily executing any armed member of the general Irish public. The Sinn Féin mayor of Limerick was also shot dead by Crown forces at this time.[99]

Ever since the summer of 1920, British attempts to force Ireland to meet its terms had increased the number of British and American foreign correspondents that visited Ireland.[100] Supporters of the Dáil knew, however, that the purpose of these men was simply to collect intelligence reports on Irish politics purely for their own governments' benefit. Therefore, they were not taken fully into their confidence.[101] The Irish correspondent of Le Temps, a semi-governmental French organ, also worked as an intelligence intermediary between the British and French governments.[102] Nevertheless, he was trusted by Michael MacWhite, who managed to cultivate some pro-Irish sympathies in southern France, including Lyon, after he addressed a French republican assembly in Bordeaux, a one-time home to fairly influential Irish merchants. MacWhite also attempted to encourage debate on the question of direct Franco-Irish trade in northern France. Yann Goblet of the University of Rennes, which also produced French publications on Ireland, supported this work and also organised regular public meetings in sympathy with Ireland in Brittany. This was probably not a potential source of strength for Ireland, however, due to Parisian antipathy to all Breton nationalists.[103]

Upon assuming direct personal responsibility for the Dáil's department of foreign affairs in February 1921, de Valera gave a French press interview in which he contrasted alleged British state support for sectarian riots in Belfast with the full civil and religious liberties offered to Irish citizens by the Irish republic. He also emphasised his belief, however, that the Anglo-Irish dispute 'can be solved definitely and completely by any of the general formulae about the rights of small nations which received almost universal recognition during the war, and were particularly approved of by the responsible statesmen of Britain.'[104] De Valera's determination to allow Ireland to adapt fully to the emerging European political order, whether it was influenced unduly by Britain or not, was reflected by his subsequent promotion of MacWhite to a diplomat in Switzerland, with the job of keeping Ireland fully informed of all developments surrounding the League of Nations initiative at Geneva.[105]

Before leaving the French capital, MacWhite together with Joseph Walshe, an ex-Jesuit now appointed to the Parisian consulate office, decided to launch an Irish cultural mission in France to 'project a distinct image of the country'.[106] This was done through the promotion of Irish arts and culture, and was based on an understanding of 'how closely intellectual esteem is related to social and trade relations'.[107] Some inspiration for this idea was drawn from a prior Canadian suggestion that a 'World Conference of the Irish Race' should be held in Montreal.[108] A new Irish organisation that was founded in South Africa to support the Irish White Cross offered to host such an occasion.[109] De Valera, however, preferred Paris as a choice of location. This was possibly because the American Relief Association had its headquarters in Paris. Certainly, the Dáil had some hopes that the separate 'American Committee for Relief in Ireland' initiative could help to encourage a process of American foreign direct investment in Ireland.[110] It seems, however, that Paris was favoured simply because of its much closer proximity to Dublin. To boost support for the Irish White Cross, Laurence Ginnell was sent to Argentina, where historic Irish émigrés had traditionally been of British imperial sympathies. Perhaps for this very reason, Ginnell was allowed to meet the Argentinian foreign minister and to organise a Buenos Aires convention in support of both the Irish White Cross and the idea of sending South American representatives to the proposed Parisian conference.[111] It was also announced that this was to become the occasion for launching a new global Irish organisation with a focus upon the world of international trade. The value that the Dáil placed in this initiative was reflected by the fact that its foreign affairs department would spend £6,000 in planning the event.[112]

Symbolically, the 'World Conference of the Irish Race' was planned to take place in January 1922 on the third anniversary of the formation of Dáil Éireann and the initial Irish republican declaration of independence. To a significant extent, however, this obscured the reality that the original Irish diplomatic mission to seek foreign powers' formal recognition of an Irish republic had already reached an unsuccessful conclusion. The evident impossibility of convincing the republican countries of America and France to defy Britain by recognising the Irish government can explain why Irish political debate now became focused almost exclusively on attempting to convince British public opinion of the justice of Irish demands. The best illustration of this trend was Aodh de Blacam's dedication of his book *What Sinn Féin Stands for: The Irish Republican Movement, Its History, Aims and Ideals, Examined as to Their Significance to the World* (Dublin, 1921) to all 'men of goodwill' throughout the British Empire.[113] It was also reflected by de Valera's suggestion to an Australian interviewer that while 'Australia, Canada and New Zealand might, in a sense, put forward a plea that they enjoy something more than independence [by being partners in a British Empire] … we in Ireland, in claiming the republic, seek simple independence and nothing more.'[114] Griffith had encouraged Irish merchants or journalists in Denmark, Italy and Argentina to affiliate themselves with the Irish department of foreign affairs, while de Valera persuaded a couple of individuals to launch diplomatic work in Spain. However, such candidates could only report on the tenor of journalism in their host countries.[115] Egyptians who sought Irish contacts were rebuffed, while the Middle East, Africa and Asia were ignored entirely. In central Europe, a couple of journalists or academics offered to do propaganda work,[116] while Gerald O'Kelly, an Irish-born Austrian count, could be said to have launched the Irish mission in Switzerland.[117] St John Gaffney, a former American consul in Munich, had expressed support for an Irish republic, but he could not be recruited for diplomatic purposes because he was an American citizen.[118] Finally, Patrick MacCartan, a former member of the IRB who visited the United States frequently, tested the possibility of receiving recognition from the USSR. After initial and seemingly positive contacts were made, the Russians decided that they valued the prospect of a British trade agreement more, and so they sent MacCartan away from Moscow without granting any recognition to the Irish republic.[119]

These diplomatic dead ends increased the relevance of British foreign office personnel in seeking to broker an Anglo-Irish understanding. Having first offered to do propaganda work for the Dáil, by February 1921 Erskine Childers had managed to persuade de Valera to employ him as a political advisor. For a time, this led John Chartres, a former colleague of Childers' in the British labour ministry, to nominally assume the responsibility of attempting to set up an Irish diplomatic office in Berlin.[120] Through Irish organisations in South Africa, British army personnel such as Maurice Moore and Tom Casement (a brother of Roger Casement's) managed to persuade de Valera to enter into communications with Jan Smuts en route to the signing of a truce-like agreement in July 1921. Under its terms, restrictions on the bearing of firearms by Irishmen were applied and secret liaison officers were appointed between the British and Irish governments for both military and policing matters. The Irish liaison officers for the army were Eamon Duggan and Robert Barton, who were also the Dáil's ministers for home affairs and agriculture respectively. The Irish liaison officers for the police were Emmet Dalton, a former British soldier, and Eoin O'Duffy, an increasingly outspoken figure regarding disturbances in Ulster, both of whom now became associates of Michael Collins.[121] Rather than reflecting on these details, Irish public opinion was inclined to simply celebrate the cessation of British coercion in July 1921. Meanwhile, notwithstanding the compromises involved, the liaison situation appeared to most Irish republican volunteers to be a welcome 'first sign of official British recognition for Oglaigh na hEireann',[122] which was the official title of the Irish republican volunteer movement that was often nicknamed the Irish Republican Army (IRA), which was the title preferred by the IRB. No political settlement had been reached, however, while the prospects for a formal institutionalisation of an independent Irish army and police force remained uncertain.

Britain had entered negotiations with de Valera on the basis of offering Ireland dominion status rather than complete independence. While the officer corps of Óglaigh na hÉireann pledged to abide by whatever the Dáil voted to accept, the effect that any Anglo-Irish agreement would have upon discipline among their own followers was far from certain, not least because the Sinn Féin organisation in the provinces acted under very different (and perhaps less disciplined) circumstances than in Dublin.[123] De Valera's initial correspondence with Lloyd George that summer was published almost immediately. Press reactions abroad were often very sceptical. The *Toronto Star* suggested that, within all the British dominions, 'everybody knows that the status offered Ireland by Lloyd George falls a long way short of being dominion status ... the half-dozen "reservations" made in the offer to Ireland make all the difference in the world'.[124] The British approach to negotiating with the Dáil stemmed partly from its greater priority of settling Anglo-American relations. In the United States, the Friends of Irish Freedom had launched a congressional campaign that called upon the new Republican administration of President Warren Harding not to compromise with Britain, nor tolerate any reduction in American naval strength, at the forthcoming Washington Naval Disarmament Conference.[125] On the British side, joining Balfour's negotiating team was Maurice Hankey, the British cabinet secretary, director of intelligence and a key figure in setting the tone for British international relations. He privately feared that commercially motivated Anglo-American tensions could lead to an actual war.[126] Just prior to Hankey's leaving for Washington D.C., his intelligence agents in Dublin reported that any forthcoming Anglo-Irish agreement would be opposed by de Valera, in a party political sense, which was seen by Britain as a development that might minimise the dominance of the Sinn Féin Party hitherto within the Dáil Éireann assembly and allow for the re-emergence of old Irish Party networks.[127] This strategy reflected Britain's approach to negotiating with a six-man team of Irish plenipotentiaries that de Valera appointed a fortnight later. Having in no sense conceded defeat, London was determined to prioritise a demand that Dublin pay reparations for alleged damages caused to Irish unionists' property during the recent independence struggle as a price for merely allowing the liaison arrangements to continue. In addition, London pressed home the Royal Navy's alleged need of three western Irish ports, encompassing the northern and southern tips of the island, in order to sustain the defence of its 'Western Approaches', stretching from the northern and southern tips of the island of Britain out to several hundred miles beyond Ireland's Atlantic coastline.[128]

Upon his release from prison in July 1921, Arthur Griffith was appointed as the Dáil's foreign minister and was now chosen by de Valera to head the Irish team of plenipotentiaries. Dublin was determined that Ireland should have the right both to be neutral in international military conflicts and to have control of its own naval defence. London was prepared to concede that its need for western Irish ports should be made temporary, pending the formal assumption by Ireland of its own naval defence. So long as London's right to these ports was conceded, however, Ireland's capacity to capitalise upon the existence of an Atlantic economy could be neutralised. A practical consequence of this would soon be felt. Entrepreneurs in Ireland that had hitherto tendered their support for Sinn Féin's trans-Atlantic ideas for the future of Irish commerce would soon withdraw that support and instead accommodate, or re-accommodate, themselves to Britain's desire that Irish business would concentrate exclusively on imperial markets.[129] On a diplomatic level, Britain had the means to potentially cement such an arrangement. Its offer to Ireland of dominion status equivalent to that of Canada would allow for an Irish admittance to the League of Nations on similar terms. This could potentially frame the future evolution of Irish economic, diplomatic and military affairs within a broader British imperial programme that was being championed not only by the Dominions Office but also by Sir Arthur Salter of the Royal Navy, who had managed to get himself appointed as the head of the economic and financial secretariat of the League of Nations.[130]

In negotiations, Griffith emphasised that Irish amenability to membership of the British Commonwealth would depend on a British recognition that Ireland could opt out of any future British war effort, and that 'on no account could I recommend any association with the Crown or the Commonwealth if the unity of Ireland were denied in form or in fact'.[131] The latter, essentially national, issue was one that Griffith believed should involve northern unionist representatives as much as the Dáil's plenipotentiaries. H.E. Pollock, the chairman of the Belfast Harbour Board and London's proposed finance minister for Northern Ireland, had argued previously that 'northern Irishmen are just as patriotic as those in the south' and 'we will welcome a chance to join it in a self-governing Ireland'.[132] Acting on the advice of the British Lord Chancellor, however, James Craig opted out of negotiating directly with the Dáil's plenipotentiaries. Whilst championing fiscal autonomy for Ireland, Griffith emphasised that Britain's demand for an Irish contribution to the British national debt was completely contrary to the fact that 'none of the dominions has any share of Britain's debt'.[133] In this matter, the combined facts of the all-island nature of the economy of Ireland and Belfast's status as an imperial city would prove problematic for Dublin. While Craig acknowledged privately that Ireland had been a victim of 'excessive payment of contribution to imperial taxation in years gone by,[134] he would soon start demanding that Ireland make a massive contribution to the British national debt, in the process placing Dublin and Belfast at loggerheads, with London acting as an unwilling intermediary.[135]

Griffith maintained that because the English king held his position purely by a parliamentary title that could be revoked, it 'follows that equality of status would make it possible for the Irish parliament to abolish the monarchy in Ireland'.[136] Craig's fears of Irish republican aspirations made him hostile to Irish claims that Article Twelve of a proposed treaty agreement, set up to deal with the northern border, should give the proposed Irish Free State within the British dominions a legal claim to a suzerainty over the whole of Ireland. Even more problematic was that Eoin O'Duffy, in his capacity as co-director of policing in Ulster, was acting as a fierce critic of the partiality of Craig's prospective northern Irish administration.[137] This fact would soon make Ulster unionists adamant that a condition of the establishment of an Irish Free State must be a legal declaration by Dublin that all republican political movements, including the secret IRB (of which O'Duffy, Collins and reputedly Griffith were also members), were illegal.[138]

The Irish negotiating team signed 'articles of agreement for a treaty' with London on 6 December 1921 on the understanding that the agreement would be binding only if it were subsequently approved by both Dáil Éireann and the Westminster parliament. A month later, the Dáil voted narrowly to accept the agreement, prompting the election of Griffith, rather than de Valera, as president. Michael Collins assumed the role as chairman of a temporary 'Provisional Government' to facilitate an administrative transfer of powers from London to an Irish Free State government. During the treaty debates and afterwards, Griffith and Collins deemed its principal selling points to be the agreement's status as a guarantor that all British armed forces would legally have to be withdrawn from the proposed Irish Free State's jurisdiction, and that the Dáil would have the capacity to exercise complete Irish fiscal autonomy and parliamentary sovereignty.[139] However, the treaty debates were characterised by comparatively little reflections on either issues of sovereignty or international affairs, with most members of the Dáil evidently being concerned solely with how they would be perceived by their constituents. Partly for this reason, Erskine Childers, who subsequently became a spokesman for de Valera's supporters who opposed the agreement, was of note for placing particular emphasis on Britain's retention of three western Irish ports as a probable negation of Ireland's right to exercise any independence in international relations.[140] Griffith evidently came to believe that Ireland's membership of the British Commonwealth could serve to guarantee its equal right to exercise an independent voice in international relations,[141] although in doing so he would seem to have underestimated the extent to which that commonwealth invariably spoke with a united political voice. By contrast, Collins argued that while 'the expression "common citizenship" in the treaty is not ideal', 'it does not attempt to confine Ireland's mother [country] claims to the states of the British Commonwealth'.[142] In making this argument, he was evidently thinking of the potential value of the planned 'World Conference of the Irish Race' in Paris, after which de Valera would return to the Irish parliament to highlight various other issues.

France welcomed the Anglo-Irish agreement. While *Le Figaro* inaccurately predicted that the Irish would soon outdo the French republic in abolishing all aristocratic titles,[143] the French Prime Minister Raymond Poincaré, on accepting a suggestion from Michael MacWhite, invited the Dáil's delegation to the World Conference of the Irish Race to the French Foreign Office at the Quay D'Orsay. On this occasion, Poincaré recalled 'the secular friendship that existed between Ireland and France in the past' and expressed his gladness that now that Ireland had reached an agreement with Britain he could express his sympathy for the Irish government 'without offending the susceptibilities of his English allies'.[144] At the time of the Parisian conference, an American-born Óglaigh na hÉireann army officer J.J. 'Ginger' O'Connell, who was deemed by the French as 'the only competent army expert in Ireland', visited the French War Ministry in the hope of initiating an agreement whereby an Irish army would purchase most its armaments from Parisian suppliers.[145] British forces, however, had not yet even begun to withdraw from the country, making this a premature action. As a result, George Gavan Duffy, the Dáil's new minister for foreign affairs, chastised both O'Connell and MacWhite.[146] This reflected a definite reality about the Anglo-Irish agreement for a treaty. Although the Dáil had ratified it in January 1922, Westminster would not even vote on it until December 1922, placing an unknown moratorium upon its eventual implementation.

Katherine Hughes and Thomas Hughes Kelly had been in Paris since the autumn of 1921 laying the basis for the weeklong conference and the associated art, drama and music festivals. This was done with support from Robert Brennan, an under-secretary of the department of foreign affairs, and Art O'Brien, the Dáil's London consul who also liaised with the Irish in the British dominions. A sad reality for the Parisian conference, however, was that although delegates were originally expected from every American state, aside from Hughes and Kelly, the only North American attendee would be de Valera's Catholic business friend John Castellini, an Italian American. Aside from the location (Paris), this happened because American political opinion was focused almost entirely upon the Washington Naval Conference. The lack of American attendance gave the conference a very imbalanced profile, with just six representatives from the Americas, including three from South America, and an extraordinarily high number of representatives from Britain, namely, thirty members of the Irish Self-Determination League of Great Britain, which almost doubled the representation from Ireland itself.[147] Furthermore, tensions developed quickly at the conference because the London representative Art O'Brien determined that the British delegates should vote *en bloc* on all proposals with a view to making the proposed global Irish organisation, to be established in the wake of the conference, both independent of the Dáil's department of foreign affairs as well as politically opposed to the whole treaty agreement. This evoked protests from the Australian, South African, Argentinian and New Zealand representatives (totalling five representatives), who were in favour of Ireland being a member of the British Commonwealth and reported that they were unwilling to cooperate with a movement such as O'Brien suggested.[148] A compromise agreement was soon arranged, but not without controversy.

Eoin MacNeill, who was intended to be minister of education in Dublin and acted as a representative of the Dáil cabinet in Paris, found some reasonable fault with the whole planning of the conference: P.J. Little, a member of the governing body of UCD who de Valera had previously sent to South Africa, appointed many proxy delegates. More controversially, MacNeill judged that Robert Brennan, on resigning as

under-secretary of the department of foreign affairs, was attempting
to use the conference not for the purpose for which the department
of foreign affairs had funded the conference – the creation of a global
Irish organisation – but instead to create a new Irish party political
movement specifically in Britain to campaign against the treaty
agreement.[149] Reflecting this, de Valera and Childers were already
launching a company in Manchester called Equity Press to publish
Poblacht na hÉireann newspapers. This included a Glasgow paper
called *Éire: the Irish Nation* (edited by P.J. Little) with a stated editorial
policy of calling on the Irish in Britain to actively campaign in British
party politics for a revision of the treaty agreement.[150] Quite illogically,
de Valera had even suggested to Brennan that he should concentrate
on creating 'an entente between ourselves, the Scotch, Welsh and the
overseas dominions as if they were nations independent of England'.[151]
The incongruity of this whole situation was judged by MacNeill to be
reflected most by the choice of a mere seven-man executive for the global
Irish organisation, to be known as 'Fine Gaedhael', in which he was to
be the only representative of the Dáil cabinet. This idea originated with
Harry Boland who, as the Dáil's former representative in the United
States, evidently desired to give maximum pre-eminence to American
businessmen John Castellini and Thomas Hughes Kelly by making
them its treasurers. The latter assured MacNeill that he would ensure
that Fine Gaedhael served its intended purposes, including Kelly's own
personal plan to fund various American university scholarships in Irish
studies. This was an educational initiative that matched the sensibilities
of Katherine Hughes, who, like MacWhite, considered the Parisian
conference a success, particularly in appealing to French opinion.[152]
MacNeill, however, considered that the four other proposed members
of the executive, namely de Valera, Brennan, O'Brien and Scotsman
Henry Hutchinson, had no purpose other than to launch a new political
movement within Britain in opposition to the Irish government.
Therefore, he reported to Gavan Duffy that 'the organisation established
in Paris is not one in which confidence can be placed'.[153] On the return
of all the Irish delegates to Dublin, however, de Valera would re-enter
the Dáil to place his case to the contrary.

The Dáil debates from February to June 1922 were often acrimonious
and usually revolved around a single point: obstructionist queries

from de Valera's supporters whether or not the Dáil was functioning as a sovereign assembly and repeated efforts by the Dáil cabinet or its supporters to explain how the transfer of powers was only beginning. Perhaps the best illustration of this was Griffith's statement that the Dáil was indeed a sovereign assembly but that Ireland's annual policing budget would cost £4 million, and until Westminster gave its formal consent to the treaty agreement (the British cabinet had arranged that this was not due to take place until one year after the agreement was signed) the Dáil's civil service could not yet count on the support of the country's financial institutions to fund such schemes.[154] Practically speaking, this meant that law and order was temporarily suspended, making London's exercise of its year-long moratorium the root of most Irish political difficulties throughout 1922. The Fine Gaedhael initiative, which all parties declared their wish to see succeed, was one matter that the Dáil felt that it could sort out by itself. One proposal made at Paris was implemented almost immediately. This was planning the holding of an Irish Olympic Games, known as the Tailteann Games, as an international tourist attraction in Dublin.[155] The first of such events would be held under state patronage in 1924 and be the largest sport event held in the world that year.[156] By contrast, state patronage was delayed for Fine Gaedhael itself. This was intended to be a permanent body to keep the Irish government in perpetual touch with an Irish diaspora which would help to promote Irish trade worldwide. De Valera requested that the cabinet provide £5,000 support immediately and typified Gavan Duffy and Griffith's hesitancy in offering funding to Fine Gaedhael, in deference to MacNeill's judgment, as ill-befitting their records in attempting to promote Ireland in international relations. In doing so, de Valera even warned: 'When the Minister of Foreign Affairs [Duffy] may find that he is not able to function and when there is a grip on him under the new Free State Constitution, you will be very glad to have some unofficial non-government machine by which Ireland's interests in foreign countries can be safeguarded.'[157]

In a manner akin to the previous initiative of the Irish White Cross, an organisation such as Fine Gaedhael needed to be a non-governmental organisation that was legally registered in each of its host countries without actually being state managed. Therefore, there was some logic in de Valera's recommendation that 'if it is valuable at all, it will be valuable because of its work as an autonomous self-supporting organisation ... the Government ... ought to retire from the business'.[158] A Dáil committee headed by Patrick MacCartan practically dismissed MacNeill's objections. Although Michael Collins, as Minister of Finance, maintained that he had agreed with Boland that Fine Gaedhael could receive some form of government loan, Boland himself declared that Fine Gaedhael could 'finance itself' without the Dáil's support. Gavan Duffy stated on 8 June that the issue was being suspended for the time being, as the next international conference under Fine Gaedhael's management was not due to take place until 1925,[159] but neither Fine Gaedhael nor a World Conference of the Irish Race would meet again. Its records indicate that Brennan wound up the association in September 1924 upon using its funds precisely as MacNeill had predicted: to form a new party political newspaper for de Valera.[160] This would seem to indicate that, contrary to Brennan's recollections,[161] a scramble for party-political capital rather than diplomatic savvy had won the day.

In the wake of the Parisian conference, Marc Sangnier had made a very sympathetic address to de Valera, in which he described him as a 'world-famed champion of liberty' and argued that 'the cause of Ireland was a cause that rightly belongs to the world'.[162] While the French national press had paid attention to Griffith, the French consul in Dublin privately considered de Valera to be 'the only real statesman that Ireland possesses'.[163] However, the outbreak of hostilities in June 1922 practically silenced for good the sympathy of international observers like Sangnier and Thomas Hughes Kelly, and also augmented the belief in Ireland that Britain was attempting to smother Irish national aspirations as much as possible. This did not work to de Valera's advantage. Instead, it simply lessened the opportunities available to present a persuasive case regarding the Irish situation. Responding to Sangnier in January 1922, de Valera had argued that Irishmen agreed that

> Their fight was not for Ireland alone ... Their fight was for the reign of true democracy and true internationalism ... The widespread influence of the Irish race would be instrumental in saving for humanity the democratic principle of which President Wilson had been the chief exponent during the war and which had been

lost at the [Versailles] peace. The Irish people were determined to save those principles for the world … France, with America, was regarded [in Ireland] as the leading nation in modern democratic ideals.[164]

British embargos on all desired Irish reforms ensured that it would take several years before the Irish Free State could start to become operational. This quickly led international observers to jump to the conclusion that 'after enjoying the doubtful dignity of being a world question the Irish problem is once more domestic'.[165] Ignoring Griffith's protests that London was breaking the spirit of the treaty agreement,[166] in early June 1922 the British government resolved to keep complete control of all Irish finances until such time as it was satisfied that Irish public opinion was not breaking the spirit of the treaty agreement and, in particular, obnoxious parties were arrested.[167] A mysterious killing in London and the kidnapping of the would-be Irish army leader J.J. O'Connell prompted the Dáil to act, but an impression soon existed, both nationally and internationally, that the proposed Free State administration was in a helpless state after the sudden deaths of Griffith, Collins and Boland and the nominal assumption of the reigns of central government by W.T. Cosgrave, a former minister for local government. Noting this trend, an American commentator pointed to the presence of George Gavan Duffy as Irish foreign affairs minister as an indication that 'the complete resources of Sinn Féin statesmanship have certainly not been exhausted'.[168] Duffy resigned suddenly, however, in September 1922 upon the creation of a new 'Department of External Affairs' under Desmond FitzGerald and Joseph Walshe that Whitehall expected to abandon any intention of upholding a separate Irish foreign policy.[169] It had been expected that peace would be restored within a fortnight of the outbreak of hostilities in late June 1922, but this would not occur until April 1923. This had a divisive and deeply traumatic effect on the Irish polity. Meanwhile, several initiatives came to a sudden halt.

Government ministers worldwide flocked to make contributions to the US journal *Foreign Affairs*, which was founded in 1922. However, despite the centrality of American opinion hitherto to the Irish struggle for independence, no Irish government minister would. Failing to find an audience, Griffith's would-be diplomatic representative in America,

Joseph Connolly (a Belfast man and future Irish senator), resolved simply to return home to Ireland. By contrast, the un-elected southern unionist leader Lord Midleton, being a known colleague of Arthur Balfour and the British Foreign Office, was actually able to acquire a hearing at the White House. He used this opportunity to express contemptuous attitudes about all Irish nationalists.[170] Thereafter, Stephen Gwynn of the British Foreign Office set a new tone for Irish political debate by writing for *Foreign Affairs* a negative portrayal of the Irish Free State compared to Northern Ireland, typifying Irish hesitancy in outlawing republican or Sinn Féin sensibilities, as well as a failure to follow in the footsteps of the late John Redmond (who died in March 1918), as being the cause of all Irish political difficulties.[171] As a result, the idea that there had been a 'victory of Sinn Féin' based on a new and more democratic international order that was inspired by American republican values would soon be silenced in Irish political debate.[172]

In the past, many Irish commentators had been fond of pointing to the historic record of Irish émigrés attaining government office in Europe, or even in the Americas, as evidence of the 'rank political heresy' of British nationalists, who held as a cardinal belief that Irishmen were unworthy, or even incapable, of 'ruling and governing at home'. Be that as it may, longstanding Irish claims to be one of the oldest and thereby one of the most suppressed nationalities in Europe had essentially rested on purely cultural premises. Traditionally, being aware of the country's complete lack of financial clout, many were actually loath to dwell on economic factors, preferring instead to assert that Irishmen 'could fight for an abstract notion – for love, for glory, for liberty; but they never knew how to take up arms for a countinghouse or a till'.[173] The Irish revolution, which was a response to America's entry into the First World War as much as it was a reaction to the 1916 Rising and Britain's frustration of Irish desires for self-government, essentially changed this situation. The unilateral setting up of an Irish parliament and civil service was directly linked with a new focus upon seeking diplomatic recognition worldwide and entering the world of international trade. This was the Sinn Féin policy of Arthur Griffith, first spelt out in 1905. Crucially, however, considerable international attention did not translate into the creation of any Irish diplomatic alliances in defiance of Britain. Ireland's trading profile also revealed very limited international interest in the country. Although the prospect of growing US trade existed, this was far from a central concern of the Americans and did not dictate their diplomatic stance. Meanwhile, the absence of a viable market for Irish goods in France cemented the French inclination to consider Ireland to be, at best, only a small potential factor in European geopolitics. As a result, there was no potential advantage to such foreign powers in taking a direct interest in the Irish case.

There had also been a local dimension to the Irish revolution. Massive recruitment of unarmed men to the volunteer movement in defiance of the British administration in Ireland shaped national perceptions of the revolution as well as levels of disappointment with its outcome. Meanwhile, ever since the 1880s, the sense of the democratic legitimacy of the Irish desire for self-government had actually rested upon the results of UK general elections, including Sinn Féin's triumphant election campaigns of 1918 and 1921. While some commentators have suggested that de Valera was simply being duplicitious, his ill-advised attempts during 1922 to capitalise upon an extant Irish capacity to work within a UK party-political framework was essentially a reflection of this electoral legacy. Privately, he would admit in later years that he knew in advance how the treaty agreement was going to be used unjustly by Britain as a weapon against Griffith and Collins rather than as an instrument to fulfil either their or the Irish parliament's declared political goals.[174] As Ireland's attempt to win recognition for an Irish republic had failed to win any international allies, the only remaining alternatives were to act as a 'restless dominion' within the British Commonwealth or else to aspire to achieve an entirely non-aligned position in international relations.[175] Such considerations would colour the history of the new Irish state up until at least the Second World War as much as a determination to sustain the ideals of Ireland's initial independence movement.

Endnotes

1 Michael Doorley, *Irish-American diaspora nationalism: the Friends of Irish Freedom, 1916–1935* (Dublin, 2005).
2 'The Pope, the President and the Peace', *Nationality*, 22 Dec. 1917.
3 *Nationality*, 21 Dec. 1918 (editorial).
4 'President Wilson and the Pope', *Irish Independent*, 14 January 1919.

5   Dáil Éireann, *Miontuaric an chead Dala 1919–1921* (Dublin, 1994).

6   Pierre-Yves Beaurepatre, 'The universal republic of the freemasons and the culture of mobility in the enlightenment', *French historical studies*, vol. 29 no. 3 (summer 2006), 407–31 Beethoven's 'Ode to Joy' would later be made the anthem of the European Union.

7   *Nationality*, 17 Mar., 9 Jun. 1917.

8   *Nationality*, 17 Mar., 31 Mar., 16 Jun. (quote), 11 Aug. 1917.

9   *Nationality*, 15 Feb. 1918 (quote).

10   *Nationality*, 26 Oct., 28 Dec. 1918.

11   *Nationality*, 9 Nov. 1918.

12   *Nationality*, 4 Aug. 1917.

13   *Nationality*, 8 Sep. 1917, 10 Nov. 1917.

14   John J. Horgan, 'Ireland and world contact', *Studies*, vol. 8 no. 29 (Mar. 1919), 35–45.

15   *Nationality*, 17 Mar., 7 Apr., 14 Apr. 1917.

16   'Ireland and the seas', *Nationality*, 3 Nov. 1917.

17   *Nationality*, 23 Jun. 1917, 8 Sep. 1917, 3 Nov. 1917, 17 Nov. 1917, 8 Dec. 1917, 28 Jan. 1918.

18   *Nationality*, 5 Oct. 1918 (quote), 20 Oct. 1917.

19   *Nationality*, 10 Aug. 1918, 23 Jun. 1917.

20   *Nationality*, 17 Mar., 7 Mar., 23 Jun. 1917.

21   Steven Watts, *The people's tycoon: Henry Ford and the American century* (New York, 2005), 230–40. 'The Women's International League for Peace and Freedom' was an outgrowth of the Woman's Peace Party, founded by Rosika Schwimmer. Ford funded and joined its Peace Ship to Europe in December 1915.

22   Pádraig Ó Siadhail, *Katherine Hughes* (Ontario, 2014).

23   Owen McGee, *Arthur Griffith* (Dublin, 2015), 155–6, 180, 196, 212, 242.

24   Michael Doorley, *Irish-American diaspora nationalism: the Friends of Irish Freedom, 1916–1935* (Dublin, 2005).

25   Elizabeth McKillen, 'Ethnicity, class and Wilsonian internationalism reconsidered: the Mexican-American and Irish-American left and US foreign relations 1914–1922', *Diplomatic history*, vol. 25 (fall 2001), 553–87.

26   Earl of Midleton, *Ireland: dupe or heroine* (London, 1932), 142–7 (quote p. 147).

27   *Nationality*, 15 Dec. 1917.

28   Walter Lippmann, 'The intimate papers of Colonel House', *Foreign affairs*, vol. 4 (1926), 383–93.

29   *Documents on Irish foreign policy*, vol. 1 (Dublin, 1998), no. 2.

30   James Quinn, 'James Bryce (1838–1922)', *Dictionary of Irish biography* (Cambridge, 2009).

31   Catherine B. Shannon, *Arthur J. Balfour and Ireland 1874–1922* (Washington D.C., 1988); Earl of Midleton, *Ireland: dupe or heroine* (London, 1932).

32   *Nationality*, 23 Jun., 30 Jun, 18 Aug., 6 Oct. 1917; Gerard Keown, *First of the small nations: the beginnings of Irish foreign policy in the interwar years 1919–1932* (Oxford, 2015), 30.

33   *Nationality*, 12 Oct. 1918 (editorial).

34   Dáil Éireann, *Miontuaric an chead Dala 1919–1921* (Dublin, 1994), minutes for 11 Apr 1919; *Documents on Irish foreign policy*, vol. 1 (Dublin, 1998), no. 4.

35   Owen McGee, *Arthur Griffith* (Dublin, 2015), 208.

36   'England, Ireland and America', *Nationality*, 16 Aug. 1919.

37 'America, Ireland and the general election', *Nationality*, 31 Aug. 1918.

38 Gerard Keown, *First of the small nations: the beginnings of Irish foreign policy in the interwar years 1919-1932* (Oxford, 2015), 42.

39 Michael Doorley, *Irish-American diaspora nationalism*, 93, 96–100, 105, 112–13.

40 G.C. Herring, *From colony to superpower: US foreign relations since 1776* (Oxford, 2008), 436.

41 Gerard Keown, *First of the small nations*, 30, 39–41, 43.

42 Earl of Midleton, *Ireland: dupe or heroine* (London, 1932), chapter 13.

43 'The coming of America', *Nationality*, 2 Aug. 1919; 'England, Ireland and America', *Nationality*, 16 Aug. 1919; 'The perils of Europe', *Nationality*, 16 Aug. 1919.

44 J.B. Duff, 'The Versailles Treaty and the Irish Americans', *Journal of American history*, vol. 55 (Dec. 1968), 582–98.

45 'Sinn Féin', *Nationality*, 12 Jul. 1919; 'Ireland and Sweden', *Nationality*, 9 Aug. 1919; 'Free Trade', *Nationality*, 16 Aug. 1919; 'The perils of Europe', *Nationality*, 16 Aug. 1919; 'Ireland and Australia', *Nationality*, 23 Aug. 1919; 'National Bank', *Nationality*, 16 March 1918; *Nationality*, 23 Aug. 1919, p. 2.

46 'Our foreign trade', *Nationality*, 23 Aug. 1919; *Young Ireland*, 10 Jan., 17 Jan., 11 Dec. 1920; *Young Ireland*, 23 May, 25 Jun., 18 Jul., 27 Aug. 1921.

47 Eoin McLaughlin and Nathan Foley Fisher, 'State dissolution, sovereign debt and default: lessons from the UK and Ireland 1920-1938', *European historical economics working paper no. 61* (August 2014), 20–4.

48 Dáil Éireann, *miontuaric an Chead Dala, 1919-1921* (Dublin, 1994), 151–3, 167–86; Lionel Smith-Gordon, *The place of banking in the national programme* (Dublin, 1921).

49 Owen McGee, *Arthur Griffith* (Dublin, 2015), chapters 8–9; Bureau of Military History WS1170.

50 Thomas J. Morrissey, *Laurence O'Neill* (Dublin, 2016), 190–1.

51 Andy Bielenberg, 'Fatalities in the Irish revolution', in J. Crowley, D. O'Driscoll, M. Murphy (eds), *Atlas of the Irish revolution* (Cork, 2017), 752–61.

52 Dáil Éireann, *miontuaric an Chead Dala, 1919-1921* (Dublin, 1994), minutes for Aug. 1919.

53 *Young Ireland*, 24 Jan. 1920; 23 May, 18 Jul. 1921.

54 Bernadette Whelan, *US foreign policy and Ireland* (Dublin, 2006), 74–80, 378, 516.

55 *Friends of Irish Freedom Newsletter*, 6 Feb. 1920.

56 For press coverage of de Valera's American lecture tours, see Dave Hannigan, *De Valera in America* (New York, 2010).

57 *Nationality*, 17 Apr., 8 Jun., 15 Jun. 1918 (quote from *New York Times*).

58 *Nationality*, 7 Sep. 1918 (quoting O'Connor in London on his return from America) In a would-be direct address to Woodrow Wilson during April 1918, de Valera had argued that 'Ireland is the acid test of England's sincerity.' *Nationality*, 21 Sep. 1918.

59 Gerard Keown, *First of the small nations*, 32–3; *Documents on Irish foreign policy*, vol. 1 (Dublin, 1998), nos 11, 59 and 67.

60 *Documents on Irish Foreign Policy*, vol. 1 (Dublin, 1998), no. 10 (quote p. 14).

61 NLI, Art Ó Briain papers, Ms8426/61, de Valera to Ó Briain, 22 Mar. 1919.

62 Robert McLaughlin, *Irish Canadian conflict and the struggle for Irish independence* (Toronto, 2011), 124. While Hughes was essentially a literary figure, Crawford had a deep interest in economics and was a former Orangeman who would establish a separate 'Protestant Friends of Irish Freedom' organisation in New York City.

63 Crawford's correspondence with Cohalan on this theme can be found within the Daniel Cohalan papers in the library of the American Irish Historical Society in New York City. I am grateful to Michael Doorley for this information. See also Robert McLaughlin, *Irish Canadian conflict*, 137–9.

64 Greg Donaghy, Michael K. Carroll (eds), *In the national interest: Canadian foreign policy, the department of foreign affairs and international trade 1909–2009* (Calgary, 2011), chapter 1.

65 Michael Doorley, *Irish-American diaspora nationalism*, 128–31 (quotes p. 129).

66 Owen McGee, *Arthur Griffith* (Dublin, 2015), 227, 228 (quote).

67 Gerard Keown, *First of the small nations*, 57–8. De Valera wrote to the Dáil cabinet in April 1920 that he believed that not alienating the church was the most essential issue. UCD, de Valera papers, P150/1132, confidential memo, 15 Apr. 1920.

68 UCD, de Valera papers, P150/1154, letter of Devoy 17 Aug. 1920 with an attached American Clan na Gael statement to the IRB Supreme Council in Dublin. Papers of the IRB were acquired by de Valera after Boland's death in 1922.

69 Michael Doorley, *Irish-American diaspora nationalism*, 140.

70 UCD, de Valera papers, P150/1125, Boland to Collins 4 Nov. 1920.

71 J. Crowley, D. O'Driscoll, M. Murphy (eds), *Atlas of the Irish revolution* (Cork, 2017), 515–19.

72 *Young Ireland*, 16 Apr. 1921. D.W. Griffith, the film director of *Birth of a Nation* (1915), was one of its earliest subscribers.

73 *Young Ireland*, 22 Jan. 1921.

74 *Young Ireland*, 12 Feb. 1921.

75 Owen McGee, *Arthur Griffith*, 230, 236–8.

76 The papers of the Irish Self-Determination League of Great Britain can be found within the Art Ó Briain papers in the National Library of Ireland.

77 Patrick O'Farrell, *The Irish in Australia* (Kensington, 1987), 280; Robert McLaughlin, *Irish Canadian conflict*, 142.

78 Robert McLaughlin, *Irish Canadian conflict*, 132–3, 140–3.

79 Patrick O'Farrell, *The Irish in Australia* (Kensington, 1987), 269–74, 284.

80 Patrick O'Farrell, *Irish in Australia*, 267; Robert McLaughlin, *Irish Canadian conflict*, 21–2, 120, 122.

81 *Young Ireland*, 28 May 1921; Patrick O'Farrell, *Irish in Australia*, 284.

82 These have been reproduced in *Documents on Irish foreign policy*, vol. 1 (Dublin, 1998).

83 *Nationality*, 17 and 31 May 1919. This reality would later be reflected in Mark Tierney (ed.), 'Calendar of Irlande, vol. 1, 2 and 3, in the Collection Europe, 1918–29 in the Archives Diplomatiques, Paris', *Collectanea Hibernica*, 21–2 (1979–80), 205–37.

84 Dáil Éireann, *Miontuaric an chead Dala 1919–1921* (Dublin, 1994), minutes for 27 Oct. 1919.

85 Dáil Éireann, *Miontuaric an chead Dala 1919–1921* (Dublin, 1994), minutes for 11 Apr. 1919.

86 Mark Tierney (ed.), 'Calendar of Irlande, vol. 1, 2 and 3, in the Collection Europe, 1918–1929 in the Archives Diplomatiques, Paris', *Collectanea Hibernica*, 21–2 (1979–80), 205–37; Gerard Keown, *First of the small nations*, 172, 177.

87 Gearoid Barry, *The disarmament of hatred: Marc Sangnier, French Catholicism and the legacy of the First World War 1914–1945* (London, 2012).

88 Pierre Ranger, 'The world in Paris and Ireland too: the French diplomacy of Sinn Féin 1919–1921', *Études Irlandaises*, vol. 36 no. 2 (2011), 7, 9, 15.

89 'France and Ireland', *Young Ireland*, 27 Mar. 1920, 30 Apr. 1921, 4 Jun. 1921.

90 Reports from over 100 such publications, published in English translation by Michael MacWhite, were reproduced in the series 'France and Ireland', which ran in *Young Ireland* from Jan. 1920 until Feb. 1922.

91 *Documents on Irish foreign policy*, vol. 1 (Dublin, 1998), no. 37 (quote pp. 70–1).

92 'France and Ireland', *Young Ireland*, 27 Mar., 17 Jul., 31 Jul., 4 Sep., 11 Sep. 1920.

93 Gerard Keown, *First of the small nations* (quote p. 52), 54–5.

94 'France and Ireland', *Young Ireland*, 10 Apr. 1920.

95 A very large collection of international press reportage on the MacSwiney hunger strike can be found in the Art Ó Briain papers in the National Library of Ireland. De Valera judged in late August 1920 that the 'worldwide publicity' generated by this protest action of Irish political prisoners in Britain going on hunger strike 'will be the nearest we can go to securing [international] intervention' in settling the Anglo-Irish dispute. Owen McGee, *Arthur Griffith*, quote p.228.

96 'France and Ireland', *Young Ireland*, 26 Mar. 1921.

97 *Young Ireland*, 2 Jul. 1921 (interview with de Valera, reproduced from the Australian press).

98 J. Crowley, D. O'Driscoll, M. Murphy (eds), *Atlas of the Irish revolution* (Cork, 2017), 390.

99 Colonel John Duggan, *A history of the Irish army* (Dublin, 1991), 28, 35–6, 50–1, 55–6, 60–2. British forces had shot dead previous mayors of Limerick and Cork cities on the charge of sympathising with rebels.

100 Maurice Walsh, *The news from Ireland: foreign correspondents and the Irish revolution* (London, 2008).

101 NLI, Art Ó Briain papers, Ms8427/26; Ms8430/12, Michael Collins to Ó Briain, 17 Jan. 1921, forwarding a communication from de Valera.

102 This was Maurice Bourgeois, who was not personally unsympathetic to Irish aims. Art O'Brien (Art Ó Briain) kept watch on him whenever he was in London and reported to Collins about him in intelligence communiqués. These telegraphed memos between O'Brien and Collins can be found in the Art Ó Briain papers in the National Library of Ireland.

103 'France and Ireland', *Young Ireland*, 10 Mar. 1920, 26 Mar., 30 Apr., 14 May 1921.

104 'France and Ireland', *Young Ireland*, 5 Feb. 1921.

105 Michael Kennedy, 'Michael MacWhite (1883–1958)', *Dictionary of Irish biography* (Cambridge, 2009).

106 Gerard Keown, *First of the small nations*, 177.

107 'France and Ireland', *Young Ireland*, 4 February 1922.

108 NLI, Art Ó Briain papers, Ms8460/46.

109 *Young Ireland*, 16 Apr. 1921; NLI, Art Ó Briain papers, Ms8460/44, Ms8425/23; Donal McCracken (ed.), *Ireland and South Africa in modern times* (Durban, 1996), 49, 55–7.

110 Owen McGee, *Arthur Griffith*, 228, 236. Griffith suggested that this could be done by American towns adopting devastated Irish towns as twin cities, in a manner comparable to what was done in post-war Britain and France. *Young Ireland*, 2 Oct. 1920, p. 1.

111 *Young Ireland*, 8 Oct., 15 Oct. 1921. The first demonstration for Irish independence in Argentina was held on 20 Jun. 1920, although it took some time for this news to reach Dublin. *Young Ireland*, 4 Sep. 1920.

112   George Gavan Duffy revealed this in the Dáil debates of 8 June 1922, which can be found at https://www.oireachtas.ie/en/debates/find/.

113   *Young Ireland*, 8 Oct. 1921 (book reviews).

114   *Young Ireland*, 2 Jul. 1921.

115   Some of the correspondence of Griffith's appointees to Denmark (Sean O'Duinn and Gearoid O'Lochlain) and Italy (Donal McHales), as well as de Valera's appointees to Spain (Máire Ní Bhriáin) and Germany (Nancy Wyse Power), can be found in the Art Ó Briain papers in the National Library of Ireland.

116   This included E.M. Aldborough, an Irish-born journalist in Austria, and Chatterton Hill, an academic in Geneva with close links to Germany. Some of their correspondence can be found in the Art Ó Briain papers in the National Library of Ireland.

117   Michael Kennedy, 'Gerald Edward O'Kelly (1890–1968)', *Dictionary of Irish biography* (Cambridge, 2009). O'Kelly would remain in Irish diplomatic circles for many years.

118   *Nationality*, 23 Mar. 1918.

119   Gerard Keown, *First of the small nations*, 59–64.

120   B.P. Murphy, *John Chartres* (Dublin, 1995).

121   Colonel John Duggan, *A history of the Irish army* (Dublin, 1991), 65–7; Sean Boyne, *Emmet Dalton* (Dublin, 2015). By the autumn of 1921, O'Duffy's status as the liaison officer for policing matters in Ulster was being mentioned frequently in the press because of his outspokenness. *Young Ireland*, 1 Oct. 1921.

122   John Duggan, *A history of the Irish army*, 70.

123   John Duggan, *A history of the Irish army*, 132, 329–30, ft.29.

124   *Young Ireland*, 1 Oct. 1921 (republished extract from the *Toronto Star*).

125   Michael Doorley, *Irish-American diaspora nationalism*, 140, 163.

126   Churchill Archives, Churchill papers, CHAR25/2, Hankey to Churchill, 4 July 1921.

127   Westminster Parliamentary Archives, Lloyd George papers, F25/1/19, Hankey to Lloyd George, 27 Sep. 1921. This item is numbered F25/1/19 but is filed at F25/2/19. The British cabinet's reliance on old Irish Party networks is evidenced in John Turner, *Lloyd George's secretariat* (Cambridge, 1980).

128   Westminster Parliamentary Archives, Lloyd George papers, F25/2/32, Tom Jones to Prime Minister, 14 Oct. 1921; NLI, Art Ó Briain papers, Ms8425/8 (copies of government reports on defence meetings).

129   A good illustration of this was John Horgan's move at this time from being a sympathetic contributor to *Studies* to being the Irish correspondent for the *Round Table*, Chatham House's journal of commonwealth affairs. Horgan also attempted to act as a champion of the legacy of the late John Redmond. J.J. Horgan, *Parnell to Pearse* (1949, 2nd ed., Dublin, 2009), biographical introduction.

130   Denis Rickett, M.C. Curthoys, 'Baron Arthur Salter (1881–1975)', *Oxford dictionary of national biography* (online edition).

131   Owen McGee, *Arthur Griffith*, 261–4 (quote p. 264).

132   *Young Ireland*, 19 February 1921 (letter of Pollock on p. 1).

133   Owen McGee, *Arthur Griffith*, 263.

134   Churchill Archives, CHAR22/11/2, Craig to Churchill, 11 Jan. 1922.

135   *Documents on Irish foreign policy*, vol. 2 (Dublin, 2002), nos 358–68.

136   Owen McGee, *Arthur Griffith*, 261–2.

137   As early as the autumn of 1921, O'Duffy was making protest speeches in Armagh that his official reports, made in his capacity as liaison officer, to British authorities on various abuses of police authority in Ulster were being completely ignored, and so

'I say that it is time we should take steps to protect ourselves.' *Young Ireland*, 5 Nov. 1921, p. 1. He continued in this tone during the spring of 1922. Although O'Duffy notoriously lacked political acumen, Northern unionists had hitherto been complicit in deliberate British efforts to destabilise the whole of Ireland, both economically and politically, by means of provoking disturbances in Ulster. Churchill Archives, Lord Hankey papers, HNKY1/5, diary entry for 7 Sep. 1920; Westminster Parliamentary Archives, Lloyd George papers, F25/1/42, Tom Jones to Lloyd George, 15 Jun. 1921 (report of Irish Situation Committee).

138   Churchill Archives, CHAR22/13/40–1, 58–60.

139   Arthur Griffith, *Arguments for the treaty* (Dublin, 1922); Michael Collins, *Arguments for the treaty* (Dublin, 1922).

140   Dáil Éireann, *Debate on the treaty between Great Britain and Ireland* (Dublin, 1922); Owen McGee, *Arthur Griffith*, 270–91.

141   Owen McGee, *Arthur Griffith*, 327–8.

142   Michael Collins, *The path to freedom* (Dublin, 1922), 43.

143   'France and Ireland', *Young Ireland*, 24 Dec. 1921. The Office of Chief Herald remained in existence in Ireland.

144   Statement made by Poincaré on the conclusion of the World Conference of the Irish Race (30 Jan. 1922), reproduced in *Young Ireland*, 11 Feb. 1922.

145   Mark Tierney, 'Calendar of Irlande, vols 9, 10 and 11', *Collectanea Hibernica*, no. 25 (1983), 209–12 (quote p. 211).

146   Gerard Keown, 'The Irish race conference 1922 reconsidered', *Irish historical studies*, vol. 32 no. 127 (May 2001), 372–3.

147   Lists of delegates can be found in NLI, Art Ó Briain papers, Ms8431/2. Correspondence from several delegates to O'Brien can be found in the Ó Briain papers.

148   Copies of this report can be found in NLI, Art Ó Briain papers, Ms8456/5–6.

149   Copies of MacNeill's report and that of other delegates at the conference can be found in NLI, Art Ó Briain papers, Ms8456/5–6.

150   NLI, Art Ó Briain papers, Ms8432/45, 8460/55, 8426/25, 8432/33, 8445/20, 8432/16. G.N. Plunkett, a one-time foreign affairs minister of the Dáil, was also a champion of this idea of focusing entirely on party politics in Britain. NLI, Art Ó Briain papers, Ms8423/13, Plunkett to O'Brien, 27 Oct.1922.

151   Gerard Keown, *The first of the small nations*, quote p. 83.

152   *Young Ireland*, 4 Feb. 1922. Excepting Marc Sangnier, who held his own reception for all Irish attendees (*Irish Examiner*, 30 Jan. 1922), no French politician appears to have taken an interest in the conference, although the French police sent some intelligence reporters. Mark Tierney, 'Calendar of Irlande'.

153   Copies of MacNeill's report and that of other delegates at the conference can be found in NLI, Art Ó Briain papers, Ms8456/5–6.

154   Speech of Griffith in the Dáil debates of 28 Feb. 1922, which can be found at https://www.oireachtas.ie/en/debates/find/.

155   Speech of J.J. Walsh in the Dáil debates of 28 Feb. 1922, which can be found at https://www.oireachtas.ie/en/debates/find/.

156   Paul Rouse, 'When Ireland's Tailteann Games eclipsed the Olympics', *Irish Examiner*, 18 Nov. 2016.

157   Speech of de Valera in the Dáil debates on Fine Gaedhael, 2 Mar. 1922, which can be found at https://www.oireachtas.ie/en/debates/find/.

158 Speech of de Valera at the Dáil debates on Fine Gaedhael, 8 Jun. 1922, which can be found at https://www.oireachtas.ie/en/debates/find/. Mary MacSwiney spoke to the same effect.

159 Speeches of MacCartan, Collins, Boland and Gavan Duffy in the Dáil debates on Fine Gaedhael, 8 Jun.1922, which can be found at https://www.oireachtas.ie/en/debates/find/.

160 NLI, Art Ó Briain papers, Mss8461/17, 8456/4, 8429/29, 8421/7, 8426/22. Fine Gaedhael's official motto was an expression of Patrick Pearse's, that 'beyond all telling is the destiny which God has in store for Ireland'.

161 Robert Brennan, *Allegiance* (Dublin, 1950), 334–6.

162 *Irish Examiner*, 30 Jan. 1922.

163 Mark Tierney (ed.), 'Calendar of Irlande, vols 1, 2, 3', *Collectanea Hibernica*, nos 21–2 (1979–80), 217.

164 *Irish Examiner*, 30 Jan. 1922. Shortly before this event, de Valera and Sangnier laid a wreath at the grave of the Unknown Soldier of France, as well as at that of the United Irishman Miles Byrne. *Irish Independent*, 30 Jan. 1922.

165 Ernest Boyd, 'Ireland: resurgent and insurgent', *Foreign Affairs*, vol. 1 no. 15 (1922), 97.

166 Westminster Parliamentary Archives, Lloyd George papers, F21/1/8, Griffith to Lloyd George, 2 Jun. 1922.

167 Churchill Archives, CHAR22/13/103–12.

168 Ernest Boyd, 'Ireland: resurgent and insurgent', *Foreign Affairs*, vol. 1 no. 15 (1922), 93–4.

169 Westminster Parliamentary Archives, Lloyd George papers, F/10/3/49, Alfred Cope to Lionel Curtis, 9 Sep. 1922; Churchill Archives, CHAR 22/14/71.

170 J.A. Gaughan (ed.), *Memoirs of Senator Joseph Connolly* (Dublin, 1996); Lord Midleton, *Ireland: dupe or heroine* (London, 1932), 149–51. Alongside Connolly, Griffith had sent another Belfast man Denis McCullough to America as a would-be diplomatic representative, but he also resigned. While Midleton was in America primarily to assist the British Foreign Office press its case upon US President Harding regarding Anglo-American naval relations, he also used this occasion to speak about Ireland.

171 Stephen Gwynn, 'Ireland: one and divisible', *Foreign affairs*, vol. 3 (1924), 183–98.

172 The last manifestation of this literary trend could be said to have been P.S. O'Hegarty, *The victory of Sinn Féin* (Dublin, 1924), although it was also deeply influenced by the acrimonious debates of 1922.

173 Owen McGee (ed.), *Eugene Davis' souvenirs of Irish footprints over Europe* (1889, 2nd ed., Dublin, 2006), 179–80.

174 Ronan Fanning, *A will to power: Éamon de Valera* (London, 2015), 258. Owen McGee, *Arthur Griffith*, chapter 12.

175 David Harkness, *The restless dominion: the Irish Free State and the British Commonwealth of Nations 1921–1931* (London, 1969).

3

Financial Quagmires and Legal Limits: Irish Free State Diplomacy, 1922–1938

Many of the founders of Dáil Éireann adopted the mindset that the Irish Free State's foreign policy should not be determined primarily by Irish membership of the British Commonwealth. Instead, it should be an expression of the Free State's own written constitution, which stated in Article Two that 'all powers of government and all authority, legislative, executive and judicial, are derived from the people of Ireland'.[1] Half of the eighteen constitutions that were studied as templates when drafting the constitution of the Irish Free State were those of republics.[2] Reflecting this, the Irish correspondent of *Foreign Affairs* during 1922 judged that 'the Free Staters, being republicans, are not prepared to destroy republicanism'.[3] America's ambassador to the United Kingdom also felt that the Irish Free State cabinet should be considered to be republican revolutionaries in their background.[4] Irrespective of the existence of a written Irish constitution, however, there was actually a very significant difference between the operations of an independent republic and membership of the British Commonwealth. Ignoring Arthur Griffith's protests to the contrary, Lloyd George explained in June 1922 that the Irish were not entitled to have 'their own ideals of political, economic and social welfare' because, according to British imperial logic, the dominions' rights in such matters were 'not based on theory but on experience': namely, the degree to which the king, or Whitehall, had first judged that it was in everyone's best political and economic interests that they begin to exercise such powers.[5] From this legal perspective, only London could represent the Irish Free State to the rest of the world by means of a proxy.

In his understanding of Irish statehood, Joseph Walshe, the secretary and practical creator of the new Irish department of external affairs, essentially subscribed to a belief in the reality of Irish sovereignty.[6] Griffith had believed that the Irish Free State constitution entitled Ireland to stand 'on equal terms with England' within the commonwealth,[7] but British Commonwealth policy regarding Ireland, upheld by the Dominions Office and the British Imperial Treasury, was always based on a hierarchy of interests that was determined by London's own foreign trade policy. Adopting this reasoning, Ireland was not regarded by London as a co-equal with Canada and Australia, let alone England, but instead as a fiscal identity comparable to New Zealand as a food supplier nation.[8] Against this backdrop, during the 1920s both leading officials and diplomats of the Irish Free State essentially learnt by a process of trial and error of various potential limits to the Irish state's legal, diplomatic and fiscal authority. This created a preoccupation with counteracting these limitations. This was partly why the Irish government became very inclined to concentrate on the League of Nations as an alternative forum to the British Commonwealth. Former American diplomat Edward House, who would be discredited under the Republican administrations of US presidents Warren Harding and Calvin Coolidge for having supposedly been led by the nose by Britain,[9] suggested during 1922 that the Irish and German cases were linked by their mutual desire to join the League of Nations and to see the United States also become a member. In any event, House predicted that membership of the League of Nations could serve as 'a God-sent haven for such states as Ireland' because if its ongoing dispute with Britain could not be solved bilaterally, 'Ireland has sought the only forum open to her where it can be done.'[10]

The importance that the Irish government attributed to the League of Nations was reflected by its decision to appoint most of its cabinet as members of its annual delegations to the league as soon as Ireland was admitted in September 1923.[11] By this time, the Dáil cabinet had also established a 'North Eastern Boundary Bureau' to seek a resolution of Ireland's partition dispute. This consisted of the legal personnel that had drafted the Free State's written constitution,[12] but it also included prominent Irish economists and, in the person of Kevin O'Shiel, a northern Irish nationalist and barrister who had formerly managed the Dáil's land courts. From his northern contacts, O'Shiel knew that many unionist businessmen were arguing privately that 'they would be better off under Dublin than Westminster', with only the budgetary logic of the British imperial treasury serving to dictate otherwise.[13] Acting on such advice, from April 1923 to January 1924, Cosgrave's cabinet considered that if a constructive customs policy was initiated, this could encourage northern businessmen to view Dublin rather than London as their natural ally and, in the process, facilitate the goal of a united Ireland. O'Shiel himself believed that Ireland's case regarding the economic and, in turn, political injustices of partition should be presented to the League of Nations itself.[14] Bruno Waller, the president of the still-extant Irish League of Nations Society, argued strongly against adopting such a stance, however, and instead advised Cosgrave's cabinet to focus simply on getting the Anglo-Irish agreement, or 'treaty', registered with the League of Nations as an internationally recognised legal agreement.[15]

The American government had some interest in establishing diplomatic and trade relations with the Irish Free State quickly. It would not do so, however, because of a combination of political disturbances in Ireland and America's felt need to defer to Britain's hesitancy in allowing a Free State government to operate freely.[16] While an Irish American contributor to *Foreign Affairs* recommended George Russell's *Irish Statesman* journal to Americans as the best guide how to 'properly envision the revolutionised Ireland of today',[17] Irish civil disturbances during 1922–3 led to the suspension of municipal government in Ireland for several years. Therefore, neither Russell's nor anyone else's ideas of economic development were likely to be implemented any time soon.[18] Russell himself would later write for *Foreign Affairs* that Ireland was the only country in Europe 'where there is neither fear nor envy, but only gratitude' for America's growing influence in international affairs. He also argued that the claim in *Foreign Affairs* by unionist propagandist Stephen Gwynn that there were two, mutually hostile, Irelands (north and south) was incorrect, and that the eclipse of partition, by means of a new federal political arrangement,[19] was likely in the near future.[20] This belief of Russell's (a native of Ulster) that the partition of Ireland could not last reflected the fact that the existence of Northern Ireland had no legal, political and cultural antecedents in history before Westminster's unilateral passing of its Government of Ireland Act in December 1920. The official title of the United Kingdom itself would not change to include Northern Ireland until 1927.[21] Its existence could not be ignored, however, while it was also clear to critics and supporters of partition alike that 'the "Ulster" problem' was 'the crux of the whole situation' in determining whether or not the fledgling Irish Free State could possess sufficient financial solvency to survive.[22]

Dublin's complaint regarding partition was not merely a question of Irish nationalism, or the fact of the existence of many unwilling residents of Northern Ireland, but it was also a practical question of economics. This was neither understood nor appreciated widely outside Ireland. To facilitate the establishment of partition, Irish banks had been ordered by Whitehall to adopt a policy whereby London-based companies should always be deemed eligible to receive preferential treatment for business loans within the Irish Free State, and that all large capital transactions between the Irish banks must be made exclusively by means of drafts drawn in Belfast directly on a London bank.[23] This practically made Belfast Ireland's banking capital on behalf of London in order to emphasise the inherent economic seniority of the intended new United Kingdom of Great Britain and Northern Ireland over the Irish Free State within the British Commonwealth. Partition soon served to create negative trading balances in both parts of Ireland, while the total volume of cross-channel trade evidently dropped by about 30 per cent.[24] This development was so acute in the Irish Free State, however, that it was unable to fund and thereby manage its own national defence. The banks refused to lend the Irish government money, necessitating that the Dáil launch three national loan schemes amongst the general Irish public to compensate for negative balance of payments in the state exchequer, which now maintained the same inverse ratio as had underpinned Whitehall's initial calculations for its intended government of Ireland bill during 1911.[25] Knowing that meat exports to Britain were then 90 per cent of all southern Irish exports, London reduced by half the price offered for Irish food exports during and after 1922. Breaking with the understanding formerly reached with (the now deceased figures of) Griffith and Collins, Britain also demanded that Ireland make a sizeable contribution to the British national debt, which was a practical denial of dominion status, but it was a feature of the original Government of Ireland Act and a backstop feature of Article Five of the Anglo-Irish agreement.[26] Against this backdrop, efforts made by the Irish Free State to develop or expand the operations of various Irish businesses during the 1920s were nearly all unsuccessful.

At the Parisian conference of January 1922, economist E.J. Riordan, who subsequently joined the Irish Free State's department of industry and commerce, had noted how Irish trade had both increased and developed a positive balance ever since the formation of the Dáil three years earlier. He also advised that 'in order to secure the permanence of shipping services with America and other countries abroad' Ireland would need to create its own mercantile marine.[27] By 1924, however, Riordan was reporting that the Irish Free State had universally negative trading balances, even with Northern Ireland, and that exports to European countries like France, Belgium and Holland were negligible.[28] Among the declared goals of the Irish Free State's new department of external affairs was to encourage 'people of the Irish race in every country' to work in support of the Irish government by dealing directly with foreign governments on behalf of Ireland because 'if the right agents can influence government personages, trade can be created'.[29] From Dublin, Sean Milroy (who attempted in vain to keep the late Arthur Griffith's publications alive) liaised with Daniel Cohalan and Lindsay Crawford, now a Free State trade agent, in New York to promote American–Irish business links. Crawford's efforts would soon be confined to the tourism industry, however, while Lionel Smith Gordon, the manager of the Dáil's National Land Bank and an advisor to O'Shiel, does not appear to have been very successful in stimulating interest in Ireland from American bankers.[30] A failure to capitalise upon such goals soon led Milroy and others to voice the opinion that department of finance policy in Dublin was evidently being unjustly determined by civil service transfers from London rather than either the Irish government or Irish public opinion.[31] If this was partly true it was also essentially unavoidable, because a new factor in determining Irish government policy was that, concurrent with Ireland's joining the League of Nations, the expectation existed in the British Dominions Office that Ireland's trading priorities and economic policy would henceforth reflect the operations of the International Labour Organisation (ILO).

Edward Phelan, the son of a Waterford mariner, had served in the British foreign office as a creator of the ILO before he assumed the position as the Irish Free State's representative on that body. Thereafter, he acted as a liaison between the Irish department of industry and commerce, external affairs and Michael MacWhite, who served as Ireland's permanent representative at the League of Nations.[32] Phelan championed the idea that the ILO was the ideal forum for the future evolution of Ireland economically, constitutionally and diplomatically, on the grounds that both the British Commonwealth and the ILO were founded on 'the same ideals' of 'a better world civilisation'.[33] He saw Ireland's common membership of the ILO as a means to guarantee the applicability of Britain's idea of a common travel area, whereby social security and employment conditions in the United Kingdom and the Irish Free State always remained uniform as a single labour market. He also celebrated the fact that the ILO, unlike the League of Nations itself (which had no specific lawmaking powers), could become a basis for influencing the drafting of international economic treaties in the British Commonwealth's best interest.[34] The capacity of London's foreign trade policy to influence the ILO stemmed from the fact that the budgets of the latter were managed by the economic section of the League of Nations,[35] which, until 1930, was led by the British Royal Navy icon Sir Arthur Salter, whose strategic economic insights played a large part in sustaining the political relevance of Winston Churchill's worldview during the interwar years. An understanding within the British Dominions Office regarding Ireland was that if Irish diplomacy and economic policy was to be defined primarily by its common membership with other British dominions of the League of Nations and the associated ILO, it could only be a side product of British foreign policy.[36] John Horgan, the new Irish correspondent for Chatham House's Round Table, saw this as a means to prevent any revival of the Sinn Féin economic nationalist policy or the establishment of separate Irish diplomatic and trade priorities from those of the British Commonwealth.[37] This naturally had significant connotations for Irish relations with the United States.

The Free State's new national loan schemes were a separate matter to the Dáil's prior loan scheme, which had attempted to sell bonds in both Britain and America. The Free State now attempted to claim these monies.[38] Thomas Smiddy, a former professor of economics at University College Cork and established colleague of the Dáil cabinet, had been in America since 1922 'looking after the financial interests of the Irish Free State'.[39] The existence of a dispute regarding the Dáil's former bond scheme in America was far from helpful, however, and prompted Irish American interest and sympathy to decline.[40] After Michael MacWhite, Ireland's permanent representative to the League of Nations, registered the Anglo-Irish treaty with the League of Nations in July 1924, Smiddy began receiving initiations to meet key US bankers, including J.P. Morgan, as a prelude to Cosgrave potentially going on a diplomatic mission to the United States.[41] The United States recognised Smiddy as Ireland's minister plenipotentiary to the United States in October 1924, during the same week as the formal institutionalisation of the Defence Forces (Ireland),[42] in the process making Smiddy the first Free State diplomat to receive official recognition. However, America would not establish its own consular office within the Irish Free State until the summer of 1927.[43] This decision was made because London was still making efforts to revise the Anglo-Irish treaty of December 1921. In the meantime, Smiddy reported with regards to the old Sinn Féin ideal of making the western ports of Ireland part of a trans-Atlantic economy that 'such an idea is at present mythical'.[44]

The Irish army initially looked to the United States as the model for its own army training courses. In its first council of defence report, issued in the spring of 1925, the Defence Forces recommended that the Irish Free State seek 'friendly and intimate relations with the USA, France and Germany', which were the principal republican powers in contemporary international relations, and pursue the goal of creating an Irish mercantile marine and naval fleet to establish a distinct Irish presence on the world stage.[45] Subsequent requests that the Free State cabinet follow the army's 'Defence Plan' to enable it to manage all issues of national defence were ignored, however, at the insistence of the new department of finance. It was adamant that Ireland had no need for anything more than reserve, or volunteer, forces to potentially assist the police in matters of internal security and that, otherwise, Ireland could rely on Britain to handle the defence of the state.[46] This served to demoralise the Irish army. It also reflected how ongoing Anglo-Irish financial negotiations were practically dictating the Irish state's evolving geopolitical identity rather than the specific desires of Irish nationalists.

In November 1925, Eoin MacNeill surprised many by resigning from both the Irish government and a Boundary Commission that was set up under Article Twelve of the treaty to consider revising the Northern Ireland border. Around the same time, reports from Dublin's finance department were convincing Cosgrave that the Free State was facing imminent bankruptcy.[47] This led to a series of 'emergency' meetings at Chequers and Whitehall, where a document entitled 'Amendment of the articles of agreement for a treaty' was agreed. Under the terms of the new Anglo-Irish treaty, the Free State definitely had to contribute to the British national debt. London offered to make this financial burden more manageable (as a sixty-year debt) in return for Dublin's promise that it would never again seek the existence of a Boundary Commission or take an interest in Northern Irish affairs.[48] This formed the precursor to the 'ultimate financial settlement' between the United Kingdom and the Irish Free State in March 1926. Under its terms, the National Land Bank was incorporated into the Bank of Ireland so that both the legal operations and financial management of the land annuities schemes that were in place since the 1880s were left unchanged.[49] The Irish state also had to pay the pensions of all Irish ex-British soldiers who had fought in the First World War and reparations to any loyalist non-residents of the state who could claim damages to their property during the Irish struggle for independence, the latter being a bill that Churchill had insisted, from July 1922 onwards, that Dublin simply must pay, essentially as a form of retribution.[50] Finally, the financing of all Irish unemployment and state pension schemes were to be regulated from London. Indeed, Griffith's old goal of nationalising the Post Office Savings Bank in Ireland had effectively been defeated as early as March 1922.[51]

An immediate consequence of these settlements was that, at James Craig's insistence, the Irish government's North Eastern Boundary Bureau was abolished. This meant that Dublin had neither the ability nor the right to acquire any information about the internal workings of Northern Ireland and all communications between the north and south of Ireland practically ceased, initiating a 'cold war' whereby any attempt to initiate cross-border communications was treated by Belfast as an intolerable security threat to Northern Ireland.[52] Perhaps the best illustration of the inequality of Anglo-Irish relations occurred when the Defence Forces' chief of staff General Peadar MacMahon (a former member of the IRB) paid a visit to the London Imperial Conference that autumn in order to raise the promise in the original treaty agreement to return control to Ireland of its entire western coastline, but the British government refused to discuss the matter.[53] The Irish army had also been subject to political hostility nationally. From some quarters, this was because some ex-British soldiers (who soon either resigned or were encouraged to resign) were allowed into the improvised 'National Army' that was assembled to put down the civil disturbances during the summer of 1922.[54] During 1924, many members of Cosgrave's own party protested when a former political follower of John Redmond was appointed as the Irish government's new minister of defence at a time of extensive army demobilisations.[55] By such time as the Irish army was formally institutionalised as the Defence Forces (Ireland) in October 1924, no ex-British soldiers were retained in either the officer corps or troops of the regular army, even if some of the army's junior technical staff were ex-British servicemen.[56] For this very reason, however, the Irish army was denounced in some other quarters on the grounds that its principal officers were evidently all former members of the IRB.[57] This resulted in the introduction of a rule that no chief of staff could serve a term longer than two years.[58] During 1927, one such officer, Sean MacEoin, would resign on coming into conflict with external affairs minister Desmond FitzGerald, who expressed the opinion that Ireland had no need for a defence budget or to entertain the idea of adopting a different foreign policy attitude, such as military neutrality, to Britain.[59] This trend provided an avenue for the political rehabilitation of Éamon de Valera. In reaction to the Anglo-Irish financial settlement of March 1926, he founded a new party called Fianna Fáil that protested against its terms.[60] The following year, de Valera re-entered the Dáil and earned the admiration of the Irish army by arguing that Ireland should have a right to determine its own foreign policy, especially in matters of neutrality, because Irish nationalism had been founded not least upon Ireland's unwillingness to either fund or fight Britain's wars.[61]

A key factor in shaping the evolution of the Irish army was the legal advice of Cahir Davitt. Contrary to the army's own desires, he believed that it was legally obliged to model itself more on the British than the American or French armies.[62] Irish army officers had first contacted the French government during 1922 and the French consulate in Dublin continued to watch the fortunes of the Irish army closely up until at least 1929.[63] Meanwhile, American military intelligence judged that the real issue facing the Irish army was its need 'to see beyond the limited field of their revolutionary experience' and that otherwise its *esprit de corps* and understanding of the need for astute diplomacy was generally strong.[64] Be that as it may, its staff almost perpetually resented the fact that the department of finance had reduced the size of the army to a force of just 5,000 men and continued to reject its pleas for additional resources in both weaponry and manpower.[65]

It was probably understood internationally that the Irish Free State could not really begin to consider entering international trading agreements until after the 1926 Anglo-Irish financial settlements were first reached. Immediately thereafter, both the Germans and the French approached the Irish government regarding the possibility of trade agreements while, from Geneva, Michael MacWhite even tested the possibility of reaching a trade agreement with the USSR.[66] During 1927, German engineers played a major role in enabling Ireland to create a novel and cost-effective hydroelectricity supply scheme. Nevertheless, the Irish department of finance rejected completely the idea of an Irish–German trade agreement because the Germans, like the French, desired that this would take the form of reciprocal tariff agreements. London made it a condition of its contemporary trade agreements that whatever terms it agreed to should also be open to all the Commonwealth nations, thereby sustaining a 'most favoured nation' agreement throughout the British Commonwealth that was based on London's foreign trade policy. The department of finance maintained that Ireland could not divert from this practice by reaching its own trade agreements.[67] This led some officials in the department of external affairs to share the army's grievance at the restrictive influence being exercised by the department of finance.[68] It also led external affairs to recruit a new legal adviser, John Hearne, who would study if the Irish state had the legal right to establish its own mercantile marine to ensure that it could operate its own export trade or if the limitations imposed by a historic British Merchant Shipping Act of 1894 still theoretically applied.[69] Following this logic, Hearne and other senior Irish legal minds would soon come to the conclusion that Ireland would probably have to create an entirely new written constitution for the Irish state if such matters were to be addressed effectively.[70]

A growing sense that the Irish Free State was being led along a course contrary to what its founders had intended was shaped by the fact that Griffith and Collins had claimed that Ireland would enjoy complete fiscal autonomy and the right to pursue its own trading priorities,[71] but they were evidently mistaken. Instead, London was successfully pressing that neither Ireland nor the dominions could have distinct economic policies, nor be a distinct player in international relations; a development that London feared would lead to the collapse of its empire.[72] Even after the United States formalised the existence of its own diplomatic office within the Irish Free State on 1 July 1927, 'US trading links [with Ireland] remained underdeveloped ... at a time when US economic horizons were expanding continually' in Europe.[73] Within ten days of the formal establishment of diplomatic relations between the American Republic and the Irish Free State, unknown assailants assassinated Kevin O'Higgins, who had just been appointed as Ireland's minister for external affairs.[74] He was then replaced by Patrick McGilligan, a former London official who had begun serving as the Irish minister for industry and commerce in the wake of the 1924 political purge of ex-IRB members from all Irish governmental offices. Historians of the British Commonwealth have described McGilligan as the true 'founder of the [Irish Free] state' because of the prominent role that he played in the imperial conference of 1926, which acknowledged that the dominions had equal status with each other in external affairs, and the imperial conference of 1930 that led to the Statute of Westminster of 1931, which acknowledged that Ireland and other dominions could advise the Crown on matters relating to their own internal affairs but not on any matters relating to their external affairs.[75] This lack of diplomatic independence governed the Irish state visit to the United States by W.T. Cosgrave in January 1928. He was invited to a state dinner at the White House and also visited Congress, but US Secretary of State Frank Kellogg acted fully on the understanding that Ireland's diplomatic identity, like that of Canada, was totally co-dependent with that of Britain.[76] Against this backdrop, the old

American Fenian idea, formerly championed by Cohalan and Devoy (who was granted an Irish state reception in 1924 and died in 1928), that the cause of Irish independence could be abetted by identifying with American foreign policy priorities effectively lost whatever limited relevance it had. Cosgrave himself expressed disappointment at not being able to 'see more of the industrial life of the United States' during his American tour for the sake of developing Irish business links with America,[77] while on a two-day visit to Canada included within the same American tour Cosgrave and FitzGerald were nearly killed when their train was derailed, purportedly by accident.[78]

Reporting on the Irish Free State at this time, the US Bureau of Foreign and Domestic Commerce judged that 'to advocate, in general, the consistent development of direct trade … is undoubtedly correct in principle', but longstanding British priorities 'which have in the past limited the development of Irish–American direct trade … surely will continue in the future to influence the majority of American exporters to sell to the new Dominion through London and Liverpool'.[79] As such, the primary significance of Cosgrave's brief American tour was essentially symbolical as the first official Irish Free State diplomatic mission to an individual state. Canada appointed its first consular representatives to non-members of the British Commonwealth during 1929,[80] and the formal establishment of Irish diplomatic relations with France, Germany and the Vatican occurred roughly at the same time.[81] A sense was now largely established in international relations, however, that Ireland could possess no foreign relations other than whatever opportunities existed to partake in multilateral actions with other British dominions at the League of Nations. A recent study has suggested that there was actually a degree of Irish contentment that relying on the Commonwealth's most-favoured nation trading option could ensure that 'the expense of maintaining an expansive infrastructure of legations and consulates was … avoided', and that this was considered to be a better situation than 'direct and formal diplomatic relations'.[82] Cosgrave adopted a different attitude, however, during a 1929 American interview. He noted that the British dominions, such as Canada and Australia, inherently regarded Britain as their 'motherland', but 'we, on the contrary, feel we are ourselves a motherland for hundreds of thousands of Irishmen … in other countries abroad'.[83]

Disappointments that faced the Irish Free State between 1922 and 1926 had prompted the Irish government to study in detail the nature of the Canadian constitution. Among its discoveries was that the British Crown had been able to commit Canada into the First World War by the King's signature alone, thereby bypassing the Canadian department of external affairs entirely, which was completely powerless in such matters.[84] Therefore, Cosgrave noted there was a potential legal problem regarding 'how the Irish Free State can remain at peace'. Emphasising that the Irish Free State still considered the partition of Ireland to be 'a grave misfortune' that should be rectified, Cosgrave was also eager, in turn, to dismiss the resulting British allegations that Ireland was, in some sense, 'not sincere' in its dealings with Britain precisely because it held this viewpoint. This reflected the fact that ministerial contact between British and Irish government officials was actually rare from the mid-1920s onwards, nominally because of ongoing British resentment about Dublin's attitude towards Northern Ireland. Meanwhile, Cosgrave noted with regards to the United States that 'we have established an Irish legation at Washington and, in accordance with our means, we are going to extend this practice'.[85]

During 1930, new Irish consular offices were created in New York and Boston while Michael MacWhite, who had hitherto been the permanent Irish representative to the League of Nations, took charge of the Irish legation at Washington, replacing Thomas Smiddy. MacWhite was practically Ireland's one diplomat of note at this time. Largely because of his work, the Irish department of external affairs had previously been able to report that 'we are recognised at Geneva as one of the main upholders of the complete independence of the smaller states',[86] while, according to Edward Phelan, not long after his arrival in the American capital, MacWhite was able to become 'one of Washington's most popular hosts' because of his social savvy.[87] Sean T. O'Kelly, a one-time colleague of MacWhite in Paris and now de Valera's agent in the United States, was far from impressed, however, deeming MacWhite's influence to be based upon the same pro-British interest groups in America that had previously supported T.P. O'Connor rather than Sinn Féin back in 1918.[88] To some extent, O'Kelly's perspective reflected the ongoing Irish interest in pursuing a contrary course to that espoused by the British foreign office, even though O'Kelly's prior attempt during 1924 to establish a common cause with the 'American Friends of Freedom for India' was actually fully in keeping with a purely internal commonwealth debate.[89]

When US Secretary of State Frank Kellogg co-signed with Aristide Briand of the French Republic a pact renouncing war as an instrument of national policy, they were awarded the freedom of Dublin (they also received a Nobel Peace Prize, as did Briand's ally Gustav Stresemann, the chancellor of the German republic). When queried if this action was taken as an illustration of Ireland's republican sensibilities, Cosgrave replied that it was an illustration purely of Ireland's co-membership with the British dominions in the League of Nations.[90] This stance reflected the reality that Irish republicanism was now considered in Irish political debate as virtually synonymous not with international relations, but instead with a desire to either deny the legitimacy of the Irish Free State or else a willingness to attempt to capitalise upon its expected collapse under British pressure. The latter expectation had been used as an excuse for de Valera's unilateral establishment of what he termed as the 'Council of State' during the autumn of 1922. During the international tourist attraction of the 1924 Tailteann Games in Dublin, de Valera's supporters had attempted to establish contact with the same foreign agents as did the governing Free State party, Cumann na nGaedhael,[91] while as late as 1929, in support of the Council of State idea, O'Kelly was attempting from America to liaise with other former Irish diplomatic personnel, such as Art O'Brien in London and Leopold Kerney, a former trade agent, in Paris. In the event of a return of de Valera to power, such men would be offered Irish diplomatic posts.[92] De Valera himself, however, was preoccupied primarily with Anglo-Irish relations.

Between 1925 and 1930, Ireland's total trade increased by 15 per cent after a three-year period when it had dropped by almost 30 per cent. This actually led Cosgrave's administration to feel that Ireland occupied a 'satisfactory position', although the state still had entirely negative balances of trade, particularly with Britain, and had recently needed to launch a third national loan simply to keep the Free State afloat.[93] The initiation of a British imperial marketing programme for advertising all Irish goods as well as extensive imports from Canada and Australia,[94] despite the fact that Ireland had no means to export goods to these countries, was not a popular policy, and reflected the reality that British Commonwealth ties offered no practical economic advantages to Ireland. Sensing this, many former supporters of Griffith and Collins transferred their allegiance from Cosgrave's party to Fianna Fáil, which promised to adopt an economic nationalist programme in keeping with the original Sinn Féin ideal to establish positive balances of Irish trade,[95] especially with Britain. Noting this trend, the British dominions secretary James Henry Thomas warned that any unilateral attempt by Dublin to diverge from London's desired economic policies for Ireland would be considered as practically an illegal negation of the treaty agreement.[96] This reality set the tone for subsequent political developments upon de Valera's return to power in 1932 as much as did the crash of the London and subsequently the New York stock markets in 1929, which initiated a long-term situation whereby virtually all countries were unable to maintain their desired prices and quantity for exports, giving birth to an era of economic protectionism and international debt crises.[97]

Long prior to the Wall Street crash, Joseph Walshe, the head of the Irish department of external affairs, recognised the reality of 'our present lopsided economic position'. While purusing 'commercial treaties with foreign countries' would be necessary to remedy this, to move in this direction first required 're-organising our trade with Great Britain'. He expected, however, that such a change could only occur 'by a slow process of evolution' due to the parity of the Irish pound (which was first established during 1927) with sterling.[98] Britain's decision in 1932 to default on its own First World War debt payments to the United States and, in turn, to initiate a protectionist trading policy against America was a uniform British Commonwealth decision taken at an Imperial Economic Conference in Ottawa, Canada. Joseph Walshe necessarily attended this conference, as did the deputy leader of the Irish government Sean T. O'Kelly, but this was actually the last imperial conference that Irish diplomatic personnel would attend. Despite it not being its legal right, a representative of Craig's Northern Ireland administration was able to gain attendance to the Ottawa conference. Stormont, which was the Northern Ireland parliament, demanded admission on the grounds that if Dublin prioritised achieving a positive balance of trade with the United Kingdom, as de Valera had intimated, this might adversely affect Belfast's power to maintain its competitive economic advantages over Dublin.[99] Craig had been promoted to the British peerage for his role in negotiating the Anglo-Irish financial settlement of 1926 that imposed the British national debt upon Dublin. After the Ottawa conference, he explained proudly at Westminster that the entire *raison d'être* of Northern Ireland was to guarantee that London could retain its desired level of power over the Irish Free State in literally all matters and at all times.[100] Understanding this, de Valera suggested to the American consul in Dublin that the primary injustice of the existence of Northern Ireland was that it was an entity that 'was conceived and initiated in bitterness and vindictive spirit'.[101]

In addition to initiating a protectionist economic policy against the United States, Britain placed a large tariff on all Irish agricultural exports during 1932. This was done less because of de Valera's abolishment of a parliamentary oath of allegiance than because of Britain's desire to punish the Irish government for having announced its intention to withhold Irish banks' land annuity debt payments to Britain. Britain's tariffs on Irish agriculture forced de Valera's government to initiate a programme of trade diversification.[102] Possibly inspired in part by a positive portrayal of the Irish Free State in *Foreign Affairs* written by Eoin MacNeill,[103] the new American government of Democratic president Franklin D. Roosevelt approached Michael MacWhite and requested a trade treaty with Ireland based on reciprocal tariff agreements.[104] Ever since the 1920s, the Irish Free State was inclined to consider its diplomatic representation in America as its most important. By 1934, it had four consular offices in the United States (Boston, New York, Chicago and San Francisco) in addition to its main office in Washington D.C. By contrast, Ireland had only one office in the other countries where it had diplomatic missions (France, Germany and the Holy See) in addition to the office of high commissioner in London.[105] The Irish department of finance, however, declared Roosevelt's idea to be impossible.[106] Thereafter, Stephen Gwynn, a veteran of the British foreign office, wrote a very negative portrayal of Ireland for *Foreign Affairs*. This inverted the reality of London's initiation of tariffs against Ireland by labelling this as a hostile 'economic war' initiated purely by Dublin that, in the process, was supposedly proving an inherent Irish incapacity for self-government.[107] Gwynn's attitude essentially reflected a British fear of Ireland's partial entry into an American, rather than purely British, economic orbit and a desire to discourage this possibility as much as possible. Indeed, in the wake of Gwynn's strident criticisms, once de Valera attempted to open trade negotiations with the USA, Roosevelt's government now declared that it could not negotiate any trading matters with Ireland or, at least, not until the Irish first reached a fresh political agreement with Britain that proved to London's satisfaction.[108] Facing such hostility, de Valera proceeded with a significant degree of caution, as would be reflected most of all by his government's attitude towards banking policy.[109]

The necessity of reforming the banking system in Ireland had long been a belief of Irish nationalists. On this question, de Valera employed as his personal advisor Thomas Smiddy, Ireland's former minister to the United States. Smiddy was an advocate of creating a new central bank in Ireland that would act like the American Federal Reserve Bank. In common with the former manager of the Dáil's defunct National Land Bank, Smiddy believed that the best alternative to the old Sinn Féin idea of bank nationalisation would be to create a central bank that would encourage bank rates for loans that were more favourable to Irish business interests, and also be more competitive than those that were on offer from London banks. This could be done without necessarily breaking the parity between the Irish pound and sterling or interfering directly with the management of the Irish commercial banks.[110] Smiddy also desired that an Irish central bank would include some government officials as directors and assume direct management of the state's exchequer account by transferring it from London to Dublin. Fearing a diplomatic crisis with Britain, however, de Valera was unwilling to defy recommendations of department of finance officials to maintain the status quo.[111] He took Smiddy's advice in only one respect, which was his suggestion that ceasing Irish payments of land annuities to Britain was a financially sound idea, as 'the retention of the payments to Britain and sweepstakes [lottery] receipts means the Irish Free State will be able to sustain an adverse trade balance … without adversely affecting our international financial position.'[112]

The international debt crisis would give rise to polarising ideological debates throughout the 1930s. Reflecting this trend, both Arthur Salter and Irish economist Joseph Johnston wrote stern critiques of both economic nationalism and state planning by associating this idea negatively and exclusively with the USSR because of its independence from the western international banking system and its declared interest in launching a five-year national economic plan.[113] Against this backdrop, it was perhaps not surprising that Dublin's contemporary wish to 're-imagine the civil service as an agent of state-driven change' was often only half-hearted in its implementation. As had been the case when Cosgrave created an agricultural credit bank as a semi-state company in 1927, when de Valera created an industrial credit bank as an Irish semi-state company in 1933 it was decided that this institution needed to have its headquarters based in London if its place in the financial world was going to be secure.[114] In the meantime, de Valera responded to Britain's tariffs against Irish agricultural exports by imposing commensurate tariffs on Irish imports of British coal and sugar while also creating a new Irish sugar company as a semi-state body. Ireland also established diplomatic relations with the Spanish republic after a short-term Irish trading agreement was reached with both Spain and Germany. However, in common with Irish trade with France and Belgium (where a new Irish diplomatic office was opened in 1932), German–Irish and Spanish–Irish trade operated according to negative trading balances for Ireland,[115] partly because 'we do not take advantage of the hints given to us in the matter and send out a trade delegation' and partly 'due to deficiencies in our supply'.[116] Since 1930, Germany was nominally Ireland's second-largest trading partner, after Britain, because unlike many European countries (most notably France) it had a sizeable market for Irish agricultural produce. Ideology did not come into the equation.[117]

Perhaps the most novel initiative of de Valera's government was the creation during 1936 of a new state airline, Aer Lingus. At the same time, a new interdepartmental 'foreign trade committee' was created. Although de Valera acted as both prime minister and minister for external affairs, responsibility for the new interdepartmental committee was withheld from external affairs because trade was not generally considered to be a proper instrument of the state's international relations for at least as long as Ireland remained a member of the British Commonwealth.[118] The fact that the Irish government chose not to purchase a shipping line that had hitherto operated most trade operating between Dublin and

Liverpool has been described as an illustration of the essentially *ad hoc* approach adopted by de Valera's government, without any overarching strategy.[119] However, the explanation for this decision, which was taken by Sean Lemass as minister of industry and commerce, was that Irish exports were still on such a small scale that direct control of such a fleet seemed to be of comparatively little practical advantage. Apart from boosting industrial employment (a task he accomplished particularly well),[120] Lemass' policy was based primarily on the idea that 'where private enterprise was unable, or unwilling, to undertake economic development', then the government should 'introduce public enterprise to fill the gap'. Irish economists typified this as mirroring 'what Arthur Griffith had sought to do', with the difference that it 'was done on a purely practical level and had no ideological significance'.[121]

By the beginning of 1937, the Irish Free State was able to report, for the first time, the existence of a positive balance of trade with Britain,[122] although appreciation for this fact was not universal. This was because it occurred at a price of temporarily reducing the country's level of total trade in the interregnum.[123] Nevertheless, maintaining this standard of keeping a positive balance of trade with Britain henceforth became a perpetual focal point of Irish economic policy even as the country sought to expand into other markets.[124] This significance of this development was it had shown that reversing British Commonwealth economic policy regarding Ireland had effectively proved necessary to ensure that Anglo-Irish trade did not serve purely British interests. However, the perpetual challenge of sustaining this situation potentially meant that efforts to expand into other markets would frequently have to take second place. This reality, combined with ongoing the parity between the British and Irish pounds, meant that Ireland still operated very much within Britain's shadow.

De Valera actually became a well-known international figure after 1932 by presiding at meetings of the League of Nations. It has been suggested that de Valera's willingness to commit Irish troops during 1934 to a league peacekeeping mission in the Saar was an illustration of a clear Irish commitment to collective security.[125] In League of Nations debates on the Italian invasion of Abyssinia, de Valera also argued that 'if we want to be realists' it was necessary to recognise that economic sanctions were practically useless unless there was a credible threat of their being backed up by military force.[126] As the League of Nations did not have a legally enforceable charter, however, it essentially embodied a principle of collective security only on a nominal, or political, level. In the wake of the league's failure to deal with the Italian–Abyssinian conflict, de Valera was essentially the first to announce that the principle of collective security was practically dead in Europe. He also utilised this occasion to express not only opposition to foreign intervention in Spain, but also to announce to the world Ireland's intention to pursue a policy of military neutrality.[127]

With regards to the ideological quarrels of the 1930s, it was perhaps of note that in welcoming the USSR to the League of Nations during 1934, de Valera expressed the hope that it would define its relations towards Europe with the same open understanding as it had recently established friendly and open diplomatic relations with the United States.[128] Like the United States, Ireland was a country that, practically speaking, had a history of relatively healthy trade unionism without any resulting ideological baggage. At the time, labour party members' professed Marxism in various European countries was less a reflection of an actual pro-Soviet internationalism than it was an expression of a romantic desire for a freedom of conscience to express entirely individualistic views on politics, without being silenced by the ever-growing trend, in all countries, of party-political opinion being governed by chief whips.[129] For this very reason, the original status of Fianna Fáil as a catch-all party for particularly outspoken TDs actually led it to being accused of Marxist tendencies.[130] To de Valera's bemusement, some British diplomats in turn attempted to interpret Irish politics through the same bipolar left–right paradigm.[131] A growing preoccupation with notions of freedom of individual conscience and social justice in contemporary political debates was generally interpreted in Ireland, however, in an entirely non-ideological fashion. In particular, some Irish academics saw this trend as a manifestation of the growth of Christian-democratic political movements in Europe in the tradition of Marc Sangnier.[132] Although the British and French media usually typified Christian democrats as being of 'the right' in an attempt to polarise opinion vis-à-vis the Soviet Union as an 'anti-Christian' power on 'the left', Irish politics did not fit easily into paradigm. Perhaps reflecting this, during 1922, Arthur Griffith, who had formerly echoed the American view that Russia was a victim of German–Austrian intrigues and civil war more than it was a proponent of international revolution, offered Irish government funds for famine relief in Russia on purely humanitarian grounds.[133] On the same political understanding of Russian geopolitics and with de Valera's encouragement, Griffith had also been responsible for initiating the Irish attempt to establish diplomatic relations with the USSR during the summer of 1920.[134]

Many Irish nationalists were disappointed that a Banking Commission of 1934–8 that had been set up by the Irish government did not lead to any specific reforms.[135] The negotiation of a new Anglo-Irish agreement between 1936 and 1938 took precedence. As part of its terms, Britain was prepared to waive its claim to the land annuities payments in return for a single lump payment by Ireland of £10 million.[136] This actually provided a little more freedom for Irish banks to manoeuvre. The Irish government was now able to convert the foreign assets of the Irish post office and trustee savings banks (which were held almost entirely in Britain) into Irish government securities for the first time, although this process, begun hesitantly in the late 1930s, would not actually be completed until 1969 when such assets were repatriated to Ireland and the Irish banking system.[137] Other Irish debts to the British state, as had been dictated as part of the 1926 agreement, were retained.[138] This reflected the fact that the policy of de Valera's government was not as confrontational as Gwynn had claimed.

Gwynn and Craig's hostility towards de Valera's government had been shaped not least by the fact that, on the level of party-political debate within Ireland, achieving a position balance of trade with Britain was often typified simplistically as an advance for Irish republicanism against British imperialism. This was reflected by de Valera's Fianna Fáil party labelling itself as 'the republican party' and the increasing willingness of Cosgrave's 'Cumann na nGaedhael Party', which was reinvented in 1934 as the 'Fine Gael: the United Ireland Party', to label itself as a 'commonwealth party', but such nomenclatures were not essentially accurate representations of the state's international relations. Economic issues aside, de Valera had practically grown to accept the British Commonwealth connection as necessary for harmonious Anglo-Irish relations.[139] On this understanding, Henry Harrison, the Irish correspondent of the London *Economist* during the mid-1930s, was actually a strong champion of de Valera's government. By the time of the Anglo-Irish negotiations of 1936–8, however, Harrison began arguing that the creation of a unitary Irish state within the commonwealth could be the ideal solution for both Britain and Ireland because of the financial burden to London in sustaining a Northern Ireland administration that was seemingly unable to deal with rising industrial unemployment. To unionists' dismay, he did so while also professing to believe that 'the moral leadership of the English-speaking world' was now being provided by the United States.[140]

London's price for re-granting Ireland control of its western ports during 1938 was the establishment of an Anglo-Irish free trade agreement that removed the prospect of any meaningful German competition with Britain within Irish markets.[141] The Irish army welcomed this removal of the British naval presence in the west of Ireland. During 1930, it had been able to fulfil its goal of creating its own military college that adopted an ancient Fianna (Fenian) slogan as its motto.[142] On a practical level, however, the Irish army was conscious of the fact that the surrender of the western ports had not altered the reality that the Irish army was practically dependent on the British market for acquiring firearms. Furthermore, on the question of military neutrality, Colonel J.J. O'Connell emphasised two factors in the face of the evident militarisation of Europe during the 1930s. First, even in the event that an Irish declaration of neutrality was recognised by all belligerents, Ireland could still end up being drawn into a major war because of a belligerent's desire to attack all food suppliers to Britain. Second, although it had been self-evident to Britain for many centuries, it had rarely, if ever, been recognised 'by the Irish people themselves' that 'Ireland was by the facts of geography a country of primary importance' in a naval sense. Adopting this logic, he emphasised that the surrender of the western ports did not inherently rule out the possibility of joint Irish military action with Britain under theoretical circumstances.[143]

The negotiations regarding Ireland's western naval ports were a part of greater negotiations stemming from de Valera's External Relations Act of 1936. Under its terms, the appointment of Irish diplomatic personnel had to be co-signed by the head of the Irish government, not by the British Crown alone. To de Valera's mind, the return of the treaty ports was essentially an extension of this External Relations

Act, under which he considered that Ireland was now 'externally associated' with the British Commonwealth rather than being subject to the prerogatives of imperial diplomacy or the will of the British Crown alone.[144] London, however, took a different view. During these negotiations, the British Dominions Office intentionally dealt almost exclusively with the office of Irish high commissioner in London. Since 1930, John Dulanty, who was actually a Manchester-born, senior British civil servant ever since the time of the First World War, had occupied this position. Dulanty's own initial unease about working for a Fianna Fáil government had been appeased when he learnt that de Valera had responded very politely to a unionist's denunciation of all Irishmen who expressed admiration for the American republic, or who did not value the British political connection alone, by noting that 'you would be surprised to know how many of my followers share that opinion.'[145] Acting on Dulanty's advice, London came to view de Valera's creation of a new written Irish constitution, to replace the Free State constitution and rename the state as Éire, as a potentially positive move. This was because if the removal of royal references within the Irish constitution satisfied Irish republican voters, the ongoing situation whereby the credentials of Irish diplomatic personnel had to be co-signed by the British Crown under the External Relations Act of 1936 was believed to ensure a continued practical supremacy for British interests, or, at the very least, a guarantor of the relevance of Britain's dominions theory, under which Britain would continue to act as the sole practical guarantor of Ireland's security.[146] Under such circumstances, if Ireland declared its neutrality in any major war it would essentially occupy the position of a 'neutralised' state rather than being a fully neutral state.[147]

De Valera's constitution enshrined in law the fact that the Irish state could not go to war without the approval of the national parliament, Dáil Éireann.[148] While a similar provision had existed in the Irish Free State constitution,[149] this was not as legally binding. As a result, many in Ireland considered that the new constitution made Éire an independent republic in all but name. The introduction of a new oath of allegiance to the Éire constitution alone by all Irish army and policing personnel was also a significant step, even if the Irish public's sense of patriotism still had no appetite for the American or French republican tradition of military conscription. Éire's 1937 constitution was also notable for emphasising the state's respect for all religious communities, including Judaism, at a time when many Europeans, being in the grip of totalitarian political ideologies, were inherently adopting an opposite viewpoint. After launching the new Éire constitution and name for the Irish state in December 1937, de Valera announced on Irish national radio that 'the chief significance of the new constitution' was 'that it bears upon its face, from the first words of its preamble to the dedication at its close, the character of the public law of a great Christian democracy' where freedom of will and individual conscience was paramount.[150] While it generated sympathetic press commentary in Belgium and Luxembourg,[151] Éire's Christian-democratic constitution, the first document of its kind, did not stimulate great public interest in Europe. The Christian-democratic political values of seeking consensus without references to ideologies and generating associated parties were active but largely marginalised by ideological battles during the interwar years and would not start to become truly popular in Europe until after the Second World War, when they would become 'the most important political movement in post-war Western Europe'.[152] In the meantime, European interest in Ireland was often lessened by a sense that it was still within the British political system.

The Irish Free State and now Éire had only a half-dozen diplomatic offices abroad, none of which were legally entitled to assume the actual role of embassies. Nevertheless the Éire constitution included an article on international relations, evidently to express a commitment to multilateral diplomacy as a significant aspect of the Irish state's sense of identity in international relations. Article Twenty-Nine of the new Éire constitution stated that 'Ireland affirms its devotion to the ideal of peace and friendly co-operation amongst nations founded on international justice and morality'; that 'Ireland affirms its adherence to the principle of the pacific settlement of international disputes by international arbitration or judicial determination'; and that 'Ireland accepts the generally recognised principles of international law as its rule of conduct in its relations with other states.'[153] The notion of 'generally recognised principles of international law', however, was more of an aspiration than a reality at this time. This can explain why Sean Lester, who would serve as the last secretary-general of the League of Nations at the same time as fellow Irishman Edward Phelan served as the director of the ILO, considered that Ireland was closer to the so-called 'utopian', as opposed to 'realist', camp in the diplomatic quarrels of the 1930s.[154] Lester had secured a seat for Ireland on the League of Nations council just prior to the 1931 crisis caused by the Japanese invasion of Manchuria, while he thereafter took up the position of League High Commissioner in the Free City of Danzig (1934–7), where he became one of the first diplomats in Europe to highlight and denounce the Nazis' persecution of the Jews.[155]

In a book dedicated to Thomas Kiernan of the Irish department of external affairs,[156] the English Catholic writer John Morton celebrated the Christian-democratic ethos of the Irish constitution as well as de Valera's allegedly unique role in giving a political voice to Christian Europe within the League of Nations throughout the 1930s. While London deemed de Valera's creation of a new Irish constitution without any references to the British Crown to be inherently a mere 'game' that could have no meaning in reality,[157] Morton argued that the removal of the old Free State constitution, which included provisions in Articles Twelve and Fifty-One regarding the role of the King of England in exercising executive authority, was a truly significant step.[158] During 1938, John Hearne, an author of the 1937 constitution, was appointed as Ireland's first diplomatic representative in Canada. Here he discovered that, in the British dominions, de Valera's speeches on the idea of a Christian commonwealth were interpreted purely as an expression of the existence of a family of nations within the British Empire that were united in their semi-religious allegiance to the English monarch. This was indeed a significant legal concept within the British Commonwealth.[159] In Hearne's experience, its impact was felt by the fact that the idea that there could be a separate Christian commonwealth, perhaps inspired by a Catholic religious faith or unrelated to the politics of either the aristocracy of Britain or the British foreign office, was both morally and intellectually inadmissible to many Canadians' minds.[160] Reflecting this, when de Valera suggested to Britain that it should reciprocate Ireland's appointment of a Canadian representative (Ireland's first representative to the dominions) by now appointing a dominions representatives to Ireland, including a formal British diplomatic minister to Ireland, London rejected this idea as both seditious and illogical on the grounds that 'the King could not appoint a Minister to himself'.[161] Post-1917,

Irish republican propaganda that announced that 'today England's foreign minister lays wreaths upon the tomb of [George] Washington but in England's secret mind Washington is a traitor still' may have been hyperbolical,[162] but it was nevertheless an accurate reflection of Ireland's familiarity with the role of the unwritten constitution of Britain in shaping British political culture, as if no country could possibly renounce an allegiance to the English king or cease to be a part of his body. As far as Joseph Walshe was concerned, this mentality was at the root of the extraordinarily patronising nature of the British government's attitude towards Ireland and, indeed, all of its former colonies.[163]

In retrospect, the principal achievement of Irish diplomacy between 1922 and 1938 was simply to guarantee that Irish political aspirations that had predated the establishment of the Irish Free State were not completely lost in the byways of British efforts to lead Ireland down an alternative course of development against its will. A tragedy in circumstances that arose from the Anglo-Irish treaty of 1921, which certainly led to the downfall of Griffith, Collins and very many others, had been the paralysis of government until such time as extensive civil service reforms were first introduced. One could well argue that it was not until 1936, when de Valera introduced the practice of interdepartmental committees to deal with matters such as external affairs and international trade, that a sound or effective balance between parliamentary and cabinet government and civil service operations within the Irish state began to be achieved. The creation of a new Irish constitution to cement this process was merely the next logical step.[164]

On an economic, political and diplomatic level, the British Commonwealth had proved to be of very limited relevance, or use, to Ireland, even if many believed that the cost of potentially pursuing an alternative direction to Britain in international relations could ultimately prove far more than it was worth. It was essentially for this reason that de Valera's mere rectification of great imbalances in Anglo-Irish relations during the 1930s was actually looked upon by many with either disfavour or extreme caution. Hitherto, Ireland could assert the right of small nations to a voice in international relations through multilateral forums such as the League of Nations, although pursuing this line of reasoning to the extent of either antagonising the great powers or adopting an entirely non-aligned position in international relations had not generally been considered a practical option. Nevertheless, a spirit of non-alignment would underpin Éire diplomacy after 1938 as it sought to conflate its desire to exercise military neutrality with continued membership of the British Commonwealth. The Defence Forces may have had the will but it certainly had not the resources to manage all issues of national defence. This prompted the declaration of a national emergency upon the outbreak of the Second World War, after which Irish public opinion would unite as never before behind the resolve to remain entirely neutral, in turn boosting significantly the degree of national interest in Ireland's international profile.[165] Partly for this reason, the period of the Second World War would be almost universally considered within Ireland as a transitional period that cemented an anti-imperial sense of Irish national identity, which, in turn, was expected to find a reflection in all aspects of Ireland's international relations. The degree to which this could lead to the development of a more extensive field for Irish diplomacy in the wake of a major international war, however, was naturally far from certain.

Endnotes

1 Eoin MacNeill, 'Ten years of the Irish Free State', *Foreign affairs*, vol. 10 (1932), 235–49.

2 *Select constitutions of the world, prepared for presentation to Dáil Éireann* (Dublin, 1922).

3 Ernest Boyd, 'Ireland: resurgent and insurgent', *Foreign affairs*, vol. 1 no. 15 (1922), 86–97 (quote p. 91); Ernest Boyd, 'Recent Irish history', *Foreign affairs*, vol. 2 no. 15 (1923), 319–29.

4 Bernadette Whelan, *US foreign policy and Ireland* (Dublin, 2006), 368, 386, 398. The American consul in Belfast was unsympathetic to the Irish Free State because he believed that, unlike Craig's followers, Dublin did not have the support of the business community.

5 Westminster Parliamentary Archives, Lloyd George papers, F21/1/7, Lloyd George to Griffith, 1 June 1922.

6 Aengus Nolan, *Joseph Walshe: Irish foreign policy 1922–46* (Cork, 1996).

7 Owen McGee, *Arthur Griffith* (Dublin, 2015), 327, 294.

8 Eoin McLaughlin and Nathan Foley Fisher, 'State dissolution, sovereign debt and default: lessons from the UK and Ireland 1920–1938', *European historical economics working paper no. 61* (August 2014), 20–4.

9 While Woodrow Wilson (who died in 1924) had received a Nobel Peace Prize for being a would-be American patron of multilateral diplomacy, House's reputation

declined greatly after the publication of his private papers. Walter Lippmann, 'The intimate papers of Colonel House', *Foreign affairs*, vol. 4 (1926), 383–93.

10 Edward House, 'The running sands', *Foreign Affairs*, vol. 1 no. 15 (1922), 7.

11 Michael Kennedy, *Ireland and the League of Nations 1919-1946* (Dublin, 1996), appendix 3.

12 L.W. White, Andrew Carpenter, 'Edward Millington Stephens (1888–1955)', *Dictionary of Irish biography* (Cambridge, 2009); Bridget Hourican, 'Ronald J.P. Mortished (1891–1957)', *Dictionary of Irish biography* (Cambridge, 2009).

13 Eda Sagarra, *Kevin O'Shiel: Tyrone nationalist and Irish state builder* (Dublin, 2013), 187, 204.

14 *Documents on Irish foreign policy*, vol. 2 (Dublin, 2000), nos 41, 188, 190 and 380.

15 Ronan Fanning, *Independent Ireland* (Dublin, 1983), 83–5; Eda Sagarra, *Kevin O'Shiel*, 204.

16 Bernadette Whelan, *US foreign policy and Ireland* (Dublin, 2006), 381; Bernadette Whelan, 'Recognition of the Irish Free State, 1924', *Irish studies in international affairs*, vol. 26 (2015), 121.

17 Ernest Boyd, 'Recent Irish history', *Foreign affairs*, vol. 2 no. 15 (1923), 327.

18 Matthew Potter, *The Irish municipal revolution* (Dublin, 2011), 280–1, 396; John Dorney, *The civil war in Dublin* (Dublin, 2017), 277.

19 Gwynn attributed the popularity of the idea of a federal union developing in Ireland not to the terms of the Anglo-Irish treaty, but instead to a mistaken notion that had once been voiced by de Valera in America: that Belfast and the northeast of Ireland should exist within a federal Irish state in a similar manner to how Quebec existed within Canada. Stephen Gwynn, 'Ireland: one and divisible', *Foreign affairs*, vol. 3 (1924), 188–9.

20 George Russell ('A.E.'), 'Twenty-five years of Irish nationality', *Foreign affairs*, vol. 7 (1929), 204–20, quote pp. 213–14.

21 Mahon Hayes, James Kingston, 'Ireland in international law: the pursuit of sovereignty and independence', in B. Tonra, M. Kennedy, J. Doyle, N. Dorr (eds), *Irish foreign policy* (Dublin, 2012), 71. The 'United Kingdom of Great Britain and Ireland' was only then renamed as the 'United Kingdom of Great Britain and Northern Ireland'.

22 Ernest Boyd, 'Ireland: resurgent and insurgent', *Foreign affairs*, vol. 1 no. 15 (1922), quote p. 94; Stephen Gwynn, 'Ireland: one and divisible', *Foreign affairs*, vol. 3 (1924), 183–98.

23 Bank of Ireland Archives, 'Synopsis of the decisions of the committee' (Irish Banks Standing Committee, 1925), 1–5.

24 Labhrás Ó Nualláin, 'A comparison of the economic position and trend in Éire and Northern Ireland', *Journal of the statistical and social inquiry society of Ireland*, vol. XVII (1945-6), 532. All-Ireland, cross-channel trade had been valued at about £150 million up to 1922, but within a few years it had dropped to about £110 million.

25 D.P. Corcoran, *Freedom to achieve freedom* (Dublin, 2013), 142, 144; *Documents on Irish foreign policy*, vol. 3 (Dublin, 2002), no. 564 (a history of the Irish Free State's national loans); Louis Cullen, *Irish national income in 1911 and its context* (Dublin, 1995); Royal Economic Society (ed.), *The fiscal relations of Great Britain and Ireland* (Suffolk, 1912).

26 *Documents on Irish foreign policy*, vol. 2 (Dublin, 2000), nos 358–68.

27 'The bright future', *Evening Herald*, 27 Jan. 1922.

28 *Documents on Irish foreign policy*, vol. 2 (2000), no. 246. H.D. Butler, *The Irish Free State: an economic survey* (Washington D.C., 1928), 67.

29 *Documents on Irish foreign policy*, vol. 2 (Dublin, 2000), no. 181.

30 Crawford's correspondence on this theme can be found in *Documents on Irish foreign policy*, volumes 2 and 3. Milroy's correspondence can be found in the Daniel Cohalan papers in the library of the American Irish Historical Society. I am grateful to Michael Doorley for the latter information.

31 Sean Milroy, *The Tariff Commission and Saorstat economic policy* (Dublin, 1926).

32 Michael Kennedy, 'Edward Joseph Phelan (1888–1967)', *Dictionary of Irish biography* (Cambridge, 2009).

33 Edward Joseph Phelan, 'Ireland and the International Labour Organisation pt. 2', *Studies*, vol. 15 no. 59 (Sep. 1926), 383, 385, 390–5, 398 (quote).

34 Edward Joseph Phelan, 'Ireland and the International Labour Organisation', *Studies*, vol. 15 no. 57 (Mar. 1926), 1–18.

35 Edward Joseph Phelan, 'Some reminiscences of the International Labour Organisation', *Studies*, vol. 43 no. 171 (autumn 1954), 255.

36 A report on the impact of the international financial crisis of 1929 on Irish trade was drafted not at the request of the Irish government's departments of external affairs, industry and commerce or even finance (which announced that 'this department is not disposed to formulate any conclusions on the subject'), but by Baron Arthur Salter, the soon-to-be-retired British secretariat of the League of Nations. *Documents on Irish foreign policy*, vol. 3 nos 530, 564.

37 John J. Horgan, *Parnell to Pearse* (1949, 2nd ed., Dublin, 2009), biographical introduction.

38 This led to a legal case against Art O'Brien in London that was first initiated just before Collins' death in August 1922. For a catalogue of the relevant legal papers, see National Library of Ireland, Art Ó Briain papers (collection list no. 150).

39 Bernadette Whelan, 'Recognition of the Irish Free State, 1924', *Irish studies in international affairs*, vol. 26 (2015), 124.

40 This created an embarrassing situation whereby Smiddy was expected to partake in British intelligence operations against New York Irish organisations with the support of the US government. Details of this campaign can be found in Whelan, *US foreign policy and Ireland*, chapter 9, and Smiddy's 1923 correspondence in *Documents on Irish foreign policy*, vol. 2 (Dublin, 2000).

41 *Documents on Irish foreign policy*, vol. 2 (Dublin, 2000), nos 212, 278, 300, 312, 320, 375.

42 The formal establishment of the Defence Forces was meant to coincide with the Ministers and Secretaries Act, which regulated the operations of the civil service. This led to the creation of a council of defence, consisting of both military and department of defence personnel. The Ministers and Secretaries Act was passed on 21 April 1924. The earliest date cited for the establishment of the Defence Forces is 10 March 1924, but 1 October 1924 has most often been cited as the formal foundation date for the Defence Forces. T.W. Moody, F.X. Martin and F.J. Byrne (eds), *A new history of Ireland, Volume VIII* (Oxford, 1989), 406–7.

43 Bernadette Whelan, *US foreign policy and Ireland* (Dublin, 2006), 504–36.

44 *Documents on Irish foreign policy*, vol. 2 (Dublin, 2000), no. 300. This was possibly partly because John Horgan was now also chairman of the Cork Harbour Board.

45 *Documents on Irish foreign policy*, vol. 2 (Dublin, 2000), no. 323.

46 Colonel John Duggan, *A history of the Irish army* (Dublin, 1991), 146–55; Eunan O'Halpin, *Defending Ireland* (Oxford, 1999).

47 *Documents on Irish foreign policy*, vol. 2 (Dublin, 2000), nos 358, 359.

48 *Documents on Irish foreign policy*, vol. 2 (Dublin, 2000), nos 352–6, 359–68.

49 The National Land Bank was purchased by the Bank of Ireland, which had managed the land purchase accounts since 1881, and reinvented as a subsidiary bank, the National City Bank, which nominally existed until 1968. Between 1922 and 1926, the principal shareholders of the National Land Bank were supporters of de Valera. Eoin Ryan, *An Irish banking revolution* (Dublin, 1995), 1–31.

50 Churchill Archives, CHAR22/14/11, Churchill to Lionel Curtis, 7 Jul. 1922; CHAR22/14/18-9 (report on Shaw Commission); CHAR22/14/32, Churchill to Hankey, 15 Jul. 1922.

51 *Documents on Irish foreign policy*, vol. 2 (Dublin, 2000), no. 385; Owen McGee, *Arthur Griffith*, 177–8, 295.

52 Michael Kennedy, *Division and consensus: the politics of cross-border relations in Ireland 1925-1969* (Dublin, 2000), chapters 1–3.

53 Colonel John Duggan, *A history of the Irish army* (Dublin, 1991), 151.

54 The foremost of these was Emmet Dalton, who was responsible for instigating the armed conflict in June 1922 but had already resigned permanently from the army by November 1922. Sean Boyne, *Emmet Dalton* (Dublin, 2015).

55 Marie Coleman, 'Peter Hughes (1878–1954)', *Dictionary of Irish biography* (Cambridge, 2009).

56 Colonel John Duggan, *A history of the Irish army*, 132, 329–30, ft. 29.

57 In the opinion of Colonel Duggan, a group of four men, Charles Dalton (brother of Emmet Dalton), Liam Tobin, Tom Cullen and Richard Mulcahy, were pressurised into engineering this controversy only so that an excuse could be found for demanding that former IRB leaders Sean O'Muirthile and Joseph McGrath were removed from government office. Colonel John Duggan, *A history of the Irish army*, 115–20, 129, 134–5, 144.

58 Eunan O'Halpin, 'The office of chief of staff in historical perspective', in Tom Hodson (ed.), *Chiefs of staff: the portrait collection of the Irish Defence Forces* (Dublin, 2012), 35–49; Colonel John Duggan, *A history of the Irish army*, 139–41.

59 Colonel John Duggan, *A history of the Irish army*, 155–59.

60 Dorothy Macardle, *The Irish republic* (London, 1937).

61 Peter Young, 'Defence and the new Irish state 1919-1939', *Irish Sword*, vol. 19 (1995), 1–10; Colonel John Duggan, *A history of the Irish army*, 155.

62 Colonel John Duggan, *A history of the Irish army*, 115–20, 129, 134–35, 144.

63 Mark Tierney, 'Calendar of Irlande, vols 9, 10, 11', *Collectanea Hibernica*, no. 25 (1983), 209–36.

64 Tom Hodson, *The College: the Irish military college 1930-2000* (Dublin, 2016), quote p. 49.

65 Colonel John Duggan, *A history of the Irish army*, 147.

66 *Documents on Irish foreign policy*, vol. 3 (Dublin, 2002), no. 122.

67 Ibid., nos 313, 315, 404, 500 and 589.

68 Ibid., no. 156; *Documents on Irish foreign policy*, vol. 4, no. 156.

69 Ibid., vol. 3, nos 241 and 300.

70 Gerard Hogan, *The origins of the Irish constitution 1928-1941* (Dublin, 2012). Hearne was later a prime mover in the creation of the 1937 constitution. Eugene Broderick, *John Hearne, architect of the 1937 constitution* (Dublin, 2016).

71   Arthur Griffith, *Arguments for the treaty* (Dublin, 1922), 26–8; Michael Collins, *The path to freedom* (Dublin, 1922), 116–17.

72   Bernadette Whelan, 'Recognition of the Irish Free State, 1924', *Irish studies in international affairs*, vol. 15 (2015), 125.

73   Bernadette Whelan, *US foreign policy and Ireland* (Dublin, 2006), 504–36 (quote p. 504).

74   John P. McCarthy, 'Kevin Christopher O'Higgins (1892–1927)', *Dictionary of Irish biography* (Cambridge, 2009).

75   David Harkness, 'Patrick McGilligan (1889–1979)', *Dictionary of Irish biography* (Cambridge, 2009), quote; David Harkness, *The restless dominion: the Irish Free State and the British Commonwealth of Nations 1921–1931* (London, 1969).

76   Francis Carroll, 'Official visits: President Cosgrave comes to Ottawa', *Canadian journal of Irish studies*, vol. 36 no. 2 (fall 2010), 174–90. The United States established its diplomatic office in Dublin at the same time as it allowed Canada to establish a diplomatic office in Washington D.C. The British and American governments considered the two developments to be directly interrelated. *Documents on Irish foreign policy*, vol. 3 no. 63.

77   *Documents on Irish foreign policy*, vol. 3 no. 132.

78   Francis Carroll, 'Official visits: President Cosgrave comes to Ottawa', *Canadian journal of Irish studies*, vol. 36 no. 2 (fall 2010), 182–3, 190.

79   H.D. Butler, *The Irish Free State: an economic survey* (Washington D.C., 1928), 86.

80   B. Tonra, M. Kennedy, J. Doyle, N. Dorr (eds), *Irish foreign policy* (Dublin, 2012), 75.

81   Ronan Fanning, *Independent Ireland* (Dublin, 1983), 85. The French government did not consider its consulate in Dublin to be a distinct office from the French embassy in London until 1929.

82   Gerard Keown, *First of the small nations: the beginnings of Irish foreign policy in the interwar years 1919–1932* (Oxford, 2015), 248.

83   'Ireland's future foreign policy: an interview with William T. Cosgrave', *Barrons*, 4 Feb. 1929, p. 5.

84   Francis Carroll, 'Official visits: President Cosgrave comes to Ottawa', *Canadian journal of Irish studies*, vol. 36 no. 2 (fall 2010), 179.

85   'Ireland's future foreign policy: an interview with William T. Cosgrave', *Barrons*, 4 Feb. 1929, p. 5.

86   Michael Kennedy, 'The Irish Free State and the League of Nations, 1922–32: the wider implications', *Irish studies in international affairs* (1992), 15, 22.

87   Edward Joseph Phelan, 'Some reminiscences of the International Labour Organisation', *Studies*, vol. 43 no. 171 (autumn 1954), 247.

88   NLI, Art Ó Briain papers, Ms8461/18, Sean T. O'Kelly to Art O'Brien, 17 Jan. 1929. The Chicago Irish Fellowship Club, which was associated with Cosgrave's tour, had supported T.P. O'Connor during 1917–18 when most Irish American organisations emphatically did not.

89   Some New Zealand politicians were speaking on behalf of India too, reflecting the degree to which this Indian debate was purely internal to the British Empire. Gerard Keown, *The first of the small nations*, 76–9.

90   'Ireland's future foreign policy: an interview with William T. Cosgrave', *Barrons*, 4 Feb. 1929, p. 5.

91   Peter Pyne, 'The third Sinn Féin party 1923–1926', *Economic and social review*, vol. 1 (1969), 29–50, esp. p. 38.

92   O'Brien and Kerney would become the Irish diplomatic representatives in France and Spain respectively during 1935 thanks to O'Kelly, who was then vice-president of the executive council of the Irish Free State.

93   *Documents on Irish foreign policy*, vol. 3, no. 564.

94   Ibid., no. 572.

95   Ciara Meehan, *The Cosgrave party: a history of Cumann na nGaedhael 1923–33* (Dublin, 2010).

96   Philip Williamson, 'James Henry Thomas (1874–1949)', *Oxford dictionary of national biography* (online edition).

97   J.J. Lee, *Ireland 1912–85* (Cambridge, 1989), 114, 190, 527.

98   *Documents on Irish foreign policy*, vol. 2, nos 310 and 38.

99   Michael Kennedy, *Division and consensus: the politics of cross-border relations in Ireland 1925–1969* (Dublin, 2000), 43–4, 49, 61, 69.

100 Northern Ireland House of Commons official report, vol. 34 col. 1095 (24 Apr. 1934).

101 Kennedy, *Division and consensus,* quote p. 43.

102 Kevin O'Rourke, 'Burn everything British but their coal: the Anglo-Irish economic war of the 1930s', *Journal of economic history*, vol. 51 no. 2 (June 1991), 357–66.

103 Eoin MacNeill, 'Ten years of the Irish Free State', *Foreign affairs*, vol. 10 (1932), 235–49.

104 *Documents on Irish foreign policy*, vol. 4 nos 182, 190, 231, 235.

105 Ibid., vol. 2 no. 278. A list of all Irish offices abroad, including their date of formation, can be found in *Documents on Irish foreign policy*, vol. 10, appendix 3.

106 Donal Lowry, 'The captive dominion: imperial realities behind Irish diplomacy 1922–49', *Irish historical studies*, vol. 36 no. 142 (Nov. 2008), 214.

107 Stephen Gwynn, 'Ireland since the treaty', *Foreign affairs*, vol. 12 (1934), 319, 326–7, 330.

108 Deirdre McMahon, *Republicans and imperialists: Anglo-Irish relations during the 1930s* (Yale, 1984), 42, 139, 146. The American consulate in Dublin privately reflected that the Irish political desire to establish a positive balance of trade with Britain at the expense of other trade was somewhat incomprehensible.

109 Edward Coyne S.J, 'Ten years of export trade', *Studies*, vol. 24 no. 95 (Sep. 1935), 459.

110 Eoin Drea, 'The role of T.A. Smiddy in Fianna Fáil economic policy-making 1932–45', *Irish studies review*, vol. 24 no. 2 (2016), 175–90. This was essentially the same policy that the First Dáil had been inclined to favour ever since the possibility of securing recognition of an entirely independent Irish republic had faded after the summer of 1920. Lionel Smith Gordon, *The place of banking in the national programme* (Dublin, 1921).

111 Ronan Fanning, *The Irish department of finance* (Dublin, 1978), 216.

112 Eoin Drea, 'The role of T.A. Smiddy in Fianna Fáil economic policy-making 1932–45', *Irish studies review*, vol. 24 no. 2 (2016), quote p. 179.

113 Baron Arthur Salter, 'The future of economic nationalism', *Foreign affairs*, vol. 11 (1932), 8–20; Joseph Johnston, *The nemesis of economic nationalism* (London, 1934).

114 Martin Maguire, *The civil service and the revolution in Ireland, 1912–38* (Manchester, 2008), 228 (quote); Mary Daly, 'The economic ideals of Irish nationalism', *Éire-Ireland* 29 (winter 1994), 77–100.

115 After 1932, Ireland imported approximately £2 million of German goods, but it did not succeed in establishing an effective export market. Mervyn O'Driscoll, *Ireland, Germany and the Nazis* (Dublin, 2004), 102–5, 118–23, 141, 162–9, 173, 200–6, 232–3, 268–9. A short-lived trade agreement was established with Spain, but this was also based on an entirely negative trade balance (of approximately £700,000). Michael Kennedy, 'Leopold Kerney and Irish–Spanish diplomatic relations, 1935–6', in D.M. Downey, J.C. MacLennan (eds), *Spanish–Irish relations through the ages* (Dublin, 2008), 193–6, 210–11.

116 *Documents on Irish foreign policy*, vol. 4 no. 229 (report of Art O'Brien from Paris).

117 Mervyn O'Driscoll, *Ireland, Germany and the Nazis: politics and diplomacy, 1919–1939* (Dublin, 2004), 46–8, 58–61, 102.

118 Mervyn O'Driscoll, 'The economic war and Irish foreign trade policy: Irish–German commerce 1932–39', *Irish studies in international affairs*, vol. 10 (1999), 74–5; Michael Kennedy, 'Joseph Walshe, Éamon de Valera and the execution of Irish foreign policy 1932–8', *Irish studies in international affairs*, vol. 14 (2003), 178–9.

119 Bryce Evans, 'A semi-state archipelago without ships: Sean Lemass, economic policy and the absence of an Irish mercantile marine', *UCD working papers in history and policy no. 6* (2012).

120 Diarmaid Ferriter, *The transformation of Ireland* (London, 2005), 371–4.

121 Patrick Lynch, 'The economic scene', in O.D. Edwards (ed.), *Conor Cruise O'Brien introduces Ireland* (London, 1969), 75–6.

122 Labhrás Ó Nualláin, 'A comparison of the economic position and trend in Éire and Northern Ireland', *Journal of the statistical and social inquiry society of Ireland*, vol. XVII (1945–6), 522.

123 Edward Coyne S.J, 'Ten years of export trade', *Studies*, vol. 24 no. 95 (Sep. 1935), 461.

124 K.A. Kennedy, T. Giblin, D. McHugh, *The economic development of Ireland in the twentieth century* (London, 1988), 183.

125 Michael Kennedy, *Ireland and the League of Nations* (Dublin, 1996), 250, 255; Michael Kennedy, 'Prologue to peacekeeping: Ireland and the Saar 1934–5', *Irish historical studies*, vol. 30 no. 19 (May 1997), 420–8.

126 J.B. Morton, *The new Ireland* (London, 1938), 103–4.

127 Martha Kavanagh, 'The Irish Free State and collective security 1930–1936', *Irish studies in international affairs*, vol. 15 (2004), 103–22.

128 J.B. Morton, *The new Ireland* (London, 1938), 102–5.

129 Maurice Duverger, *Political parties: their organisation and activity in the modern state, with a foreword by D.W. Brogan* (2nd ed. English language translation, London, 1959), viii–ix, xxxii–iii.

130 J.P. O'Carroll, John Murphy (eds), *De Valera and his times* (Cork, 1983), 134–59.

131 *Documents on Irish foreign policy*, vol. 6 no. 37.

132 Gearoid Barry, *The disarmament of hatred: Marc Sangnier, French Catholicism and the legacy of the First World War 1914–1945* (London, 2012). Irish Catholic opinion did not tend to regard Marxism as an ideological threat to religion in the same way as liberalism and republicanism had been considered in the nineteenth century, when church–state relations were a far more polarising issue, particularly within the UK and France. R. Dudley Edwards (ed.), *Ireland and the Italian Risorgimento* (Dublin, 1960), 66–73.

133 *Documents on Irish foreign policy*, vol. 1 no. 274.

134 Michael Quinn, *Irish–Soviet diplomatic and friendship relations 1917–1991* (Maynooth, 2016), 11.

135 Mary E. Daly, *Industrial development and Irish national identity, 1922–1939* (Syracuse, 1994), 16; Joseph Lee, *Ireland, 1912–1985* (Cambridge, 1989), 109–10, 144–5.

136 Kevin O'Rourke, 'Burn everything British but their coal: the Anglo-Irish economic war of the 1930s', *Journal of economic history*, vol. 51 no. 2 (June 1991), 357–66.

137 Padraig McGowan, *Money and banking in Ireland* (Dublin, 1990), 33.

138 Henry Harrison, *Ulster and the British Empire: help or hindrance?* (Bristol, 1938), appendix 2.

139 Deirdre McMahon, *Republicans and imperialists: Anglo-Irish relations during the 1930s* (Yale, 1984), 224–5.

140 Henry Harrison, *Ulster and the British Empire: help or hindrance?* (Bristol, 1938) quote from the opening dedication to F.D. Roosevelt.

141 Mervyn O'Driscoll, 'The economic war and Irish foreign trade policy: Irish–German commerce 1932–39', *Irish studies in international affairs*, vol. 10 (1999), 71–89.

142 This is reproduced as the opening dedication of Colonel John Duggan, *A history of the Irish army* (Dublin, 1991). For the history of the military college, see Colonel Tom Hodson, *The College: the Irish military college 1930–2000* (Dublin, 2016).

143 J.J. O'Connell, 'The vulnerability of Ireland in war', *Studies*, vol. 27 no. 125 (Mar. 1938), 125–35; 'Can Ireland remain neutral in war?', *Studies*, vol. 27 no. 108 (Dec. 1938), 647–55.

144 Donal Lowry, 'The captive dominion: imperial realities behind Irish diplomacy 1922–49', *Irish historical studies*, vol. 36 no. 142 (Nov. 2008), 202–26.

145 *Documents on Irish foreign policy*, vol. 3 no. 609.

146 Donal Lowry, 'The captive dominion: imperial realities behind Irish diplomacy 1922–49', *Irish historical studies*, vol. 36 no. 142 (Nov. 2008), 202–26; Michael Kennedy, 'Joseph Walshe, Éamon de Valera and the execution of Irish foreign policy 1932–8', *Irish studies in international affairs*, vol. 14 (2003), 180-1.

147 Patrick Keatinge, *A singular stance: Irish neutrality* (Dublin, 1984), 4.

148 Brian Doolan, *Principles of Irish law* (6th ed., Dublin, 2003), 18.

149 B. Tonra, M. Kennedy, J. Doyle, N. Dorr (eds), *Irish foreign policy* (Dublin, 2012), 72.

150 J.B. Morton, *The New Ireland* (London, 1938), quote p. 97.

151 Mervyn O'Driscoll, Dermot Keogh, Jerome aan de Wiel (eds), *Ireland through European eyes: western Europe, the EEC and Ireland 1945–1973* (Cork, 2013), 256, 295.

152 Richard Vinen, *A history in fragments: Europe in the twentieth century* (London, 2000), 359, 383 (quote).

153 *Bunreacht na hÉireann* (Dublin, 1937), article 29, sections 1–3, p. 96.

154 Gerard Keown, 'Sean Lester: journalist, revolutionary, diplomat, statesman', *Irish studies in international affairs*, vol. 23 (2012), 149.

155 Gerard Keown, 'Sean Lester: journalist, revolutionary, diplomat, statesman', *Irish studies in international affairs*, vol. 23 (2012), 143–54.

156 At the time of writing, Kiernan was a member of staff of the Irish diplomatic corps in London, but he would soon be transferred to the Holy See. He was the husband of the popular singer Delia Murphy.

157 *Documents on Irish foreign policy*, vol. 6 no. 37 (Sir John Maffey to Anthony Eden).

158 J.B. Morton, *The New Ireland* (London, 1938), 95–6.

159 Norman Bonney, *Monarchy, religion and the state: civil religion in the United Kingdom, Canada, Australia and the Commonwealth* (Manchester, 2013).

160 *Documents on Irish foreign policy*, vol. 6 no. 68.

161 *Documents on Irish foreign policy*, vol. 6 no. 37 (Sir John Maffey to Anthony Eden).

162 *Nationality*, 24 Nov. 1917 (editorial).

163 Although he had been the Irish official with perhaps the most cordial relationship with the British dominions office, Joseph Walshe felt that 'every advance in the form of Irish freedom ... had been met by an unbelievable narrow-mindedness and rigidity of outlook' on behalf of Britain. *Documents on Irish foreign policy*, vol. 6 no. 15.

164 Martin Maguire, *The civil service and the revolution in Ireland, 1912–38* (Manchester, 2008).

165 Search results analytics for the term 'external affairs' in the *Irish Independent* (Irish Newspaper Archive) and in *The Irish Times* (ProQuest Historical Newspapers) shows that the Irish press did not begin to pay regular attention to the activities of the Irish department of external affairs until the 1940s, and that this level of interest was both sustained and grew thereafter.

4

A Spirit of Non-Alignment: Ireland in and out of the British Commonwealth, 1938–1955

I reland believed that it needed to establish a common cause with other neutral countries if its stance was to be understood and respected internationally. For this reason, the decision of Arnold Toynbee, an icon of Britain's Chatham House, to establish a small 'Irish Institute of International Affairs' in Dublin just as the Second World War was approaching was not looked upon by the Irish government with favour.[1] The Irish government intended to present its neutral stance as 'a positive and active peace policy', but propagating this view within the British Commonwealth was 'taken as a criticism'. As soon as the Second World War broke out, it bred definite resentments, including misleading attempts to portray Irish nationalists as pro-German.[2] This effectively repeated Ireland's experience during the First World War. The fact that Ireland had very limited and weak diplomatic representation also meant that it had little means to counteract this trend. Efforts to boost Ireland's relationship with neutral Spain, previously based on trading agreements established while Spain was still a republic, failed because of the presence of past republican fighters from Ireland in Franco's jails.[3] Ireland had no diplomatic representation in neutral Scandinavia, even if it did have a friendly, but informal, relationship with Finland.[4] Efforts were made to create new Irish diplomatic offices in the neutral countries of Switzerland and Portugal, but their operations remained only nominal. Therefore, it was decided that the only neutral country that Ireland could hope to reach a significant understanding with was the United States.

Ireland's policy towards the United States tended to focus more on the potential value of Irish lobby groups in America than on dealing directly with the American government itself.[5] For instance, acting on Joseph Walshe's advice, de Valera had made a series of radio news broadcasts that were addressed specifically to an Irish audience in America, and these continued throughout the war. In the late 1930s, Walshe had hoped that these could influence 'the responsible American press' to consider the potential value of a united Ireland 'as a factor of world peace'.[6] Joseph Cudahy, the American minister to Dublin during the 1930s, took notice of this trend.[7] However, President Roosevelt, in appointing the Irish American Joseph Kennedy (father of John F. Kennedy) as America's ambassador to Britain, stressed that even if the American government might discuss Ireland informally with Britain, it would not discuss or raise Anglo-Irish relations as a formal, or diplomatic, issue because it was considered to be a purely internal British Commonwealth matter.[8]

Robert Brennan became the new Irish minister at Washington D.C. at the end of 1938.[9] After the European war broke out, he attempted to secure American recognition of Irish neutrality and encouraged neutral America to send its merchant ships to Irish ports. The American government replied that while it 'had sympathy with neutral countries' it considered that Ireland and 'other European neutrals' were practically within a combat zone. Therefore, Irish ports should be considered as effectively closed for American commerce for the duration of the war.[10] This encouraged the Irish government to continue focusing on 'Irish America'. With the assistance of the American-Irish, Ireland was able to charter an American ship to sail under Ireland's neutral tricolour to ensure that some trans-Atlantic trade, such as imports of maize and fertilisers, continued.[11] Echoing American pacifism during the early stages of the First World War, the American government appointed a representative to the Vatican during 1939 so 'that the President and the Pope can work more easily to bring about that international peace which both so ardently desire'. America did so whilst refraining from allowing a papal nuncio to establish himself in the United States. This situation would continue until 1984 because, in Brennan's words, Americans 'base their objection [to a nuncio] on the grounds that freedom loving Americans dislike the idea of church and State being linked'.[12] American Catholic cardinals of Irish descent entered into direct communications with Brennan. They professed to be concerned less with international relations, however, than combating the 'false [moral] standards' of rich 'robber barons' that were judged to be too influential in American life.[13] Meanwhile, Dublin's prior efforts during the 1930s to rekindle a sense of Irish identity amongst the Irish population in the United States partly paid off when they chose to express strong support for both American and Irish neutrality.

The principal threat to American neutrality was reputedly the degree of popular support for repeating the highly profitable example during the First World War of removing the embargo on the sale of American munitions to the Allies.[14] In opposition to this trend, Daniel Cohalan's *Gaelic American*, which was no longer a significant publication (it would cease publication in 1953 not long after Cohalan's death), argued that Britain had tricked America into entering the First World War and thereafter forced America to foot Britain's bills by defaulting on its debt repayments during 1932. He predicted that the same thing would happen again. Brennan and his small staff of Irish consular officials knew enough about American government attitudes, however, to understand that the possibilities of an Anglo-American alliance were always governed far less by the situation in Europe than in the Far East.[15] Deteriorating US–Japan relations, arising from growing US influence in Asia, was the American government's greatest concern. Japan's 1911 international trade treaty had involved both the USA and the United Kingdom but it was due to end in January 1940. A Japanese attack on Hawaii in December 1941 would draw America into the war. Thereafter, the *Gaelic American* expressed its total support for the American war effort whilst continuing to defend the logic of Irish neutrality.[16]

Expecting that 'this war would lead to a new world order', Joseph Walshe believed that an effort should be made to rely on the 'immense importance of Ireland's position in the English speaking Catholic world',[17] while de Valera had the foresight to consider the possibility 'if the present war is followed by a close European federation'.[18] On the same day as Britain and France declared war on Germany, de Valera introduced the Emergency Powers Act in the Dáil as a national legal instrument to ensure that Irish neutrality operated effectively at home, including in the media. Irish diplomatic staff in Berlin, Paris and Rome kept Dublin quite well informed of developments on the continent. Meanwwhile, the legal advisor to Ireland's diplomatic staff, Michael Rynne, ensured that Ireland's declaration of neutrality, which was based upon an elaboration of Hague Convention rules, was sent to all foreign powers.[19] Closer to home, however, Anglo-Irish relations soon became strained.

Although Britain rejected de Valera's call to establish a British diplomatic presence in Ireland, within a month of the outbreak of the war it did appoint a 'special representative' to Dublin, Sir John Maffey, in order to facilitate effective wartime communications between Dublin and London.[20] This arrangement initially worked quite well. However, Winston Churchill, a critic of the 1938 Anglo-Irish agreement, was elected as British Prime Minister in May 1940. In the wake of the shocking fall of Paris and the Royal Air Force's defensive 'battle of Britain' that summer and autumn, Churchill resumed his old criticisms of Ireland, complaining in the House of Commons that the denial to Britain of Irish ports was hampering Britain's defence. He purposively timed his remarks to coincide with the November 1940 US presidential election. Reflecting British commercial influence within the United States, this claim almost immediately evoked a very sympathetic response in an ostensibly liberal American press. Stephen Gwynn of the British Foreign Office had recently used *Foreign Affairs* to claim that James Craig was once again proving his sterling patriotism during times of war in contrast to the Irish government, whose true colours as irresponsible charlatans was being illustrated by de Valera's efforts to seek the protective benefits of British Commonwealth membership without being willing to pay anything in return.[21] The failure of anyone from the Irish government to write for US journals such as *Foreign Affairs* may well have served to validate Gwynn's propaganda in American eyes. Certainly, it would seem to have influenced David Gray, a relative of Eleanor Roosevelt who was now appointed as the new US minister to Ireland. Even prior to America's entry into the war in December 1941, Gray encouraged the sending of American army technicians to Northern Ireland. Reputedly, mild Irish press criticisms of the arrival of American troops in Northern Ireland in early 1942 (which led to the construction of a new naval base in Derry) increased Churchill's capacity to dictate what attitude the United States should adopt towards Éire,[22] although the *American Journal of International Law* emphasised that the stance of the Irish government must be fully respected.[23]

Some British Foreign Office historians have celebrated the degree to which Churchill practically exercised a directing influence over Roosevelt,[24] although this perspective was certainly prone to exaggeration: American foreign policy, whether under Democratic or Republican administrations, was naturally determined primarily by American self-interest rather than national biases.[25] Furthermore, America was keen to reverse the anti-American, British Commonwealth consensus that had been established at Ottawa during 1932. The essential issue for Ireland with regards to the operations of Anglo-American relations was that it did not result in its own distinct voice being either silenced or ignored. In its intelligence communications with the American government, Britain deliberately downplayed the extent to which Ireland was a friendly neutral in the war.[26] Robert Smyllie, the editor of the strongly pro-Commonwealth *Irish Times*, was not happy about the operations of wartime press censorship in Ireland. Nevertheless, he was so irked that Ireland's neutral, yet essentially pro-Allies, stance was misrepresented abroad that he soon decided to employ more Irish nationalist staff.[27] Immediately after the war, he would also highlight to the US journal *Foreign Affairs* why all Irishmen had been inclined to share de Valera's stance during the war:

> The late Arthur Griffith, father of the Sinn Féin movement, said that the British had built a paper wall around Ireland; on the inside they painted what they wanted the Irish to know about the rest of the world, on the outside what they wanted the rest of the world to know about Ireland. During the war this system operated in striking fashion ... Americans may not realise that Éire has no news agencies of her own ... The result had been that during the war Éire found herself virtually dumb, while she was being subject to widespread and sometimes even vindictive misrepresentation.[28]

Although he exaggerated the numbers involved, Smyllie highlighted that de Valera had allowed those Irishmen who desired to enlist in British armed forces abroad to do so; that Ireland supplied massive amounts of both food and labour for Britain; and that, no matter what the British government may have claimed in either its secret or public communications with its Allies, a positive diplomatic relationship existed between the British and Irish governments during the war. Ireland 'was of greater assistance to the Allies as an official neutral than she could have been as an active belligerent' while Axis diplomats were left alone and expatriated European diplomats were feted in Dublin.[29]

Strident American press criticisms of Irish neutrality had led to the creation of an 'American Friends of Irish Neutrality' organisation as early as November 1940. This body had no formal link with the Irish ministry in Washington, which chose to work instead with four American Democratic senators to promote the cause of Irish neutrality.[30] Nevertheless, it mounted a fairly effective press campaign before it was ultimately disbanded upon America's entry into the war in December 1941.[31] The latter development actually did much to counter anti-Irish propaganda in America. This was because it led Churchill to accept a judgment that his own military chiefs of staff had already fully accepted as early as 1938: being vulnerable to German attacks, the southern Irish ports were actually far less valuable to Britain's defences than its bases in Northern Ireland, where Sir Basil Brooke, a nephew of the chief of staff of the British imperial army, would soon succeed to the position of Prime Minister (a position he would hold for twenty years).[32]

It could well be argued that the reality of Éire's position was not a militarily neutral country but rather a 'neutralised state', operating on the assumption that outside powers would act as a guarantor of Irish security in return for Ireland's refusal to enter into any diplomatic alliance with which the more powerful partners in this agreement did not approve.[33] Since 1926, a government policy had been established of depriving the Irish army of resources while prioritising the recruitment of reserve volunteer forces to assist the police in matters of internal security only. This policy of utilising reserve forces had been implemented during 1934 with particular success by de Valera, who also launched annual 1916 commemorations and military pension schemes to bring about a rapprochement between what had been typified during 1922, rightly or wrongly, as opposing sides in an Irish civil war.[34] The significant threat to its neutrality during 1940 and 1941 necessitated that the Irish government promote both extensive army recruitment (up to 40,000 men) and compile more detailed military intelligence reports regarding the possibilities of invasion. An invasion was feared not only from Germany but also from the supposedly 'neutralising' power of Britain. Like James Craig (who died in November 1940), the Canadians had initially been prepared to call for an invasion of Éire.[35] In the wake of the departure of Henry Harrison, the London *Economist* also called for an invasion of Ireland or, at the very least, to subject Ireland to a very punishing economic blockade.[36] In the face of this hostility, de Valera told Sir John Maffey that Ireland would 'fight to the death' any attempt to interfere with its independence. However, an absence of military supplies (for which Ireland had been purposively made dependent on the British market) soon meant that de Valera had to admit to Maffey that the Irish army could not cope against even a 5,000-man invasion force, if it was well armed, and that in the event of a German invasion the Irish army could probably only hold out for a single day before needing the assistance of British troops from Northern Ireland.[37]

Perhaps the greatest illustration of Ireland's lack of preparedness for war was that efforts to create the basis of an Irish navy were not made until after the war had broken out.[38] Ireland acquired three armoured patrol vessels, which were less well equipped than other nations' armed merchant ships on the Atlantic or the Mediterranean. It also acquired six torpedo boats, but these were unequipped to deal with submarines. Neither the army nor the coastguard service had 'trained personnel' for military intelligence purposes. Instead, both had to rely on an extensive staff of volunteers, who operated without equipment, for the purposes of spotting belligerents' presence, on many thousands of occasions, in the air or at sea. Reflecting this, in addition to the maximisation of the strength of the Defence Forces to 40,000 men, by 1942 the Irish state's voluntary reserve forces had been boosted from 13,000 to nearly 100,000 men.[39] For this very reason, the defence of Irish neutrality during the period of 'The Emergency' made about as deep an impression on the Irish political imagination as had the mass enrolment of volunteers to resist the imposition of British martial law after 1920. All belligerents who landed in Ireland were duly interned, while the Irish army would fire nine times upon unidentified aircraft during the key period of 1940–1.[40]

An attempt had been made to provide an intelligence system for a nascent Irish army during 1919–22, but after 1926 Irish military intelligence was essentially non-existent. Instead, there were only two men who acted as liaisons for the police and army respectively in matters of internal security alone. For the duration of the war, however, the Irish army would recruit an intelligence staff of approximately forty men under a central command of six. These men played a relatively effective part in decoding international ciphers and radio signals. Upon being told by London that German intelligence was using disaffected Irish expatriates in Britain (members of an 'IRA' secret society)[41] for espionage purposes, a liaison system for receiving some information from British military intelligence was also necessarily developed.[42] From an intelligence point of view, some British historians have argued that Ireland could have benefited diplomatically from abandoning its policy of neutrality during or after 1942, once the war became concentrated away from the Western Front.[43] However, the Irish army remained certain that 'an attack on this country by the Axis powers remains a constant danger' while there was also still a possibility of an Allied attack, for 'so long as these powers are unable to overcome the menace of the submarine to their Atlantic shipping lines a change of policy might occur at any time'.[44] The Irish army had to deal with occasional accidental bombings of Ireland by either Allies or Axis aircraft for the duration of the war. Not until the beginning of 1944 did it feel confident that 'the Allied Powers seemed to have at last mastered the submarine menace to their Atlantic shipping'.[45] Nevertheless, a nadir of Irish relations with the Allies occurred very soon thereafter.

In February 1944, US envoy to Ireland David Gray demanded that Ireland unilaterally close all diplomatic offices of the Axis powers within its territories. Gray feared an intelligence leak in the months leading up to a forthcoming Allied invasion of France, which took place that June. Churchill also spoke in the House of Commons of his intention to isolate Ireland by imposing economic sanctions, blocking all Irish trade except for what was 'necessary' purely for Britain, if it did not unilaterally suppress the Axis powers' diplomatic offices in Ireland.[46] Hitherto, Joseph Walshe had shouldered the burden of explaining the

Irish government's position to both the Germans and the British, each of which cynically attempted to play upon Dublin's desire to end partition. On the one hand, Walshe informed the Germans that Ireland fully intended to continue to supply food to Britain as a neutral. On the other hand, he informed Britain and America that Ireland would be unable to explain its policy of neutrality to all sides if it ever chose to expel the Axis diplomats.[47] This was also why Ireland worked to ensure that its few diplomatic offices on the European continent remained operative throughout the war. This included the Irish legation in Berlin, which was destroyed by a bomb in November 1943. This office attempted to assist Jewish refugees and also issued intelligence reports to Dublin on German plots to kill Adolf Hitler that, in turn, were secretly shared with the Allies.[48]

In the opinion of the Irish army, America became complicit with Britain in implementing 'a whole succession of measures ... designed to isolate this country from the rest of the world to the uttermost extent' in the wake of Ireland's refusal to expel Axis diplomats.[49] This was not necessarily an exaggerated complaint. For the duration of the war, Sean Lester of the Irish government, as the last secretary-general of the League of Nations in Geneva, and fellow Irishman Edward Phelan, as the director of the ILO (although Phelan was not a member of the Irish government's staff), played a key role in keeping the machinery of international law alive, to facilitate a revival of multilateral diplomacy, until such time as the United Nations could be launched in San Francisco during the spring of 1945. In the wake of de Valera's condemnation of the Nazi invasions of Belgium and Holland, Lester and Phelan had concentrated most of their efforts on the lowlands countries, which were now considering establishing a new Benelux customs union. However, they also crossed the continent and the Atlantic several times to sustain old networks of multilateral diplomacy before and after the Allies' liberation of France indicated that the war would soon draw to a close. In recognition of their work, both men were awarded honorary doctorates, abroad and at home, once the war ended in April 1945.[50] Despite this fact, however, the great powers decided that neither man nor indeed any Irish representative should be allowed admittance to the initial assembly of the United Nations (UN), evidently because it was decided to exclude all neutrals. This development served to make government opinion in Ireland somewhat uneasy regarding the country's probable place in the post-war international order.[51]

Ireland's own little masterplan for contributing to a post-war peace settlement ever since the summer of 1944 was to launch a European relief aid programme, although Ireland did not have the shipping facilities necessary to transport relief aid goods by itself. This programme was particularly appreciated in the Netherlands and, to a lesser extent, in Belgium, two countries that had appointed counsels to Dublin in the past, although Ireland (which closed its Belgian office during the war) had yet to appoint diplomatic representatives to either country.[52] Despite improved relations with Ireland, however, sections of the press in both countries found it hard to believe that the Irish had not been pro-Axis during the war, not least because of the influence of British media. Ireland's role in expelling German spies both during and after war went unnoticed. Meanwhile, although de Valera retained a quite positive reputation in the continental press, the purely protocol visit that he made to the German legation in Dublin in April 1945 may have helped to sustain rumours thereafter that Ireland actually became a haven for Nazi war criminals.[53] Otherwise, the Irish relief aid scheme launched in 1945 served to improve Ireland's traditionally weak relationship with Italy, while the highest degree of Irish relief aid (equivalent to $2 million) was sent to what would become West Germany. Only a minimal degree of Irish aid reached central or eastern Europe.[54]

Hitherto, Ireland had tended to view its performance in the League of Nations, including the naval disarmament conferences of the 1920s, as an expression of its own independent values.[55] Practically speaking, however, its co-dependent foreign policy status with the British Commonwealth had slowly but surely moulded its outlook, as was reflected by the fact that Michael MacWhite (who served as Ireland's minister in Italy until his retirement in 1950)[56] came to share the British desire that America would involve itself in European security as early as the 1930s.[57] Joseph Walshe retired as general secretary of Ireland's department of external affairs after the war ended in order to take up a diplomatic role at the Holy See.[58] In the past, the republics of America and France had tended to view Walshe's viewpoints as obscurantist to the point of being nearly incomprehensible. For instance, ignoring the advice of Sean Murphy, Ireland's minister in France (who necessarily relocated to Vichy after the fall of Paris), Walshe's sympathetic attitude towards the Vichy government in France during the war had not been well thought out. Reflecting this, although Murphy was able to persuade Charles de Gaulle, who admired de Valera personally, to recognise the Irish ministerial presence in France and to respect Ireland's wartime stance of neutrality after the liberation of Paris in August 1944, the actual staff of the French foreign ministry remained far less sympathetic.[59]

Banking on its role in arming the Allies, from 1945 onwards the United States took an approach towards international relations that was shaped not least by its desire to undo the imperial tariff scheme that the British Commonwealth had adopted against the United States at the Ottawa conference of 1932.[60] Britain, however, was in no hurry to call another imperial conference with a view to reaching an intra-commonwealth agreement in such matters. This was because it viewed Ottawa as having been a decisive moment in strengthening the unitary voice of its Commonwealth.[61] Nicholas Mansergh, an Irish-born member of the British Dominions Office and the official historian of the Commonwealth,[62] was determined that this prerogative should also govern Britain's policy towards Ireland. In particular, he judged that the peculiar fiscal identity of the Irish state, including its economic dependency on the British market for food exports, should be used as a weapon against it to ensure that Ireland was kept as closely tied to the British Commonwealth as was possible.[63] For the same reason, John Horgan, the Irish correspondent of Chatham House's Round Table, wrote books at this time that demonised the founders of Dáil Éireann in 1919 on the grounds that 'they sacrificed Irish unity for Irish sovereignty and attained neither' whilst simultaneously recommending, illogically, that Ireland must never diverge from the politics that had acquired pre-eminence in the period between the deaths of Charles Stewart Parnell (1891) and Patrick Pearse (1916) or, in other words, when Ireland was still ruled directly by Britain.[64] A heavy role for the United States in the post-war financial reconstruction of Europe, however, had the potential to neutralise Horgan and Mansergh's ideas.

In 1946, Frederick Boland, the new general secretary of Ireland's department of external affairs, appointed more commercial attachés to boost Ireland's international profile. He also opened new missions in Sweden, Australia and Argentina and launched departmental brainstorming conferences, reputedly to undo the legacy of Walshe or de Valera's past example of relying 'solely on his own opinion'.[65] Boland, however, was also highly conservative. Being the son of a former leading department of finance official, he did not consider either Ireland's relief aid programme or its interdepartmental foreign trade committee as matters that should concern his department.[66] As late as 1938, the Irish department of finance was basing its reasoning almost entirely upon precedents that had existed during the First World War.[67] A sterling area crisis caused by Britain's wartime debts to the United States soon meant, however, that Ireland could no longer rely on Britain to convert Ireland's sterling balances in Britain into dollars to enable Ireland to trade internationally. Therefore, Ireland had to consider major alternations in the state's financial management, such as repatriating the country's sterling assets,[68] as well as changes to the country's overall trading priorities in order to overcome Ireland's lack of foreign currency reserves.[69]

The idea that the American dollar should serve as the key currency in underwriting the future international financial order was practically born at an international monetary conference that was held during 1944 in Bretton Woods, a small village in the American state of New Hampshire. America succeeded in persuading European representatives, Britain's commonwealth partners of Canada and Australia and even some Japanese representatives to partake in this plan. The choice of the Californian city of San Francisco for the initial meeting of the United Nations (UN), which thereafter established its headquarters in New York City, also belied America's desire to reinvent forums of multilateral diplomacy. This was done by expanding upon the essentially Eurocentric vision of the now defunct League of Nations by creating a much wider variety of affiliated international organisations, a new human rights charter and, last but not necessarily least, an academic journal *International Organization* (New York) that would become a vehicle for a new, American-inspired international relations theory. Post-war recruits to Ireland's diplomatic staff, including Conor Cruise O'Brien (a recent transfer from the department of finance), would soon devote their minds to attempting to understand this new dispensation, although Ireland's seemingly fixed place within the sterling area partly limited its scope of vision.[70]

De Valera's Irish relief aid programme of £3 million, first launched in April 1945, was completely overshadowed three years later by an American relief aid programme of $13 billion. This was inspired by George Marshall, the US military's chief of staff. This American aid was to be distributed by a European Relief Programme (ERP) and to work in conjunction with an Organisation for European Economic Cooperation (OEEC). The Benelux countries who had been recipients of Irish aid expected Irish participation in the new OEEC. As early as July 1947, however, Frederick Boland disappointed them by emphasising that Ireland was not enthusiastic about their idea of a European customs union. In making this argument, Boland was reflecting the thinking of both the Irish department of finance and the British imperial treasury, which considered the question of Ireland potentially becoming involved in American reconstruction plans for Europe only from the point of view of its own advantage.[71] Britain was deeply suspicious that participation in any European customs union programme might undermine its own sovereignty. The Conservative Party feared for the unity of the British Commonwealth. The British Labour Party was more fearful of 'surrendering their key nationalised industries to European control at a time when continental Europe seemed dominated by capitalist Christian-democratic governments'.[72] The significant degree to which British industries had already been nationalised was a major reason why Marxist rhetoric, or an affected fascination with the USSR, was relatively prevalent in Britain, as was the case in France, because Russia's status as a major country outside the international monetary system had facilitated a degree of nationalisation and state-planning there ever since the 1930s.[73]

John Hearne in Ottawa, Francis Cremins in Berne and Sean Lester in New York acted as Ireland's initial advisors on the UN. They believed that the capacity of the war's victorious powers to veto UN Security Council decisions was 'inherent mischief' that was designed to guarantee inequality of juridical status in international relations and a resultant continuation of war. In addition, the fact that Russia's veto upon Irish membership of the UN was motivated by its desire to trade off the admission of small western European nations into the UN with that of small eastern European nations seemed to Irish eyes to make the whole idea of a 'United Nations' forum meaningless. Unconvinced that an effective forum for multilateral diplomacy on issues of collective security existed, Ireland concentrated on joining various other international bodies in the wake of the Second World War, more than doubling its membership of such bodies over the next ten years to include seventy-five organisations relating to agriculture, industry, transport and medicine. Meanwhile, among neutral countries with comparable concerns to Ireland, the Irish government saw few legal role models, with the possible exception of Sweden.[74]

After 1945, the Irish army desired to retain a level of government support akin to what it had received during the war. It did this by emphasising the fact that even neutral countries generally needed some degree of conscription to sustain their defence forces in times of peace. Such appeals, however, went unheeded: its ranks were reduced to just 8,000 men while its additional wartime supplies were simply sold off.[75] The Irish naval service that was created during the war was allowed to survive, although its funding was cut to a minimum.[76] The Irish army was initially quite sceptical about an alleged new ideological divide in international affairs. It noted that 'it is becoming more apparent that all nations are being forced into the adoption of one of the widely conflicting ideological positions which are rapidly dividing the people of the world into two hostile camps', but it detected an air of unreality about this whole process.[77] Within a couple of years, however, the army was arguing that 'our defence policy should be based on the realities of our situation in Western Europe'. To this end, it suggested allowing access to Ireland's airfields and ports to those countries that were in the process of forming an American-led North Atlantic Treaty Organisation (NATO) mutual defence organisation in reaction to the fact that the USSR, eager to recuperate from the fact that Russia had suffered the greatest losses during the war, was in no hurry to withdraw its military forces from eastern Europe.[78] This change in the Irish army's attitude may have reflected a manipulative influence exercised by a new American Central Intelligence Agency (CIA),[79] which hoped to make the Catholic Church and Ireland an ally of its plan to promote an international European Youth Campaign (EYC) which was based, in part, upon the idea that 'European unification offered a place within the Western system for neutrals' such as Ireland. During the 1950s, this would lead to the creation of an Irish wing of the EYC that had its own journal known as *Commentary*.[80] This development was looked upon sympathetically by the Irish government. Dublin resented, however, that the ex-Allies, adopting a traditional British tactic to neutralise Ireland, were also arguing that munitions could not be sold to Ireland unless it first joined their common security plans.[81] This attempt to coerce the Irish government made the Irish army desirous of purchasing its firearms from neutral Sweden instead.[82]

Pope Pius XII informed Irish diplomat Joseph Walshe that, although he had no desire to encourage this trend, the American government desired that he appoint Catholic cardinals in the US but not in Ireland so that these American cardinals could exercise some leverage over the Irish church with a view to potentially exerting an influence upon Irish politicians.[83] The CIA may well have judged that appeals to Christian-democratic sensibilities could be a good means to persuade Ireland to join a pro-American, or pro-western, and anti-Soviet bloc. It has been suggested that Irish Catholic bishops and the American CIA together persuaded the Irish government to secretly offer some financial assistance to Italian Christian democrats in the first major post-war Italian general election.[84] Whatever the case, contemporary US suggestions that Ireland could be a particularly good member of the United Nations Educational, Scientific and Cultural Organisation (UNESCO) were evidently ignored by the Irish government solely because it did not want to have to expand the department of external affairs' budget to cover the financial cost of joining such organisations.[85] Another seeming reflection of Irish apathy was that on being invited to attend Council of Europe meetings it would initially send only non-governmental personnel;[86] an action that might well have appeared like a deliberate snub.

John Costello of Fine Gael, a former Irish attorney general and legal colleague of John Hearne and Michael Rynne in Geneva, was made the prime minister (a position known since 1937 as 'Taoiseach') of an Irish coalition government that was returned after the February 1948 Irish general election. Costello professed to be a strong believer that Ireland should now look to the American republic with a view to expanding the Irish state's capacity to be an exporting nation.[87] Meanwhile, de

Valera, the outgoing Taoiseach and minister for external affairs, went on a month-long tour of the United States before spending over a month in Australia and New Zealand and a final couple of days in India on a sort of unofficial world tour that had evidently been planned by external affairs prior to de Valera's removal from office. Conor Cruise O'Brien recalled that the purpose of de Valera's international tour was to justify both Ireland's policy of wartime neutrality and its official constitutional stance since 1937 in referring to the island of Ireland as a 'national territory' without making an actual legal claim over Northern Ireland. At a time when the minority Fine Gael government in office was believed to be in favour of Ireland joining NATO, de Valera's tour was intended to focus minds on other matters. In O'Brien's opinion, the publicity surrounding de Valera's world tour of 1948 'must be recorded as a brilliant and unqualified success' in sustaining Irish support for the policy of military neutrality, and was made effective largely because 'the Irish people trusted Mr. De Valera judgment on international affairs far more than they trusted that of anyone else'.[88] De Valera's tour, however, was not entirely without controversy. While he effectively explained the Irish policy of neutrality to the new US president Harry Truman, in his speeches before an Irish American audience de Valera actually typified the partition of Ireland as illegal (on the grounds that nobody had actually voted for it in 1920), a line of propaganda that, not surprisingly, de Valera did not repeat when he visited loyalist Australia.[89] Foreign powers were not willing to antagonise Britain by being associated in any way with such a stance. Therefore, the French, who (like the Americans, the British and the Dutch) were engaging in NATO exercises within Northern Ireland, purposively chose not to thank Ireland for its relief aid programme.[90] They also resented criticism of plans for European defence cooperation by Frank Aiken, who later became an Irish minister for external affairs. Aiken believed that 'competition in building up arms was so intensive' that it could mean that the Second World War would never truly end.[91]

De Valera's Irish American speeches on partition, as well as a similar British lecture tour that winter, were motivated partly by a desire to demobilise cross-border sympathy for a new Clann na Poblachta party in Ireland whose leader Sean MacBride had actually been made Ireland's minister for external affairs under the new Fine

Gael-led coalition government. In the autumn of 1948, in between de Valera's Australian and British lecture tours, this Fine Gael–Clann na Poblachta–Labour coalition government repealed de Valera's External Relations Act of 1936, in the process removing Ireland from the British Commonwealth and giving to Éire a new official description as 'the Republic of Ireland'.[92] As Taoiseach, John Costello maintained that the Republic of Ireland Act was a natural evolutionary process for the Irish state. The chief significance of its introduction was that, henceforth, both Ireland's diplomatic personnel abroad and foreign diplomatic personnel in Ireland itself could assume, for the first time, the formal title of ambassadors, as they now invariably did, thereby initiating a new era of direct diplomatic relations for Ireland itself. Reflecting this, Ireland's fourteen consular offices abroad now became residences for fourteen different Irish ambassadors. A position of president had been created under Ireland's 1937 constitution. This legal office acted primarily as a final reviewer and signatory of Irish legislation in a manner comparable to a British monarch. However, it could now potentially assume a diplomatic role for the first time. This would be reflected by the invitation of Sean T. O'Kelly, as Irish president, to the French republic in 1950 and the US president's issuing congratulations to the Irish government for introducing the Republic of Ireland Act through that office.[93] Paradoxically, however, the proclamation of an Irish republic did not essentially amount to a total break from the British Commonwealth in Irish diplomats' minds.

After 1949, Frederick Boland, whom MacBride now appointed as Ireland's ambassador to London, expected that Ireland would continue to be invited to Commonwealth conferences to determine a common economic policy.[94] In the light of the ongoing parity between the British and Irish pounds, such connections could even seem necessary to Irish politicians. There was also a question of established civil service traditions. Under de Valera's tutelage, external affairs had tended to see Ireland's membership of the British Commonwealth as a necessary platform to exist if there ever was to be a unitary Irish state. An Anti-Partition League had developed within Northern Ireland since 1945. However, all Irish political parties tended to be fearful of instability if some kind of cross-border alliance developed among Irish nationalists that did not reflect actual government policy on this question. Hence, just prior to the return of nine Anti-Partition League MPs in Northern Ireland in February 1949, an all-party 'anti-partition fund' was established in Dublin in order to emphasise the belief that Dáil Éireann alone must be *the* forum for determining Irish public attitudes to the partition question.[95]

Sean MacBride, the minister for external affairs at the time of the Republic of Ireland Act, was not in any real sense a radical in terms of Anglo-Irish relations. Whitehall's unpopular response to the Republic of Ireland Act was to pass an Ireland Act (1949). This declared that common citizenship rights (related to work and social security permits) must continue to exist for all British and Irish citizens in both countries, irrespective of Ireland's non-membership of the commonwealth.[96] This British legal development was something for which MacBride actually sought to claim credit.[97] Reflecting this, the chief significance of MacBride's tenure as minister for external affairs was that it coincided with Ireland's initial efforts to adapt to the post-Bretton Woods international financial order. This task was made difficult because the existing north–south, as well as east–west, dynamics of Ireland's economic relationship with the United Kingdom was not very favourable to Irish interests. Northern Ireland had experienced massive industrial unemployment between 1924 and 1939, but the development of a munitions industry in the north during the Second World War did much to revive its industrial production so that, in its volume of total trade, Northern Ireland now almost doubled the trading activity of Éire.[98] Irish food exports to Britain received a significantly lesser price during and after the war. Partly as a result, total Irish exports (£40 million) were now less than a third of Northern Irish exports (£140 million).[99] For Dublin, this was a shocking imbalance.

The relative fortunes of Northern Ireland were also shaped in part by the dynamic of Dublin–London banking relations. Belfast's status as a clearing house for all large Irish bank transactions within the Republic of Ireland helped to give an inherent pre-eminence to British business interests within the markets of the southern Irish state. Being subject to a 'wider imperial banking structure dominated by the Bank of England', Irish banks had resisted all plans to establish a central bank until a Central Bank of Ireland was established in 1943 as part of a 'global financial reconstruction' plan of the Bank of England that was inspired not least by John Maynard Keynes of the British imperial treasury. Ninety-nine per cent of Irish government assets and securities were still banked in England rather than in Ireland on the grounds that a repatriation of the state's assets could potentially disrupt the existing north–south and east–west dynamics of Ireland's fiscal relationship with the United Kingdom to Belfast's potential disadvantage.[100] The new interparty government of 1948–51, acting partly upon the advice of a new finance department official named T.K. Whitaker, became willing to attempt to modify this situation. One reason for this development was that MacBride had been invited to become a vice-president of the Organisation for European Economic Development and, in this capacity, he became an advocate of the Council of Europe plan for European economic integration.[101] MacBride also hoped that Ireland could be a recipient of an American grant to boost its level of industrial production. Instead, Ireland was initially offered only a sizeable loan ($130 million) over a three-year period on the understanding that this financial assistance to Ireland could also assist the post-war revival of the British economy. This understanding also influenced an Anglo-Irish trading agreement that was reached during the summer of 1948.[102]

Ireland's American loan was used to create, for the first time, an Irish Central Statistics Office (CSO); an expansion of the country's electricity supply board and telephone networks; and the development of new forestry and local-authority housing schemes. The most significant change, however, was a new emphasis on foreign direct investment. This was reflected by the fact that the Industrial Development Association, which was focused primarily on promoting domestic businesses, was now undervalued compared to a new Industrial Development Authority (IDA) that was created purely to promote foreign direct investment in Ireland.[103] This took place ten years before an International Development Authority was launched in Washington D.C. as a partner of the International Bank for Reconstruction and Development to create a new World Bank Group. Another significant new development was the use of a small American grant of $18 million during 1950 to create Córas Tráchtála as a new Irish Export Board. Córas Tráchtála owed its existence almost entirely to a felt need to increase the willingness of American banks to offer credit (or a 'dollar-earning capacity') to Irish firms through enhancing direct Irish trade with the United States. Irish exports increased, but this greater Irish receptivity to a North American market worked primarily to the advantage of American, or even Canadian, rather than Irish firms.[104] Meanwhile, the department of finance resisted MacBride's desire to make either economic planning or trading matters a prerogative of the department of external affairs.[105] Reflecting this, Irish government fiunding for Córas Tráchtála was permitted only if it reported to the department of industry and commerce alone. In turn, this department directed the Irish Export Board's agents to focus exclusively on acting as a one-to-one advisor to potential exporters.[106] The significance of this development was that unlike most other countries' export boards, including that of the United Kingdom and France, the Irish Export Board was never allowed to operate as an instrument for the existence of a national trading policy involving coordinated cross-departmental planning to achieve national economic goals. In fact, such planning practically did not exist at an Irish governmental level, notwithstanding the nominal existence of a commercial staff at the new Iveagh House headquarters of the department of external affairs. This was because the Irish government believed in a *laissez faire* attitude of total non-intervention in the private sector, meaning the government possessed no role in trading matters except to evaluate the situation 'in the light of Ireland's foreign exchange position'.[107]

Major General Liam Archer, a former 1916 rebel who had served in the Defence Forces for decades before being appointed as the new chief of staff of the Irish army after the Republic of Ireland Act, was considered by British military intelligence to be 'an ardent republican'.[108] However, the government showed no inclination after 1948 to rename the Defences Forces (Ireland) as an Irish republican army partly for cultural reasons associated with that nomenclature. The Irish army itself generally contained within its ranks men who identified strongly with its antecedents in Irish republican volunteer forces (this was perhaps particularly true of its earliest officers during the 1920s and 1930s)[109] and men who identified primarily with the contemporary military geopolitics that were shaping international relations (an essential qualification for senior officers in later years) without necessarily having a high level of retrospective regard for the levels of professionalism that had been exhibited by the original Irish republican volunteer movement. The evidently pro-NATO sympathies of Irish army officers during 1949 were not shared by Sean MacBride, who recalled that he found it inappropriate to discover that Irish army intelligence 'seemed to be much more interested in Cold War politics' than it was in its need to manage issues of national security, which, to MacBride's mind, meant being prepared for any potential eventuality surrounding the Irish land border.[110] Contrary to MacBride's claims, the small and illegal 'IRA' secret society did not disappear in 1949; instead, it issued a public proclamation stating that the Republic of Ireland Act did not create a free Ireland because of the reality of partition and it started recruiting members for the purpose of creating a violent protest regarding that border.[111] Meanwhile, calls by the actual Irish republican army for increased funding to allow it to develop its capacity to properly handle all matters of national defence continued to be ignored by the department of finance.[112] The consensus that the Irish army should exist only as an auxiliary to the police in matters of internal security reflected an unwillingness of the Irish government to develop a truly comprehensive national and international defence policy. In a few individuals' cases, this may actually have served to abet an 'IRA' underground through frustrating the expression of an Irish patriotism by means of the actual army of the Republic of Ireland.[113]

Britain's post-war success in creating a new welfare state, including free healthcare under a National Health Service as well as free education, contrasted greatly with the situation in Éire, where many Irish people now came to the conclusion, essentially for the first time, that the reliance upon voluntary and religious organisations for (virtually unreformable) health, welfare and educational services was not necessarily a good idea. Meanwhile, a very sizeable drop in Irish wages during the war continued, leading to the likelihood of more strikes, but primarily to increased emigration. As a result of these trends, Ireland's new diplomatic status in the wake of the Republic of Ireland Act did not lead to any great celebrations of the country's progress. Instead, it actually led many commentators to seriously question the viability of the Irish state, as if the Irish government's retention of a common labour market or travel area with Britain was intended only to ensure that the expense of 'a more imaginative approach to economic and social policy on the part of politicians and civil servants' could be avoided.[114] As if to validate this claim, for the first and last time (until the twenty-first century), a 'Commission on Emigration and Other Population Problems' sat between 1948 and 1954, but it actually advised that no policy decisions should be taken. Instead, it determined that a cultural effort should be made by the Irish government to persuade the Irish public that moving to London and the development of an Irish community in Britain should never be considered by the general Irish public as being equivalent to emigration.[115] Over the next decade, almost 400,000 people would end up leaving the country, often against their will, and they left almost entirely for England. Although Portugal, Spain, Italy, Greece and even Scotland lost a similar number of residents to emigration during this period, because of Ireland's small size, virtually no country experienced a comparable wave of emigration, which amounted to almost one-sixth of the entire population of the Irish state.[116]

Northern Ireland introduced legislation to bring itself into line with British welfare legislation (including the new National Health Service), but it legally restricted the employment of all southern Irish workers.[117] As such, the common travel area and common labour market with Éire applied to the island of Britain rather than the United Kingdom per se. Areas for cross-border cooperation between semi-state companies, such as the creation of an Erne hydroelectric scheme and Lough Foyle fisheries commission (both of which covered each side of the border in the northwest) or joint management of the Great Northern Railway (the chief transport link between Dublin and Belfast in the northeast),[118] were regulated by Northern Ireland legislation alone.[119] Irish semi-state companies such as an Irish Sugar Board, an Irish Turf Board and new transport companies, Córas Iompair Éireann (CIE) and Irish Rail (which was made dependent on leasing vehicles from British Rail), had no influence upon the north, but they were traditionally a source of much employment in the south. However, the department of finance favoured cutting back on funding for all Irish semi-state companies. This unpopular decision helped to ensure that Costello's coalition government was not returned to office in 1951, while MacBride would never again hold an Irish governmental office. He could be said to have been of some note as a minister for external affairs primarily because he promoted the Council of Europe and welcomed the establishment of both the European Convention on Human Rights and the European Court of Justice.[120]

Nicholas Mansergh encouraged Frederick Boland, the Irish ambassador to London, to consider Irish–Indian parallels in terms of their relationship with the British Commonwealth. This was done to reflect the fact that London had informed the Irish government that 'her relations with the United Kingdom are [to be] conducted not through the Foreign Office but through the Commonwealth Relations Office' and 'that no effort should be made to define our position more precisely'.[121] This diplomatic ambiguity was primarily of London's rather than Dublin's making. Frank Aiken, the minister for external affairs for the incoming Fianna Fáil government, queried Lord Salisbury, Secretary of State for commonwealth relations, as to why the British government insisted on being 'a queer people' in that 'they went to the greatest possible lengths to avoid a written internal constitution' and were still playing a game regarding 'the Crown and commonwealth relations' with regards to Ireland. In response, Salisbury emphasised strategic rather than economic considerations as the British government's chief reason for desiring to keep a close tab on the Irish state.[122] However, a crisis in Ireland's balance of trade figures at this time was often perceived in Dublin to have been a situation that was deliberately manipulated by Britain in order to cripple the Irish state. More undeniable was the reality that disturbing imbalances in the Irish state's economic performance were evidently not remedial by means of promoting its existing export-orientated firms. Córas Tráchtála offered valuable assistance to many individual traders and also played a part in developing a larger class of professionally trained Irish marketing agents (many of whom subsequently became Irish company directors), but it made little direct impact on the state's overall balance of trade because most Irish exporting companies were little more than cottage industries when compared to their international competitors.[123] Meanwhile, although Córas Tráchtála established about twenty offices abroad during the 1950s, Irish embassies maintained no contact with it because they considered their sole goal to be to partake, if possible, in the multilateral forum of the United Nations while Irish embassies abroad possessed no dedicated trade agents.[124]

Against this backdrop, Sean Lemass, as minister for industry and commerce, judged that the best solution for Ireland's balance of trade difficulties was to promote its tourism industry because it 'offers an opportunity of expansion and the prospect of a quicker return than any other trade'.[125] The development of an Irish Tourist Association and an Irish Tourist Board was closely related to the development of Aer Lingus, which suceeded after 1945 in persuading the American government to allow the development of a transatlantic air service to and from Shannon airport,[126] which was made a permanent base for the display of Irish-made goods. During 1949, the head of the 'travel development section' of the European Economic Cooperation Administration had visited Dublin and arranged for the general assembly of the 'International Union of Official Travel Organisations', which represented thirty-eight countries, to hold their world convention in Dublin the following year. In response, Lemass worked after 1951 to amalgamate the Irish Tourist Association and Irish Tourist Board to create Bord Fáilte Éireann. Its marketing wing, Fógra Fáilte, would soon be led by T.J. O'Driscoll, who had recently served as Ireland's first ambassador to the Netherlands. Pan American Airlines provided the inspiration for the launch during 1952 of an annual Irish festival for tourists ('An Tostal'). Although shortlived, this made the principle of government expenditure to promote the tourism industry and urban development (including 'tidy town initiatives') a more established feature of Irish civil service thinking.[127] This tourism initiative was also supported by a Fine Gael government that was returned to office in 1954 and was of note for establishing a German–Irish aviation agreement to stimulate foreign direct investment from West Germany.[128]

By the mid-1950s, a sufficient amount of the Irish state's sterling assets had been repatriated in order to make Ireland's adaption to the new American-inspired international order more feasible. Nevertheless, by such time as Ireland was admitted to the United Nations in New York in December 1955, divisions existed within the Irish government itself regarding what precisely the country's place in the international arena should be. At a time when the 'Warsaw Pact', an eastern European collective security arrangement, was being created by the USSR to rival the American-led NATO alliance, should Ireland aspire to the position of an entirely non-aligned state in international relations

in order to express its disapproval for this trend? Eighteen years of
Éire diplomacy had seemed to pivot on Ireland's peculiar status as a
country that was professedly without but was practically within the
British Commonwealth's diplomatic orbit. As the activities of Chatham
House demonstrated, many British commentators continued to view
Ireland in this light, even after it left the commonwealth in 1949.[129]
De Valera had long since realised that the idea he first entertained on
Erskine Childers' advice during 1921 that Ireland could be 'externally
associated' with the commonwealth was essentially a legal nonsense.[130]
Meanwhile, Mansergh's suggestion of an Indian parallel because of
India's anomalous new identity as a republic within the commonwealth
was practically irrelevant because there were neither economic nor
diplomatic ties between the two countries.[131] The real issue facing
the Irish state was whether or not its place in the international order,
economically and in turn diplomatically, counted for anything, or was
it to be only a political entity under the indirect control of the United
Kingdom of Great Britain and Northern Ireland? The irony in the Irish
state's position in this regard was that its prior concentration during
the 1930s on attaining a positive balance of trade with Britain had been
motivated by a desire to lessen Britain's powers of manipulation within
the Irish state, but Ireland's position in broader international markets
remained so weak that it still operated very much under Britain's
shadow. Reflecting this, the notion of establishing a completely separate
Irish currency did not have as many supporters as might conceivably
have been expected.

Liam Cosgrave, a son of W.T. Cosgrave (who had retired in 1944),
served as Irish minister for external affairs from 1954 until 1957. He
initially relied largely upon the advice of Frederick Boland in attempting
to decide what Ireland's foreign policy should be. Boland would
be chosen as Ireland's first permanent representative at the United
Nations, where he would ultimately distinguish himself as a frequent
chairman of its meetings prior to his retirement in 1963. Since 1950,
however, he had endeavoured with much success to make the position
of Ireland's ambassador to Britain, rather than its ambassador to the
United States or any European power, the most influential position
within Ireland's nascent foreign service of ambassadors.[132] In this, he
was supported by Conor Cruise O'Brien, who judged that the delay of

Ireland's admission to the UN was actually opportune because it was not until 1955 that 'Ireland's international status was no longer a matter of internal controversy.'[133] This introverted perspective reflected the fact that O'Brien and, to a lesser extent, Boland, had been preoccupied since 1950 with the fact that a new 'Sinn Féin' party was being created within the Irish state that was led by a former MP from Northern Ireland.[134] Controversially, this was reputedly affiliated with a new 'IRA' secret society. The wartime economic boom for Northern Ireland was disappearing, while tensions were brewing in Ulster due to the absence of an effective labour party. Boland saw this trend as evidence that 'IRA activity is bound to be a constantly recurring problem,'[135] while O'Brien felt that if an 'IRA' secret society which was allegedly active in the south was responsible for attacks on Northern Ireland, this would probably result in 'the ending of partition by the reoccupation of the Twenty-Six Counties [Éire]' by the British army.[136] This fear persuaded O'Brien that Ireland must look upon its prior participation as a member of the British Commonwealth in multilateral diplomatic forums (most notably during de Valera's presidency of the League of Nations during the 1930s) as the ideal role model for Ireland's future performance on the world stage.[137]

De Valera had ceased his career in external affairs in 1948 at the age of sixty-five. Together with Joseph Walshe, who retired from the Irish diplomatic service in 1954 (and, rather inappropriately, was soon buried in a Commonwealth War Graves cemetery in Cairo),[138] he had shaped the fundamentally Christian-democratic identity of the Irish state. In the post-1945 world, however, de Valera was not inclined to see this as a bridge between Ireland and the European continent. Partly reflecting Mansergh's influence, he was fearful of Ireland becoming too insecure, or isolated, on the international stage if it was not associated in some way with the British Commonwealth.[139] In the Irish public mind, however, de Valera and Frank Aiken were generally considered to be Irish republicans who were preoccupied most with finding more effective measures for promoting Irish defence. Reflecting this, Aiken had rejected the American idea of a mutual security act with Europe in October 1951 less in principle than because of foreign powers' unwillingness to allow Ireland to purchase munitions (Ireland had no munitions industry of its own) unless it joined NATO on *their* terms.[140]

Some British historians have argued that this stance of Aiken's was typical of 'a dismal and nervous outlook on the external world' adopted by Ireland in the wake of its adoption of the Republic of Ireland Act that was 'fuelled by the construction of a hermitage Ireland', but this was essentially a distorted view. Most foreign diplomats understood that for Ireland to desire to control its own armaments programme was not the stance of 'a hermitage Ireland' but simply a logical expression of national self-interest.[141] If there was a 'nervous outlook on the external world' by Irish government ministers throughout the 1950s, this was primarily the result of an acute awareness of Ireland's very insecure trading profile. Anticipating a British embargo on Irish trade, efforts had been made to establish Irish Shipping as a semi-state company after 1939, while the occasion of Ireland's admittance to the United Nations in 1955 coincided with the passing of an Irish Mercantile Marine Act that established unequivocally the totally independent legal status of Irish shipping.[142] This was a rather belated move. Its significance was perhaps no longer so great in the light of the growing importance of the aviation industry, but it had potential ramifications for improving Ireland's future relations with both Europe and the United States. A combination of underdeveloped Irish shipping and the absence of a business-friendly banking system had been a major factor in causing America to abandon its initial interest in promoting US foreign direct investment in Ireland after 1949.[143]

An Irish acceptance of plans for western European integration was reflected by Liam Cosgrave's formal announcement at the outset of 1956 that Ireland's policy at the UN would be shaped by the fact that 'we belong to the great community of states made up of the United States of America, Canada and Western Europe'. Cosgrave's fear of Ireland being potentially defenceless in an international conflict had made him personally in favour of Ireland joining NATO,[144] but he emphasised that the official policy of the state was 'to maintain a position of independence ... in a just and disinterested way' in terms of giving vocal expression to the distinct priorities and identity of the Irish state at the UN.[145] This reflected the reality that, from 1946 until 1955, Ireland had been aware that if it was admitted to the UN only as a member of a particular bloc, as the USSR had desired, this could perpetually deny Ireland its capacity to ever exercise any kind of independent voice. The Irish government was determined that Ireland's admission to the UN during 1955 would not be understood in these terms, but this prompted Britain to typify Ireland as occupying an 'absurd' position of 'a non-aligned country in a Europe split by NATO and the Warsaw Pact'.[146] One could well argue, however, that Ireland was less 'non-aligned' with the international community before and after 1949 than it was simply searching for a new means of effective alignment outside the peculiar dynamics of British Commonwealth, if that were possible. In particular, if a 'shift of emphasis towards an economic foreign policy' would slowly but surely become a 'hallmark of Ireland's place in the world' from 1949 onwards, the relative places of 'Dublin and London in the "Pax Americana"' was still being determined largely by the fact that 'the United Kingdom's adaptation to these new [American-led] circumstances was not without trauma'. In turn, the degree of Ireland's ongoing economic co-dependence with Britain, stemming not least from Ireland's membership of the sterling area, meant that 'Ireland's accommodation to the post-war world was equally tentative'.[147] Membership of the Council of Europe was practically Ireland's only outlet for considering alternative ideas or options.

Dean Acheson, an anglophile US Secretary of State from 1949 until 1953, was one of a number of senior American officials who were becoming inclined to view the British Commonwealth as an essentially defunct entity, so much so that Britain's ongoing attempts 'to play a separate power role – that is, a role apart from Europe; a role based on a "special relationship" with the United States; a role based on being the head of a "Commonwealth"' was 'about to be played out'.[148] This American bias reflected the fact that its post-war diplomacy was shaped not least by its desire to undo permanently the legacy of the Ottawa conference of 1932. The Bretton Woods conference essentially accomplished this goal. While Ireland had no great reason to quarrel with this impetus, conventional logic in Irish government circles made the interrelated issues of Ireland's membership of the sterling area and the partition question a central consideration. For this reason, the post-1955 period would be characterised by a period of hesitant political experimentation in Ireland. Outside the circle of Ireland's food exporters to Britain, this process was generally considered in Ireland to be an extension, rather than a retraction, of the initiatives first launched during the 1930s, as a new emphasis upon attracting foreign investment to Ireland was pursued with much the same goal as the pro-industry campaigns of the 1930s: namely, 'hastening the decoupling of the Irish economy upon its almost total dependence on the United Kingdom' with the specific end goal of enabling Ireland to find better options for its own prosperity and, in turn, asserting the independence of its own voice in international affairs.[149] On this level, the period between 1956 and 1968 would generally be considered in Ireland a purely positive one in terms of advertising Irish values to the rest of the world. However, while its performance at the UN and Ireland's new national economic development plans would attract the interest of both the United States and Europe during the 1960s, this process did not lead to significant growth in the actual scale of Irish diplomatic activity.[150] This indicated that Ireland's role in international relations was unlikely to become greater until its status as a European country first attained much greater definition.

Endnotes

1   Mick McCarthy, *International affairs at home: the story of the Irish Institute of International Affairs* (Dublin, 2006).

2   *Documents on Irish foreign policy*, vol. 6 no. 68 (quotes); R.M. Smyllie, 'Un-neutral Neutral Éire', *Foreign affairs*, vol. 24 (1946), 317–26.

3   *Documents on Irish foreign policy*, vol. 6 nos 22, 47, 61, 76, 99, 100. The Irish minister in Spain, Leopold Kerney, took charge of this mission, but he proved ill equipped for the role. He entered into communication with some of Frank Ryan's 'IRA' associates without his department's approval or knowledge, which later proved embarrassing. *Documents on Irish foreign policy*, vol. 10 nos 262, 264, 211.

4   *Documents on Irish foreign policy*, vol. 6 no. 80.

5   *Documents on Irish foreign policy*, vol. 3 nos 106, 167, 193, 198.

6   Michael Kennedy, 'Joseph Walshe, Éamon de Valera and the execution of Irish foreign policy 1932–8', *Irish studies in international affairs*, vol. 14 (2003), quote p. 181.

7   Judith Devlin, H.B. Clarke (ed.), *European encounters* (Dublin, 2003), 191–2.

8   Donal Lowry, 'The captive dominion: imperial realities behind Irish diplomacy 1922–49', *Irish historical studies*, vol. 36 no. 142 (Nov. 2008), 214.

9   After the cessation of Fine Gaedhael in September 1924, Brennan had worked as a fund collector for Fianna Fáil in the United States and the first general manager of the *Irish Press* before becoming secretary to the Irish legation at Washington D.C. in February 1934. He became the minister at Washington in late 1938.

10 *Documents on Irish foreign policy*, vol. 6 nos 16, 41, 45, 57, 69, 71, 73, 74.

11 Michael Funchion (ed.), *Irish American voluntary organisations* (Connecticut, 1983), 36. A transatlantic flying boat service, based in Foynes, Co. Limerick, also operated during the war.

12 *Documents on Irish foreign policy*, vol. 6, no. 101.

13 Ibid., no. 87.

14 Ibid., no. 8, 12, 49. Irish diplomatic staff in America identified press magnate William Randolph Hearst as the most influential champion of keeping the arms embargo in place.

15 Ibid., no. 8, 12, 49.

16 Michael Funchion (ed.), *Irish American voluntary organisations* (Connecticut, 1983), 34–8; Brian Hanley, "'No English enemy … ever stooped so low": Mike Quill, de Valera's visit to the German legation and Irish-American attitudes during World War II', *Radharc*, vol. 5–7 (2004–6), 245–64.

17 *Documents on Irish foreign policy*, vol. 6, no. 15.

18 Ibid., no. 78 (a report by Walshe on de Valera's views).

19 The reports of William Warnock (Berlin), Sean Murphy (Paris) and Michael MacWhite (Rome), as well as Michael Rynne (Dublin), can be found in *Documents on Irish foreign policy*, vol. 6. Warnock fell ill after the bombing of the Irish legation in Berlin in November 1943, prompting his replacement by Con Cremin.

20 *Documents on Irish foreign policy*, vol. 6 no. 37.

21 Stephen Gwynn, 'Ireland and the War', *Foreign affairs*, vol. 18 (1940), 305–13.

22 Brian Girvin, *The emergency: neutral Ireland 1939–45* (London, 2006), 284–300.

23 Robert Wilson, 'Questions relating to Irish neutrality', *The American journal of international law*, vol. 36 no. 2 (Apr. 1942), 288–91.

24 David Stafford, *Roosevelt and Churchill: men of secrets* (London, 1999), 235.

25 G.T. Dempsey, review of 'Dublin's American policy', in *Irish historical studies*, vol. 31 no. 124 (Nov. 1999), 583–4. Dempsey was a member of America's diplomatic service.

26 Eunan O'Halpin, 'Irish–Allied security relations and the American note crisis: new evidence from British records', *Irish studies in international affairs*, vol. 11 (2000), 71–83.

27 Terence Brown, *The Irish Times: 150 years of influence* (London, 2015), 144–9, 166–9, 174.

28 R.M. Smyllie, 'Un-neutral Neutral Éire', *Foreign Affairs*, vol. 24 (1946), 317–26, quote p. 317.

29 Ibid., 320–6, quote pp. 325–6.

30 *Documents on Irish foreign policy*, vol. 10, no. 210.

31 Funchion (ed.), *Irish American voluntary organisations*, 34–8.

32 Patrick Keatinge, *A singular stance* (Dublin, 1984), 16.

33 Ibid., 4.

34 J.P. Duggan, *A history of the Irish army*, 156–71; Tom Hodson, *The college* (Dublin, 2016), 63.

35 Emma Cunningham, 'Ireland, Canada and the American note', in D. Keogh, M. O'Driscoll (eds), *Ireland in World War Two: neutrality and survival* (Cork, 2004), 143–58. After these initial strident criticisms, the Canadians would set up their own office of high commissioner in Ireland in March 1940 to appease Éire.

36 Frederick Boland, then assistant secretary of the department of external affairs, was particularly peeved about this. *Documents on Irish foreign policy*, vol. 10 no. 210. He would recall that the extent of criticisms of Ireland after the fall of Paris was what cemented Irish public opinion behind the policy of neutrality perhaps more than anything else.

37 Michael Kennedy, Victor Laing (eds), *The Irish Defence Forces 1940–1949: the chief of staff reports* (Dublin, 2011), xviii (quote), xxiv, xxv. In Irish law, the chief of staff of

the Irish army, although the professional head of the Defence Forces, is not by law a commander, but instead is the chief military advisor to the Irish minister for defence.

38 Tom MacGinty, *The Irish navy: golden jubilee of the Irish naval service* (Tralee, 1995).

39 Patrick Keatinge, *A singular stance: Irish neutrality* (Dublin, 1984), 19.

40 Michael Kennedy, Victor Laing (eds), *The Irish Defence Forces 1940–1949: the Chief of Staff reports* (Dublin, 2011), 20–1, 64, 78–80, 87–91, 235–6. Some warning shots were also fired from Dublin and Waterford whenever ships attempted to pass too close to the Irish coast without permission.

41 From Britain, some members of an underground organisation styling itself as 'Óglaigh na hÉireann IRA' developed communications with Germany. J.P. Duggan, *Neutral Ireland and the Third Reich* (Dublin, 1975). An IRA secret society also existed in Ireland, but this was practically suppressed by de Valera during the earliest stages of the war using political intelligence alone.

42 Maurice Walsh, *G2 in defence of Ireland: Irish military intelligence 1918–45* (Cork, 2010), 160–98.

43 Brian Girvin, *The emergency: neutral Ireland 1939–1945* (London, 2006), ix–xiii.

44 Michael Kennedy, Victor Laing (eds), *The Irish Defence Forces 1940–1949: the chief of staff reports* (Dublin, 2011), 181.

45 Ibid., 277.

46 D. Keogh, M. O'Driscoll (eds), *Ireland in World War Two* (Cork, 2004), 156.

47 Aengus Nolan, 'A most heavy and grievous burden: Joseph Walshe and the establishment of sustainable neutrality, 1940', in D. Keogh, M. O'Driscoll (eds), *Ireland in World War Two: neutrality and survival* (Cork, 2004), 126–43, esp. 129–32, 134; Patrick Keatinge, *The formulation of Irish foreign policy* (Dublin, 1973), 111. Walshe's mere willingness to consider that either side could lose the war was why Gray and others thought he was too 'anti-British' in his attitudes. Privately, Walshe felt that neither America nor Britain would invade Ireland for fear of causing a pro-Irish backlash in America.

48 Niall Keogh, 'Con Cremin, Berlin and *die billige gesandtschaft*', in D. Keogh, M. O'Driscoll (eds), *Ireland in World War Two: neutrality and survival* (Cork, 2004), 159–72.

49 Michael Kennedy, Victor Laing (eds), *The Irish Defence Forces 1940–1949: the chief of staff reports* (Dublin, 2011), 365.

50 Gerard Keown, 'Sean Lester: journalist, revolutionary, diplomat, statesman', *Irish studies in international affairs*, vol. 23 (2012), 143–54; Mervyn O'Driscoll, Dermot Keogh, Jerome aan de Wiel (eds), *Ireland through European eyes: western Europe, the EEC and Ireland 1945–1973* (Cork, 2013), 256–7; Michael Kennedy, 'Edward Joseph Phelan (1888–1967)', *Dictionary of Irish biography* (Cambridge, 2009).

51 B. Tonra, M. Kennedy, J. Doyle, N. Dorr (eds), *Irish foreign policy* (Dublin, 2012), 79–80.

52 Mervyn O'Driscoll, Dermot Keogh, Jerome aan de Wiel (eds), *Ireland through European eyes: Western Europe, the EEC and Ireland 1945–1973* (Cork, 2013), 245–90.

53 Mervyn O'Driscoll, Dermot Keogh, Jerome aan de Wiel (eds), *Ireland through European eyes*, 24–5, 143, 145, 190, 196–7, 200–9, 248, 259, 261. The Irish government had denounced the Italian legation in Dublin publicly when it issued pro-Axis propaganda during the war, but a few senior ex-Nazi German officers were able to buy land in Ireland after the war. This was briefly a source of a little controversy, both nationally and internationally.

54 Mervyn O'Driscoll, Dermot Keogh, Jerome aan de Wiel (eds), *Ireland through European eyes*, 24–5, 135–8, 141–2.

55 Michael Kennedy, *Ireland and the League of Nations* (Dublin, 1996).

56 MacWhite received some honours from the Americans and French governments, as well as from the Italian government, upon leaving the Irish diplomatic service. Michael Kennedy, 'Michael MacWhite (1880–1958)', *Dictionary of Irish biography* (Cambridge, 2009).

57 *Documents on Irish foreign policy*, vol. 3 no. 137. Edward Phelan encouraged this trend during the 1930s by means of the ILO. The British foreign office succeeded in recruiting Daniel Binchy, a former Irish minister to Germany (1929–32), as one of its chief research officers at the time of de Valera's constitutional reforms of 1936–8. Tom Garvin, *The lives of Daniel Binchy: Irish scholar, diplomat, public intellectual* (Dublin, 2016), 108.

58 Walshe had always been inclined to pay attention to the stance of various papal nuncios. During the war, his department relied partly on such men to act as neutral couriers of letters between the Irish consuls in Europe. References to papal nuncios in volumes 6 and 7 of *Documents on Irish foreign policy* are usually made specifically in this context.

59 Robert Patterson, 'Ireland, Vichy and post-liberation France 1938–50', in M. Kennedy, J. Skelly (eds), *Irish foreign policy 1919–1966* (Dublin, 2000), 96–114.

60 Charles Maier, 'The politics of productivity: the foundation of American international economic policy after World War II', *International organization*, vol. 31 no. 4 (autumn 1977), 607–33.

61 Francine McKenzie, 'Renegotiating a special relationship: the Commonwealth and Anglo-American economic discussions, September–December 1945', *The journal of Imperial and Commonwealth history*, vol. 26 no. 3 (1998), 71–93.

62 Keith Jeffery, 'Nicholas Seton Mansergh (1910–91)', *Dictionary of Irish biography* (Cambridge, 2009).

63 Nicholas Mansergh, 'Ireland: the republic outside the commonwealth', *International affairs*, vol. 28, no. 3 (Jul. 1952), 277–91.

64 John J. Horgan, *Parnell to Pearse* (1949, 2nd ed., Dublin, 2009), quote 354. Previously, Horgan had been the chief Irish critic of de Valera for having practically made a desire to end partition part of the diplomatic and constitutional identity of the Irish state. See, for instance, Horgan's contribution to Michael Tierney, A.H. Ryan, R.M. Henry, John Horgan, Daniel Binchy, 'Partition and a policy of national unity', *Studies*, vol. 24, no. 93 (Mar. 1935), 1–24.

65 T. Geiger, M. Kennedy (eds), *Ireland, Europe and the Marshall Plan* (Dublin, 2004), 104–11 (quote p. 110).

66 Michael Kennedy, 'Frederick Boland (1904–85)', *Dictionary of Irish biography* (Cambridge, 2009).

67 D. Keogh, M. O'Driscoll (eds), *Ireland in World War Two*, 48–62.

68 T.K. Whitaker, 'Ireland's external assets', *Journal of the statistical and social inquiry society of Ireland*, vol. 102 (1948–9), 192–209.

69 Till Geiger, 'Why Ireland needed the Marshall Plan but did not want it: Ireland, the sterling area and the European Recovery Program 1947–8', *Irish studies in international affairs*, vol. 11 (2000), 193–215.

70 C.C. O'Brien, *Writers and politics* (London, 1965); C.C. O'Brien, 'Ireland in international relations', in O.D. Edwards (ed.), *Conor Cruise O'Brien introduces Ireland* (London, 1969).

71   T. Geiger, M. Kennedy (eds), *Ireland, Europe and the Marshall Plan*, 66–7, 81-101.

72   J.W. Young, *Britain and European unity 1945–1999* (2nd ed., London, 2000), quote p. 31.

73   Maurice Duverger, *Political parties: their organisation and activity in the modern state, with a foreword by D.W. Brogan* (2nd ed. English language translation, London, 1959); Paul Kennedy, *The rise and fall of the great powers* (London, 1988), 483, 491.

74   J.M. Skelly, 'Ireland, the department of external affairs and the United Nations 1946–55', *Irish studies in international affairs*, vol. 7 (1996), 64–7 (quote p. 64), 74–7; Patrick Keatinge, *A singular stance* (Dublin, 1984), chapter 3.

75   Michael Kennedy, Victor Laing (eds), *The Irish Defence Forces 1940–1949: the chief of staff reports* (Dublin, 2011), 410–11, 616.

76   John Treacy, 'Caveat emptor: building Ireland's small navy 1945–1949', *Defence Forces review* (2016), 141–53. Like the army, the navy had needed to purchase its supplies from Britain by means of John Dulanty, the Irish high commissioner in London.

77   Kennedy, Laing (eds), *The Irish Defence Forces 1940–1949: chief of staff reports*, 518.

78   Ibid., 615.

79   Elizabeth Keane, 'Coming out of the cave: the first inter-party government, the Council of Europe and NATO', *Irish studies in international affairs*, vol. 15 (2004), 169, 180–2, 184, 187–8.

80   B.A. McKenzie, 'The European Youth Campaign in Ireland: neutrality, Americanisation and the cold war 1950 to 1959', *Diplomatic History*, vol. 40 no. 3 (2016), 421–44 (quote p. 439).

81   *Documents on Irish foreign policy*, vol. 10, nos 28, 41–2, 192.

82   Ibid., no. 32.

83   Aengus Nolan, *Joseph Walshe: Irish foreign policy 1922–1946* (Cork, 1996), 315, 321.

84   Mervyn O'Driscoll, Dermot Keogh, Jerome aan de Wiel (eds), *Ireland through European eyes*, 147–8. Being eager to appeal to Catholic sensibilities, Sean MacBride, who became minister of external affairs in February 1948, certainly agreed with this plan, but this may not have constituted actual government support. Michael Kennedy, 'Irish foreign policy 1919–73', in T. Bartlett (ed.), *Cambridge history of Ireland*, vol. 4 (Cambridge, 2018), 625. American CIA financial support for Italian Christian democrats in 1948 has been typified as that organisation's 'first major covert operation'. G.C. Herring, *From colony to superpower: US foreign relations since 1776* (Oxford, 2008), 621.

85   J.M. Skelly, 'Ireland, the department of external affairs and the United Nations 1946–55', *Irish studies in international affairs*, vol. 7 (1996), 67–73, 75–9.

86   Elizabeth Keane, 'Coming out of the cave', 170–1, 173, 175. The first Irish attendees were Michael Tierney of UCD and James Douglas, a banker and elderly senator.

87   Charles Lysaght, 'John Aloysius Costello (1891–1976)', *Dictionary of Irish biography* (Cambridge, 2009).

88   C.C. O'Brien, 'Ireland in international affairs', in O.D. Edwards (ed.), *Conor Cruise O'Brien introduces Ireland* (London, 1969), 124–7.

89   Stephen Kelly, 'A policy of futility: Éamon de Valera's anti-partition campaign 1948–51', *Études Irlandaises*, vol. 36 no. 2 (2012), 1–13. De Valera's Australian tour was held at the invitation and under upon the auspices of the, by now, very elderly figure of Archbishop Daniel Mannix of Melbourne. When some American congressmen offered to explain Ireland's complaint regarding partition during 1951, Sir Basil Brooke immediately decided to pay a well-publicised protest visit to America. *Documents on Irish foreign policy*, vol. 10 nos 43, 34–6.

90 Mervyn O'Driscoll, Dermot Keogh, Jerome aan de Wiel (eds), *Ireland through European eyes: western Europe, the EEC and Ireland 1945–1973* (Cork, 2013), 77, 82–3.
91 *Documents on Irish foreign policy*, vol. 10 no. 147.
92 T.W. Moody, F.X. Martin, F.J. Byrne (eds), *A new history of Ireland*, vol. 8 (Oxford, 1989), 431.
93 M. Kennedy, J. Skelly (eds), *Irish foreign policy 1919–1966* (Dublin, 2000), 115; D. Keogh, F. O'Shea, C. Quinlan (eds), *Ireland in the 1950s* (Cork, 2004), 195. In 1958, Sean T. O'Kelly became the first Irish president to make a state visit to the United States.
94 *Documents on Irish foreign policy*, vol. 10 no. 141.
95 T.W. Moody, F.X. Martin, F.J. Byrne (eds), *A new history of Ireland*, vol. 8 (Oxford, 1989), 431; Stephen Kelly, 'A policy of futility: Éamon de Valera's anti-partition campaign 1948–51', *Études Irlandaises*, vol. 36 no. 2 (2012), 1–13; NLI, Sean O'Mahony papers, Ms44080–1.
96 T.W. Moody, F.X. Martin, F.J. Byrne (eds), *A new history of Ireland*, vol. 8 (Oxford, 1989), 432.
97 Sean MacBride, *That day's struggle: a memoir 1904–1951* (Dublin, 2005), 159–61.
98 Labhrás Ó Nualláin, 'A comparison of the economic position and trend in Éire and Northern Ireland', *Journal of the statistical and social inquiry society of Ireland*, vol. XVII (1945–6), 517, 520.
99 Labhrás Ó Nualláin, 'A comparison of the external trade of the twenty-six and six counties of Ireland', *Studies*, vol. 41 no. 161 (Mar. 1952), 1–24, especially p. 8.
100 Eoin Drea, 'The Bank of England, Montagu Norman and the internationalisation of Anglo-Irish monetary relations 1922–1943', *Financial history review*, vol. 21 no. 1 (2013), 59–76, quotes p. 63, 71.
101 Sean MacBride, *That day's struggle: a memoir 1904–1951* (Dublin, 2005), 180–9.
102 Till Geiger, Michael Kennedy (eds), *Ireland, Europe and the Marshall Plan* (Dublin, 2004), 22–3.
103 The old Industrial Development Association would even end up being disbanded during 1961. Records of the IDA (1905–61) are now held in the National Archives of Ireland.
104 For instance, during the first year of Córas Tráchtála's operations in 1951, Irish exports to the United States and Canada doubled up to £1m, but imports from the United States and Canada became as high as £15m. Michael MacCormac, 'Crisis in Ireland's balance of trade', *Studies*, vol. 49 no. 159 (Sep. 1951), 266–7.
105 Anthony J. Jordan, *Sean MacBride* (Dublin, 1993), 102–3.
106 Brian O'Doherty, a former director of Córas Tráchtála, to author (phone interview, Mar. 2018).
107 *Documents on Irish foreign policy*, vol. 10 nos 177 (quote), 306.
108 Kennedy, Laing (eds), *The Irish Defence Forces 1940–1949: chief of staff reports*, xvii (quote).
109 Terence O'Reilly, *Our struggle for independence: eye witness accounts from the pages of An Cosantóir* (Cork, 2009). *An Cosantóir* was founded as the magazine of the Defence Forces in December 1940 by Colonel Michael Costello.
110 Sean MacBride, *That day's struggle: a memoir 1904–1951* (Dublin, 2005), 192–3.
111 Brian Hanley, *The IRA* (London, 2015), 117–29.
112 John P. Duggan, *A history of the Irish army* (Dublin, 1991), 175, 222–32.

113 Patrick Maume, 'Sean Cronin (1922–2011)', *Dictionary of Irish biography* (online edition).

114 Enda Delaney, 'The vanishing Irish: the exodus from Ireland in the 1950s', in D. Keogh, F. O'Shea, C. Quinlan (ed.), *Ireland in the 1950s: the lost decade* (Cork, 2001), 81–2, quote p. 86.

115 Tracey Connolly, 'The commission on emigration 1948–1954', in D. Keogh, F. O'Shea, C. Quinlan (ed.), *Ireland in the 1950s: the lost decade* (Cork, 2001), 87–104. This attitude continued to exist in later decades. Ronan Fanning, *Independent Ireland* (Dublin, 1983), 118.

116 Enda Delaney, 'The vanishing Irish', 80–6.

117 T.W. Moody et al. (eds), *A new history of Ireland*, vol. 8, 429–31.

118 Michael Kennedy, *Division and consensus: the politics of cross-border relations 1925–69* (Dublin, 2000), chapters 4–6.

119 The key legislation in this respect was the Northern Ireland Act of 31 July 1947. T.W. Moody, F.X. Martin, F.J. Byrne (eds), *A new history of Ireland*, vol. 8 (Oxford, 1989), 430.

120 M. Kennedy, E. O'Halpin, *Ireland and the Council of Europe* (Strasbourg, 2000); Elizabeth Keane, 'Coming out of the cave', 175, 178.

121 *Documents on Irish foreign policy*, vol. 10, no. 116.

122 Ibid., no. 150.

123 Brian O'Doherty, a former director of Córas Tráchtála, to author (phone interview, Mar. 2018).

124 A suggestion during 1955 that the American office of Córas Tráchtála should be made co-residents with the Irish consular offices in New York City was evidently dismissed at the Irish embassy's request. *Documents on Irish foreign policy*, vol. 10 no. 384.

125 Irene Furlong, 'Tourism and the Irish state in the 1950s', in D. Keogh, F. O'Shea, C. Quinlan (ed.), *Ireland in the 1950s: the lost decade* (Cork, 2001), 164–86, quote p. 173.

126 Andrew Sanders, 'Landing rights in Dublin: relations between Ireland and the United States 1945–72', *Irish studies in international affairs*, vol. 28 (2017), 147–71.

127 Irene Furlong, 'Tourism and the Irish state in the 1950s', 170–9.

128 Mervyn O'Driscoll, *Ireland, West Germany and the new Europe 1949–1973* (Manchester, 2017).

129 Sean MacBride, *That day's struggle: a memoir 1904–1951* (Dublin, 2005), 167–79; Nicholas Mansergh, 'Ireland: the republic outside the Commonwealth', *International affairs*, vol. 28 no. 3 (Jul. 1952), 277–91.

130 David McCullagh, *De Valera: rule 1932–1975* (Dublin, 2018), 267–9.

131 There was a history, however, of Indian nationalists being interested in Irish developments. Kate O'Malley, *Ireland, India and Empire: Indo–Irish radical connections 1919–1964* (Manchester, 2008).

132 Michael Kennedy, 'Frederick Boland (1904-85)', *Dictionary of Irish Biography* (Cambridge, 2009).

133 O.D. Edwards (ed.), *Conor Cruise O'Brien introduces Ireland* (London, 1969), 127–8.

134 The MP in question was called Padraig McLogan.

135 *Documents on Irish foreign policy*, vol. 10, nos.322, 370. Boland reported frequently between 1951 and 1955 on the activities of the Anti-Partition League in Britain.

136 Ibid., no. 317 (quote); C.C. O'Brien (ed.), *The shaping of modern Ireland* (London, 1960), 173.

137 C.C. O'Brien, 'Ireland in international relations', in O.D. Edwards (ed.), *Conor Cruise O'Brien introduces Ireland* (London, 1969), 106–17.

138 Walshe was en route between South Africa, where he went for health reasons, and Rome when he took ill and died in Cairo. Michael Kennedy, 'Joseph Patrick Walshe (1886–1956)', *Dictionary of Irish biography* (Cambridge, 2009).

139 Michael Kennedy, Eunan O'Halpin, *Ireland and the Council of Europe* (Strasbourg, 2000).

140 *Documents on Irish foreign policy*, vol. 10 nos 66, 67, 133.

141 Kris Brown, 'A hermitage Ireland: a foreign policy of despair? 1951–5', *Irish studies in international affairs*, vol. 10 (1999), 106 (quote). NATO membership could have meant that Ireland could not have prevented any allied (including UK) command bases and armaments being installed on its territory. A combination of the ethos of its prior independence struggle and the fact that, unlike the rest of Europe, Ireland had no experience of (friendly or foe) foreign troops on its soil during the war, coloured its perspective on NATO. In recognition of Irish sensibilities, the US respectfully appointed William Taft (a son of the chief US opponent of NATO and grandson of President Taft) to Dublin in 1949 and as its ambassador to Ireland in 1954.

142 http://www.irishstatutebook.ie/eli/1955/act/29/enacted/en/html. *Documents on Irish foreign policy*, vol. 10 no. 210.

143 Anne Groutel, 'American Janus-faced economic diplomacy towards Ireland in the mid-1950s', *Irish economic and social history*, vol. 43 no. 1 (2016), 3–20.

144 Michael Kennedy, Eunan O'Halpin, *Ireland and the Council of Europe* (Strasbourg, 2000), 105.

145 C.C. O'Brien, 'Ireland in international affairs', quote p. 128.

146 Elizabeth Keane, 'Coming out of the cave', 188.

147 Patrick Keatinge, 'Unequal sovereigns: the diplomatic dimension of Anglo-Irish relations', in P.J. Drudy (ed.), *Ireland and Britain since 1922* (Cambridge, 1986), 147, 150.

148 Rueben Wong, Christopher Hill (eds), *National and European foreign policies* (London, 2011), quote p. 73.

149 D. Keogh, F. O'Shea, C. Quinlan (ed.), *Ireland in the 1950s* (Cork, 2001), quote p. 117.

150 The only new Irish embassies opened in this period were Nigeria (1960), Denmark (1962), India (1964) and Australia (1965).

5

Introducing Ireland to the United Nations and the European Community, 1955–1968

Between 1957 and 1961, the principal focus of the United Nations (UN) was its expansion to include many small nation–states. This was perhaps fortunate for Ireland because, as a result, it would enjoy a fairly significant profile at the UN during the initial stages of its membership. By contrast, introducing Ireland to the European community would prove to be a much more difficult challenge. A process of Irish integration into western Europe had been encouraged by the United States on a cultural level.[1] However, 'Europe and a wider world' had played 'no part' in the thinking of the Irish department of finance to date.[2] A turning point occurred during 1957 when Ireland joined the International Monetary Fund (IMF). The IMF existed to survey member states' performance in order to assist them manage their balance of payments difficulties. Although inspired largely by American or British economists, it always chose European directors. Gunnar Myrdal, a representative of neutral Sweden, was its director when Ireland joined. He criticised the Irish government for looking no further than its currency union with Great Britain and, in turn, prioritising 'restoring Ireland's pre-war trading relationship with Britain' rather than paying attention to the prospect of multilateral trade agreements that were being raised by the post-war creation of a General Agreement on Tariffs and Trade (GATT).[3] This sought consensuses on most-favoured-nation trading agreements that could be made operable on an intercontinental level, effectively replacing traditional preferential trade agreements with a more 'global', or universal, conception of free trade that was not governed exclusively by national preferences. From this new European perspective, Ireland appeared to be a very hesitant player in international relations.

In the wake of the Treaty of Rome that led to the establishment of the European Economic Community (EEC) in 1957, Myrdal was surprised to discover that the Irish government's interdepartmental foreign trade committee, first established in 1936, was under the department of the Taoiseach and ministry of commerce rather than external affairs. It was also far from active because most senior Irish government officials had no interest in its operations.[4] Its leader, economist Patrick Lynch, would serve as a bank director, a chairman of Aer Lingus and a member of virtually all the Irish government advisory committees relating to the Organisation for Economic Cooperation and Development (OECD), but he was not involved in external affairs.[5] Timothy O'Driscoll, the first director of Córas Tráchtála, acted as Ireland's consultant to the UN and the Ford Foundation on the tourism industry, but this was done exclusive of his brief tenure in the department of external affairs. Government policy was still practically based on a belief that Ireland's foreign relations should not be influenced by commerce.[6] Reflecting this, directors of Irish semi-state companies attended new multilateral economic forums rather than government ministers. Michael Sweetman, the foreign-trade advisor of the Federation of Irish Industries and chief propagandist of the Irish Council of the European Movement, also acted independently of the Irish government, although his cousin Gerard Sweetman was the Fine Gael minister of finance who brought Ireland into the IMF.[7] Contemporary Irish intellectuals were more interested in the national applicability of social-democratic theories, such as the search for a morally 'just society', than they were in international relations, and this served to limit the significance of efforts by a rejuvenated Irish diplomatic staff to develop a distinct Irish strategy regarding the UN and Europe, as much as did Irish diplomats' own failure to focus on developments such as the creation of the World Bank Group during 1960.[8]

Con Cremin, who served as general secretary of the Irish department of external affairs (1954–63),[9] was a skilled diplomatic reporter on themes such as US attitudes regarding the Vatican, British attitudes towards Europe and greater European discussions on defence, but he did not employ economic analyses in his reporting.[10] His successor as departmental secretary Hugh McCann (1963–74), a graduate of the London School of Economics, had served as Ireland's first representative on the Food and Agricultural Organisation (FAO), which existed to promote the commercialisation and mechanisation of agriculture in the Third World and to regulate the supply and demand of food on a global level, and he also served as an ambassador to Britain (1958–63).[11] Although these men believed that Ireland should act within an essentially pro-American and western bloc in international affairs, the absence of an economic strategy to the department of external affairs meant that its operations hardly reflected the international priorities of, for instance, the United States in such matters. Meanwhile, the post-war determination of the British Dominions Office that 'we do not want to give the Éire government the opportunity of rebuffing us' and that 'cooperation with her in an international organisation is the best means of promoting cooperation in, for example, defence and economic matters, which is valuable for purely British reasons', continued to be made quite effective by Britain's evidently successful insistence that Ireland deal with Britain exclusively through internal channels, rather than the British Foreign Office, up until such time as the British Dominions Office amalgamated with the British Foreign Office during 1968.[12] In this way, the evolution of the British Commonwealth still exercised a significant, if indirect, influence that was designed to minimise the relevance of the Republic of Ireland Act to Ireland's future political evolution.

Frank Aiken, who acted as Ireland's minister for external affairs from 1957 to 1969, was considered to be a politician very akin to Éamon de Valera. The Irish public expected him to act as a steady moral voice whenever he was speaking on their behalf on the international stage. On a national level, Aiken was perhaps best known for being an essentially middle-class Catholic that came from a northern Irish nationalist background. In his understanding of either northern or international affairs, however, Aiken was never well attuned to economic matters.[13] Patrick Lynch, the chief economic advisor to the Irish government, was unsure if the trend whereby 'large scale capital investment for development purposes in Ireland has become respectable' should be viewed as a form of 'radicalism' akin to discarded 'visions of Arthur Griffith' or as a reason to embrace a contemporary Marxist idea that the root of Ireland's difficulties was that it 'remains a complacent middle-class society'.[14] The latter strain of thought perhaps reflected contemporary French propaganda, which maintained that all politics is 'the interplay between Right and Left' whilst also conveniently asserting that 'the French Left, like France itself, is at the heart of the European'.[15] Perhaps the best illustration of Irish conservatism, however, was that new efforts by finance (itself a highly conservative department) to adapt to international circumstances soon 'evoked a desultory response from other departments', who preferred to retain 'a rather parochial attitude' and to resist all ideas of reform.[16]

During the late 1950s, Conor Cruise O'Brien managed to get himself appointed head of the UN section of the Irish department of external affairs. In his own estimation, he and Aiken were the co-custodians of an Irish tradition of giving expression to a purely independent stance on international affairs up until the early- to mid-1960s.[17] Unlike Aiken, however, O'Brien was a rather egocentric man who was intellectually rooted in British conservatism. Being a literary critic, he was also overly preoccupied with literature as a mode of political analysis.[18] Be that as it may, he would soon find himself at the centre of the first major UN controversy in which Ireland became involved.

The main issues at the UN when Ireland first took its seat in the General Assembly (situated alphabetically between Iran and Israel) were disruptive events in the Middle East and many different applications for UN membership in Africa. The new state of Israel, which was invaded by five Arab states within twenty-four hours of its establishment in 1948, was eager to establish bilateral ties with Ireland, while, in general, the Arab world welcomed Ireland's admission to the UN in the belief that it would be a good critic of colonial imperialism.[19] The Irish, however, did not wish to become a partisan for either side. John Hearne, who served as ambassador to the United States during the 1950s, felt that the Middle East was being turned into 'a witch's cauldron' because of a balance of power based upon a damaging Russian and American arms race.[20] Such concerns would not start to become prevalent in the United States until the 1970s.[21] In the meantime, O'Brien voiced similar concerns regarding the operations of the process of decolonisation

in Africa.[22] Ireland cited the UN Charter as the basis of its criticism
of the Israeli-backed British and French invasion of Egypt after the
Egyptians attempted to nationalise the Suez Canal in 1956. This was in
keeping with America's stance. In endeavouring to exercise a distinct
voice, Ireland emphasised the fate of refugees as the most central
issue in determining the possibilities of establishing a durable peace
in the Middle East. This Irish stance did not win much international
appreciation, however, because Ireland was a late party to the 1951
UN Convention Relating to the Status of Refugees and had, as yet, no
asylum policy itself. This was why Ireland had been able to offer only
minimal protection to Hungarian refugees, in the wake of a recent
failed effort to undo the Russian occupation of their country, as well as
to Jewish refugees during the 1940s.[23]

De Valera, who had been a good friend to the chief rabbi of Ireland
(who was also the father of a future Israeli president), deliberately sent
kosher food to Europe as part of Ireland's relief-aid programme.[24] He had
also visited Israel with an Irish Jewish TD shortly after Britain offered
de jure recognition to the Israeli state in 1950. Ireland's own diplomatic
stance regarding Israel, however, was shaped almost entirely by the
Catholic Church's concern for the fate of religious sites in Palestine. As
a result, the Irish government would not offer *de jure* recognition to
the Israeli state until after the conclusion of Vatican II in 1962, while
formal Irish diplomatic relations with Israel would not actually begin
until 1974.[25] The Jewish population of Ireland, which peaked during
1946 at 4,000 before declining thereafter, had always been small. If a
culture of anti-Semitism existed in Ireland, it had often been expressed
within the context of Anglophobic and umbrella Catholic criticism of
freemasonry; a way of life that attracted many Jews and that, in Ireland,
was most often associated with a Protestant business elite,[26] with an
Anglo-Catholic worldview, that wrote on international affairs for
the *Irish Times* newspaper.[27] Many individuals from this same social
background were either attracted to or were actively encouraged to join
Ireland's department of external affairs.[28] This perhaps reflected the
degree to which an active, or stakeholder, interest in international affairs
was comparatively slight amongst Ireland's predominantly Catholic
population, prompting in turn the Irish department of external affairs
to maintain a very low public profile.[29]

The 'Irish Institute of International Affairs', founded by Arnold Toynbee in 1937, had replaced Bruno Waller's old Irish League of Nations Society. It reinvented itself after 1945, under the guidance of a former ILO official, as the International Affairs Association. It attracted only small audiences, however, consisting almost exclusively of retired Irish diplomats or British and Irish academics. Its practical affiliation with Chatham House's Royal Institute of International Affairs, which had been under the direct control of the British Foreign Office during the war, made it the subject of controversy in Dublin after it invited Jan Masaryk, a Czech minister in exile and future founder of the World Federation of United Nations Associations, to speak before the society without first seeking the permission of the Irish department of external affairs.[30] This World Federation had invited the International Affairs Association to become an affiliated member during 1953, not long after it held some pioneering conferences on American foreign policy, but the society collapsed thereafter because of Catholic disapproval of the tenor of the society's subsequent debates about countries like Yugoslavia, a home of recent racial–religious conflict. At a time when American Catholic opinion, which had been to the fore in calling for world peace during the era of the Kellogg–Briand Pact,[31] had shifted into adopting polemical cold war mentalities, the Irish 'Catholic Association for International Relations', as well as some Irish Catholic newspapers, often became quite histrionic in their attitudes by aping such attitudes.[32]

While an Irish Council of the European Movement was launched in early 1954, an 'Irish United Nations Association' could not be launched until 1959, by which time Aiken was perhaps best known in Ireland for having argued before the UN that 'there are sins that are common both to the Communistic and to the non-Communistic states'.[33] Along with Sweden, Ireland was the only western country that was willing to discuss the admission of the People's Republic of China into the UN. This was done less in defiance of the US policy of confining Chinese representation to Taiwan, which was the home of an expatriated Chinese government, than to mobilise the international community into condemning China on the grounds of its suppression of religious freedoms in Tibet.[34] Ireland generally saw this issue of religious freedoms as being connected with the operations of all humanitarian missions abroad.[35] Otherwise, it soon became quite well known at the UN for its regular support for the Relief and Works Agency. This made Ireland the sixth-largest contributor to relief aid within the entire UN in terms of percentage of its gross national product.[36] Ireland's other claim to fame was its consistent call for the non-proliferation of nuclear weapons. This was an Irish policy that, not surprisingly, was supported by the now pacifist nation of Japan.[37] Aside from a tradition of Irish missionary work, another small, yet significant, factor in contributing to Ireland's emerging humanitarian profile was its efforts, despite the weakness of its own army, to bring greater definition to the UN's potential role as a peacekeeper. After 1958, Aiken oversaw the sending of Irish army officers abroad to serve in UN observation group missions. This occurred first in the Lebanon, in the wake of the creation of the United Arab Republic of Syria and Egypt, and subsequently in the Congo. Here Irishmen became central to a controversy that, as one Irish army officer noted, was rooted in the fact that 'the term "peacekeeping" as a form of conflict control is not even mentioned, much less described, in the UN Charter ... [but] Dag Hammarskjöld [the Swedish secretary-general of the UN] felt that a new chapter of the Charter was needed' to remedy this fact. Along with neutral Sweden, Ireland was one of the few European countries that agreed with this assessment.[38]

Nine members of an Irish patrol serving in the Congo were killed in an ambush in November 1960 and the return of their bodies to Dublin was the occasion of one of the largest state funerals in Irish history. Thereafter, the UN realised the necessity of better-armed troops in the Congo, while veteran Irish general Sean MacEoin was made the nominal commander of the UN troops. The assassination of the Congolese prime minister in February 1961 prompted Hammarskjöld to decide to authorise the use of force. He also persuaded the Irish government to remove Conor Cruise O'Brien from his position as assistant secretary of the Irish department of external affairs so that he could serve as the UN's official representative in the Congo. The root of the whole controversy was that although Belgium had allowed Congolese independence the previous summer, with the support of the British and the French, Belgian industrial interests in the Congo hired mercenaries to promote the partition of the Congo by creating a breakaway state of Katanga. This created a civil war-like situation. In

September 1961, a company of a hundred Irish soldiers stationed at Jadotville attracted international attention by repelling a Katanga force of 2,000 men. O'Brien and the Swedish commander of the UN forces simultaneously authorised an attempt to arrest the Katanga leaders. This failed because the British embassy offered protection to the Katanga rebel leaders. Within twenty-four hours of a battle involving joint Irish–Swedish forces (in which three Irish soldiers were killed), Hammarskjöld himself was killed in a plane crash (which O'Brien, amongst others, doubted was an accident) after he defied the British by attempting to fly out to the Congo himself.[39] Irish troops, while suffering a total of twenty-six casualties, continued to serve in the Congo until the defeat of Katanga in 1963, but levels of international controversy over the Congo conflict meant that it did not boost the credibility of the UN as a peacekeeper.

Despite his being awarded a Nobel Peace Prize, Britain was adamant that Hammarskjöld was entirely at fault. Emphasising that it is 'a purely administrative role … which is representative of no sovereign interest', Britain argued that the UN secretariat 'is no more fitted to deal with political crises – as opposed to the supervision of the world's administrative services – than the [UN] General Assembly'. Therefore, any effort by the UN secretariat to step beyond this role by determining upon a policy, as if the UN was an embryonic 'world government', must 'end by being discredited and destroyed'.[40] The Congolese controversy also served to terminate O'Brien's career as an Irish diplomat. After writing a book justifying his actions in the Congo, he spent the rest of the decade in academic circles, first as a chancellor of the University of Ghana (1962–5) and then as a humanities lecturer in New York University. Mirroring Hammarskjöld's sensibilities, O'Brien argued that the UN was achieving what the League of Nations had failed to achieve, namely 'a life and an apparent volition of its own' through its sensitivity to 'the opinions of the smaller, formerly subject, nations', so much so that their combined voices at the UN could potentially resist the imperial ambitions for which 'the great power systems strive, especially in Africa and Asia'.[41] By contrast, Britain maintained that the veto that the great powers could exercise by means of their permanent representation on the UN Security Council was entirely just because it served to guarantee that the UN should 'only be able to work effectively in the contingencies for which it was intended, to avoid or suppress the use of force in issues in which a Great Power was not involved'.[42]

O'Brien's subsequent emergence as the highest-profile Irish writer on international relations indirectly highlighted a peculiarity of the Irish diplomatic world, which was the absence of any diplomats with public profiles as authors. For instance, although some of his diplomatic speeches were later converted into Irish publications,[43] Éamon de Valera never wrote. This was also true of Frank Aiken, who shared de Valera's belief that public discussion of Ireland's international relations, even in the Dáil, was something that was best avoided.[44] The justification for this belief was a sense that geopolitical realities governing the Irish state were matters that 'few Irish policymakers outside the military and diplomatic nexus understood'.[45] However, this understandable culture of secrecy encouraged many in the Irish state to suspect that the Irish government was deliberately masking *realpolitik* behind Anglo-Irish relations – as if the country's army and diplomacy were being neutralised to an even greater extent than was popularly understood – just as a deep distrust, or distaste, for a southern Irish political culture of secrecy was the essential basis of Northern Ireland's extant British loyalism, perhaps even more so than some Ulstermen's pride in past, or present, imperial service.[46]

De Valera's fixed idea from the time of his 1920 Cuban proposal up until his retirement was that if Ireland never allowed itself to be used as a base for an attack upon Britain, the latter would be willing to recognise Ireland's right to possess its own distinct constitution.[47] However, the degree to which this principle attained supremacy over all other Irish governmental considerations, both economically and diplomatically, meant that the potential development of a different course of political evolution, based on a perpetually evolving international economic order that inherently underpins all nations' foreign policies, was almost completely overlooked by the Irish government. This was a reason for de Valera's great hesitancy, or lack of initiative, in the wake of the Republic of Ireland Act in 1948.[48] Sean Lemass replaced de Valera as Taoiseach in 1959 and he attributed 'the incapacity of the government under his [de Valera's] leadership to do things that had to be done' primarily to 'defects of co-ordination in government' on a national level.[49]

Lemass' vision for a better-coordinated government policy was revealed during 1961 when he transferred Maurice Moynihan, hitherto secretary to the department of the Taoiseach (a position equivalent to cabinet secretary in Irish governmental practice), to the position of governor of the Central Bank of Ireland. In this capacity, Moynihan worked closely with Donal Carroll in his position as the new governor of the Bank of Ireland and chairman of the Irish Banks Standing Committee. Carroll did not agree with the policy of all his predecessors of keeping the Irish banks' reserves in London and refusing to meet the borrowing requirements of the Irish state. To reverse this trend, the Irish government decided to keep its exchequer account with Carroll's Bank of Ireland, to transfer the bank's external reserves from the Bank of England to Moynihan's central bank in Dublin and to create a new affiliated branch, the Investment Bank of Ireland, which employed purely American consultants. The aim was to instigate an Irish monetary policy whereby the Central Bank would concentrate primarily on foreign exchange markets, as opposed to just the sterling area, and to promote cooperation between Irish state and commercial banking to a degree that had never been witnessed before.[50] A launch of Irish government securities also served to stimulate greater activity in a traditionally dormant Irish Stock Exchange.

On a national level, Carroll's own business enterprises had been the chief advertiser in the post-1916 Irish republican press. This may partly explain why he was a firm believer in the economic reasoning that had motivated the initial formation of Dáil Éireann in 1919: 'No nation which exports its money to the detriment of its own industry can be surprised if the people also leave it. They have, in fact, no practical alternative.'[51] Indeed, once the Irish government's sterling assets started to be repatriated after 1961, the great wave of Irish emigration during the 1950s reversed so that, by the end of the decade, the country's population was growing for the first time in over a century. Moynihan encouraged Irish cooperation with all central bankers internationally by affiliating the Central Bank of Ireland with the Bank for International Settlements. He judged that foreign direct investment in Ireland, as well as a general 'growth in the volume of world trade', should be encouraged to ensure a rapid growth in Irish state revenue by means of corporate taxation of both national and international companies.

Creating an open economy was also seen to be a means to maximise not only Irish state revenue but also public expenditure.[52] This was essentially contrary to the British treasury goal of a strict programme of national public expenditure control and resisting the influence of all supranational structures in the worlds of international banking or credit that it did not control.[53] Britain's desire to forecast international market trends was governed almost exclusively by its desire to retain its own strategic advantages.[54] By contrast, Ireland's ambition was simply to solve its balance of payments difficulties.

Within two years, Moynihan's directive to Irish banks to increase the levels of credit they offered to the Irish public and private sectors by 10 per cent served to convert a £42 million deficit in the Irish state's balance of payments into an Irish surplus of £10 million.[55] T.K. Whitaker's 1958 white paper *Economic Development* did not suggest any national banking reforms and he did not believe that most Irish commercial banks would be prepared to support Carroll and Moynihan's programme.[56] Whitaker's plan was to give indirect state assistance to private enterprise in agriculture and, to a lesser extent, tourism and industry by means of grants, loans and tax incentives. As such, it was not essentially a major alternation to Irish government policy during the 1930s, with the single exception of its prioritisation of agriculture. Be that as it may, it would later be typified as a blueprint for Ireland's future political evolution.[57] The essential reason for this was that second and third programmes for economic expansion, based on national banking reforms with a macro-economic and internationalist focus, would not outlive Whitaker's replacement of Moynihan as governor of the Central Bank of Ireland and the subsequent removal of Donal Carroll from his position as director of the Bank of Ireland and chairman of the Irish Banks Standing Committee during 1969. This was done on the grounds of the perceived disruptive effect that their policy was having on Anglo-Irish relations by undermining Belfast's practical status hitherto as the banking capital of the island of Ireland.[58] To undo this trend and prevent the development of an all-island economy that was regulated more by Dublin, Britain would favour introducing direct rule over Northern Ireland.[59]

Carroll's 1962 programme for economic expansion was based on the necessity of setting 'national and sectoral growth targets' purely in the light of the international situation.[60] Within five years, his programme saw national income levels increase fourfold; gross national product levels rise by 4.5 per cent (twice the OECD average); a rise of merchandise exports by 10 per cent a year to attain a strong positive balance of trade in that area; and the 'highest level ever' of Irish governmental financial reserves. Based on such results, Carroll believed that it was now fully realised in Ireland that 'no society can prosper if economic policy, monetary policy and banking practice are in conflict'. On inviting European and American bankers to Dublin to discuss the role of the banking system in economic planning, Carroll emphasised that, for the first time in Ireland, 'the Central Bank is in tactical control of the monetary sector' and 'the government is in strategic control of economic activity'. Independent commercial banks remained 'free, albeit in a limited way, to carry on their businesses within these parameters'. As a result of this new policy, Irish bankers were now 'equipped ... to participate in complex macro-economic discussions' with international partners in a manner which they were never able to do in the past, when they 'were not prepared to accept that economic planning had any practical value' and simply did not understand that proper 'macro-economic theory envisages that the growth of savings will be invested in the economy' for national developmental purposes.[61]

Carroll's policy was based upon logical precepts and an expectation that Ireland would become a member of the EEC 'before 1970'. Be that as it may, it was perhaps too drastic a change to command widespread public support from the commercial banks' principal existing shareholders. In addition, the fact that London acted as the banker for the sterling area ensured that most Irish banks still 'use the London money market to preserve their liquidity'. Carroll saw this as evidence that 'there is a very real conflict between the application of the economic plan and banking practice', but he expected that this problem would be short lived.[62] Although he had cooperated with Carroll in repatriating some banks' sterling assets, T.K. Whitaker was determined to cut back on Irish public expenditure and to reassert the total independence of the banking sector, not least by asserting that only a strictly non-governmental Economic and Social Research Institute (ESRI) could give sound advice.[63] Meanwhile, the prioritisation of 'inducements ... to foreign industrialists to provide Ireland with the enterprise that Griffith hoped Irishmen would display for themselves' was widely considered to be creating imbalances. Most of the 200 industrial undertakings launched in Ireland between 1959 and 1967 were set up with 'foreign capital participation'. While income levels in Ireland were boosted by the fact that exports in manufactured goods rose in the decade after 1955 from £13 million to £81 million, 75 per cent of Irish exports still went to the United Kingdom and thus Ireland was still incredibly vulnerable to British economic manipulation at any time the United Kingdom chose to exercise this power.[64] European awareness of this fact was sufficient to ensure that their appreciation for the distinct identity of the Irish state often remained weak.[65]

Ireland's extraordinarily small diplomatic corps meant that its capacity to launch an international charm offensive was never strong. Perhaps realising this, veteran Irish diplomat Thomas Kiernan decided as part of his final role as ambassador to America (1960–4) to persuade the American Columbia Broadcasting System (CBS) to do a television series on Ireland. The result was actually very disappointing, however, because the Americans decided to portray Northern Ireland as a model of industriousness that was being subject to Catholic religious persecution from the rest of Ireland.[66] In deference to British Commonwealth diplomatic protocols and London's Ireland Act of 1949, which declared that Ireland must never be considered to be a foreign country, the American CIA had decided that intelligence communications with the Irish government should operate only via the American embassy in London rather than the American embassy in Dublin. This was a fact that the Irish army necessarily, if somewhat reluctantly, had to accept as part of its own very limited intelligence operations.[67] Thomas Kiernan's second attempt at a charm offensive was rather more successful, however, which was to encourage John F. Kennedy to go on the first formal diplomatic visit to Ireland by an American president. Although the film industry in Ireland itself was still managed primarily within Britain, Ireland had recently launched a national television service as an extension of its radio service, leading to the establishment of Raidió Teilifís Éireann (RTÉ) in place of Raidió Éireann. This would serve to maximise the impact of Kennedy's arrival.[68]

In itself, Kennedy's presidency illustrated all the internal paradoxes of American foreign policy since the Second World War, during which

America had seen its gross national produce rise from $886 million to a staggering $135 billion that, in turn, allowed it to exercise an economic leverage over Europe.[69] On the one hand, Kennedy gave voice to a utopian UN idealism that made perhaps an even greater impact on international opinion than had Woodrow Wilson's speeches over forty years previously.[70] On the other hand, Kennedy struggled to come to terms with the CIA's preoccupation with international arms races and resulting proxy wars, as well as the role that such actions had in creating internal intelligence scares in domestic American politics essentially for the first time.[71] As a result, in American governmental circles, Kennedy was frequently perceived to have 'reacted to crises and improvised responses on a day-to-day basis, seldom examining the implications of his actions', because of his tendency to rely upon rhetorical impulses rather than strategic insights.[72] Kennedy's Irish state visit was only one aspect of his European tour of June 1963. This had two dimensions: first, coming to terms with the recent erection of the Berlin Wall; and second, squaring his commitment (stemming from a recent scare in Cuba) to implement a treaty that banned nuclear bomb testing with meeting Britain, France and Israel's ongoing desire for full nuclear armament capabilities.

In his speech before Dáil Éireann, Kennedy expressed an unqualified appreciation for the fact that by having recently 'modernised your economy', Ireland was now 'moving in the mainstream of current world events'. 'As a maker and shaper of world peace', Kennedy claimed that 'Ireland has already set an example and a standard for other small nations to follow', not least through the UN, 'the major forum for your nation's greater role in world affairs', to which 'Ireland is sending its most talented men to do the world's most important work – the work of peace.' Echoing Hammarskjöld, Kennedy also argued before the Dáil that

The United Nations must be fully and fairly financed. Its peacekeeping machinery must be strengthened. Its institutions must be developed until some day, and perhaps some distant day, a world of law is achieved. Ireland's influence in the United Nations is far greater than your relative size ... I speak of these matters today – not because Ireland is unaware of its role – but because I

think it important that you know that we know what you have done
... The peace-keeping machinery of the United Nations cannot
work without the help of the smaller nations, nations whose forces
threaten no one and whose forces can thus help create a world in
which no nation is threatened.[73]

Speaking before the UN General Assembly three months later, Kennedy
went so far as to argue that the UN should utilise satellite technology
to create a global communications system with a tripartite goal of
environmental protection, food distribution in the Third World and the
development of 'a genuine world security system'. For these reasons, he
also called for the removal of all the financial restrictions that had been
imposed upon UN budgets in the wake of Hammarskjöld's death.[74]
However, Kennedy himself was assassinated shortly thereafter.

As the Irish president, de Valera had welcomed Kennedy to Ireland,
but he could not make the return compliment of addressing a joint
session of both US houses of Congress until six months after Kennedy's
death. By this time, de Valera (who also chose to visit Canada) was
eighty-two years old. Speaking in Washington, he recalled the
inspiration that Ireland's freedom fighters had drawn from Woodrow
Wilson; argued that the United Nations, having come into being 'as the
result of American influence', was the only real hope for world peace;
and cited appreciatively a speech of the late President Kennedy, when
he said 'he wished for an America whose military strength would be
matched by its moral strength'. From Ireland's point of view, de Valera
judged that 'it is a great comfort to know that a nation like yours is
thinking at that level'.[75] Reflecting Frank Aiken's sensibilities, de Valera
gave no publicity to Cold War shibboleths during his speech. This was
partly why Washington, like London, tended to view Taoiseach Sean
Lemass with more sympathy.[76] In the wake of Kennedy's visit, Lemass
was made the front-cover subject of America's *Time* magazine, albeit
accompanied by a cartoon leprechaun.[77] In private, Lemass judged
Kennedy to be a man purely of outward charm rather than of any real
substance.[78] Although he spoke to Kennedy regarding the UN, Lemass'
scepticism regarding its relevance made him look upon Aiken's tendency
to swallow its professed idealism with little sympathy. Reflecting this,
he reined in Aiken's temptation to use the UN to give voice to criticisms

of Britain and Europe's past record of colonial imperialism in Africa and the Middle East, judging this inclination to be entirely foolish in the light of Ireland's attempt to join the EEC.[79]

Some Irish historians have argued that Aiken adopted a virtually non-aligned stance at the UN.[80] His expression of appreciation for anti-colonial nationalism, however, was actually fully in keeping with both Kennedy's outward political façade and the drive to expand UN membership to include Africa and Asia during the early 1960s.[81] Kennedy's prioritisation of the UN and Ireland's part in it would lead many future Irish historians to consider the period up until his death as marking the high point of Irish involvement in the UN. In retrospect, however, the years between 1956 and 1963 may have appeared exceptional for Ireland only because it was in this period of UN expansionism that the theme of small nations' involvement was usually made a major topic of discussion. In the wake of Kennedy's death, this focus would switch to an almost exclusive focus upon the development of regional economic commissions that were held under UN auspices, but in which the World Bank rather than the UN played the directing role.[82] Meanwhile, notwithstanding certain freedoms of expression exercised, there are reasons to judge that Ireland's role at the UN during the 1960s was essentially just what the United States always wanted it to be. This was perhaps best reflected by Aiken's refusal to criticise US policy in Vietnam.[83] In general, America valued the UN most as a means to make its diplomacy with the USSR visible to the world. This was possible through the participation of Nikita Khrushchev who, unlike his predecessor Joseph Stalin, was perpetually open to diplomacy. The Anglophile Irish diplomat Frederick Boland had been chosen by both the USA and USSR as a good president, or chairman, for UN debates during 1960. For this reason, Boland had even been considered as a potential successor to Dag Hammarskjöld as UN secretary-general during 1961, just prior to Ireland serving a half-term on the UN Security Council (1962–3). Boland chose to retire, however, just before Kennedy's visit to Dublin in June 1963.[84]

Closer to home, France's decision in January 1963 to veto Britain's EEC membership application without vetoing the Irish application served to highlight certain Irish priorities. Although he appointed a permanent representative to Brussels and opened diplomatic relations with Denmark, acting on the advice of T.K. Whitaker, Lemass decided that Ireland must not accept membership of the EEC if Britain was not a member. In addition, he arranged an Anglo-Irish free trade agreement with a focus on agricultural produce. This was done to appease Irish farmers, but it was generally read throughout the EEC as evidence that Ireland was more interested in strengthening its historic relationship with the United Kingdom than it was in cultivating a new relationship with Europe.[85] At a time when American influence in international monetary markets was prompting Australia to follow Canada out of the sterling area, Ireland was seemingly drawing closer to the British Commonwealth. Be that as it may, 'in pursuance of our intention to participate in international trade', it was also decided at this time not to contemplate 'freedom of trade in industrial goods with the UK' until 1975, by which time it was expected that both countries would already be operating under EEC free trade rules for at least a few years.[86] The significance of this decision was it reflected Dublin's recognition that the potential of Ireland's agrarian economy had already been fully exploited, as 'it could not provide additional exports nor could it generate further employment'. Therefore, the development of its industrial economy, with a focus upon American and European markets, was going to remain its priority.[87]

Sean Lemass was popular in British governmental circles for signing the Anglo-Irish free trade agreement. However, unlike either the British or de Valera,[88] Lemass was very willing to contemplate that Irish membership of the EEC could ultimately lead to a common foreign policy with the Europeans. After going personally on various diplomatic missions to the continent,[89] Lemass judged that Britain had no other policy regarding the European common market 'except to destroy it' or, at least, 'to slow down its development in some way' in order to 'change its character'.[90] Despite American pressure upon Britain to join the EEC, Britain had not been prepared to contemplate applying for EEC membership until it first tested whether or not its 'European Free Trade Association' initiative, with an eye to federating the Benelux countries with Scandinavia, could outmanoeuvre it. Although unsuccessful, this British project had embodied a logic based upon the geographical status of the UK and, indeed, Ireland as northern Europeans. Meanwhile, Britain's refusal to join the European Coal and Steel Community (which, it anticipated, could lead to a common European defence programme) was not the actual reason why French president Charles de Gaulle vetoed British membership. Rather, de Gaulle objected to London's effort to acquire special trading privileges for the entire British Commonwealth within the EEC. This would have not only given the British imperial market a supremacy of interests over each individual partner within the EEC but it would also have likely caused the entire European common market to collapse by giving the British common market, i.e. the commonwealth, an unfair advantage through simultaneously being a member and the chief competitor of the European common market.[91]

In deference not least to Sir Basil Brooke of Northern Ireland (who retired in 1963), British diplomatic protocol referred to the Irish state only by its Gaeilge name of 'Éire' on the grounds that to refer to it by its English name of 'Ireland' might seem to give credence to the idea that the national territory of Ireland could theoretically someday encompass Northern Ireland as well. This scruple was sufficient to ensure that, despite initial moves in 1946, full diplomatic relations could not be initiated between Ireland and Australia until 1965, when the combination of the Anglo-Irish free trade agreement, the establishment of an Irish embassy in India and the creation of a new diplomatic office of Secretariat of the British Commonwealth led Britain's closest partners to entertain a possible re-embracing of Ireland.[92] To encourage this trend, all the British Commonwealth partners continued to offer Ireland preferential access to their markets after 1949. However, this policy was essentially made ineffective because of the practical disappearance of a specific free trade agreement for the commonwealth during the 1950s. Having left the sterling area, Canada and Australia would make no effort to clarify their subordinate position to the British Crown until the 1980s, when they reaffirmed their commitment to the ongoing health of the concept of a British family of nations sustained by Anglo-catholic values, common laws and a common diplomacy, even as American financial influence within these territories grew.[93] A South African failure to abide by these moral standards was generally considered in Britain to be both the justification and the explanation for its parting from the British Commonwealth in May 1961. A speech by Conservative Prime Minister Harold Macmillan in Capetown in February 1960 that adopted this moral viewpoint would later be cited as an exemplary expression of the relevance of a British worldview based upon a united Protestant–Christian family of British nations on the world stage,[94] a tradition of thought that also made England a valued educational base for many American Protestant missionaries. Curiously, Macmillan's visit also marked the occasion of the appointment of an honorary Irish consul to South Africa, which had a long tradition of Ulster Protestant missionary work, but Ireland would not establish full diplomatic relations with South Africa until 1994 and in the interregnum acted chiefly as a critic of its apartheid regime.[95]

Although Irish diplomats welcomed the establishment of relations with both India and Australia during the mid-1960s, the British Commonwealth was naturally a much more relevant concept to Northern Ireland than the Republic of Ireland by the 1960s. All British dominions were technically subjects of the Crown alone, which was also the head of the Church of England, rather than the sovereign United Kingdom parliament. Nevertheless, conferences between commonwealth prime ministers for purposes of cooperation on economic and military matters was still the essential basis of its politics. In return for the commonwealth's supply of 'bases and manpower', Britain provided them with 'a world-encompassing navy capable of defending the rest of the Commonwealth'. In return for the commonwealth's supply of 'much of the food and raw materials it needed', the UK 'provided them with manufactured goods, capital and the facilities of an established network of financial and commercial contacts' worldwide. The withdrawal of South Africa from the commonwealth was typified in London as practically an expulsion because it had failed to abide by the new commonwealth policy of making efforts to oppose distinctions of race or religion amongst its subjects. This new policy was designed to enable the commonwealth to act as a united British diplomatic voice at the United Nations (a key concept to the subsequent evolution of the 'Commonwealth of Nations') but it was not popular either in Australia or in Northern Ireland while, in the light of the contemporary plight of immigrants from the British West Indies (Jamaica), it was perhaps not very popular in England itself either.[96]

Within Northern Ireland, Sir Basil Brooke had maintained the Orange Order tradition that because only a Protestant can legally serve as the British monarch, only Protestant subjects of the Crown can be loyal enough to maintain true law and order in Northern Ireland and thereby be trustworthy enough to bear arms or serve in its police forces. Brooke's successor Terence O'Neill was also a Berkshire-educated British army officer who was well known for adopting a Churchill-like tone (and accent) in his public addresses through his new Ulster Television (UTV) network. Be that as it may, he was very conscious that Britain's efforts to improve the commonwealth's international image at the UN was inadvertently creating negative publicity for his Northern Irish parliament. This was because it oversaw very poor community relations stemming from sectarian-based discriminations in politics (as represented by the existence of gerrymandered electoral constituencies) as well as in employments within both the public and private sectors. At the request of the Church of Ireland (a member of the Anglican communion), O'Neill would invite Lemass to Belfast in January 1965 in the hope of remedying this poor image. To this end, Timothy O'Driscoll created a joint North American tourism campaign between Northern Ireland and Éire during 1966,[97] but O'Neill's principal hope was that Lemass could encourage Northern Irish nationalist representatives to identify far more with the Stormont assembly. O'Neill was actually subjected to attack from Northern Ireland unionists, however, for merely acknowledging the existence of a Dublin government. This was because no public meeting with Irish government personnel had been held since 1925, while hitherto no British prime minister had ever formally acknowledged the existence of an Irish government by actually visiting Dublin.[98] Partly due to ill health, Lemass decided to retire from politics during 1966, once the Anglo-Irish free trade agreement became fully operational, while Frank Aiken, who was not a fan of the Northern Ireland administration, continued to serve as Ireland's minister for external affairs under a new government led by Jack Lynch.

Lynch's new finance minister Charles Haughey sympathised more with Donal Carroll's than T.K. Whitaker's stance regarding banking and economic planning. Be that as it may, Haughey actually cited Walt Rostow, an economist then serving as America's national security advisor, as his chief inspiration in championing a programme of government that was based upon economic planning and yet did not 'indicate any particular ideological bent'. His aim was to boost national income generation by building a society that was based upon the mass public consumption of goods and yet did not rule out enhancing governments, employers and trade unionists' understanding of the value in subscribing to a common programme for economic development with a shared concern for the state's balance of payments situation.[99] Speaking alongside Haughey, an American banker suggested in Dublin that the best means of achieving better collaboration between banking and government was neither the nationalisation model of the USSR nor 'the other extreme' of traditions in Britain and Ireland, 'where the banking structure has developed with almost no official guidance', but rather 'a dual banking system', allowing for a degree of state and free enterprise. This had particularly suited the United States because of its need for an effective balance between the operations of federal and state governments, but he believed that it could also serve Ireland well, a country that he suggested (notwithstanding the presence of a senior British treasury official at the same conference) had once been subject to 'tyrannical dictation by an oppressive central government' of which 'Americans as well as Irishmen once had some experience'.[100] French foreign ministers started making regular visits to Ireland in the wake of US President Kennedy's arrival in 1963. On one such occasion, the French foreign minister raised the idea of creating a European currency with Haughey.[101] Haughey's subsequent public identification with Rostow, however, would make it seem unlikely that he sympathised with this idea because Rostow was actually the chief advocate of a pro-British and anti-French American policy regarding European integration in opposition to de Gaulle's desire to minimise European reliance on America for defence purposes.[102]

The dramatic turnaround and improvement in the Irish state's economic performance after the 1962 programme for government led to creation of a third *Economic Development* programme during 1967, which was designed to prepare for a joint Irish and British entry into the EEC. During 1962, Chatham House's *The World Today* cited as 'particularly interesting' Lemass' remark that joint British and Irish entry into the EEC could mean that 'all economic arguments in favour of partition would disappear'.[103] In drastic contrast to the situation just after the Second World War, by 1967 Northern Ireland feared that the republic was on a road that could soon lead it to outperform the north economically, now that it had repatriated much of its sterling assets and had greater direct access to foreign currency markets.[104] Although Stormont had viewed Lemass' Anglo-Irish free trade agreement as a means to restore its competitive advantages over Dublin, many Belfast journalists believed that Terence O'Neill's initiation of Belfast–Dublin communications was motivated primarily by 'the North's desire to share in the Republic's economic expansion'.[105] If Britain and Ireland joined the EEC at the same time, this would mean the creation of an all-Ireland free trade area that could potentially benefit all parts of the island without the existence of any direct means for Belfast to counteract the republic's seemingly higher rate of growth. Therefore, it was feared that EEC membership could ultimately result in the reunification of Ireland if this trend was not resisted. For this reason, armed loyalist groups were formed in opposition to O'Neill's initiation of political communications with Dublin.[106] In turn, a new American-inspired civil rights movement that was created at the outset of 1967 to demand the introduction of a 'one man one vote' system in Northern Ireland would be treated as a form of Irish nationalist conspiracy by popular Ulster Protestant street preachers such as Ian Paisley.[107]

On the suggestion of T.K. Whitaker, Dublin had recently initiated a policy of promoting greater economic cooperation with northern unionists, such as the development of cross-border electricity facilities, less to foment change than to simply cease the cold war in north–south relations.[108] As soon as the Irish government launched its 1967 programme for government, however, O'Neill felt it necessary to refuse to ever visit Dublin again. In public, he claimed that Irish governments were inherently capable only of begging or 'cardboard box' economic policies and asserted that 'those who see Europe as the setting for a united Ireland were following an old time-worn path of self-delusion. Let me say it quite clearly and firmly for all the world to hear and understand: Ulster – whether within the European Community or outside it – will always remain British.'[109] At Jack Lynch's request, O'Neill did meet the Taoiseach briefly in Belfast a month later. Having practically withdrawn the drawbridge, however, no Irish prime minister would be allowed to visit Northern Ireland again for another twenty-three years.[110]

Notwithstanding this northern debate, neither British nor Irish membership of the EEC was a foregone conclusion. In Britain's case, this was because of its primary allegiance to the Commonwealth. In

Ireland's case, although political support for the Irish Council of the European Movement was growing,[111] government policy on Europe had not developed much further than the holding of occasional bilateral meetings between the Taoiseach and the British Prime Minister on the latest European developments. London called these meetings to request that Dublin refuse to listen to French and West German suggestions of different timescales for British and Irish entry.[112] In the light of these trends and Ireland's (partly chosen) economic dependence upon Britain, the six members of the European community expected that 'as a member of the EEC, Ireland would remain within the British orbit, no matter how strong the Christian-democratic philosophy of all three of its major parties'.[113]

In general, countries with Christian-democratic governments, such as Italy and West Germany, were the European countries that were inclined to look upon Ireland most sympathetically. They also viewed the Irish performance at the UN in New York as evidence that its non-membership of NATO did not mean that it was uncommitted to European security considerations. West Germany even considered that the influence of the Irish community in the United States could serve to increase European influence upon the United States once Ireland was admitted into the EEC.[114] In the wake of France's rejection of Britain's application in 1963, West Germany had also promoted the idea of holding perpetual EEC consultations with all potential applicants. This had prompted Hugh McCann, secretary to the Irish department of external affairs, to consider some form of Irish 'external association' with the EEC, essentially as an interim arrangement, but London strongly discouraged this idea. Meanwhile, Denis McDonald, Ireland's most significant ambassador on the continent (he served as Ireland's ambassador to France and subsequently to Italy), realised that the most critical task facing the Irish government with regards to the EEC was to learn how to understand and adapt to France's priorities.[115]

Ireland's dependence on the food industry had always inherently limited its economic relevance to Europe and particularly France. Beef exports to West Germany, which had recently grown fourfold to £5 million a year, constituted Ireland's largest single European market. This trade, however, operated purely by means of British transport companies. Indeed, the Anglo-Irish free trade agreement of 1965 was

Michael MacWhite (left) with Frank Kellogg, US secretary of state (1929). Initially the chief Irish republican propagandist on the European continent (1919–21), MacWhite served as the Irish Free State's representative at the League of Nations (1923–9) and minister to the United States (1929–38), before his final posting as Éire's minister to Italy (1938–50).

Éamon de Valera's re-election in 1932, after Britain controversially defaulted on its debt repayments to the United States, enhanced his international profile, as did his subsequent chairing of meetings of the League of Nations at Geneva.

The formation of Aer Lingus (1936) and creation of Dublin Airport (1941) helped to compensate for a major weakness in the Irish state's international identity: underdeveloped Irish shipping.

A new image for Ireland: a detail from a 1938 publication that advertised the Christian-democratic ethos of the new Éire constitution as a link between the Irish state and pacifist opinion right across Europe.

Left to right: Robert Brennan, Sean T. O'Kelly and John Hearne in Washington D.C. just prior to the outbreak of the Second World War. As Ireland's representatives, Brennan and Hearne explained the Irish policy of neutrality during and after the war respectively, while O'Kelly would become the first Irish president to represent that office by means of a state visit.

Frank Aiken (right), the first signatory of the important Nuclear Non-Proliferation Treaty (1968), was an outspoken champion at the United Nations of the idea of a Middle East peace process from the late-1950s onwards.

US President John Fitzgerald Kennedy was the first significant head of state to make a state visit to Ireland (1963). Kennedy spoke before the Dáil, laid a wreath in memory of Ireland's 1916 rebels at Arbour Hill, and is seen here decorating a monument in Wexford to John Barry, an Irish-born founder of the US navy.

The National Monument on Merrion Square, Dublin, commemorates all Irish soldiers who have been killed on UN peacekeeping missions abroad since 1958.

Garret FitzGerald (left), who was Ireland's first president of the European Council, introducing Taoiseach Liam Cosgrave to US President Gerald Ford and US Secretary of State Henry Kissinger (right) at the White House (1976).

Peter Sutherland (centre), a former Irish attorney general and future director-general of the World Trade Organisation, was at the heart of Ireland's European policy and greater orientation towards international financial markets from the mid-1980s onwards. He is seen here listening to Lawrence Summers, then deputy secretary of the US treasury, at a World Economic Forum.

Irish foreign minister Dick Spring (right) meeting the new US president Bill Clinton for the first time (1993) while Noel Dorr looks on in the background. Clinton later typified his decision to appoint a special peace envoy to Northern Ireland as being motivated by his sense that Ulster and the Balkans were the two trouble spots in the greater European project of political and economic integration.

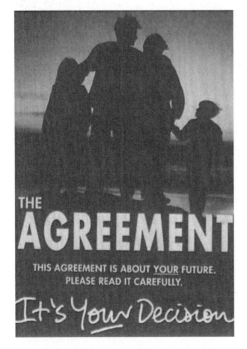

Registered at the UN with the British and Irish governments as its co-guarantors, the Good Friday Agreement of 1998 was nevertheless based on the principle that the future of Northern Ireland must be entirely the decision of its own inhabitants.

Left to right: Chris Patten (EU commissioner for external relations), Brian Cowen (Irish foreign minister), Colin Powell (US secretary of state) and Javier Solana (EU high representative for foreign policy) in Washington for a new US–EU ministerial summit (March 2004).

A second such summit, attended by Romano Prodi (, Commission) and George Bush (US president), was held recognition of Taoiseach Bertie Ahern's (right) chairing (during which nine new entrants were admitted into the 1

In te
Europe
(1961–3),
here seen se
involvement in
Irish soldiers hav

Mary Robinson (left), a former Irish president and UN commissioner for human rights, meeting with an aid worker from Trócaire (2011), an Irish non-governmental organisation founded in 1973. Greater participation by Ireland in African developmental aid programmes has been expected at the UN to be a prominent feature of Ireland's foreign policy ever since 1968.

rms of manpower, Ireland has made one of the highest contributions in to UN peacekeeping but, after its initial battle experience in the Congo Ireland has usually avoided sending combat troops. Irish troops are ving on a UN mission in East Timor (2001) but its most consistent UN peacekeeping has remained in Lebanon, where almost fifty been killed.

partly designed to enable the transfer of Irish food produce to the European continent via British transportation. Coming ten years after the introduction of the now-forgotten Irish Mercantile Marine Act (Irish Shipping had been reduced to only a nominal existence),[116] this type of co-dependent Irish behaviour did not impress European governments. The resulting boost in Anglo-Irish trade also served to weaken a German–Irish Trade Association that had been established during 1964 to promote trade in manufactured goods (totalling £2.5 million a year). Meanwhile, as France, like the United States, was an entirely self-sufficient country in the food industry, Irish exports and total trade with France remained extremely small (£24,000).[117] Therefore, the French business community was not inclined to believe that Ireland was economically fit for EEC membership. Knowing this, Irish semi-state companies such as Córas Tráchtála and the IDA responded by opening Parisian offices during the 1960s. However, the Irish department of industry and commerce actually encouraged European traders to deal with Ireland only 'as a negligible appendix of their trade with Britain', and this dissuaded French businesses from dealing with the individual Irish trade agents that had been sent to Paris by Córas Tráchtála and the IDA.[118] Even prior to the Anglo-Irish free trade agreement of 1965, Ireland had decided to grant preferential treatment to imports from the United Kingdom, but the EEC was in favour of Ireland abandoning this preferential system should it become a member.[119]

In contrast to the sorry state of Irish–French trade relations, on a purely diplomatic level France had some interest in Ireland. Although he viewed Lemass to be a spineless puppet of Britain, President Charles de Gaulle admired Aiken and de Valera's moral integrity and considered that Ireland could be a good diplomatic ally of France, even though France was not entirely convinced that Ireland's professed willingness to allow US planes to land at Shannon Airport was a genuine expression of Ireland's commitment to western Europe's defence.[120] When a French foreign minister visited Ireland for the first time in 1964, he purposely dealt with Aiken and de Valera rather than Lemass. Upon the latter's retirement, de Gaulle, who had some Irish ancestors and even considered retiring to Ireland, reaffirmed that France had 'no major difficulty with Ireland's joining the Community' even as he vetoed British membership of the EEC for a second time. During 1967, the French foreign minister told Haughey on a visit to Dublin that whenever France had told Whitehall that Britain's potential terms of admission to the EEC must be equal and offer no greater privileges to those on offer to Ireland, Britain had reacted with great anger, deeming this idea to be 'an insult'.[121] It is likely that this French observation was partly affectation to curry Ireland's favour, however, because France's neighbouring Benelux countries evidently had an astute understanding of British priorities, including with regards to Ireland.

In Holland, the press often adopted a British view of Ireland (which was also popular in Anglophile America) of having a very unfavourable attitude towards all things Irish except for its literature.[122] More significantly, the Dutch considered the Belgian statesman Paul-Henri Spaak, certainly not the French, to be the true architect and the practical leader of the European community. Reflecting the Benelux countries' close economic relationship with Britain, both the Dutch and Belgians had purposively made state visits to Northern Ireland during the 1950s at the request of Sir Basil Brooke whilst ignoring the existence of the Republic of Ireland entirely. During the 1960s, they accepted the view that the British and Irish cases regarding the EEC were inherently one and, therefore, encouraged the Irish government to follow Britain's lead.[123] Like Britain, the Benelux countries had a healthy banking relationship with the United States and viewed British entry into the EEC as a means to combat French and West German power over the EEC. As an extension of this position, the British held, as a fixed principle, that Ireland should never be allowed to fall under a Franco-German, as opposed to a British, influence by means of the EEC.[124] Although Belgium deeply resented Ireland's role during the UN Congo crisis, it did not view its negative attitude to Irish EEC applications as an extension of this stance. Instead, Belgium judged its attitude to be rooted entirely in the reality of an 'Atlanticist' politics that Spaak, a founder of the Western European Union (WEU) defence agreement, had fully supported as a means to make Brussels a 'centre of the Atlantic world' and, in turn, allow Belgium to punch above its weight through supranational forums. A means to this end was to make Britain a bridge between the United States and western Europe through the operations of the banking institutions of Amsterdam and the Hague. Like Brussels and London, these had been sympathetic towards Britain's unsuccessful European Free Trade Area initiative involving Scandinavia.[125]

Ireland imported £3 million of goods (fertiliser and metals) from Belgium annually but exported only £800,000 of goods (cattle and horses). This Irish dependence on a livestock trade was judged by Belgium to be proof that Ireland was unfit for EEC membership. Belgium also judged that Ireland's professed interest in an eventual reunification of Ireland was inherently nonsense. The fact that 75 per cent of Irish exports still went to Britain ensured that 'England is holding Éire in its hand' at Dublin's own request, and that any divergence from British economic plans for Ireland would be tantamount to 'suicide' for the southern Irish state. During 1960, a Belgian intelligence source even claimed that 'Dublin proposed to London to transfer its imports from the Continent to Great Britain in case an Anglo-Irish economic entity was created' to supercede the existence of the Irish state entirely.[126] Even though a Belgian king did make a first official visit to Ireland in May 1968, this train of thought made the Belgians very dismissive of both Ireland and Irish politicians.[127] The root of its 1960 intelligence claim was evidently the fact that T.K. Whitaker had proposed during 1960 that Ireland must join Britain's European Free Trade Association if it was to retain a preferential access to British markets. The Irish decision not to sign up to the evolving General Agreement on Tariffs and Trade until after an Anglo-Irish free trade agreement was first reached in 1965 was motivated by the same consideration.[128]

At the outset of 1968, the EEC had planned to launch a massive propaganda campaign to entice all potential applicants for membership. This initiative was quickly halted, however, because of widespread internal disturbances that also had foreign policy implications.[129] A growing tradition of intelligence cooperation between the United States and all the British Commonwealth countries, first launched in 1946, did not prevent many countries from receiving mixed signals during 1968. Most notably, the liberal side of international academia, with some encouragement from sections of the international press, shook the republican certainties of life in France and America as student protestors, allegedly seeking 'an elusive third way between capitalism and communism', effectively turned de Gaulle from a figure of national pride into one of ridicule (he would soon be forced to retire), while major student protests against the American army in the United States coincided with the assassinations of presidential candidate Robert Kennedy (brother of John F. Kennedy) and civil rights leader Martin Luther King.[130] Britain had just decided to amalgamate its former dominions and commonwealth office with its foreign office so that its commonwealth could respond as a unified voice to a programme of 'global [economic] partnership' that *International Organization* had just announced as the diplomatic strategy of the future.[131] Reflecting Ireland's vulnerability, conterminous adjustments in international monetary markets would cause Ireland's relative economic boom between 1962 and 1967 to reverse dramatically.

Having attained a healthy balance of payments surplus of £10 million at the outset of 1967, during 1968 Ireland's balance of payments slid out of control to a deficit of £22 million that would grow to a 'very worrying' £55 million deficit in 1969.[132] This led to T.K. Whitaker, a firm believer in concentrating exclusively on London's financial markets to ensure Irish financial stability, being appointed as the new governor of the Central Bank of Ireland, but deficits continued to grow, leading to ever-rising government borrowing.[133] Meanwhile, violent street protest politics had erupted in Northern Ireland. Attacks upon civil rights marchers in Derry during October 1968 prompted Taoiseach Jack Lynch to request that London take some preventative actions, but this action evoked fierce protests that Dublin had no right to speak about purely internal United Kingdom affairs. On his return from Honolulu and the Irish consulate in San Francisco, where he had examined the possibility of Irish participation in Pacific trade, Lynch naively suggested that harmonious north–south relations, based on mutual understanding, should be possible to attain during 1968 in what was widely being called a year for championing human rights. However, the new Northern Ireland premier Brian Faulkner immediately typified Lynch's remark as an intolerable criticism of the integrity of British civics and, in turn, called for a cessation of all political communications with Dublin.[134] Acting on the advice of London financiers, some in Belfast were growing convinced that the future presented no middle ground between complete dependence on London or absorption into an Irish republic. Reflecting this, by the winter of 1968–9 London had decided to send more British army troops into Ulster and to restore direct rule over Northern Ireland, in the process disbanding the Stormont assembly and removing the anomalous position that had existed since the 1920s whereby Ulster uniquely had a devolved parliamentary assembly within a United Kingdom political system that was not actually devolved.[135]

Historian Michael Kennedy has judged that the Irish government was in no sense prepared for the great disruption in Anglo-Irish relations after the outbreak of the Troubles in Northern Ireland during the summer of 1969, not least because – in a necessary deference to Stormont's protocols – it essentially had no policy regarding Northern Ireland hitherto, a fact that many northern nationalists had always lamented.[136] Complacent Irish attitudes at the time were perhaps best reflected by the publication of a book by a Scottish academic in which retired Irish diplomats, foreign correspondents, economists and directors of Irish tourist and airline companies presented a seemingly entirely positive, prosperous and peaceful vision of Ireland's future.[137] One reason for this expectation of a lasting peace was that ever since John F. Kennedy's treaty banning nuclear bomb testing had been signed by the US, the USSR and the UK in August 1963, it was widely perceived that a period of détente was emerging in cold war politics. Aiken's consistent support for restricting the spread of nuclear weapons had been entirely in keeping with this trend. In recognition of this, Aiken was asked to be the first signatory of the subsequent Non-Proliferation Treaty. This was signed in Moscow in July 1968 and would be widely considered as having initiated a process that 'converted the acquisition of nuclear weapons by a state from an act of national pride in 1960 to an act contrary to international law in 1974'.[138] This also potentially meant that arms races could henceforth be only a source of UN criticism. In general, the Irish public welcomed this development as much as the rest of the international community. However, it actually attracted less attention nationally during 1968 than a mixed public reaction to the fact that Aiken also supported Paul Keating, Ireland's only African ambassador, when he sided with the Nigerian government against Biafra rebels that had received sympathy from Irish missionaries who were promptly expelled from Nigeria.[139] This evoked a debate on the relative merits of state and voluntary aid, while it also saw an expansion in the number of religious voluntary bodies in Ireland that desired to aid the victims of famine in Biafra.[140]

Uncertainty regarding the future political direction of Ireland had created a fairly vibrant national debate at the time of the Irish government's fiftieth-anniversary celebrations of the 1916 Rising. However, this debate also produced some surprising consequences. For example, reversing his former stance as an Irish spokesman, Conor Cruise O'Brien stated that he now regretted ever having served an Irish government and he began identifying himself from New York University as an ideological Marxist in criticism of Ireland's alleged subservience to US foreign policy.[141] Meanwhile, Irish national pride in the Defence Forces' role in the Congo during the early 1960s had not led to any significant improvement in the army's fortunes. The Defence Forces was so deprived of resources that most of its weaponry was, by now, over twenty years out of date, while Irish defence budgets frequently extended no further than a bare minimum to facilitate the perpetual survival of a permanent reserve force (Fórsa Cosanta Áitiúil, or FCA). This trend perhaps reflected the fact that Ireland's post-1964 UN peacekeeping mission in Cyprus, where 9,000 members of the Defence Forces would serve up until 1974, involved purely unarmed policing responsibilities. In the light of the national policy of the army being expected to serve only as an aide to the civil power of the Irish police, its capacity to handle more difficult missions was certainly open to question. In this sense, Ireland's non-participation in NATO was partly an extension of its own peculiarly limited national defence policy.[142]

Reflecting on Irish diplomacy in general since the 1920s, Michael Kennedy has judged that although Ireland's 'fear of empires and encumbering alliance led it to follow a very singular stance which did bring with it international recognition' at the UN, 'the great secrecy with which Irish foreign policy was conducted' had only served to create a situation whereby 'meaningful debate was stultified' and 'public opinion was often indifferent'. Therefore, 'Irish foreign policy showed a mixed balance sheet overall', and it was not until fresh approaches were taken during the 1970s that 'the lacklustre approach of the previous fifty years' would begin to be acknowledged by Irish governments.[143] Although he had practically retired from public speaking in 1966, Éamon de Valera (who ultimately died in 1975 at the age of ninety-three) remained the Irish president up until 1973. After 1969, in witnessing what he described as 'these terrible times', he would occasionally counsel Irish government ministers to follow his old dictum that solutions to difficulties in Anglo-Irish relations, stemming not least from the Northern Ireland situation, were not to be found by throwing everything back into a melting pot.[144] This was precisely what Irish government ministers were generally encouraged to do, however, because of London and Belfast's insistence that returning peace to Northern Ireland, as well as avoiding resulting instability across the entire island, was somehow entirely dependent on Dublin's compliance with their will.[145] It is hardly surprising, therefore, that Irish diplomacy during the 1970s would often be characterised by a sense of crisis management, responding to outside developments over which it had no control but that seemed to threaten the very integrity of the state. The growing European dimension to Irish politics essentially became the vehicle that allowed Ireland to adapt to the new global partnership strategy that would characterise the post-1968 international order. Reflecting this, a Belfast scholar would judge that not until its first presidency of the European Council in 1975 did Ireland find proper channels for its diplomacy – far removed from the 'acrimony and claustrophobia' that had always characterised Anglo-Irish relations – that could allow it to assume a balanced international role for the first time.[146] Be that as it may, the ebb and flow of the Northern Troubles usually made it seem necessary for the Irish government to prioritise instead its respective bilateral relations with Britain and the United States if it was to find the political equilibrium that it both needed and desired.

Endnotes

1   B.A. McKenzie, 'The European Youth Campaign in Ireland: neutrality, Americanisation and the Cold War 1950 to 1959', *Diplomatic history*, vol. 40 no. 3 (2016), 421–44.

2   Ronan Fanning, *The Irish department of finance 1922–1958* (Dublin, 1978), 626.

3   Michael Kennedy, Deirdre McMahon (eds), *Obligations and responsibilities: Ireland and the United Nations 1955–2005* (Dublin, 2005), 51.

4   Michael Kennedy, Deirdre McMahon (eds), *Obligations and responsibilities*, 31, 35, 37, 42, 46–7.

5   L.W. White, 'Patrick Lynch (1917–2001)', *Dictionary of Irish biography* (Cambridge, 2009).

6   T. K. Whitaker, 'Timothy O'Driscoll (1908–98)', *Dictionary of Irish biography* (Cambridge, 2009).

7   Tom Feeney, 'Gerard Sweetman (1908–70)', *Dictionary of Irish biography* (Cambridge, 2009); Shaun Boylan, 'Michael Sweetman (1935–72)', *Dictionary of Irish biography* (Cambridge, 2009).

8 The diplomatic tradition of conceiving of the world purely in terms of the economic output levels of regions was associated with a 'global partnership' system launched in 1968. It could well be dated, however, to the creation of the World Bank Group during 1960 and the subsequent development of regional development policies at the UN. Roy Blough, 'The World Bank Group', *International organization*, vol. 22 no. 1 (winter 1968), 152–81; Michael Brauninger, Henning Vopel, 'Globalisation, trade and growth: a macroeconomic perspective', *Intereconomics* (May–June 2009) 185–92.

9 Cremin succeeded two old republicans (Sean Nunan and Sean Murphy) who had acted in an essentially caretaker role as departmental secretaries since 1951.

10 Niall Keogh, *Con Cremin: Ireland's wartime diplomat* (Cork, 2006), chapters 6–8.

11 Michael Kennedy, 'Hugh McCann (1916–86)', *Dictionary of Irish biography* (Cambridge, 2009).

12 M. Kennedy, D. McMahon (eds), *Obligations and responsibilities*, 9 (quote), 28–31, 47–51.

13 Bryce Evans, Stephen Kelly (eds), *Frank Aiken: nationalist and internationalist* (Dublin, 2014).

14 Patrick Lynch, 'The economic scene', in O.D. Edwards (ed.), *Conor Cruise O'Brien introduces Ireland* (London, 1969), 78. This idea did much to revive interest in the writings of James Connolly in Ireland during the 1960s, with even Lynch typifying him as a 'great revolutionary Marxist'. Ibid., 76.

15 Jean-Jacques Servan-Schreiber, *The American challenge* (1st English translation, London, 1968), 164. The author was a key figure in shaping French foreign policy during the 1950s and 1960s.

16 Peter Murray, *Facilitating the future?: US aid, European integration and Irish industrial viability 1948–1973* (Dublin, 2009), 196.

17 C.C. O'Brien, 'Ireland in international affairs', in O.D. Edwards (ed.), *Conor Cruise O'Brien introduces Ireland* (London, 1968), 129–34; J.M. Skelly, *Irish diplomacy at the United Nations* (Dublin, 1997), 19–20.

18 Frank Callanan, 'Conor Cruise O'Brien (1917–2008)', *Dictionary of Irish biography* (Cambridge, 2009); Eamon Delaney, *An accidental diplomat* (Dublin, 2001), 15.

19 Michael Kennedy, Deirdre McMahon (eds), *Obligations and responsibilities*, 54–6.

20 Ibid., 16, 18–19, 21, 23 (quote).

21 Edward Kennedy, 'The Persian Gulf: arms race or arms control?', *Foreign affairs*, vol. 54 no. 1 (Oct. 1975).

22 C.C. O'Brien, *Writers and politics* (London, 1965).

23 Pia Phiri, 'UNHCR, international refugee protection and Ireland', in U. Fraser, C. Harvey (eds), *Sanctuary in Ireland* (Dublin, 2003), 115.

24 The rabbi in question was Isaac Herzog.

25 Dermot Keogh, 'Making Aliya: Irish Jews, the Irish state and Israel', in D. Keogh, F. O'Shea, C. Quinlan (ed.), *Ireland in the 1950s: the lost decade* (Cork, 2001), 252–72. Irish-Jewish emigrants to Israel would form an Israel–Ireland Friendship League in 1969, five years before diplomatic relations formally began. However, the first Israeli embassy was not established in Dublin until 1993, while Irish diplomatic representatives to Israel were non-residents of Israel up until 1996.

26 Some Irish government ministers, including Sean Lemass, joined the Knights of St Columbanus, a lay Catholic fraternal organisation that concentrated on rivalling the established role that the freemasons played as a lay Protestant fraternal organisation

specifically within the Irish business world. David Dickson, *Dublin* (London, 2014), 490.

27 D. Keogh, F. O'Shea, C. Quinlan (ed.), *Ireland in the 1950s: the lost decade* (Cork, 2001), 273–4.

28 Eamon Delaney, *An accidental diplomat* (Dublin, 2001), 23.

29 Michael Kennedy, 'Irish foreign policy 1919–1973', in Thomas Bartlett (ed.) *Cambridge history of Ireland*, vol. 4 (Cambridge, 2017), 604–5.

30 Mick McCarthy, *International affairs at home: the story of the Irish Institute of International Affairs* (Dublin, 2006), 88–132, esp. 104–5. The former ILO official who revived the society as the International Affairs Association was Ron Mortished.

31 See, for example, Catholic Association for International Peace, *A Catholic program for world peace* (Washington D.C., 1930), which also includes a list of associated books from that period.

32 Mick McCarthy, *International affairs at home: the story of the Irish Institute of International Affairs* (Dublin, 2006), 145–8, 192–8, 226–39.

33 O.D. Edwards (ed.), *Conor Cruise O'Brien introduces Ireland* (London, 1968), quote p. 129.

34 Michael Kennedy, Deirdre McMahon (eds), *Obligations and responsibilities*, 183–6, 237–8.

35 Later, in 1981, Ireland's Declan O'Donovan chaired the UN committee on human rights that introduced a declaration against intolerance of religions.

36 Michael Kennedy, Deirdre McMahon (eds), *Obligations and responsibilities*, 60.

37 Department of foreign affairs and trade, *Celebrating sixty-years: Ireland–Japan diplomatic relations* (Dublin, 2017), 9–11.

38 J.P. Duggan, *A history of the Irish army* (Dublin, 1991), 236–42, 249 (quote).

39 Ibid., 250–8, 276; Frank Callanan, 'Conor Cruise O'Brien (1917–2008)', *Dictionary of Irish biography* (Cambridge, 2009).

40 F.H. Hinsley, *Power and the pursuit of peace: theory and practice in the history of relations between states* (Cambridge, 1963), 344–5.

41 C.C. O'Brien, *Writers and politics* (London, 1965), 245–6.

42 F.H. Hinsley, *Power and the pursuit of peace: theory and practice in the history of relations between states* (Cambridge, 1963), 340.

43 De Valera's speeches at Geneva between 1932 and 1938 were published as Éamon de Valera, *War and Peace* (Dublin, 1944). After his retirement, a former secretary to the department of the Taoiseach, Maurice Moynihan, produced *Speeches and statements of Éamon de Valera 1917–1973* (Dublin, 1980).

44 Ronan Fanning, 'Francis Thomas Aiken (1898–1983)', *Dictionary of Irish biography* (Cambridge, 2009).

45 Michael Kennedy, 'Irish foreign policy 1919–1973', in Thomas Bartlett (ed.), *Cambridge history of Ireland*, vol. 4 (Cambridge, 2017), 604–5, ft. 4 (quote).

46 Alvin Jackson, 'Ireland, the Union and the Empire 1800–1960', in Kevin Kenny (ed.), *Ireland and the British Empire* (Oxford, 2004), 123–53; Alvin Jackson, 'Unionism and the future of the Union', in Robert Savage (ed.), *Ireland in the new century* (Dublin, 2003), 43–66.

47 Ronan Fanning, 'Small states, large neighbours: Ireland and the United Kingdom', *Irish studies in international affairs*, vol. 9 (1998), 21–9.

48 Ronan Fanning, *Éamon de Valera: a will to power* (London, 2015), 186, 189, 225, 252–3, 268.

49   Ronan McGreevy, 'The Lemass tapes: a complex relationship', *The Irish Times*, 2 June 2018.

50   David O'Mahony, *The Irish economy* (2nd ed., Cork, 1964), 100; Institute of Bankers in Ireland, *Economic planning and the banking system* (Dublin, 1968), 31.

51   Lionel Smith-Gordon, *The place of banking in the national programme* (Dublin, 1921), 6–7 (quote). Carroll's cigarette company was the chief advertiser in Arthur Griffith's journals *Nationality* and *Young Ireland*, which featured a perpetual large advertisement for Carroll's cigarettes (often with Irish republican slogans encompassed within the advertisement's text), as well as advertisements for the Dublin drapery firm of J.T. Lemass (father of Sean Lemass), beside Griffith's editorials each week.

52   Maurice Moynihan, 'The role of a central bank', in Institute of Bankers in Ireland, *Economic planning and the banking system* (Dublin, 1968), 13–27, especially pp. 16–18.

53   L.P. Thompson McCausland, 'Planning in an international monetary system', in Institute of Bankers in Ireland, *Economic planning and the banking system* (Dublin, 1968), 117–29. McCausland, then chief consultant to the British treasury, was formerly the chief advisor to the Bank of England.

54   Samuel Brittan, *The Treasury under the Tories 1951–1964* (London, 1964).

55   Maurice Moynihan, 'The role of a central bank', in Institute of Bankers in Ireland, *Economic planning and the banking system* (Dublin, 1968), 21–2, 23 (quote), 26.

56   Deirdre McMahon, 'Maurice Moynihan (1902–99)', *Dictionary of Irish biography* (Cambridge, 2009); Shaun Boylan, 'Donal Carroll (1928–2000)', *Dictionary of Irish biography* (Cambridge, 2009).

57   Michael Mulreany (ed.), *Economic development fifty years on 1958–2008* (Dublin, 2009).

58   Anne Chambers, *T.K. Whitaker* (Dublin, 2014), chapters 8–9.

59   Ronan Fanning, 'Playing it cool: the response of the British and Irish governments to the crisis in Northern Ireland 1968–9', *Irish studies in international affairs*, vol. 12 (2001), 57–85, especially pp. 62–4.

60   D.S.A. Carroll, 'The function of an independent commercial banking system', in Institute of Bankers in Ireland, *Economic planning and the banking system* (Dublin, 1968), 29–48.

61   Ibid., 33–7.

62   Ibid., 37.

63   Anne Chambers, *T.K. Whitaker* (Dublin, 2014), 217–9, 227–9.

64   Patrick Lynch, 'The economic scene', in O.D. Edwards (ed.), *Conor Cruise O'Brien introduces Ireland*, 79 (quotes); Brian Girvin, Gary Murphy (ed.), *The Lemass era* (Dublin, 2005), 87.

65   Mervyn O'Driscoll, Dermot Keogh, Jerome aan de Wiel (eds), *Ireland through European eyes: western Europe, the EEC and Ireland 1945–1973* (Cork, 2013), 270–81.

66   Brian Girvin, Gary Murphy (ed.), *The Lemass era* (Dublin, 2005), 191–214, especially pp. 207–14.

67   *Documents on Irish foreign policy*, vol. 10 nos 326, 339–41, 366. From 1927 up until 1949, American diplomatic representatives in Ireland had been known as 'envoy extraordinary and ministerial plenipotentiary', which is a rank below ambassador. After 1950, they were known as ambassadors although their official title was actually 'ambassador extraordinary and plenipotentiary'.

68   Brian Girvin, Gary Murphy (ed.), *The Lemass era* (Dublin, 2005), 166–90.

69 G.C. Herring, *From colony to superpower: US foreign relations since 1776* (Oxford, 2008), 597.

70 Jeffrey D. Sachs, *To move the world: JFK's quest for peace* (London, 2013).

71 This was also the context of Joseph McCarthy's politics. G.C. Herring, *From colony to superpower*, 635–7, 642, 654–5.

72 G.C. Herring, *From colony to superpower*, 703–29, quote p. 729.

73 Jeffrey Sachs, *To move the world: JFK's quest for peace* (London, 2013), 180–9.

74 Jeffrey Sachs, *To move the world: JFK's quest for peace* (London, 2013), 200–10.

75 Maurice Moynihan (ed.), *Speeches and statements of Éamon de Valera 1917–1973* (Dublin, 1980), 599–602, quote p. 601.

76 Brian Girvin, Gary Murphy (ed.), *The Lemass era* (Dublin, 2005), 88–9.

77 *Time*, 12 July 1963.

78 Ronan McGreevy, 'Lemass tapes made public', interview on 'Today with Sean O'Rourke', RTÉ Radio One, 4 June 2018.

79 Bryce Evans, Stephen Kelly (eds), *Frank Aiken: nationalist and internationalist* (Dublin, 2014), 33–7, 252.

80 During 1957 Aiken suggested that there should be military disengagement from central Europe and the Middle East. During 1961, he criticised apartheid in South Africa and expressed support for self-determination for Algeria. Michael Kennedy, 'Irish foreign policy 1919–73', in T. Bartlett (ed.), *Cambridge history of Ireland*, vol. 4 (Cambridge, 2018), 629.

81 G.C. Herring, *From colony to superpower*, 711–15.

82 *International organization: the global partnership*, vol. 22 no. 1 (winter 1968).

83 O.D. Edwards (ed.), *Conor Cruise O'Brien introduces Ireland* (London, 1968), 129, 133–4.

84 Michael Kennedy, 'Frederick Boland (1904–85)', *Dictionary of Irish biography* (Cambridge, 2009). For the remainder of the decade, Ireland's representative at the UN was Denis Holmes, later Ireland's ambassador to India, and subsequently Con Cremin.

85 Mervyn O'Driscoll, Dermot Keogh, Jerome aan de Wiel (eds), *Ireland through European eyes: western Europe, the EEC and Ireland 1945–1973* (Cork, 2013).

86 Institute of Bankers in Ireland, *Economic planning and the banking system* (Dublin, 1968), 14, 33.

87 B. Girvin, G. Murphy (eds), *The Lemass era* (Dublin, 2005), 28.

88 Maurice Moynihan (ed.), *Speeches and statements of Éamon de Valera*, 576–7.

89 Patrick Hillery, 'Negotiating Ireland's entry', in J. Dooge, R. Barrington (eds), *A vital national interest: Ireland in Europe 1973–1998* (Dublin, 1999), 18–19.

90 'The Lemass tapes: gospel according to Lemass', *The Irish Times*, 2 June 2018.

91 Graeme Moodie, *The government of Great Britain* (London, 1964), 177–8, 181–5.

92 Patrick O'Farrell, *The Irish in Australia* (Kensington, 1987), 305–6.

93 The key legislation in this regard was the Canada Act of 1982 and the Australia Act of 1986.

94 Brian MacArthur (ed.), *The Penguin book of twentieth-century speeches* (London, 1999), 286–91.

95 D.P. McCracken (ed.), *Ireland and South Africa in modern times* (Johannesburg, 1996), 36–7. This book was also volume three of a journal entitled *South African–Irish Studies*. An Irish anti-apartheid movement was first established in 1964.

96   Graeme Moodie, *The government of Great Britain* (London, 1964), 181–5 (quotes p. 183).

97   Michael Kennedy, *Division and consensus: the politics of cross-border relations 1925–1969* (Dublin, 2000), 260. Aer Lingus would open a Belfast office in 1967.

98   Ronan McGreevy, 'The Lemass tapes: meeting with O'Neill met stiff opposition', *The Irish Times*, 2 June 2018.

99   C.J. Haughey, 'The scope of economic planning', in Institute of Bankers in Ireland, *Economic planning and the banking system* (Dublin, 1968), 1–12 (quote p. 1).

100   E. Sherman Adams, 'Effects of public policies on commercial banking', in Institute of Bankers in Ireland, *Economic planning and the banking system* (Dublin, 1968), 129–44 (quote p. 130).

101   Mervyn O'Driscoll, Dermot Keogh, Jerome aan de Wiel (eds), *Ireland through European eyes*, 115–18.

102   L.N. Piers, 'Transatlantic relations in the Johnson and Nixon eras', *London School of Economics research online* (2010).

103   J.R. Lambert, 'Enlargement of the Common Market: Denmark, Norway and Ireland', *The world today*, vol. 18 no. 8 (Aug. 1962), 350–60 (quote pp. 353–4).

104   K.A. Kennedy, T. Giblin, D. McHugh (eds), *The economic development of Ireland in the twentieth century* (London, 1988), 101–102.

105   Emmet O'Connor, 'Division and consensus' (book review), *Irish political studies*, vol. 15 no. 1 (2000), 235.

106   Noel Dorr, *Sunningdale: the search for peace in Northern Ireland* (Dublin, 2017), chapter 1.

107   Michael Kennedy, *Division and consensus: the politics of cross-border relations 1925–69* (Dublin, 2000), 262–71.

108   Ibid., 279–80, 293–9.

109   *The Irish Times*, 15 Nov. 1967, quoted in Terence Brown, *The Irish Times: 150 years of influence*, 261.

110   The next visit was by Charles Haughey in April 1990. O'Neill did visit Dublin once more, in January 1968. Michael Kennedy, *Division and consensus*, 301, 303, 367.

111   Miriam Hederman O'Brien, 'The role of the European movement', in J. Dooge, R. Barrington (eds), *A vital national interest: Ireland in Europe 1973-1998* (Dublin, 1999), 5–7.

112   D.J. Maher, *The tortuous path: the course of Ireland's entry into the EEC 1948-73* (Dublin, 1986), 235–6.

113   Mervyn O'Driscoll, Dermot Keogh, Jerome aan de Wiel (eds), *Ireland through European eyes: western Europe, the EEC and Ireland 1945-1973* (Cork, 2013), quote p. 152.

114   Ibid., 49, 149–54, 177.

115   Ibid., 165–7, 172–3, 178–9.

116   Irish Shipping Ltd., first established in 1939, had fallen into disrepair by the 1960s, although it did not ultimately collapse until 1984. Brian Fitzgerald, 'Ireland – an islander's perspective', *Defence Forces review* (2016), 192.

117   Mervyn O'Driscoll, Dermot Keogh, Jerome aan de Wiel (eds), *Ireland through European eyes*, 53–5, 98–9, 110–11.

118   Ibid., 110–11.

119   J.R. Lambert, 'Enlargement of the Common Market: Denmark, Norway and Ireland', *The world today*, vol. 18 no. 8 (Aug. 1962), 358.

120 Mervyn O'Driscoll, Dermot Keogh, Jerome aan de Wiel (eds), *Ireland through European eyes*, 100–9 (quote p. 106).

121 Ibid., 109–19 (quotes p. 115, 116, 118). De Gaulle paid a month-long non-diplomatic visit to Ireland during 1969 in the wake of his retirement as French president. He died the following year at the age of seventy-nine.

122 Ibid., 217–30 (quote p. 221). Holland had its own branch of the Orange Order, while its press often maintained that Ireland had made no contribution to the world except for creating 'a couple of million narrow-minded emigrants'.

123 Ibid., 228–9, 234–41, 278–9. A Dutch agriculture minister was alone in dissenting from this view, suggesting that Ireland could be suited for membership of the Common Market regardless. Although a Dutch shipbuilding firm was established in Cork in 1962, the IDA was not receptive to Dutch business.

124 J.W. Young, *Britain and European unity 1945–1999* (2nd ed., London, 2000), 188.

125 Mervyn O'Driscoll, Dermot Keogh, Jerome aan de Wiel (eds), *Ireland through European eyes*, 270, 277.

126 Ibid., 270–81, quotes p. 271, 272.

127 Ibid., 277–9.

128 Frank Barry, 'Trade, investment, integration: the economics of Irish foreign policy', in B. Tonra, M. Kennedy, J. Doyle, N. Dorr (eds), *Irish foreign policy* (Dublin, 2012), 185–6.

129 Mervyn O'Driscoll, Dermot Keogh, Jerome aan de Wiel (eds), *Ireland through European eyes*, 241–2.

130 G.C. Herring, *From colony to superpower: US foreign relations since 1776* (Oxford, 2008), 751.

131 *International organization*, vol. 21, no. 1 (1968).

132 Mervyn O'Driscoll, Dermot Keogh, Jerome aan de Wiel (eds), *Ireland through European eyes*, 59.

133 Anne Chambers, *T.K. Whitaker* (Dublin, 2014), 221–4.

134 Michael Kennedy, *Division and consensus*, 308–11.

135 Ronan Fanning, 'Playing it cool: the response of the British and Irish governments to the crisis in Northern Ireland 1968–9', *Irish studies in international affairs*, vol. 12 (2001), 57–85, especially pp. 62–4.

136 Michael Kennedy, 'This tragic and most intractable problem: the reaction of the department of external affairs to the outbreak of the troubles in Northern Ireland', *Irish studies in international affairs*, vol. 12 (2001), 87–95; Michael Kennedy, *Division and consensus*.

137 This was *Conor Cruise O'Brien introduces Ireland*, published by Andre Deutsch Ltd, and edited by Owen Dudley Edwards, a Scottish academic who had served as American correspondent of *The Irish Times* between 1959 and 1965 and, like O'Brien himself, had also been a lecturer in American universities. The full list of personnel who assisted in the production of this book, which had a red-haired Irish fashion model on its front cover, can be found in its introduction.

138 Jeffrey Sachs, *To move the world*, 127, 139–43 (quote p. 141).

139 Michael Kennedy, 'Paul Keating (1924–80)', *Dictionary of Irish biography* (Cambridge, 2009); Ronan Fanning, 'Francis Thomas Aiken (1898–1983)', *Dictionary of Irish biography* (Cambridge, 2009).

140 T. Bartlett (ed.), *Cambridge history of Ireland*, vol. 4 (Cambridge, 2018), 634. Africa Concern (later Concern Worldwide) was established in Dublin in response to the

Nigerian civil war. Gorta, an Irish organisation for distributing food in Africa, was founded in 1965 in response to the situation in Tanzania and subsequently Nigeria. Irish medical missionary work in Africa was a feature of the 1969 documentary *The flying doctors of East Africa* by maverick German film director Werner Herzog.

141 Frank Callanan, 'Conor Cruise O'Brien (1917–2008)', *Dictionary of Irish biography* (Cambridge, 2009); O.D. Edwards (ed.), *Conor Cruise O'Brien introduces Ireland* (London, 1968), 129, 133–4.

142 Patrick Keatinge, *A singular stance* (Dublin, 1984).

143 Michael Kennedy, 'Irish foreign policy 1919–1973', T. Bartlett (ed.), *Cambridge history of Ireland*, vol. 4 (Cambridge, 2018), 630–1, 637–8 (quotes).

144 Ronan Fanning, *A will to power: Éamon de Valera* (London, 2015), 256–7.

145 Noel Dorr, *Sunningdale: the search for peace in Northern Ireland* (Dublin, 2017).

146 E.M. Browne, 'Ireland in the EEC', *The world today*, vol. 31, no. 10 (Oct. 1975), 424–32, quote p. 431.

6

Small Worlds: Globalisation, the Northern Question and Irish Crisis Diplomacy, 1968–1982

The 'global partnership' system was a reaction to the fact that the value of the UN as a forum for multilateral diplomacy was considered to have declined significantly. Hitherto, the UN had been used for both national statements of intent by 'Third World' powers and, reflecting J.F. Kennedy's naïve rhetoric, the expression of fanciful notions of a world security system that would override the prerogatives of the great powers. An alternative system was deemed necessary to undo these trends. The envisioned global partnership involved a division of the world into a multitude of regions and was designed to regulate the relationship between great and small powers on every continent through stimulating joint commitments between donors and recipients of developmental aid, in turn making the donors the effective moulders of the international order. Spokesmen for the great powers believed that this programme, sponsored by the UN, would consummate the 'burgeoning efforts of the last twenty-five years to organise world society' by promoting genuine concern for less well-developed regions in a manner that would be acceptable to all. This trend was not universally welcomed. In America, the war in Vietnam did much to raise doubts regarding the viability of all foreign aid programmes, which were widely considered to be a continuation of 'the paternalistic and somewhat condescending humanitarianism' evident in both past colonisation ventures and in the ongoing tradition of 'private charitable and missionary activities' in the Far East.[1] By contrast, small European nations such as Ireland tended to view participation in multilateral development aid programmes as a means to occupy a relatively secure place in the international order. Reflecting this, between 1968 and 1975 the Irish state would make an official developmental aid policy a significant aspect of both its diplomatic identity and its exchequer management, in the process meeting an expectation within both the UN and the EEC that Ireland would henceforth play the role of a perpetual northern hemisphere contributor to developmental aid in Africa.[2]

During the Arab–Israeli conflict of 1967, Ireland's status as a small nation with very limited influence was highlighted by the fact that, although Frank Aiken's emphasis upon the Middle Eastern refugee question won him praise from both Arnold Toynbee and US Secretary of State Dean Rusk, Ireland was deemed a moral hypocrite by others for not being a contributor to the UN's refugee fund.[3] Slowly but surely such criticisms of Ireland lessened after 1968, while Ireland's approach to questions of human rights would henceforth be shaped increasingly by the multilateral system implicit in UN development aid programmes. Reflecting its acute poverty for much of the twentieth century, Ireland itself was actually a recipient of aid from the UN Special Fund up until 1961.[4] After 1968, however, it could potentially see itself as occupying a 'middle power' status at the UN through its responsibility of acting as an intermediary between the so-called developed and developing worlds. Hitherto, Irish activists in developmental aid consisted primarily of religious missionaries abroad. Such men and women continued to exercise an influence upon the Irish public's worldview up until the 1980s, but their significant decline in both influence and numbers from the late 1960s onwards was nevertheless a very perceptible trend.[5] After 1973, Trócaire, an organisation of lay volunteers set up by the Catholic Church with a focus upon the 'Third World', often served to highlight cases of the abuse of human rights to Irish diplomatic staff and, in turn, encouraged the Irish department of foreign affairs to take specific actions.[6] If such activities were appreciated in Ireland, however, the attitude of other states towards Ireland would be governed primarily by the degree to which it was judged to be conforming with UN expectations.

On an intellectual level, the global partnership system was justified by international academia in two notable ways. First, economists began treating the notion of a 'global economy' and the questions of individual liberty and welfare as inherently interconnected concepts that were rooted in a common concern for 'happiness'.[7] This effectively revived the old political concept of utilitarianism. Second, sociologists and international relations theorists pioneered a new language of 'transnationalism' and 'soft power' as euphemisms for the supposedly positive effects of the globalisation agenda in creating a more universal sense of values around the same time that the American dollar, having initially set the international gold standard at Bretton Woods in 1944, left the gold standard and adopted a new floating exchange rate system.[8] Profitable 'soft power' tools of persuasion, such as international entertainment industries and the associated youth cultures they promoted, were also used to promote this message of the inherent interdependence of all peoples and the benevolence of multinational corporations.[9] This was done even to the point of promoting internal criticisms of national governments. Notoriously, the student protests of 1968, most notably in Paris, had accepted uncritically a supposed inherent polarity between 'left' and 'right' in both politics and brain functions. This had been typified by French Gaullist republicans as a conspiracy, but the soft power of international academia and the media successfully portrayed them as a purely spontaneous expression of a justly indignant humanity.[10] As a result, both de Gaulle's growing criticisms of the international monetary system and the likelihood that France would drop out of the North Atlantic Treaty Organisation (NATO) before that treaty could be renewed in 1969 were defeated.[11] De Gaulle had also been willing to encourage east–west trade with the USSR by means of a Franco–German partnership in order to heal divisions within Europe and resist economic dependence on the United States, but this led the Americans to turn against their traditional European republican ally and call upon Britain to take the lead in promoting European integration instead.[12] De Gaulle's growing willingness to pursue a policy of détente with Russia had also offended Israel, which now viewed France as having turned from an ally into an enemy in Israel's struggle with the Arab world.[13]

The Russians' obstinance in not joining the International Monetary Fund (IMF) and World Bank federation that underpinned all international trade utilising American dollars was the real basis of both cold war politics and the internal divide within Europe.[14] In Ireland, Haughey's public identification with Rostow rather than de Gaulle intimated Ireland's pro-American priorities, while a growing influence of American academia upon Irish diplomats would be reflected by the emergence of Edward Brennan, a former understudy of American international relations theorist Hans Morgenthau, as a significant figure behind Ireland's EEC negotiations.[15] Like the French and Germans, the Irish government had been open since the 1950s to the idea of instigating more trade with the eastern bloc without necessarily promoting, or taking part in, strategic intelligence wars, which was the favoured option of Britain and the United States.[16] Nevertheless, recent events in Czechoslovakia and elsewhere naturally encouraged Irish government ministers to revive their well-founded belief, which was shared by many central and eastern Europeans, that a naked military imperialism was at the heart of Russian foreign policy. Taoiseach Jack Lynch consciously sought to echo the global partnership rhetoric during 1968 by typifying it as an 'international year of human rights', but he did so while also praising the Ulster civil rights movement, which drew inspiration from the African American movement of Martin Luther King.[17] The opinion of the Northern Ireland parliament of the Ulster civil rights movement was that it was unnecessary and practically seditious in its insulting attitude towards the British state, but Frank Aiken sympathised strongly with the civil rights marchers, who identified unequal voting rights, based on property ownership, to be at the heart of Ulster's problem of ghettoised communities and gerrymandered politics.[18] In April 1969, Aiken decided to speak directly to the UN secretary-general about the Ulster civil rights movement, but this offended London deeply.[19] Two months later, Lynch decided not to reappoint Aiken as Ireland's minister for external affairs, evidently because of Ireland's need for a more European-focused foreign minister at a time when negotiations regarding Ireland's entry into the EEC were about to begin.[20]

Eamonn Gallagher, a former official in Ireland's Parisian embassy, advised Aiken's successor Patrick Hillery about Ulster by drawing upon his business connections in the northwest of Ireland.[21] This included

John Hume, a French-language teacher from a working-class background who, after forming a successful credit union in Derry, was elected as the president of the Credit Union League of Ireland, which was an all-Ireland body. Hume laid out an essential premise of his future political career when he argued at Queen's University Belfast during 1965 that the regional development policies now favoured by both the UN and the EEC were of inherent relevance to Northern Ireland because they were a potential remedy for the huge neglect by Stormont hitherto of the historic city of Derry and most areas in the west of Ulster.[22] A lifelong pacifist, Hume was elected to Stormont in 1968 to represent the civil rights marchers and thereafter visited the United States where he met Sean Donlon, the Irish consul at Boston, who introduced him to John McCormack, the speaker of the US House of Representatives. By now a retiring figure, McCormack had long advised Irish diplomats to focus upon dealing directly with Washington rather than whatever political influence Irish emigrants may have had in the United States.[23] A sense of rapport with Hume's political vision developed quickly among Irish diplomats not least because Garret FitzGerald, a Fine Gael foreign affairs spokesman and fellow 'social democrat', shared Hume's attitude towards the EEC and also believed that a tripartite political relationship, involving both the British and Irish governments as well as the EEC, was the best model for Northern Ireland's future development.[24] Hume warned Eamonn Gallagher, however, that the unionist political establishment at Stormont was adamant that the initiation of tripartite talks regarding Northern Ireland, involving Dublin in any way, must never be allowed to take place.[25]

By the summer of 1969, Stormont was willing to request that both army troops and gas weapons would be used against the civil rights marchers in Derry. Being aware of this, Patrick Hillery told the British Foreign Office that it should persuade the British Home Office, which was in charge of UK internal security, to do all in its power to prevent this, but no action was taken. On 12 August, police attacks on civil rights groups led to three days of rioting in Derry and, in turn, pogroms in Belfast. These events affected about ten thousand people and were partly televised and broadcast internationally. London's failure to heed Dublin's concerns prompted Jack Lynch to make a national television address about the Irish government's determination to take

a stand in the matter (this included establishing field hospitals along
the northern border to treat any victims who decided to flee across the
border), while Hugh McCann, Hillery's secretary, called on London
to apply for the appointment of a UN peacekeeping force in Northern
Ireland.[26] Instead, London placed the British army in full control
of all northern policing. Thereafter, nothern nationalist politicians
began making frequent requests to Dublin for assistance.[27] As finance
minister, Charles Haughey had the unenviable task of chairing an Irish
government subcommittee that considered the feasibility of offering
financial assistance to representatives of civil rights groups. This could
potentially be deemed illegal interference by London. This question
was made even more problematic because three Northern nationalist
MPs, supported by three Irish TDs from border constituencies, actually
suggested purchasing armaments.[28]

Dublin's concern that the Troubles in Northern Ireland could easily
spill across the border led the Irish army to consider the theoretical
possibility of crossing the border to contain such unrest, although
it was adamant that this should not be done. Instead, it judged that
preventing all illegal arms trafficking should be the priority.[29] Around
this time, a Donegal TD, who claimed to have been thinking only of
the Irish army, contacted a Belgian arms dealer who was also known to
the Belgian intelligence services, which were then in favour of Ireland's
admission to the EEC only if it followed Britain's lead.[30] Oliver Wright,
a distinguished British diplomat who had led the reorganisation of the
British Foreign Office during 1968, had recently been assigned to work
with a pro-reform Northern Ireland section of the British Home Office,
and Dublin welcomed the fact that he was open to talks with the Irish
government. Wright rectified a major source of Northern grievances in
November 1969 by removing unequal voting rights in local government
elections, while he also arranged for the future disbandment of the
B-Special auxiliary police force in Northern Ireland, which, for the
previous fifty years, had operated exclusively on the Orange Order
principle that because only a Protestant can legally serve as the British
monarch, only Protestant subjects of the Crown can be loyal enough
to maintain law and order.[31] Shortly after Wright's departure in March
1970, however, a story about an unsolicited Belgian arms importation
attempt was leaked to the press and resulted in a highly publicised trial.

This saw no convictions (no arms were actually imported) but generated enough negative publicity to force government resignations, including that of Haughey as finance minister. A cultural expectation that the Irish army must purchase its arms supplies only in Britain may have added to this controversy, although it became a highly sensitive issue primarily because Stormont linked this development to the launch of a 'Provisional IRA' conspiracy in Belfast in December 1969. Henceforth, claims that support for this conspiracy existed on *both* sides of the border became the basis for perpetual and strident criticism of the Irish government, both nationally and internationally, by Ulster unionists for so long as a secret IRA society could be said to exist.[32]

During September 1969, Patrick Hillery had attempted, albeit in vain, to raise the idea of sending a UN peacekeeping force to Northern Ireland at both the UN Security Council and UN General Assembly meetings in New York. This prompted London to warn Dublin that it would attack the Irish government diplomatically for having an unjust anti-British bias if it persisted in such actions at the UN, but Dublin would not rule out raising its concerns regarding Ulster at the UN again.[33] Thereafter, the creation of a 'Provisional IRA' conspiracy in Belfast became a basis for London to demand total security cooperation between Dublin and London. The experience of past Irish governments had indicated to it that the secret 'IRA' society was a tool of British intelligence services,[34] while Hillery's own view was that 'the British in many ways created the IRA'.[35] Be that as it may, Dublin did not have persuasive powers to present a different case to Britain internationally regarding Irish security considerations, not least because of Ireland's non-membership of NATO and the fact that the Royal Navy and Royal Air Force always allowed its NATO partners to use Northern Ireland facilities. Reflecting this, even though it was not considered to be a single political entity, the US state department still spoke of 'the strategic unity of the British Isles' in geopolitical terms.[36] Therefore, regardless of the actual provenance of the secret 'IRA' society, Ireland practically had an obligation to fall into line with whatever Britain declared to be their mutual security concerns if Ireland was not to alienate Britain's strategic partners.

Although Britain inherently rejected Dublin's idea of creating a UN peacekeeping force in Northern Ireland, British military intelligence (which favoured but seemingly did not adopt telephone-tapping as a secret intelligence tool within the Republic of Ireland) saw parallels between the Troubles in Northern Ireland and those in Cyprus, with the obvious distinction that Britain had withdrawn from the latter in 1959.[37] In 1964, Ireland had been among the first four countries (alongside Canada, Denmark and Finland) to send UN peacekeeping troops to Cyprus, where an Irish army officer would later serve as the UN force commander.[38] However, both the British and Irish governments would often declare themselves to be equally unimpressed with the other's record in handling civil–military relations between 1970 and 1974.[39] The apparent necessity and yet seeming impossibility of reforming policing on *both* sides of the border was constantly raised as an issue. In the south, this prompted the Taoiseach's department to involve itself directly in the Justice department's internal security policy and increased greatly the pressure on the Irish police forces (An Garda Síochána) to act as political intelligence gatherers.[40] During the early 1970s, at the time when 650 people were killed as a result of a breakdown of police and community relations within Northern Ireland, security cooperation between the north and south operated via their respective police forces and did not involve the Irish military,[41] while in the south an anti-state campaign was directed by three different secret 'IRA' societies that issued death threats to the Irish justice minister.[42] In keeping with London's wishes, since 1926 Dublin had continued a prior practice in civil–military relations that had existed under the original Union of 1801–1920 whereby troops stationed specifically in Ireland were to act purely as 'an aid to the civil power' of the police for matters of internal security but were not to be relied on for matters of national defence, including the direction of security, or intelligence, services.[43] Legally, therefore, the only assistance that the Irish Defence Forces could provide to An Garda Síochána was manpower and expertise in handling crisis situations.[44] Withholding from the army the responsibility of managing national defence created a culture of vulnerability in Dublin that to Northern Irishmen unfamiliar with the internal dynamics of the Irish state could appear to be a mask for subterfuge or else a sign of pure moral cowardice.[45] For the Irish army itself, it was 'painful for members of Óglaigh na hÉireann [the Defence Forces] to see the once honourable name of the IRA – integral to its traditions – so sullied and traduced' by 'illegitimate revolutionary organisations' within Northern Ireland, although confidence nevertheless remained high that 'the Defence Forces are truly the people's army'.[46]

At a governmental level at least, the Northern Troubles did not affect Ireland's relations with its would-be EEC partners. The Germans anticipated no difficulty in Ireland joining the EEC while the French kept up regular official state visits to Ireland. Notwithstanding de Gaulle's departure, the French continued to welcome intimations by Patrick Hillery and Eamon Kennedy, the Irish ambassador to France, that Irish interests within the EEC would be distinct from those of Britain.[47] At a press level, however, Ireland's international reputation suffered badly at this time because of its inability to disprove Belfast and London's claim that it was somehow morally responsible for the Northern Troubles.[48] To counteract this trend, during the summer of 1970 Noel Dorr, an official in Ireland's Washington embassy, was recalled to Dublin to work with Ireland's London embassy in an attempt to persuade more foreign correspondents to act as Dublin correspondents. An American agency was also employed to handle the Irish government's press on the European continent, although this practice was soon discontinued due to unsatisfactory results. It was deflating for the Irish government that new Dublin correspondents within the international media tended to be interested only in Northern Ireland affairs. Not only did they generally ignore all Irish government press statements but also (in common with established London correspondents of American and European journals) they invariably adopted London's official line of adopting a critical attitude towards the Irish government for occupying a supposed moral low ground.[49] Lacking the means to create an international Irish press, for the remainder of the decade, Irish diplomatic staff generally attempted to coax, or work with, select journalists and newspaper editors abroad who were deemed to be sufficiently sympathetic and influential to be useful, but this approach did not nullify the reality that the international community as a whole generally received Irish news only by proxy, via London.[50]

Economically, the Northern Troubles had both a local and an all-island dimension. After Ireland relocated the source of Irish banks' liquidity from London to Dublin in the late spring of 1969,[51] a recently introduced cross-border electricity service was sabotaged by militant British loyalists who feared the possibility of an Irish economic penetration of Northern Ireland. Meanwhile, irrespective of Dublin's complete lack of jurisdiction within Northern Ireland, the great visibility in the international media of the outbreak of violence on the island of Ireland meant that there was every reason to believe that the recent rise in tourism and foreign direct investment within the Irish state's jurisdiction was going to be reversed dramatically.[52] On a commercial level, the American government's primary interest in Ireland was the relevance of trans-Atlantic aviation to American business and, to a lesser extent, American tourism. This policy was focused upon Dublin rather than Belfast. It formed the backdrop to the appointment of a new American ambassador to Ireland in April 1969 and the inclusion by US President Richard Nixon, who had met Irish political leaders on a few occasions in the past, of a state visit to Dublin within his European tour of October 1970.[53] Henry Kissinger, the new American national security advisor, advised Nixon to emphasise how American–Irish relations were 'warm and non-partisan' on the grounds that 'we have a sympathetic interest in Ireland's extensive involvement in world affairs'. At the same time, however, Kissinger emphasised that America should renegotiate the American–Irish aviation agreements, first launched in 1945, whereby Ireland had attained landing rights in New York, Boston and Chicago (it was also pressing for landing rights in California), but was denying American airlines the right to land directly in Dublin rather than just at Shannon Airport.[54] To sell this idea, the US emphasised reasonably the boost to Dublin tourism that would arise from its proposal.[55] As it had done consistently for the past decade, however, Dublin argued that the existing situation was necessary to sustain because Shannon Airport was central to its plans for the economic development of the west of Ireland. An additional factor that Dublin did not emphasise, but which was no doubt fully realised by the Americans, was that British airlines had a significant monopoly of Dublin Airport's business, and the Irish government was fearful that altering this situation in any way could result in a severe economic reaction from British investors.[56]

There was also an American dimension to the Northern Ireland Troubles. Dublin raised its concern with America that private fund-raising for the 'Provisional IRA' could exist within the United States.[57]

The American government was already attempting to instigate legal proceedings against suspect parties,[58] although, bizarrely, an American Fulbright scholar of international relations had recently written a well-publicised panegyric about the new secret Provisional IRA society which accepted its highly questionable self-definition at face value.[59] In August 1971, America used the occasion of Irish protests against Britain over the introduction of internment without trial in Northern Ireland as the moment to press home its own demands, announcing that Aer Lingus would be denied landing rights in New York in one year's time if American commercial airlines continued to be denied landing rights in Dublin. In an act of competition with Dublin, Belfast responded by intimating its desire to enter into the same trans-Atlantic aviation market for the first time. Meanwhile, in support of both Belfast and British business interests in Dublin, Canadian airlines began competing with the Americans for landing rights in the Irish capital. Irish procrastinations in meeting the Americans' demand was sustained partly by an illogical belief that American–Irish politicians would prefer an aviation agreement that worked more to Dublin than to Washington's commercial advantage. As Kissinger expected, however, Dublin would begin to relent as the August 1972 deadline approached.[60]

Within Northern Ireland, the new Social Democratic Labour Party (SDLP), which was inspired largely by John Hume, withdrew from Stormont in protest against the British army's shooting of two unarmed civilians in Derry. After it protested outside that assembly against the introduction of internment (claiming, amongst other things, that this action by London was serving only to give the Provisional IRA its excuse to exist), Stormont practically labelled the SDLP as seditious. In response to the introduction of internment, Sean Donlon left Ireland's consular office in Boston to join a four-man diplomatic team in Dublin that advised Jack Lynch on Northern Ireland. On the grounds that Northern nationalists had no means of making such a complaint, Donlon raised the issue of prison beatings and alleged tortures committed by British security forces within Northern Ireland with the European Court of Human Rights, thereby giving birth to a lengthy legal case.[61] This accusation of uncivilised behaviour by the British army was considered inadmissable by London, although the fact that the Irish government purposively employed a former British army psychologist to present its case in Europe helped to deflect criticisms. While this case was taking place, ex-Irish diplomat Sean MacBride, a champion of the European Court of Human Rights, was awarded both a Nobel Peace Prize and a Lenin Prize for having inspired Amnesty International,[62] while ultimately the European Court of Human Rights would find the British army in Northern Ireland guilty of torture before revising this judgment two years later by ruling that it had been guilty only of degrading and inhuman practices in its treatment of ordinary Northern Irish civilians under the internment regime.[63]

Although London had been ready to consider introducing direct rule from Westminster as early as the spring of 1969, Ulster unionists feared that the disbandment of Stormont could remove the source of their power. In particular, it might cause the future of Anglo-Irish relations and Northern Ireland to be determined primarily by London and Dublin, without Stormont possessing its usual leverage to shape the nature of that relationship purely to its own and London's advantage.[64] T.K. Whitaker was sensitive to these unionist concerns. He practically initiated a Dublin policy of seeking to establish a rapport with Northern unionists, nominally on the grounds that an aspiration for a united Ireland would be inherently meaningless if such a rapport did not exist. During his tenure as Central Bank governor (1969–76), he continued to advice such a course whilst also performing his principal responsibility, which earned him almost universal respect in Dublin, of balancing the Irish effort to meet the challenge of preparing for EEC membership with the challenge of rising government debts.[65] On the northern question, Whitaker favoured supporting liberal Northern unionists and issued a veiled criticism of both Eamonn Gallagher and John Hume on the grounds that they had been allegedly guilty of 'too much ad-hocing ... too much reliance on any one man's personal contacts or judgments, particularly if they arise from "us" rather than "them" sources'.[66] Hume and Gallagher had favoured dealing directly with London to encourage the introduction of a proportional representation voting system in Northern Ireland on the grounds that the 'winner takes all' system of majority governments was unsuited to a society as deeply divided as that in Ulster. Implicit in this concept was a degree of power sharing. London's response to this idea during

1971 had been to organise meetings at Chequers, first between the Tory Prime Minister Edward Heath and Brian Faulkner and later between Heath and Jack Lynch.[67]

At this time, Lynch was seeking meetings with all Northern Irish parties with a view to drafting an all-Ireland statement in favour of non-violence and political equality.[68] Following this line of reasoning, on visiting Chequers with Donal O'Sullivan (Ireland's ambassador to the UK), Lynch had suggested to Heath that some kind of all-Ireland council could be created, with London acting in an advisory role. Heath responded, however, by repeating his demand that the Irish government must respect the Home Office's judgment regarding the necessity of the internment policy within Northern Ireland and, in turn, not give any moral credibility to the SDLP's stance of passive resistance to that policy. Meanwhile, Heath judged that if the idea of an all-Ireland council could possibly make some sense as a consultative forum on purely economic matters, it could not possibly make any legal sense because of the inherent sovereignty of the Westminster parliament within the United Kingdom. Subsequent press reactions to the Chequers meetings had an unfortunate impact. The mere fact that the Irish government had been consulted by London regarding Northern Ireland during September 1971 led to the creation thereafter of an armed Ulster Defence Association (UDA) in protest against this development. Reputedly, it soon acquired as many as 50,000 members.[69]

During the winter of 1971, Patrick Hillery renamed his department as 'foreign affairs' on the grounds that the title 'external affairs' was an outdated British Commonwealth terminology (curiously, the 'official' Irish language title of his department was left unchanged).[70] Thereafter, his department published Lynch's recent speeches on the Northern question in book form, which was actually the first time that this had been done for an Irish prime minister. Foreign affairs also published in Britain an Irish assessment of Stormont. While this was designed primarily to influence British opinion, it was also sent to Ireland's American embassy, after which parts of it were read out before Congress.[71] Eamonn Gallagher's impromptu Northern Ireland section of the foreign affairs department was replaced by a new 'Anglo-Irish relations' division, while Gallagher himself was relocated to become the leader of foreign affairs' new European division a few weeks before

Hillery signed an EEC accession treaty on 22 January 1972. Under its terms, Ireland was able to obtain a transitional arrangement to allow it to maintain its existing aids and incentives for industrial development, as well as a leeway of a few years to change its existing trading laws to meet all European common market standards.[72]

The United Kingdom signed an EEC accession treaty on the same day as Ireland, but Anglo-Irish relations would face their severest strain just one week later after the British army shot dead thirteen civil rights marchers in Derry. The Irish government responded by holding a national day of mourning and announced that it intended to withdraw its ambassador from London as a protest. Before this action could be taken, however, the Irish government was taken by surprise by a mob's attack on the (temporarily vacant) British embassy in Dublin, which was burned down after the police guarding it were overwhelmed. In response, London demanded the introduction of a new 'common law enforcement area' to encompass both the United Kingdom of Great Britain and Northern Ireland and the entirety of the legal jurisdiction of the Republic of Ireland to ensure all hostile anti-British elements within the latter were contained indefinitely. After also threatening to introduce severe economic sanctions against Ireland, London proceeded directly with its plans for direct rule, disbanding Stormont on 24 March 1972 and creating a new secretary of state for Northern Ireland so that a new Northern Ireland Office, directed by a British cabinet member, now took all decisions relating to the government of Northern Ireland.[73]

In the wake of British army outrages on civilians in Derry, American senator Ted Kennedy invited John Hume to meet him at the Irish embassy in Bonn, West Germany. Hume had previously declined an invitation from prominent Democratic congressman Tip O'Neill to address Congress on the Northern Troubles, but he used this occasion to express his opinion to Kennedy that if there was to be any chance of an improvement in the situation in Northern Ireland the Americans would have to learn to understand the full complexity of the political situation while also ensuring that neither arms nor money could possibly be sent from America to suspect parties.[74] The disbandment of Stormont prompted the US journal *Foreign Affairs* to invite Jack Lynch to make a contribution, which was the first time such an invitation was extended to an Irish prime minister. While Lynch's article essentially took the form of a lengthy essay on Irish history (thereby possibly bewildering many of its American readers), its core argument was that Stormont had indeed been a flawed institution and that a new and better relationship, constitutional or otherwise, between Dublin, Belfast and London was now likely in the context of joint EEC membership and the applicability of regional development policies.[75] That autumn, the new Northern Ireland Office prepared a government paper that suggested Dublin could have a consultative role to play in the creation of a new form of Northern Ireland assembly in the light of the 'special relationship' that existed between Britain and Ireland. Dublin welcomed this development, seeing it as a vindication of its raising the idea of an all-Ireland council at Chequers one year previously, and this led to the holding of joint British and Irish governmental meetings in London that November.[76]

Another effort to reach a rapprochement in Anglo-Irish relations during 1972 was the creation, independently of the Irish department of foreign affairs, of a British–Irish Association that concentrated on the financial world.[77] This initiative was supported by Whitaker as well as Fine Gael activist Garret FitzGerald, whose recent book *Towards a New Ireland* provided a well-received analysis of both Northern Ireland and the Republic of Ireland. Significantly, FitzGerald highlighted the perpetual foreign policy quagmires facing the Irish republic in diverting from Britain's desired economic policy for Ireland due to the existence of all-Ireland institutions in the worlds of banking and trade unionism.[78] FitzGerald's argument in this regard, however, differed from that of his party leader Liam Cosgrave, who saw the existence of such all-Ireland institutions, as well as the all-Ireland basis of both the Christian churches and Irish sporting organisations, as entirely unproblematic and a reflection of Irish social unity rather than a practical limitation upon Dublin's freedom of action.[79]

Unlike London, Dublin had required a constitutional referendum to facilitate EEC membership. In May 1972, over 80 per cent of Irish voters had supported the idea. This served to strengthen FitzGerald's resolve to focus on the question of Europe. His efforts to be a particularly outspoken Fine Gael commentator on foreign affairs at this time were probably enhanced by the fact that his predecessor was killed on his

way to a meeting of a Canadian–Irish business enterprise; a close party
colleague, who had also been the chief promoter of the European
movement in Ireland, was killed in a London plane crash (along with
eleven other senior Irish businessmen) while on his way to Brussels
in June 1972; and Ireland's ambassador to the Netherlands was killed
in a car crash very shortly thereafter.[80] When FitzGerald became the
new Irish foreign affairs minister upon the election of a Fine Gael–
Labour coalition government in March 1973, he preoccupied himself
primarily with adjusting Ireland to EEC political structures and
diplomatic practices. However, when the British foreign secretary re-
emphasised that so long as Ireland kept its case against the British
army at the European Court of Human Rights London would seek
to convince the rest of the world that Dublin, certainly not itself,[81]
was responsible for sustaining the IRA, FitzGerald was adamant that
Ireland would not drop its European case and that he intended to
visit Northern Ireland regularly to highlight Dublin's concern for the
welfare of its citizens.[82]

The implementation of direct rule by Westminster over Northern
Ireland in March 1972 essentially did more to create a period of crisis
diplomacy for the Irish government than the outbreak of the Troubles
on the streets of Derry and Belfast in August 1969. This was because
the existence of all-Ireland banking and trade union institutions meant
that this development had direct economic connotations for the Irish
state that could not possibly be ignored. Within a year, economic
pressures led to the amalgamation of the Dublin Stock Exchange with
that in London while, in the wake of the introduction of direct rule in
Northern Ireland, London sought to court both Conor Cruise O'Brien
and Erskine Childers, then the Tánaiste or deputy prime minister under
Jack Lynch, to act as its confidential advisor.[83] On making a brief return
into Irish politics via the Irish Labour Party, O'Brien was able to get
himself appointed as the Irish government's new official spokesman
on the Northern question within the coalition government. After
embarking on a new career as a British journalist, in his subsequent
writings O'Brien essentially inverted the Christian-democratic identity
of the Irish state by arguing that Irish people were, in comparison to
UK citizens, inherently only a 'nominally Christian' people and, in
turn, a pathologically false Irish view of England was the logical cause

of all violence.[84] The fact that an Irish government minister engaged in such irrational polemics arguably reflected a level of disarray in Irish government thinking at this time, which did not impress significant sections of Irish public opinion.

A memoir by Noel Dorr indicates that Dublin was inclined to misinterpret the reference to 'an Irish dimension' within the Northern Ireland Office's constitutional paper as raising the possibility of bipartite rule. In turn, some senior Irish government officials became inclined to think of Dublin's own (entirely separate) Council of Ireland idea in terms of a related constitutional experiment, akin to a new Anglo-Irish treaty that might possibly draw on EEC structures as a model. In the past, Whitaker had been adamant that Ireland should be open to exploring every conceivable possibility, including potentially sharing Irish sovereignty with Britain under a Benelux type of arrangement separate from the existence of the EEC. In support of this idea, some Irish legal minds had even peculiarly suggested that the Irish finance minister should be made a permanent member of a 'Council of Ireland' under British sovereignty. This was an idea that Brian Faulkner was naturally keen to encourage and that evidently motivated his willingness to engage regularly with Irish government ministers at this time. Not surprisingly, however, such attitudes were criticised sternly by Dermot Nally, a new secretary of the department of the Taoiseach, who became the practical coordinator of the Irish government's policy towards both the EEC and the Northern question for the next twenty years.[85] The UK had never considered giving cross-border bodies executive authority because it legally could not do so because of the inherent supremacy of Westminster parliament, as well as the unitary legal status of the Crown, within the unwritten British constitution. The Irish government was invited, however, by the Northern Ireland Office to take part in Anglo-Irish talks that also involved all sympathetic Northern Irish parties in Sunningdale, England on 6 December 1973. In preparation for these talks, Edward Heath made the first ever visit of a British prime minister to Dublin, albeit in secret, to meet the new Taoiseach Liam Cosgrave, who had recently emphasised to Faulkner that the Irish government wanted to see law and policing in Northern Ireland internationally monitored and not under exclusive British control.[86]

The Irish delegation to Sunningdale focused on the potential role of the EEC as an overarching political structure. This reflected the fact that, beyond its purely economic status as a common market, the European Community was very much an evolving political entity. It also embodied a constitutional paradox. The Benelux countries of Belgium, the Netherlands and Luxembourg were constitutional monarchies, as were the new additions during 1973 of the United Kingdom and Denmark, but the largest countries in the EEC – France, Italy and West Germany – were republics. While the Christian-democratic political tradition in Europe was perhaps evenly scattered across the continent, governing parties in this tradition were generally returned only within republican countries, which could now be said to include Ireland. Be that as it may, ever since his arrival at Brussels, Garret FitzGerald had identified most with representatives of the Benelux countries, who were perhaps the most eager to court Ireland because of its status as a fellow small nation. This can explain why FitzGerald suggested to Heath that the Luxembourg foreign minister could chair the Sunningdale talks.[87] Heath immediately rejected this idea as unconstitutional and, on chairing the Sunningdale talks himself, the British Prime Minister emphasised that he considered Dublin's 'Council of Ireland' idea only as a potential cost-saving measure for London in regulating its relations with Ireland. The Northern Ireland secretary of state dismissed as illegal the suggestions of FitzGerald and Hume that EEC regional development policies could possibly apply to Northern Ireland, while when Hume suggested that the European Court of Human Rights could be made a basis for harmonising British and Irish laws to deal with political violence, the British attorney general, Heath and Faulkner were as one in noting that this was impossible because the United Kingdom, by its very constitutional nature as a common law country (as were Ireland and the United States), could never become part of a codified European legal system.[88]

For its own part, the Irish government was very conscious that if any legal agreement was signed at Sunningdale this could end up being declared unconstitutional by its own courts.[89] Under the circumstances, the most that could be done was to produce an agreed communiqué that recognised each state's existing constitutional position. As an extension of Dublin's continued *de facto* acceptance of the legal status of Northern Ireland, London stated that if the people of Ulster ever decided in favour of a united Ireland, 'the British government would support that wish'. Dublin considered that if this agreed communiqué was made the basis of a formal agreement, then its principles could be registered in international law under Article 102 of the UN charter.[90] In reaction to this fact, however, the Ulster Unionist Party reversed its decision to consider sharing power with the SDLP in a proposed new Northern Ireland Assembly. This led necessarily to Faulkner's resignation as party leader, although he remained a nominal leader of a power-sharing executive for creating a new assembly up until May 1974. Under the Sunningdale agreement, John Hume was supposed to become Northern Ireland's minister for commerce.[91] A new British Labour government agreed with Faulkner, however, that the idea of power sharing with Irish nationalists should be disbanded permanently, not least because, in opposition to this idea, Ulster loyalists had recently called a successful and violent general strike across the whole of Northern Ireland. In protest against a growing trend of British consultations with the Irish government, they also placed car bombs in both Dublin and Monaghan, killing thirty-three people.[92]

Retrospectively, Dublin tended to view the Sunningdale experiment positively as establishing a precedent of London's recognition of the existence of an 'Irish dimension' to the Northern question. However, the Sunningdale conferences were, in several respects, only a stopgap measure deployed by the British civil service until the process of fully implementing direct rule was complete.[93] International observers probably anticipated this development. Even though the issue had also been settled as early as the spring of 1972, the American government would not allow its commercial airlines to land in Dublin Airport until May 1974 or until the Sunningdale agreement collapsed.[94] Specifically for Dublin, the fallout from the dismissal of the power-sharing idea was perhaps more problematic than its failure. Like the Northern Ireland Office but unlike the Irish government, Harold Wilson, the new British Labour Party prime minister, had held secret meetings with the 'Provisional IRA' in the past.[95] He now decided to legalise both the loyalist paramilitary Ulster Volunteer Force (UVF) and a new, small Belfast 'Sinn Féin Party' that, according to Dublin's intelligence, was secretly under the Provisional IRA's command. This prompted

FitzGerald, while in Washington on an EEC-related mission, to attempt
to persuade Henry Kissinger, the US secretary of state, to use his
influence to oppose this British decision, albeit in vain.[96]

The Irish government's position regarding the secret 'IRA' society
had always been unequivocal: every member of An Garda Síochána
and the Defence Forces had sworn an oath to uphold the constitution
of the Republic of Ireland. Therefore, for any government, public body
or public representative to give recognition to a body that was both
illegally and inaccurately professing to be acting in the name of an
Irish republic was a direct attack on the institutions of the Irish state
itself, as well as the legal bases upon which all Irish ambassadors, as
well as all foreign ambassadors to Ireland, had operated ever since
the Republic of Ireland Act. However, the existence of all-island trade
union, banking and academic networks meant that the Irish state
was often not respected in this regard.[97] Sections of the media began
adopting the language of the Belfast-led Sinn Féin Party, treating the
terms 'republican' and 'republicanism' as synonymous with the illegal
'IRA' society; denouncing An Garda Síochána for either alleged police
brutality or unjustly liaising with forces north of the border against the
'IRA'; and attacking the Irish government for using censorship laws to
prevent the northern Sinn Féin Party from using Irish national media
outlets, the latter being a decision that may have actually backfired
by serving to boost sympathy for Sinn Féin amongst southern trade
unionists, particularly in Dublin.[98]

All Irish governments and even the Irish army were painfully aware
of how ghosts of what was often misleadingly typified as an Irish civil
war could possibly end up being revived.[99] In various communities, it
was never forgotten that many republicans had been arrested before the
British army and its perceived eyes and ears (the police) could be fully
withdrawn from the Irish state's jurisdiction during 1922. Adopting
the attitude that the nature of the root can inherently be told by its
branches, this led to the creation of a minority, yet persistent, political
subculture in Ireland which maintained that the legitimacy of the forces
of law and order in the Irish state were always open to question.[100]
As early as 1972, Gerry Adams of Belfast, who soon began to rise as
the new leader of the Northern Sinn Féin Party, had been negotiating
with the British Labour Party to seek official political recognition of

the Provisional IRA and, in particular, its arrested members.[101] While this would become the touchstone of the position of the Northern Ireland Sinn Féin Party, Adams would also attempt to convince people within the republic's jurisdiction that there was no essential difference between these Provisional IRA volunteers in Belfast and the original founders of the Irish army in Dublin on the grounds that both acted as 'a voluntary political structure' and 'in a fairly haphazard way', and that 'the type of struggle involved ... is nothing like joining a "regular" army'.[102]

The Irish army's role in policing the troubles had been slight up until 1974 when, as a response to a partial breakdown in Anglo-Irish negotiations, its troops were recalled from Cyprus, partly at the suggestion of T.K. Whitaker.[103] This would lead to an increase in its number of battalions in the border regions; more regular patrolling and searching of all Irish border areas; the provision of permanent guards at vital installations of the Irish state (a trend that would encourage the creation of an Army Ranger Wing in 1980);[104] and an enhancement of the coastguard services provided by the Irish navy, which would assist the police in uncovering and arresting 'Provisional IRA' arms agents on a few significant occasions.[105] A side product of this development, however, was that the Irish army was not allowed to resume its UN peacekeeping operations until 1978, when it began sending its troops back to the Lebanon. In the meantime, its enforced concentration exclusively upon a perceived threat from within Irish society practically boosted an unhealthy cultural tension in Ireland, sustained in part by a corrosive tradition of British and Irish journalism which argued that the Irish state should always be characterised first and foremost by 'the repression of the sort of activities' that the Irish state's own founding fathers had mistakenly been prepared to entertain.[106] Meanwhile, Northern Ireland unionists' ongoing desire to prevent the free movement of labour across the border was practically sustained by the claims of the Provisional IRA before the British and, in turn, the international media that it was secretly being directed by Dublin to establish an all-island and southern worker-controlled Marxist state by means of an armed campaign.[107] A common view in Belfast was that an east–west divide existed on the island of Ireland, both in Northern Ireland and in the republic, because of Britain's desire to remain the pivot of the Irish economy, and this was also an explanation for reputed higher levels of sympathy for the IRA in the western half of the island or else among poor western migrants to eastern Irish or British cities.

Ireland's assumption of the presidency of the European Council of (foreign) Ministers in January 1975 served as a welcome respite from Northern propaganda wars.[108] Since 1972, the feasibility of creating a monetary union and actual European Union before 1980 had often been discussed at Brussels. As a vice-president of the council, Patrick Hillery chaired a European committee set up to examine the possibility of establishing a common welfare-orientated 'social action programme' for Europe. Efforts to promote the ideal of a common EEC social policy were largely ignored, however, because the major powers were still preoccupied with Saudi Arabia's initiation of an oil crisis in 1973 by denying its exports to the pro-Israeli west.[109] As chairman of the European Council, Garret FitzGerald expressed strong Irish support for the idea of a coordinated European response to all matters with due regard to the equality of both weak and strong member states in opposition to a push by Britain, France and West Germany, as the three most powerful member states, to dominate the proceedings.[110] A European Council decision that a Regional Development Fund should apply to Italy, the United Kingdom and Ireland was opposed by Britain on the grounds that this amounted to an illegal interference in its own internal affairs. Indeed, Britain sought to renegotiate its terms of membership almost as soon as it entered the community. It desired to give the entire British Commonwealth equal access to the European common market because if Britain prioritised access to the European common market over the operations of the British (commonwealth) common market, this would create significant challenges for the British Foreign Office. The resulting political tensions necessitated that a national referendum take place in Britain during June 1975. Both the Ulster Unionist Party and sections of British labour were adamant that Britain must leave the European community immediately, just as Sinn Féin and sections of the Irish Labour Party called on Ireland to do the same, but Britain voted to remain.[111] Just prior to the British referendum, FitzGerald announced that if Britain withdrew from the European community Ireland would still remain, while the Irish president symbolically paid a state visit to all EEC institutions to advertise the distinctiveness of Ireland's own membership of the community. Combined with recent French naval visits to Ireland and the creation of an Alliance Francaise in Dublin, this trend led to suspicions in Belfast and London that an unwelcome and secret Franco-Irish diplomatic entente must be in place. However, it was the Germans and the Dutch, rather than the Irish or the French, who had raised the idea at Brussels that a regional development policy should apply to both sides of the Irish border. They had done so purely on the premise of the community's guiding principle 'that border areas within the EEC should be treated as special cases in an attempt to mitigate the anomalous effects of national frontiers', but Britain had already decided on a policy of direct rule over Ulster as 'a permanent solution' to what it saw as its Irish question.[112]

Key achievements of FitzGerald's six-month presidency of European council of foreign ministers included the initiation of small-scale regional development programmes; the Lomé Convention agreement that initiated EEC relations with forty-six countries of the Third World; the creation of an EEC–Israel trade agreement; and a Helsinki agreement for the normalisation of existing east–west relations. For Ireland itself, this trend allowed for the initiation of direct diplomatic relations with Austria, the USSR, Israel and Japan during 1974, with the latter development essentially serving as a prelude to the establishment of Irish diplomatic relations with the People's Republic of China during 1979.[113] In the wake of pioneering visits by FitzGerald Irish government ministers were now expected by the EEC to go to the Middle East to represent essentially European trading interests in a diplomatic fashion. This trend led to the establishment of new Irish embassies in Egypt, Saudi Arabia, Iran and Greece and had some potentially positive connotations for the activities of the IDA and Córas Tráchtála. By the time of Ireland's second presidency of the European Council (July–December 1979), however, a combination of poor Anglo-Irish relations and the ongoing economic impact of the post-1973 oil crisis was making the Irish government acutely aware of the country's great vulnerability, particularly on an economic level.[114] This was a trend that the perpetual rise of regional development aid received from the EEC between 1975 and 1981 did comparatively little to alleviate,[115] although on the balance Ireland was able to initiate some new and advantageous economic policies at this time. The European Community's common agricultural policy saw a dramatic rise in the prices offered for Irish food exports; total Irish foreign trade (now amounting to about £400 million) rose from about 40 to over 70 per cent of the country's gross domestic product; while a new concentration upon achieving a positive balance of trade specifically with Europe rather than Britain would be achieved by 1980 at a time when Northern Ireland began to develop a severe balance of payments deficit of about 30 per cent.[116]

In the give and take of EEC membership, not every development was necessarily positive for Ireland. Eamonn Gallagher would serve for over a decade as a leader of a European fisheries commission after he played a prominent role during 1975–6 in negotiating EEC trade agreements with the Arab world, the United States and Canada.[117] Purely in his capacity as an Irishman, however, Gallagher was disappointed to discover that UN-inspired rules, dating from the late 1940s, for the operations of the law at sea practically outlawed Ireland from assisting its own chronically underdeveloped fishing industry under a 'north–west Atlantic fisheries' system, prompting Gallagher to grow increasingly disillusioned with what he once described as 'this new restrictive age'.[118] Meanwhile, British Labour's combination of intensely nationalist scepticism regarding Europe and (supposedly ideologically Marxist) hatred for the republicanism of the United States often found an outlet in Sinn Féin, the mainstream Irish national media, the Irish Labour Party (which had actually opposed Ireland's entry into the EEC)[119] and even in Irish women's groups, despite the fact that EEC membership was doing much to promote women's rights in Ireland.[120] In the wake of the UN's 1968 Declaration on the Elimination of Discrimination against Women, Ireland had seen the election to parliament in Ulster of Bernadette Devlin, a teenage female civil rights worker, and the beginning of a political career in Dublin for a young, Harvard-educated believer in the 1968 creed that the law existed solely to promote social change, Mary Bourke, who would later go on to become Ireland's first female president under the name Mary Robinson.[121] Throughout the 1970s, the Irish department of foreign affairs facilitated Irish women's groups in attending the UN's women-only conventions.[122] The idea of purposively dividing humanity according to sex for political purposes (represented by some contemporary academics' illogical championing of a conflict between feminism and humanism) was often considered in Ireland to be a false division, engineered to create new societal divisions, both nationally and internationally, to compensate for the decline of politicians' ability, post-détente, to literally hold everyone on the planet to ransom with a perpetual fear of both ideological and physical wars. Where action did need to be taken, however, was in the field of actual legal discrimination, particularly in the workplace.[123] On this level, Robinson was one of the first Irish barristers to focus on relevant European legislation.[124] During the late 1970s, a few more women emerged as significant figures in Ireland's department of foreign affairs,[125] but this essentially belied the fact that Ireland still had a very low percentage of women active in political life.[126]

At the outset of the American bicentennial year of 1976, a philanthropic 'Ireland Fund' was established in America by the Rooney family, owner of the Super Bowl champion Pittsburgh Steelers, and Tony O'Reilly, a prominent Irish businessman in America.[127] Drawing his inspiration from the successful example of the American United Jewish Appeal in supporting Israel, O'Reilly's Ireland Fund would absorb a pre-existing American Irish Foundation (first founded during John F. Kennedy's visit to Ireland during 1963) to become the 'American Ireland Fund' and make voluntary donations of $5 million a year to Ireland.[128] While O'Reilly was a strong supporter of the trend of American investment in Ireland, his belief in the strong link between peace and prosperity meant that he was also sympathetic to the idea of dealing with Northern financiers and stimulating the operations of an all-island economy in an entirely non-ideological fashion.[129] Such trends reflected the perspective of a recent *American Foreign Policy Library* study of Ireland, which suggested that 'the most important relations of Americans to Ireland always have been informal, spontaneous and familial', not least because 'formal diplomatic relations' have not been 'important enough' to merit their prioritisation.[130] In addition to all the usual diplomatic courtesies (including an address by Cosgrave before the US Congress), the actual bicentenary of the American declaration of independence during 1976 was marked by a joint Irish and American–Irish academic effort to publish a series of volumes to celebrate the historic connections between what some people described as the two republics.[131] Meanwhile, in the French republic, Pierre Joannon, an Irish consular officer who later founded an Ireland Fund of France, launched *Études Irlandaises*.[132] In this way, the relationship between the Republic of Ireland and the American and French republics was effectively celebrated during 1976. Just a fortnight after the American bicentennial, however, these positive developments were seemingly negated and Ireland was thrown into a security crisis after the British ambassador to Dublin was assassinated by the 'Provisional IRA', which announced thereafter from Belfast that it had launched 'a long war'. In turn, this announcement was used by the new British Prime Minister Jim Callaghan as his justification in declaring that both Britain and Ireland must henceforth be as one in seeking to destroy their common enemy of 'republicanism'.[133] This was effectively a propaganda tool to equate any lack of cooperation between Britain and Ireland with clandestine sympathies for the IRA.

During the autumn of 1976, the recently marginalised figure of John Hume accepted a fellowship at Harvard University's Center for International Relations and renewed his association with Irish diplomatic staff in America. Together, they encouraged the development of a new American political pressure group consisting of Senators Edward Kennedy and D.P. Moynihan (a recent US representative at the UN), New York state Governor Hugh Carey and Boston Congressman Tip O'Neill who, most significantly, would become speaker of the US House of Representatives upon the assumption of the US presidency by Jimmy Carter during January 1977. By August 1977, President Carter had been persuaded by this group to issue a statement on Ireland, in the process effectively becoming the first American president to ever do so unilaterally.[134] He called for the establishment of a just and representative government in Northern Ireland that could command the support of the Irish as much as the British government and noted that, in such an event, America would offer investment schemes for Northern Ireland.[135] Irish diplomatic staff in America such as ambassador Sean Donlon (a former student at Maynooth College alongside Hume), political officer Michael Lillis and press officer James Sharkey (a native of Derry) believed with Hume that the solution to the Northern question was to rely on diplomacy and, in turn, to speak in the language of an agreed Ireland that was based on peace, reconciliation and social and economic justice. Hume's resolve in this regard was increased further after he worked for a time with Ireland's European commissioner in Brussels. Northern Ireland became entitled to return representatives to the European Parliament during 1979, and, upon his election, Hume would champion the EEC frequently as the finest peace process in modern history.[136]

While some have suggested that his initiative can be attributed partly to Irish diplomatic efforts,[137] President Carter viewed his Irish statement purely in the light of his own diplomatic goal of promoting the United States' international record as a champion of human rights.[138] By contrast, the Irish reaction to his initiative served to revive public debate on the potential role of a pro-Irish lobby group within the United States. The combination of the Eisenhower administration's over-preoccupation with internal security as a means of preserving 'the good life' in America, Harry Truman's prior initiation of a foreign policy for Europe and the legacy of F.D. Roosevelt's championing of welfarism (a politics that was now the principal basis of Tip O'Neill's American support) had allowed the Democratic Party to capture both the liberal intellectual and social-democratic American political audience. By the 1970s, Irish perceptions of the United States were filtered largely through this lens. Be that as it may, as Speaker of the US House of Representatives, Tip O'Neill was also naturally open to getting senior Republican Party members involved in his envisioned 'Friends of Ireland' group in the US Houses of Congress.[139] This would prove to be valuable, but this initiative faced competition from a controversial rival lobby group that won some support from Congressmen of Jewish and Italian American backgrounds. The 'Irish National Caucus' and its associated 'ad hoc' congressional group was led by men who believed, first and foremost, that neither neutral nor diplomatic language was ever appropriate when speaking of British misgovernment in Northern Ireland. This attitude was largely the result of poor political leadership, and the existence of this body generally served only to embarrass Tip O'Neill or else to deny to the Irish government some additional sympathisers in Congress.[140]

After paying a visit to Ireland, Tip O'Neill suceeded in getting an American law passed in August 1979 which banned the sale of all firearms to Northern Ireland, including to the Royal Ulster

Constabulary.[141] This reflected Edward Kennedy's drive to increase levels of regulation upon all American arms sales abroad, including to the Middle East,[142] although it was understood by some to be a sign of a growing American interest in the Northern Troubles on terms that were not necessarily favoured by Britain.[143] Only a few days later, the 'Provisional IRA' killed Lord Mountbatten and as many as eighteen British soldiers on a single day,[144] and this led O'Neill to be subject to criticism in some quarters for having prevented the sale of American firearms to Northern police forces. He was also subject to criticism from other quarters, including Sean McManus, the leader of the Irish National Caucus and a controversial priest who had been banished from Ulster by the Catholic Church because of his very close familial and thereby personal association with the IRA.[145] Prior to forming the Irish National Caucus, McManus had been associated with an Irish Northern Aid Committee (NORAID) in New York that was accused publicly of sending supplies to the IRA.[146] Its great notoriety, however, belied the nature of virtually all contemporary non-governmental organisations that were in any way associated with Ireland. While many of these were inclined to adopt an entirely independent moral stance on international relations, they invariably did so on purely humanitarian grounds, in the process often reflecting an ongoing tradition of peacekeeping Irish missionary work.[147] When Charles Haughey became Taoiseach for the first time in December 1979, the visibility of vocal divisions within the Irish community in America prompted him to threaten to dismiss Donlon for failing to rectify this divide before he essentially learnt from experience the validity of Donlon's judgment regarding the untrustworthiness of the Irish National Caucus. From 1981 until 1987, Donlon would serve as general secretary of the Irish department of foreign affairs.[148]

Ireland's entry into the European Monetary System (EMS) in 1978 after it removed all its tariff barriers with an eye to both the European and American markets was essentially a turning point in the history of the Irish state.[149] It motivated Ireland's subsequent breaking of the parity between the Irish pound and the British pound for the first time in over 150 years.[150] At a time when balance of payments crises were leading many states to rely more on national banking schemes than the advice of the IMF,[151] it was widely believed in Belfast and London that

Ireland's entry into the EMS was an effort by France and Germany to separate Ireland from the United Kingdom rather than a purely Irish decision. The new British Prime Minister Margaret Thatcher visited Dublin for a European Council of Ministers meeting in November 1979. Aside from criticising the Irish government, she called for drastic changes to Britain's requirements to contribute to EEC budgets and in the EEC's relations with the Middle East.[152] Ever since 1973, most of Europe, including Ireland, was forced to rely on increasingly expensive Russian oil imports,[153] while instability in the international monetary system had led many to fear a deep economic recession. It was not essentially until after 1979, however, that Ireland began to experience real problems after prolonged strikes hit the British and, in turn, Irish labour markets.[154] During 1980, Haughey faced the largest protest demonstrations in the history of the Irish state over rising income taxes, while the simultaneous launch of hunger strike protests by IRA prisoners in Northern Ireland played a large part in exciting Irish public opinion. Britain's determination to keep very close economic ties to Ireland was illustrated that December when, aside from the Northern Ireland secretary of state, the British chancellor of the exchequer and British foreign secretary joined Thatcher on a mission to Dublin. This was a totally unprecedented development and it would appear to have been a successful mission. Thereafter, both governments issued statements that they were committed to recognising 'the totality of relationships' that existed between the United Kingdom and Ireland and that they were going to hold more intergovernmental conferences in the future to mitigate potentially divergent policies towards Europe.[155]

Owing to the Northern hunger strikes, the Irish public generally interpreted these statements purely in the light of their desire for a resolution of the Northern Ireland Troubles. During 1981, the death of ten IRA hunger strikers in Northern Ireland created a genuine strain in Anglo-Irish relations (Irish American protests were also common),[156] although the degree of public sympathy evoked within Northern Ireland itself was undoubtedly their most significant result.[157] In the wake of the Anglo-Irish summit of December 1980, there would be three changes of Irish government within just eighteen months. Financial pressure being exercised upon Dublin would soon create a fiscal crisis, so much so that a revival of unemployment and, in turn, emigration to Britain on a scale not witnessed since the mass exodus of the 1950s would actually become a defining Irish social experience of the 1980s.[158] This had not been expected. During 1982, Haughey's criticism of Thatcher's policy regarding the Anglo-Argentine Falklands War defied the advice of both the Irish ambassador to Britain and the EEC, which had been willing to impose sanctions on Argentina.[159] The new US president Ronald Reagan also defied Thatcher by criticising the Falklands War,[160] although Haughey's motive was probably simple resentment at the economic pressures being placed upon Ireland by Britain.[161]

By 1982, Ireland was in a somewhat paradoxical situation. In Germany, hitherto unsympathetic press agencies were adamant that Ireland had now become a model European nation,[162] although the growing recession within Ireland was leading many Irish people to question that judgment. While the United Kingdom was hyper conscious that its own 'freedom of manouevre in European, let alone global, affairs is seriously circumscribed' compared to yesteryear, Ireland's approach to Europe had been governed by the fact that it 'has none of the great powers' preoccupations with grandeur, real or imaginary', meaning in turn that it was 'able to confront problems with solutions that attract no suspicion of self-interest' and, at least potentially, a significant degree of original thought. However, an unchanged reality that still practically defined Ireland's status as a small nation was that 'neither in the Dáil nor among the public at large is there much interest or expertise in foreign affairs'. Therefore, the question of Ireland's role in international affairs was still seen within Ireland to be the prerogative exclusively of 'a small circle of cognoscenti', consisting of diplomats and select figures within Ireland's aviation and agricultural industries.[163] This government tradition would begin to be challenged during the 1980s.[164] A pervasive sense still existed, however, that both Ireland and Northern Ireland essentially occupied their own small worlds. This was perhaps sustained by the fact that the role of multinational businesses in shaping the globalisation debate ever since 1971 was widely considered to have simply passed Ireland by. The fact that outrages in Northern Ireland, rather than the fortunes of the Irish state, grabbed most international headlines regarding Ireland throughout the 1970s was not helpful. 'Provisional IRA' propaganda of word and deed emanating from Northern Ireland 'leveraged the political system' into unjustly making this Ireland's claim to fame.[165] After 1978, the director of Ireland's first multinational company outside the food industry (a packaging business) was asked to take a lead in modernising Ireland's communications industry, but he was neither involved in nor interested greatly in international affairs.[166]

An Irish Institute of Public Administration had been founded during 1957 to coincide with the Treaty of Rome and Ireland's entry into the IMF, but twenty-five years later there was still a very notable absence of scholarly studies of Ireland's approach to foreign policy. In the past, de Valera had considered the Éire constitution of 1937 and the Anglo-Irish agreement of 1938 to have been his crowning achievement, but his creation thereafter of a joint British–Irish school of Irish historical studies to oversee literally all university writings on Ireland had actually served to silence all scholarship specifically on the theme of Irish statehood. Only after Ireland's decision to join the EMS in 1978 would efforts be made within Irish academia to write about either the history or current state of Ireland in the context of international law and international relations.[167] Initial authors tended to be preoccupied primarily with perceived legacy issues, such as the degree to which Ireland was still trapped within a British system of 'unequal sovereigns' or the extent to which Ireland's self-definition ever since 1936 as a militarily neutral country was truly 'a singular stance'.[168] In keeping with broader international trends, security debates would become more prevalent within Ireland during the 1980s. Be that as it may, it would not essentially be until after a European Monetary Union was formed in 1994 that a significant expansion in the number of studies of Ireland's role in international affairs occurred. This reflected the extent to which the intervening period was one in which the political order within Ireland as much as the rest of Europe was slowly but surely being reinvented according to a new paradigm, not least due to the process of European integration and its interconnection with the global partnership system that had been launched during 1968.

Endnotes

1 M.F. Millikan, 'An introductory essay: the global partnership', *International organization*, vol. 22 no. 1 (winter 1968), 1–2. Missionaries often served as America's contacts within the Far East.

2 Kevin O'Sullivan, 'Biafra to Lomé: the evolution of Irish government policy on official development assistance 1969-1975', *Irish studies in international affairs*, vol. 18 (2007), 91-107; Kevin O'Sullivan, 'Between internationalism and empire: Ireland, the like-minded group and the search for a new international order 1974-1982', *The international history review*, vol. 37 no. 5 (2015), 1083-101.

3 Bryce Evans, Stephen Kelly (eds), *Frank Aiken, nationalist and internationalist* (Dublin, 2014), 292-302.

4 B. Tonra, M. Kennedy, J. Doyle, N. Dorr (eds), *Irish foreign policy* (Dublin, 2012), 154.

5 Joe Humphreys, *God's entrepreneurs: how Irish missionaries tried to change the world* (Dublin, 2010). From the 1960s until the 1980s, Ireland's new national television service, RTÉ, ran a documentary series, *Radharc*, that often paid attention to the work of missionaries in the Third World.

6 Brian Maye, *The search for justice: Trócaire: a history* (Dublin, 2010).

7 P.A. David, M.V. Reder (eds), *Nations and households in economic growth* (New York, 1974).

8 Joseph Nye, Robert Keohane, 'Transnational relations and world politics', *International organization*, vol. 25 no. 3 (1971), 721-48. The American dollar formally left the gold standard in 1971, but had practically ceased to be convertible into gold during 1968. J.G. Ruggie, 'International regimes, transactions and change', *International organization*, vol. 36 no. 2 (spring 1982), 405-8.

9 G.C. Herring, *From colony to superpower: US foreign relations since 1776* (Oxford, 2008), 439-40, 914, 921.

10 Jeremi Suri, *Power and protest: global revolution and the use of détente* (Harvard, 2003). It has often been suggested that the United Kingdom was the only major power to escape internal civil disruption during 1968, although this argument essentially ignores the existence of Northern Ireland as part of the United Kingdom.

11 Jean-Jacques Servan-Schreiber, *The American challenge* (London, 1968); L.N. Piers, 'Transatlantic relations in the Johnson and Nixon eras', *London School of Economics research online* (2010).

12 Paul Kennedy, *The rise and fall of the great powers* (New York, 1988), 518-20; John Pinder, *The European Union* (Oxford, 2001), 13-16.

13 Dan Senor, Saul Singer, *Start-up nation: the story of Israel's economic miracle* (New York, 2009), 178-80.

14 Paul Kennedy, *The rise and fall of the great powers* (London, 1988), 483, 491; W.F. Mondale, 'Beyond détente: towards international economic security', *Foreign affairs*, vol. 53 no. 1 (Oct. 1974). The partition of Germany and the promotion of trade between West Germany and neutral Austria served to undo historically strong German-Russian trading links that Britain had opposed.

15 Brennan would also later become Ireland's first (and strictly pro-western) ambassador to the USSR (1974-80). Michael Quinn, *Irish-Soviet diplomatic and friendship relations 1917-1991* (Maynooth, 2017), 103, 159.

16 *Documents on Irish foreign policy*, vol. 10 nos 306 and 320; Michael Quinn, *Irish-Soviet diplomatic and friendship relations 1917-1991* (Maynooth, 2017), chapter 8.

17 Michael Kennedy, *Division and consensus: the politics of cross-border relations 1925-1969* (Dublin, 2000), quote p. 311.

18 Austin Currie, 'Civil rights movement', in Sean Farren, Denis Haughey (eds), *John Hume: Irish peacemaker* (Dublin, 2015), 55-70.

19 Michael Kennedy, *Division and consensus*, 324-31.

20 T. Bartlett (ed.), *Cambridge history of Ireland*, vol. 4 (Cambridge, 2018), 633.

21 Terry Clavin, 'Eamon Gallagher (1926–2009)' and 'Redmond Gallagher (1914–2006)', *Dictionary of Irish biography* (online edition).

22 Sean Farren (ed.), *John Hume in his own words* (Dublin, 2018), 29; Sean Farren, Denis Haughey (eds) *John Hume: Irish peacemaker* (Dublin, 2015), 55–6.

23 Sean Donlon, 'John Hume and the Irish government', in Sean Farren, Denis Haughey (eds), *John Hume: Irish peacemaker* (Dublin, 2015), 88–9.

24 Garret FitzGerald *Towards a new Ireland* (Dublin, 1972); Sean Farren, Denis Haughey (eds), *John Hume*, 84–5; Garret FitzGerald *All in a life* (Dublin, 1991), chapter 4.

25 Noel Dorr, *Sunningdale: the search for peace in Northern Ireland* (Dublin, 2017), chapter 2.

26 Michael Kennedy, *Division and consensus: the politics of cross-border relations 1925–1969* (Dublin, 2000), 323, 332–6.

27 Michael Kennedy, *Division and consensus*, 337–45.

28 Stephen Kelly, *Fianna Fáil, partition and Northern Ireland 1926–1971* (Dublin, 2013), 314.

29 Michael Kennedy, *Division and consensus*, 347; Dan Harvey, *Soldiering against subversion: the Irish Defence Forces and internal security during the troubles 1969–1998* (Dublin, 2018).

30 Mervyn O'Driscoll, Dermot Keogh, Jerome aan de Wiel (eds), *Ireland through European eyes: Western Europe, the EEC and Ireland 1945–1973* (Cork, 2013), 288–9. The arms dealer was Albert Luykx. The Donegal TD was Neil Blaney, a former minister for posts and telegraphs.

31 Noel Dorr, *Sunningdale: the search for peace in Northern Ireland* (Dublin, 2017), chapter 2.

32 Stephen Kelly, *Fianna Fáil, partition and Northern Ireland 1926–1971* (Dublin, 2013) 316–23.

33 Michael Kennedy, *Division and consensus*, 349–52, 355–6.

34 Ronan McGreevy, 'The Lemass tapes: IRA infiltrated by British secret service', *The Irish Times*, 2 Jun. 2018. During the late 1950s, the secret 'IRA' society had operated a border campaign that was trained or directed by two mavericks: first, Eric Dorman-Smith, a lecturer in British military colleges at Chatham who rose to the rank of brigadier in the British army during the Second World War before, in the wake of the Republic of Ireland Act, moving to Ireland under the false name 'O'Gowan' and attempting to build up a network of political contacts; and second, Sean Cronin, a man who wrote on international affairs for *The Irish Times* before controversially and defiantly claiming in court that the secret 'IRA' society actually had a mandate for its campaign from the ethos of the Irish constitution itself. Patrick Maume, 'Eric Dorman-Smith "O'Gowan" (1895–1969)' and 'Sean Cronin (1922–2011)', *Dictionary of Irish biography* (online edition). Largely under Cronin's direction, this campaign continued intermittently between December 1956 and February 1962.

35 John Walsh, *Patrick Hillery: the official biography* (Dublin, 2008), quote p. 527.

36 Ronan Fanning, 'The Anglo-American alliance and the Irish question in the twentieth century', in H.B. Clarke, Judith Devlin (eds), *European encounters* (Dublin, 2003), 203–11 (quote p. 203).

37 Peter Wright, *Spy catcher* (London, 1987), 358–9. In late November 1973, Dublin discovered that the direct connection between Ireland's London embassy and a telegraph-printing machine at Iveagh House in Dublin had been tapped by a third

party. Noel Dorr, *Sunningdale: the search for peace in Northern Ireland* (Dublin, 2017), chapter 15.

38 J.P. Duggan, *A history of the Irish army* (Dublin, 1991), 259–62, 276. The Irish force commander of the UN troops in Cyprus from 1976–81 was General James Quinn, who had also been deputy chief of staff under General Sean MacEoin when the latter commanded UN troops in the Congo.

39 Noel Dorr, *Sunningdale: the search for peace in Northern Ireland* (Dublin, 2017).

40 Ibid., chapter 4.

41 Ibid., chapter 13.

42 Desmond O'Malley, *Conduct unbecoming: a memoir* (Dublin, 2014), 78–87.

43 D.N. Haire, 'In the aid of the civil power, 1868–1890', in F.S.L. Lyons, R.J. Hawkins (eds), *Ireland under the Union* (Oxford, 1980); E.A. Muenger, *The British military dilemma in Ireland* (Dublin, 1991). In the past, the tradition of withholding from the army the responsibility of managing national defence had made de Valera fearful that mentioning this fact could make any Irish government as unpopular with the Irish public as John Redmond had been during the First World War. This was why he favoured an exaggerated degree of secrecy regarding the Irish state's approach to international relations. Ronan Fanning, *Éamon de Valera: a will to power* (Dublin, 2015), 189–93, 213.

44 Dan Harvey, *Soldiering against subversion: the Irish Defence Forces and internal security during the troubles 1969–1998* (Dublin, 2018).

45 Alvin Jackson, 'Ireland, the Union and the Empire 1800–1960', in Kevin Kenny (ed.), *Ireland and the British Empire* (Oxford, 2004), 123–53; Alvin Jackson, 'Unionism and the future of the Union', in Robert Savage (ed.), *Ireland in the new century* (Dublin, 2003), 43–66.

46 J.P. Duggan, *A history of the Irish army* (Dublin, 1991), 280–8, 294–5 (quotes pp. 281–2, 288, 294).

47 Mervyn O'Driscoll, Dermot Keogh, Jerome ann de Wiel (eds), *Ireland through European eyes: Western Europe, the EEC and Ireland 1945–1973* (Cork, 2013), 57–60, 120–7.

48 Fergal Lenehan, *Stereotypes, ideology and foreign correspondents: German media representations of Ireland 1946–2010* (London, 2016).

49 Noel Dorr, *Sunningdale: the search for peace in Northern Ireland* (Dublin, 2017), chapter 3.

50 Ibid., chapter 15; Michael Fitzpatrick, *John Hume in America* (Dublin, 2017).

51 Padraig McGowan, *Money and banking in Ireland* (Dublin, 1990), 85–9.

52 Michael Kennedy, *Division and consensus*, 361–5.

53 Andrew Sanders, 'Landing rights in Dublin: relations between Ireland and the United States 1945–72', *Irish studies in international affairs*, vol. 28 (2017), 147–71. As vice-president under Dwight Eisenhower's administration (1953–61), Nixon met Irish politicians such as John A. Costello and President Sean T. O'Kelly during Irish state visits to America, while Nixon had also met Sean Lemass on an unofficial trip to Dublin during 1966. Jack Lynch would make a reciprocal visit to the White House in March 1971.

54 Andrew Sanders, 'Landing rights in Dublin: relations between Ireland and the United States 1945–72', *Irish studies in international affairs*, vol. 28 (2017), 150–6, 160, 162, 169.

55　The US had calculated that Ireland was within the seven most popular American tourist destinations. Andrew Sanders, 'Landing rights in Dublin', 151.

56　Irene Furlong, 'Tourism and the Irish state in the 1950s', in D. Keogh, F. O'Shea, C. Quinlan (eds), *Ireland in the 1950s: the lost decade* (Cork, 2001), 164–86. By 1972, nine airlines had landing rights at Dublin Airport, including five British ones and one each from Spain, Italy, Germany and Sweden, but none from the United States. Andrew Sanders, 'Landing rights in Dublin', 167.

57　Desmond O'Malley, *Conduct unbecoming: a memoir* (Dublin, 2014), 93–5.

58　Michael Funchion (ed.), *Irish American voluntary organisations* (Connecticut, 1983), 201–2.

59　J. Bowyer Bell, *The secret army: the IRA 1916–1970* (London, 1970). An Irish journalist T.P. Coogan would publish a book of a similar kind around the same time for London publishers.

60　Andrew Sanders, 'Landing rights in Dublin: relations between Ireland and the United States 1945–72', *Irish studies in international affairs*, vol. 28 (2017), 154, 166–70.

61　Noel Dorr, *Sunningdale: the search for peace in Northern Ireland* (Dublin, 2017), chapter 4.

62　Ronan Keane, 'Sean MacBride (1904–1988)', *Dictionary of Irish biography* (Cambridge, 2009).

63　Aisling O'Sullivan, Roja Fazaeli, 'Multilateralism, human rights and the 1970s: insights from Ireland's role in the evolution of the human rights field', *Irish studies in international affairs*, vol. 29 (2018). The army psychologist was a Professor Robert Daly.

64　Noel Dorr, *Sunningdale*, chapters 5–7.

65　Anne Chambers, *T.K. Whitaker: portrait of a patriot* (Dublin, 2014), chapter 8.

66　Anne Chambers, *T.K. Whitaker: portrait of a patriot* (Dublin, 2014), quote p. 281.

67　Noel Dorr, *Sunningdale*, chapters 5–7.

68　John Lynch, *Speeches and statements on Irish unity and Anglo-Irish relations, August 1969–October 1971* (Dublin, 1971), 60–6, 77–82.

69　Noel Dorr, *Sunningdale*, chapters 5–6.

70　John Walsh, *Patrick Hillery* (Dublin, 2008), 170–1.

71　Noel Dorr, *Sunningdale*, chapter 4.

72　T. Bartlett (ed.), *Cambridge history of Ireland*, vol. 4 (Cambridge, 2018), 633.

73　Noel Dorr, *Sunningdale*, chapters 6–8.

74　Maurice Fitzpatrick, *John Hume in America* (Dublin, 2017), 30–7. John Dumbrell, 'The United States and the Northern Irish conflict 1969–94', *Irish studies in international affairs*, vol. 6 (1995), 107–13.

75　John M. Lynch, 'The Anglo-Irish problem', *Foreign Affairs*, vol. 50 no. 4 (Jul. 1972), 601–17. Dorr played a role in writing this *Foreign affairs* article, while Hugh McCann, Eamonn Gallagher and T.K. Whitaker played an editorial role in its creation. Noel Dorr, *Sunningdale*, chapter 9.

76　Noel Dorr, *Sunningdale*, chapters 9–11.

77　Chambers, *T.K. Whitaker*, 299–310.

78　Garret FitzGerald, *Towards a new Ireland* (Dublin, 1972), 58–60.

79　Speech of Liam Cosgrave, reproduced in Noel Dorr, *Sunningdale*, chapter 13.

80　See the *Dictionary of Irish Biography* entries for 'Gerard Sweetman (1908–70)', 'Michael Sweetman (1935–72)' and 'Eoin MacWhite (1923–1972)', who was the son of former Irish diplomat Michael MacWhite.

81 In a recent high-profile Dublin legal case, two English bank robbers in Ireland revealed that they were working for both British intelligence and the IRA. This almost led to a diplomatic incident, although the Irish government, upon sentencing the criminals Kenneth and Keith Littlejohn, decided to let the matter drop. Noel Dorr, *Sunningdale*, chapter 15.

82 Garret FitzGerald, *All in a life* (Dublin, 1991), chapter 5.

83 Noel Dorr, *Sunningdale*, chapters 10–11; Frank Callanan, 'Conor Cruise O'Brien (1917-2008)', *Dictionary of Irish biography* (Cambridge, 2009).

84 Conor Cruise O'Brien, *Neighbours* (London, 1980), quotes pp. 17, 61.

85 Noel Dorr, *Sunningdale*, chapters 11–14.

86 Ibid., chapter 15. For security reasons, the Heath–Cosgrave meeting on 17 September 1973 was held in the Irish air force's base at Baldonnell, County Dublin.

87 Garret FitzGerald *All in a life*, 123, 211.

88 Noel Dorr, *Sunningdale*, chapter 17.

89 Garret FitzGerald *All in a life*, 222. Conscious of the fact that the Sunningdale meeting was held on the anniversary (6 December) of the Anglo-Irish treaty agreement of 1921 and Britain's acceptance of the Irish Free State constitution in 1922, the large Irish delegation, including the attorney general, had actually been granted plenipotentiary powers to sign an agreement. Noel Dorr, *Sunningdale*, chapter 15.

90 Noel Dorr, *Sunningdale*, chapter 18.

91 Michael Fitzpatrick, *John Hume in America* (Dublin, 2017), 159–62.

92 Noel Dorr, *Sunningdale*, chapters 19–21.

93 Ibid., chapter 21.

94 Andrew Sanders, 'Landing rights in Dublin', 170.

95 The National Archives (Kew), PREM 15/1009, cited in Noel Dorr, 'A year in the life: behind the scenes in Irish foreign affairs in 1972', *Irish studies in international affairs*, vol. 28 (2017), 141–3.

96 Thomas Bartlett (ed.), *Cambridge history of Ireland*, vol. 4 (Cambridge, 2018), 456–8. FitzGerald spoke with Kissinger at Washington D.C. on 8 January 1975.

97 Maurice Moynihan, *Speeches and statements of Éamon de Valera 1917–1973*, 580–8.

98 Diarmaid Ferriter, *The transformation of Ireland* (Dublin, 2005), 632–3. The media ban on Sinn Féin continued until 1994.

99 J.P. Duggan, *A history of the Irish army* (Dublin, 1991), 295.

100 Areas of Ireland that had witnessed cruel atrocities during 1922-3 – perhaps most notably County Kerry – were often the most prone to perpetuating this bitterness. Kerry had served as a home for small IRA-related printing presses ever since the 1940s.

101 The National Archives (Kew), PREM 15/1009, cited in Noel Dorr, 'A year in the life: behind the scenes in Irish foreign affairs in 1972', *Irish Studies in international affairs*, vol. 28 (2017), 141–3.

102 Gerry Adams, *Free Ireland* (2nd ed., Dingle, 1995), 62, 64 (quotes); Fr. J.A. Gaughan, review of J.P. Duggan's *A history of the Irish army*, in Studies, vol. 80, no. 320 (winter 1991), 441.

103 Anne Chambers, *T.K. Whitaker: a portrait of a patriot* (Dublin, 2014), 299.

104 J.P. Duggan, *A history of the Irish army* (Dublin, 1991), 280–8, 294–5.

105 Tom MacGinty, *The Irish navy: golden jubilee* (Tralee, 1995), chapters 15 and 18. The navy were able to expose Belfast Sinn Féin–IRA activist Joe Cahill in 1973, after he

attempted to import arms from Libya, and Kerry Sinn Féin–IRA activist Martin Ferris in 1984, after he attempted to import arms from America.

106 O.D. Edwards (ed.), *Conor Cruise O'Brien introduces Ireland* (London, 1968), 105.

107 Richard English, *Armed struggle* (London, 2003), 232, 345–6.

108 E.M. Browne, 'Ireland in the EEC', *The world today*, vol. 31 no. 10 (Oct. 1975), 424–32.

109 John Walsh, *Patrick Hillery: the official biography* (Dublin, 2008), 370–9.

110 Tony Brown, *The first presidency: Ireland's presidency of the council, January–June 1975, parts 1–3* (Dublin, 2013), 6–8, 10–12 (part one), 2–4 (part two).

111 Ibid., part two, 8–15.

112 E.M. Browne, 'Ireland in the EEC', *The world today*, vol. 31 no. 10 (Oct. 1975), 424–32.

113 Michael Quinn, *Irish–Soviet diplomatic and friendship relations*, chapters 4–6; Tony Brown, *The first presidency: Ireland's presidency of the council, January–June 1975*, part three (Dublin, 2013); Department of foreign affairs and trade, *Celebrating sixty-years: Ireland-Japan diplomatic relations* (Dublin, 2017).

114 Desmond O'Malley, *Conduct unbecoming: a memoir* (Dublin, 2014), 103–15.

115 Diarmaid Ferriter, *The transformation of Ireland* (London, 2005), 683.

116 Kieran Kennedy, T.A. Giblin, Deirdre McHugh (eds), *The economic development of Ireland in the twentieth century* (London, 1988), 179, 183; John Bradley, 'The Irish–Northern Irish economic relationship, the Belfast Agreement, UK devolution and the EU', *Ethnopolitics*, vol. 17 no. 3 (2018), 268–72.

117 Terry Clavin, 'Eamonn Gallagher (1926–2009)', *Dictionary of Irish biography* (online edition).

118 Eamonn Gallagher, 'The north Atlantic fisheries', in J. DeCourcy Ireland, D.C. Sheehy (eds), *Atlantic visions* (Dún Laoghaire, 1989), 105–7 (quote p. 106).

119 For the most part, this opposition was expressed as a fear that joining the EEC would force Ireland to abandon its military neutrality. Patrick Keatinge, *A singular stance* (Dublin, 1984), 28.

120 J. Dooge, R. Barrington (eds) *A vital interest: Ireland in Europe 1973–1998* (Dublin, 1999), 224–36.

121 John Horgan, *Mary Robinson: an independent voice* (Dublin, 1997), 13–28.

122 Aisling O'Sullivan, Roja Fazaeli, 'Multilateralism, human rights and the 1970s: insights from Ireland's role in the evolution of the human rights field', Royal Irish Academy multilateralism and interdependence conference, 2 May 2018.

123 The Unfair Dismissal Act of 1977 and the Maternity Protection of Employees Act of 1981 were among the first pieces of Irish legislation to deal with such questions. Mary Redmond, *Dismissal law in the Republic of Ireland* (Naas, 1982).

124 Mary Robinson, *Everybody matters: a memoir* (London, 2013), chapters 5 and 8.

125 The 1970s women diplomats in question were Anne Anderson, who later became Ireland's first female ambassador to the United States, Marie Cross, an Irish delegate at the United Nations who later became Ireland's first ambassador to Czechoslovakia (1993), and Thelma Doran who, during the 1990s, served as Irish ambassador to China, Poland and Norway. In 1978, Anderson and Doran joined the Irish staff of the 'European Political Cooperation' network of the EEC under Noel Dorr. In the post-1945 period, the only women in the Irish department of external affairs had been Josephine MacNeill and Sheila Murphy.

126 Diarmaid Ferriter, *The transformation of Ireland* (London, 2005), 722–4. At the time, only five of 148 TDs (members of the Irish parliament) were women. Prior to Ireland's

joining the EEC, all Irishwomen had a legal obligation to retire from the civil service upon marrying.

127 This philanthropic Ireland Fund, later renamed the 'American Ireland Fund', would continue to be managed by the Rooney family, while Dan Rooney would later be appointed US ambassador to Ireland (2009–12). Niall O'Dowd, 'Dan Rooney, NFL legend, Ireland Fund founder, former US ambassador, passes', *Irish Central*, 13 Apr. 2017. O'Reilly had worked initially for Irish semi-state companies before becoming the founder of 'Kerrygold' (an Irish butter export company), and then a director, later the chairman, of Heinz food company in Pittsburgh, Pennsylvania.

128 Ivan Fallon, *The player: the life of Tony O'Reilly* (London, 1994), 309–12.

129 A.J.F. O'Reilly, 'Letter from America', in Michael D'Arcy, Tim Dickson (eds), *Border crossings: developing Ireland's island economy* (Dublin, 1995), 3–7.

130 D.H. Akenson, *The United States and Ireland* (Harvard, 1973), ix. From 1934 to date, American ambassadorial envoys to Ireland have never been drawn from the staff of career US diplomats.

131 D.N. Doyle, O.D. Edwards (eds), *America and Ireland 1776–1976: the American identity and the Irish connection* (Connecticut, 1980).

132 Jane Conroy (ed.), *Franco-Irish connections: essays, memoirs and poems in honour of Pierre Joannon* (Dublin, 2009). *Études Irlandaises* was published at the University of Rennes, which had been a base of support for the first Irish diplomatic mission to France after 1919. See chapter two.

133 Richard English, *Armed struggle* (London, 2003), 212–13.

134 John Dumbrell, 'The United States and the Northern Irish conflict 1969–94: from indifference to intervention', *Irish studies in international affairs*, vol. 6 (1995), 114–25.

135 Michael Fitzpatrick, *John Hume in America* (Dublin, 2017), 53–8.

136 Sean Farren, Denis Haughey (eds), *John Hume: Irish peacemaker* (Dublin, 2015), 89–90.

137 P.J. McLoughlin, Alison Meagher, 'The 1977 "Carter Initiative" on Northern Ireland', *Diplomatic history*, vol. 43 no. 4 (2019).

138 Michael Fitzpatrick, *John Hume in America* (Dublin, 2017), 58–69.

139 Ibid., 85.

140 J. E. Thompson, 'Irish National Caucus', in M.F. Funchion (ed.), *Irish American voluntary organizations* (Connecticut, 1983), 177–83.

141 Michael Fitzpatrick, *John Hume in America*, 82.

142 Edward Kennedy, 'The Persian Gulf: arms race or arms control?', *Foreign affairs*, vol. 54 no. 1 (Oct. 1975), 14–35.

143 Luke Devoy, 'The British response to American interest in Northern Ireland 1976–1979', *Irish studies in international affairs*, vol. 25 (2014), 221–38.

144 Richard English, *Armed struggle*, 220.

145 Sean McManus, *My American struggle for justice in Northern Ireland* (Cork, 2011).

146 Members of NORAID were brought before a congressional hearing in 1975 after denunciations by both the Irish and British governments. J.T. Ridge, 'Irish Northern Aid Committee', in M.F. Funchion (ed.), *Irish American voluntary organizations* (Connecticut, 1983), 200–3.

147 Brian Maye, *The search for justice: Trócaire: a history* (Dublin, 2010).

148 Michael Fitzpatrick, *John Hume in America*, 77–81, 84.

149 John O'Hagan, 'The Irish economy 1973–2016', in Thomas Bartlett (ed.), *Cambridge history of Ireland*, vol. 4 (Cambridge, 2017), 500–26.

150 Padraig McGowan, *Money and banking in Ireland* (Dublin, 1990), 85–9. These policies were all opposed by Sinn Féin, which nevertheless (and unusually) published a pamphlet during 1977 entitled *The Banks* that practically called for a revival of the original Sinn Féin policy, largely unspoken of since the 1930s, of bank nationalisation.

151 B.J. Cohen, 'Balance of payments financing: evolution of a regime', *International organization*, vol. 36 no. 2 (spring 1982), 457–78.

152 Michael O'Kennedy, 'The evolution of economic and budgetary policy 1973–83', in J. Dooge, R. Barrington (eds), *A vital interest: Ireland in Europe 1973–1998* (Dublin, 1999), 269–81.

153 Irish imports of Russian oil had grown from £1.5 million in 1973 to £20.5 million in 1977. Michael Quinn, *Irish–Soviet diplomatic and friendship relations*, 156.

154 Frank Barry, John Bradley, 'On the causes of Ireland's unemployment', *The economic and social review*, vol. 22 no. 4 (July 1991), 253–86.

155 Stephen Kelly, 'The totality of relationships: the Haughey–Thatcher relationship and the Anglo-Irish Summit, 8 December 1980', *Éire-Ireland*, vol. 51 no. 3–4 (fall/winter 2016), 244–73.

156 An archive of press reactions can be found at the New York University Internet site '1981 Hunger Strikes: America Reacts'.

157 This would become a defining moment in the history of Northern Ireland Sinn Féin, allowing it to develop a profile, or public voice, that could not easily be suppressed thereafter. Gerry Adams, *Free Ireland* (2nd ed., Dingle, 1995). The first Northern Ireland hunger striker who was elected to parliament purely as a protest vote was Bobby Sands. Two hunger strikers were also elected within the republic as a protest vote.

158 Frank Barry, John Bradley, 'On the causes of Ireland's unemployment', *The economic and social review*, vol. 22 no. 4 (July 1991), 253–86, especially pp. 263–4, 266, 268, 270–2.

159 Richard Burke, 'European special envoy (1982–1985)', in J. Dooge, R. Barrington (eds), *A vital interest: Ireland in Europe 1973–1998* (Dublin, 1999), 257–60; Michael Kennedy, 'Eamonn Kennedy (1921–2000)', *Dictionary of Irish biography* (Cambridge, 2009).

160 Richard Aldous, *Reagan and Thatcher: the difficult relationship* (London, 2012), 85–90. Notwithstanding Reagan's stance, the US navy did offer some assistance to the Royal Navy in the conflict.

161 At the time of Haughey's visit to the White House for Saint Patrick's Day in 1982, some Ulster unionists had started claiming that the American government was behind the IRA. Adrian Guelke, 'The American connection to the Northern Ireland conflict', *Irish studies in international affairs*, vol. 1 no. 4 (1984), 27–39, especially pp. 27–8.

162 Fergal Lenehan, *Stereotypes, ideology and foreign correspondents: German media representations of Ireland 1946–2010* (London, 2016).

163 E.M. Browne, 'Ireland in the EEC', *The world today*, vol. 31 no. 10 (Oct. 1975), 424–32.

164 Michael D. Higgins, 'The case for an Oireachtas foreign policy committee', *Studies* (spring 1988), reproduced in Michael D. Higgins, *Causes for concern* (Dublin, 2007), 201–5.

165 'Interview with Sean O'hUiginn', Edward Kennedy oral history project (PDF available online), quote p. 5.

166 Michael Smurfit, an English-born Irish businessman, had taken advantage of the 1973 amalgamation of the Dublin and London stock exchange to launch his business before, in return, offering a company directorship to Jack Lynch (who subsequently retired) as a sinecure. Michael Smurfit, *A life worth living: the autobiography* (Cork, 2014), 137, 141, 253.

167 Ciaran Brady (ed.), *Interpreting Irish history* (Dublin, 1994). The first journal on this theme, *Irish studies in international affairs*, was launched in 1979. This was published by the Royal Irish Academy, an all-Ireland body that had been based in Dublin since 1785.

168 Patrick Keatinge, *A singular stance: Irish neutrality in the 1980s* (Dublin, 1984); Patrick Keatinge, 'Unequal sovereigns: the diplomatic dimension of Anglo-Irish relations', in P.J. Drudy (ed.), *Ireland and Britain since 1922* (Cambridge, 1986). See also Keatinge's pioneering books, *The formulation of Irish foreign policy* (Dublin, 1973) and *Amongst the nations* (Dublin, 1978).

7

Ireland and the Reinvention of the European Political Order, 1982–1994

The European political order after 1982 was still defined largely by the Helsinki Act that had been signed during Ireland's European Council presidency in 1975 and that had come into being shortly after the European Economic Community (EEC) was first granted 'observer status' at the United Nations (UN). The Helsinki agreement had recognised the ongoing validity of an east–west political divide on the European continent, represented primarily by the continued existence since the 1950s of NATO and the Warsaw Pact as two distinct collective security arrangements. The post-1973 boom for the Russian oil industry meant that economic production outputs within the eastern bloc were now slightly stronger than within the EEC. This was why the Helsinki debate had been held and why an emphasis upon the role of multinational businesses in pushing a transnational agenda was so prevalent within the west.[1] Ireland's diplomatic connection to this whole process was the European Political Cooperation (EPC) committee. This trans-national intelligence committee operated in French, consisted exclusively of diplomatic staff and had been inspired by Étienne Davignon, an aristocratic Belgian foreign secretary. Ireland partook in eight EPC working groups.[2] From 1974 until 1980, the EPC's principal Irish member had been Noel Dorr who, after serving as Ireland's permanent representative at the UN (1980–3) and ambassador to Britain (1983–7), would later become general secretary of Irish department of foreign affairs (1987–95).[3] Dorr was conscious that 'for much of the time and on many issues ... a small state's foreign policy is necessarily reactive', but he was nevertheless a firm believer that Ireland's membership of the European Community was helping to ensure that its overall diplomatic approach was 'positive' through maintaining a symbiotic connection with the heart of greater international developments. This process 'added substance and depth to Ireland's foreign policy'.[4] Meanwhile, combining Ireland's intended role as an intermediary between the developed and developing world with ongoing efforts to sustain the initiative of the nuclear Non-Proliferation Treaty of 1968 had coloured Ireland's UN policy throughout the 1970s.[5]

During 1981, upon Ireland being granted a temporary seat on the UN Security Council for the first time in twenty years, Dorr had criticised Israeli policy towards the Lebanon, where William Callaghan, an Irish lieutenant-general, now commanded the UN peacekeeping forces (approximately 700 Irish soldiers had served in the Lebanon since 1978 and Irish forces would remain there for decades, suffering a total of forty-seven casualties). Combined with consistent Irish championing of relief for refugees in Palestine,[6] this trend sometimes strained Irish–Israeli relations.[7] In keeping with the attitude of its EEC partners, however, Ireland did not essentially have an anti-Israeli policy, having refused to support a UN resolution against Zionism in 1975.[8] In 1979 and again in 1981, the Fianna Fáil foreign minister Michael O'Kennedy, an outspoken supporter of Palestine, had also spoken of Ireland's willingness to take part in a defence of the EEC from any military attack. By 1982, General Carl O'Sullivan, a recently retired chief of staff of the Irish Defence Forces, was calling publicly for a reconsideration of Ireland's non-membership of NATO. At meetings of the EPC, however, Ireland would join those countries that insisted that political, as opposed to military, cooperation should be the limit of the EEC's defence considerations.[9] Indeed, the chief significance of the EPC was essentially its role in sharing information regarding the probable evolution of east–west European relations on a purely economic and political level. In this regard, an unexpected consequence of Russia's post-1973 invasion of the European energy market was that the ageing Soviet leader Leonid Brezhnev, who died in 1982, struggled to counterbalance this development with the highly nationalised economic system that the ruling Russian politburo kept in place. This served to open the door for closer east–west European economic ties, a reformist impulse within Russia itself and a consequent probable reinvention of the European political order by purely economic means.[10]

During 1976, Noel Dorr and Edward Brennan, the Irish ambassador to the USSR and a member of the east-European section of the EPC, brought Garret FitzGerald, Paul Keating (the then secretary-general of foreign affairs) and an agent of Córas Tráchtála to Moscow on a trade mission. On this occasion, Andrei Gromyko, the Soviet foreign minister, expressed the opinion that Ireland occupied an entirely anomalous position in the international order. He typified it as adopting a non-aligned position, but it paradoxically refused to join the post-1961 Non-Aligned Movement at the UN, which consisted mostly of Third World countries that were undergoing a process of decolonisation.[11] Since the days of Lemass, the Irish government had attempted to convince the international community that Ireland was entirely committed to Europe and was certainly not a non-aligned country. This claim was made on the grounds that Ireland could contribute more effectively to the 'support of the principles for which the free democracies stand outside NATO than within it'.[12] Few, if any, states gave much credence to this claim, however, because being a member of the European Community and yet not being a partner in NATO was unusual. Ever since 1978, Ireland's status as one of the most demilitarised countries in the world was also perpetually open for all to see. This was because the International Bank For Reconstruction and Development, or 'World Bank', was now publishing figures of each country's defence spending as well as information regarding the size of its military forces as a percentage of its total financial and human resources.[13] Irish advocacy of disarmament even to the point of being unwilling to properly sustain its own army at home[14] – a development that seemed entirely illogical to neutral countries such as Switzerland and Sweden – often made Ireland's rhetoric of favouring disarmament seem to others to be a mask for 'an abdication of political responsibility', as well as a major 'policy gap with regards to national defence', but stimulating political debate within Ireland itself upon this reality was extraordinarily difficult. In itself, this development was probably a legacy of the degree to which de Valera's longstanding secrecy regarding his desire to maintain Ireland as a neutralised, as opposed to a strictly neutral, state had engendered deep public misunderstandings, as well as the rise of some myopic civil servants, within Ireland itself.[15]

General O'Sullivan's pro-NATO statements were criticised greatly in the Dáil because Irish law forbids soldiers from expressing political opinions. The still Eurosceptic Irish Labour Party, as well as a new pro-European Green Party, often conflated their support for Irish military neutrality with championing non-aligned movements and moral support for all anti-nuclear power lobby groups. Since 1979, an Irish Committee for Nuclear Disarmament (which was first founded in 1958 but was practically dormant after 1968) had acquired about 5,000 members. It frequently picketed both foreign embassies and the Irish department of foreign affairs in disapproval of their toleration of the militarism of the great powers. In the wake of President Reagan's championing of a new nuclear deterrent programme during 1983, such voluntary groups often portrayed America to be the chief aggressor in international relations. This trend was something that an official visit to Ireland that year by American vice-president George Bush did little to alter.[16]

Lack of transparency regarding how funds of the Irish state's developmental aid programme were being distributed would motivate a Labour Party demand for the creation of an all-party 'foreign policy committee' of the Irish houses of parliament, encompassing both the government and all parties of the opposition.[17] Ireland's development aid programme had recently been encouraged by the EPC committee to extend its focus from Africa to Latin America. In itself, this trend could involve an implicit or direct criticism of US foreign policy.[18] The role of religion in shaping Irish attitudes to international affairs was perhaps made most evident during the 1980s. In Ireland, family law remained conservative (two-thirds of voters rejected abortion and divorce laws during the mid-1980s) but the Irish state was actually 'one of the least confessional in Europe, with no official church'.[19] This can perhaps explain why the prevalent labour reaction against a supposed establishment ethos of Christian-democratic governments in Europe during the 1970s had not been very noticeable in Ireland. Instead, in the wake of Pope John Paul II's popular visit in 1979 (the first-ever papal visit to Ireland), contemporary Irish intellectuals were more likely to speak of the virtues of a Christian socialism.[20] A similar spirit perhaps underpinned the most notorious, Irish-inspired, non-governmental initiative of the mid-1980s. In response to a growing famine in Somalia, Irish, or Irish-born, entertainers would play a large part in creating rock music festivals for charity purposes, leading to the initiation of 'Band Aid' and 'Live Aid' events abroad, to which Ireland was the highest per capita donor. However, unlike the avowed Marxism of the highly profitable 'punk rock' music industry in Britain, these Irish initiatives bore no ideological slogans.[21] Throughout the 1980s, the Irish Labour Party's foreign affairs spokesman Michael D. Higgins, who later became an Irish president, actually used an Irish rock music magazine *Hot Press* as his vehicle, but in doing so he expressed primarily a humanitarian concern for all developing countries.[22] His envisioned parliamentary joint committee on foreign affairs, however, would not be established in Ireland until 1993, while it was not until the creation of a Human Rights Unit of the Irish department of foreign affairs in 1997 that it began to develop a formal association with the rising number of non-governmental organisations in Ireland.[23]

By 1983, John Hume was a European and a Westminster parliamentary representative as well as a critic of London and Dublin's uninspired talk of creating a new Northern Ireland assembly purely as a means to contain a protest vote that was caused by the 1981 hunger strikes. The latter saw Sinn Féin acquire a brief peak in electoral support (which would not be repeated for another fifteen years), although it still did not possess one-third of the following of Hume's SDLP. The essential reason for this was Hume's perfectly honest explanation of a sad fact of Northern Ireland's existence: almost three-quarters of the £427 million invested in Northern Ireland since 1968 had needed to be spent on repairing 'industrial and commercial damage caused by paramilitary bombing', creating an almost zero-sum result for nationalist areas like his own constituency of Derry and Strabane. This trend had ensured that in Northern Ireland 'the skilled and professional emigrate, while the economy stagnates and the semi-skilled and unskilled swell the unemployment lines, as well as the ranks of parliamentary organisations'.[24] Illustrating his willingness to prioritise a cross-community political vision, Hume invited Ian Paisley of the rising Democratic Unionist Party (DUP) to join him on a brief Ulster investment promotion tour of North America during September 1983, although all unionists refused to accept the Irish government's invitation to join Hume in a New Ireland Forum at Dublin Castle. This was an attempt to bring about an effective north–south Irish political dialogue and it met between May 1983 and February 1984. It coincided with a Danish-led and Hume-inspired EEC investigation into circumstances in Northern Ireland. This used as its premise the fact that 1984 was intended to be a special year for celebrating the cultural diversity of Europe. Hume would welcome the publication of a New Ireland Forum Report in May 1984, but he was privately disappointed with its conclusion. Dublin viewed the Northern question as a purely constitutional issue that could only have three possible legal solutions: a single united Ireland; a federal government for the island of Ireland; or joint British and Irish sovereignty over Northern Ireland.[25] By contrast, Hume's purpose in arranging discussions with parties within the Irish state was to see the emergence of a planned 'process of building a new Ireland' in which 'there are no longer any unconditional guarantees' for any one party, but rather 'there are guarantees [of rights] for all' as an expected outcome.[26]

Writing for *Foreign Affairs*, Hume had accused both the British and Irish governments of an inability to understand Ulster. London's use of a majority rule claim as an embargo on change and Dublin's 'hint of irredentism' and 'ambiguity' were, to his mind, a mirror of each other's unwillingness to see Ulster in the light of the reality of its inhabitants' lived experience. Regarding the unionist majority within Northern Ireland, Hume noted that its political leaders, or at least its spokesmen within an emerging Ulster academia, were 'justly proud' of their 'contribution to the world' in previous centuries. By now, however, these men felt that 'a British retreat from a world view' was the most probable explanation for its uncharacteristic inability to find a practical solution to Northern Ireland's problems. Hume judged that a logical conclusion that could be drawn from this trend was that both the USA and EEC should act on the premise that for them to take an interest in Northern Ireland's problems was both 'historically inevitable and perfectly legitimate', not least because it could provide London and Dublin with the 'courage' necessary to begin to look to the wider world in the search for a workable solution. Hume maintained that a challenge for Ireland as a whole was to begin to draw its inspiration primarily from international affairs, not least by asking in the light of the success of the USA and EEC in creating 'a unity in diversity' within their own jurisdictions whether or not 'is it too much to ask that we on this small island do precisely the same thing?'[27]

As the leader of a new Fine Gael government (1983–7), Garret FitzGerald spoke before a joint session of the US Houses of Congress in March 1984. With the encouragement of James Sharkey, the political officer of the Irish embassy at Washington D.C., he called upon the American government to pay particular attention to the New Ireland Forum initiative.[28] Within a month of the publication of the New Ireland Forum Report that May, Ronald Reagan paid a four-day state visit to Ireland while on his way to attending a French-inspired commemoration of the fortieth anniversary of the American naval landing in Normandy and the resulting liberation of France. On being received by Irish president Patrick Hillery at Shannon Airport, Reagan echoed J.F. Kennedy by speaking in praise of Ireland's role in international councils and UN peacekeeping, and also spoke about the strength of American–Irish friendship. By contrast, on addressing a joint session of the Irish houses of parliament three days later, Reagan concentrated primarily on justifying US foreign policy. In doing so, he perhaps anticipated that anti-nuclear power protest demonstrations would be held regarding his visit.[29] In general, however, as had been the case even with the Vietnam War, the American government was generally well aware that popular excitement about US foreign policy abroad, even when it was negative, was, in itself, a reflection the success of its 'soft power' initiative of making purely American concerns seem to foreigners like it was equally their own.

Reagan had recently allowed for the establishment of a papal nuncio in America for the first time, just two years after Britain formally instigated full diplomatic relations with the Vatican for the first time since the English Reformation. While speaking in the Dáil, Reagan stressed the central role of religion in combating totalitarian political ideologies, not least in Latin America. Contrary to popular opinion, he also emphasised that recent American nuclear-deterrent initiatives, such as meeting the Soviets and European leaders under IMF and UN auspices at Stockholm and Geneva respectively, were aimed purely at disarmament. In both his Shannon and Dublin speeches, Reagan emphasised America's total opposition to all forms of terrorism in

Northern Ireland.[30] However, while he suggested at Shannon that American investment in Ireland could help to remedy the conflict,[31] in the Dáil he spoke only about the potential role of trans-national businesses in promoting better foreign relations in general. American investment in Ireland had increased from approximately $72 million during the 1960s (in the process helping to create over 10,000 jobs) to about $4.6 billion in 1984, which in turn helped to create 37,000 jobs as a result of the operations of 350 American firms within Ireland.[32] This showed that, despite the Irish government's fears or even expectations during the early 1970s, the Northern Troubles had not served to lessen American investment in Ireland. Finally, in a brief reference to the New Ireland Forum Report, Reagan emphasised that the US 'will not interfere in Irish matters' but would nevertheless offer its 'goodwill and support' in the work of peace.[33]

Another context of Reagan's visit was that Ireland was about to succeed France, which was re-emerging as the principal continental ally of Reagan's Republican administration, as the holder of the presidency of the European Council (July–December 1984). Since the second oil crisis of the late 1970s, the EEC was widely considered to be suffering from a form of 'sclerosis', having fallen well behind the productivity of countries like the United States and Japan, but Ireland's presidency of the European Council coincided with a fresh sense of purpose and direction.[34] Garret FitzGerald renewed the Lomé agreement between the EEC and Africa, helped to boost plans for the accession of Iberia into the European community and supported the creation of a European currency unit. A European 'committee of institutional affairs' was also created to look at the best means of drafting a new legal treaty between EEC member states to overhaul, or expand, the existing Treaty of Rome (1957) with a view to creating a formal European Union. Led by Jim Dooge, a former Irish minister for foreign affairs, this committee laid the basis for a 'Single European Act', signed in February 1986, which was widely seen to have simply streamlined the operations of the European common market, but it actually marked the moment when the EPC was fully incorporated into EEC law for the first time.[35]

While John Hume had seen the New Ireland Forum initiative to be a purely north–south matter, Garret FitzGerald and the Irish department of foreign affairs used the occasion to promote a simultaneous British–

Irish dialogue in keeping with the Thatcher–Haughey initiative of 1980. This was done by arranging talks between two veterans of the Sunningdale negotiations over a decade earlier, namely British Cabinet Secretary Robert Armstrong and Dermot Nally who, as secretary to the department of the Taoiseach, was practically the Irish cabinet secretary. These inter-cabinet talks were still taking place in November 1984 when, shortly after the bombing of a British Tory party conference in Brighton, Margaret Thatcher declared that all suggestions of the New Ireland Forum Report were inherently out of the question.[36] Being in America at the time, John Hume responded by requesting Tip O'Neill, who had remained the Speaker of the US House of Congress under the Republican administration, to persuade Reagan to advise Thatcher to be far more attentive to Irish considerations. Although Reagan had recently rejected Ted Kennedy's longstanding idea of appointing a special American peace envoy to Northern Ireland, on meeting Thatcher in Washington the following month, Reagan emphasised to her 'the desirability of flexibility on the part of all the involved parties … in resolving the complex situation in Northern Ireland' and that the American government considered the Irish government to be its friend as much as it did the British government.[37]

This gentle American pressure on London soon began to have an impact.[38] On being invited by O'Neill to speak before the Joint Houses of Congress in February 1985, Thatcher now recognised the significance of the New Ireland Forum Report and practically made an unprecedented admission by a British government by acknowledging that it had never believed that the government of the Irish republic was in any sense morally responsible for Northern Irish terrorism. The British embassy in Washington was still secretly attempting, however, to persuade Reagan not to support FitzGerald's idea of creating a new Anglo-Irish agreement that would allow for the Irish government to have a voice in shaping Northern Irish affairs. Tip O'Neill worked successfully to resist this push, however, and so Thatcher ended up signing an Anglo-Irish agreement with FitzGerald on 15 November 1985. This was subsequently registered in international law at the United Nations and was welcomed publicly by Reagan.[39] Be that as it may, the Washington correspondent of *The Irish Times* responded by publishing a book on the history of American–Irish relations that argued that Washington's indifference to poor Irish immigrants in America, as well as its alleged history of 'pro-British' rather than 'pro-Irish' behaviour, was proof that President Reagan's support of the Anglo-Irish Agreement was not made with Ireland's best interests at heart.[40] American diplomats tended to view the popularity of such arguments in Ireland as an indication that Irish analysts were intellectually incapable of distinguishing between the priorities of Britain and that of all other countries in international relations and that (no different from other countries) American foreign policy, whether under Democratic or Republican administrations, was naturally determined at all times by practical issues of national self-interest, rather than national biases, and an expectation of bilateral benefits and increased mutual understanding arising from its dealings with any individual country in international relations, including Ireland.[41]

As it did not originate purely with London, the Anglo-Irish Agreement could have been typified as an actual achievement of the Irish department of foreign affairs. From the Irish government's point of view, its chief significance was that Britain was now legally obliged for the first time to take into consideration any expressed concerns, or advice, regarding Northern Ireland that emanated from the Irish government. These concerns would be voiced via a new small secretariat, stationed at Maryfield, Belfast.[42] Of perhaps even greater consequence for the chances of peace in Northern Ireland, however, was that an 'International Fund for Ireland' was established that could allow American state investment in Northern Ireland to take place. This practically consummated a suggestion first made by US president Jimmy Carter in 1977 but which had remained dormant ever since. This was a separate matter to the entirely voluntary 'American Ireland Fund' that had been launched by Tony O'Reilly in 1976 and that now inspired similar bodies within a half-dozen other countries, including within the British Commonwealth.[43]

Hitherto, the possibilities of establishing American businesses in Northern Ireland, including a very expensive and yet unsuccessful attempt to establish a sports-car factory in west Belfast,[44] were dependent on a case-by-case analysis of the degree to which it suited the UK market as a whole. However, Senator Ted Kennedy, Mark Durkan of the SDLP and Michael Lillis of the Irish department of foreign affairs now encouraged Congress in America to recommend an annual blanket expenditure of $20 million a year. A desire for no undue American influence in its internal affairs can explain why the British Commonwealth countries of Canada and New Zealand responded by launching a rival initiative. The essential issue with regards to the 'International Fund for Ireland', however, was that its mere existence recognised that the economy specifically of Northern Ireland was both a special case and an international issue. Reflecting this, in addition to American and British Commonwealth funding, the International Fund for Ireland would soon be made open to European funding. This effectively realised Hume's goal that European regional development policies could begin to apply to Northern Ireland around the time that the Single European Act was ratified in February 1986.[45] Such financial developments, arising from the Anglo-Irish Agreement of 1985, could benefit all Ulster parties, but hostility was very strong from all unionists, who staged a symbolic walkout from Westminster in protest against Thatcher's signing of the Anglo-Irish Agreement. It was particularly intense among DUP supporters who, in calling for the agreement to be scrapped, burnt Irish tricolours at massive open-air rallies in Belfast and repeated more forcibly than ever their claim that the Irish government was the sole and perpetual cause of terrorism within Northern Ireland for supposedly allowing the secret IRA society a safe haven within the republic's jurisdiction.[46]

By 1985, Ireland's trade with the United Kingdom had dropped to about one-third of its total trade and the country was focused primarily on the broader European market.[47] This was not reflected, however, in contemporary scholarship. In the wake of the Anglo-Irish Agreement, a five-volume publication of Cambridge University Press was issued that initiated within academia 'Irish Studies Programmes' that defined the experience of Ireland, and that of all Irish immigrants in America and the British Commonwealth, in the light of continuities in the British historical experience. It was argued that Britain's non-membership of the European Monetary System (EMS) inherently created financial instability in Ireland, reflected by constant fluctuations in the value of the Irish pound, and therefore Ireland must reverse its prior decision to join the EMS.[48] In opposition to European harmonisation programmes, it was advised that direct Irish legal and financial emulations of the

British social security system must continue. Finally, it was stressed that Ireland must follow Britain's EEC policy more closely and use the opportunity of inter-governmental conferences ever since December 1980 primarily to reconcile its diplomatic stance more fully with that of Britain.[49]

Gemma Hussey, an intensely pro-European leader of the Irish Senate who was also Ireland's leading feminist politician during the 1980s, attributed these trends to the 'almost complete lack of interaction between groups which should be working together – business, industry, universities, civil service, politicians', with the inevitable end result that there was an over-reliance in Ireland on the opinions of others, as well as an unduly insecure and fragmented approach towards governance.[50] As if to remedy this trend, her Fine Gael party, while it had always identified itself as Ireland's most pro-European party, now practically became a champion of European federalism. It celebrated the fact that its party member Peter Sutherland, an ex-Irish attorney general, had recently become the chief aide of European Commission president Jacques Delors in promoting not only the Single European Act but also in bringing about much closer relations between the European Commission and the European Parliament.[51] However, although Ireland had nominally chaired the September 1984 European Council sessions that led to the initiation of European currency plans, the Central Bank of Ireland, in common with the Bank of England, was evidently the only central bank of an EEC-member state that was not a player in the successful German-led push thereafter in stimulating continent-wide support for creating a European Central Bank.[52] Therefore, bodies such as the Irish Economic and Social Research Institute (ESRI) were acutely aware that, in the absence of relevant knowledge regarding the true dynamics of the European project, only a great deal of uncertainty could exist in Ireland regarding the country's evolving relationship with the European Community.[53] In practice, the ESRI, an influential non-governmental and academic organisation, judged the government's pro-European stance to be more politically motivated than economically sound and, on this basis, was actually inclined to call for a means to hold the state's foreign trade policy to account, deeming any focus outside the UK to be unwise.[54] Irish economic instability would crush the pro-European Fine Gael government in January 1987, prompting

Garret FitzGerald to soon retire altogether from politics, albeit not from journalism.

The influence of London financial markets was such that, up until the late 1980s, the Irish banks tended to view the 'maximum currency instability for Ireland' after it left the sterling area in 1979 as essentially an unwise gamble that had been taken by pro-Europeans due to 'a perceived political and diplomatic imperative'.[55] As 'the credibility benefits of Ireland's membership of the EMS were delayed by about a decade',[56] in the meantime the country was often torn between those who saw rising national debt, emigration and unemployment figures (akin to the situation during the 1950s) as being the result of susceptibility to British economic pressures or else an inevitable consequence of a foolish desire to decrease such bonds. A significant factor shaping such considerations was that the EMS 'has hardly ever been free from government intervention',[57] while the practice of state regulation of banking, first initiated in Ireland during 1962, had been practically undone in Ireland after 1969 and would not be restored again until, in rather different circumstances, after 1998. The impact that this great volatility had on Ireland's international reputation during the 1980s can be witnessed in an American study of Ireland from this time that suggested that, in the light of the Irish tendency to adopt purely reactive and piecemeal economic policies, all orthodox thinkers of international relations believed that Ireland should be considered as occupying a similar position to 'the semi-developed countries of Latin America', 'using the easy credit thrust upon it' for little other than to 'minimise the social dislocation caused by the process of integration into the international community' whilst exhibiting no constructive capacity for strategic thinking, either nationally or internationally.[58]

During the 1980s, the world of Irish retail banking was notable for the assistance it gave to new medium-sized Irish businesses, such as supermarkets, although the historic monopoly of UK firms within the Irish retail market was never actively resisted and so was always liable to be reasserted forcibly with just subtle market pressures.[59] Combined with the Irish agricultural industry's reliance on the British food market and, in particular, British transport and food-processing firms, this reality was sufficient to convince the UK that it could still forever lead Ireland wherever and whenever it willed. Aside from defining Ulster unionism, this belief also shaped a cultural mentality that a recent British ambassador to Dublin had described as the UK's perpetual 'Isle of Wight syndrome': 'to forget entirely that Ireland is independent'.[60] Patrick Keatinge, the leader of the Royal Irish Academy's international affairs committee, suggested that the fact that 'the relevant machinery of government in Dublin is on a significantly smaller scale' was sufficient to ensure that Ireland was bound to follow Britain's lead with regards to critical matters such as the EPC.[61] Meanwhile, the Irish government's direct diplomatic involvement in supporting the Single European Act belied a degree of Irish opposition to this trend.

Raymond Crotty, an Irish lecturer in agrarian economics and a future advisor to the World Bank, challenged the passing of the Single European Act on the grounds that the legalisation of Ireland's involvement in the EPC impacted on Irish sovereignty and so should have been made the subject of a national referendum. Together with Anthony Coughlan, a Trinity College Dublin political scientist and champion of British Labour propaganda regarding Ireland,[62] Crotty had been a campaigner against Irish entry into the EEC as early as 1972 and his appeal to the Irish Supreme Court was successful, thus necessitating that an Irish referendum on the Single European Act (SEA) be held in May 1987.[63] A pro-European vision was not very widely accepted by the Catholic Church in Ireland because Irish Catholic organisations and newspapers, feeling a sense of duty to the Catholic population on the much more populous island of Britain and being conscious that the Irish ecclesiastical capital (Armagh) was located within Northern Ireland, took their cues on civil relations largely from UK organisations, such as Civitas. Dermot Keogh, an Irish graduate of the European Institute in Florence and author on Irish relations with the Vatican,[64] noted at the time how various international developments tended 'be the focus of criticism [in Ireland] from the well intentioned and the concerned alike for as long as the process is perceived as being "Masonic"'.[65] Pádraig MacKernan, Ireland's permanent representative at Brussels, argued that neither the SEA nor the EPC served to undermine Ireland's right to exercise an independent diplomatic stance because joining a forum for foreign policy consultation in no sense created a compulsion to follow other countries' dictates.[66] The public voted in favour of the government's acceptance of the act by a large margin, although few during the referendum were convinced that the Irish public had any real conception of the European community's status as an evolving political and legal, as opposed to purely economic, entity.[67] The Irish government's official case in the referendum was that 'approving the Single European Act ... will be a vital step forward in Ireland's economic development' by safeguarding the operations of regional development funds, while 'co-operation is limited to foreign policy issues of general interest, including the political and economic aspects of security. The *military* aspects of security are deliberately omitted from this co-operation'.[68]

The New York and London stock exchange crash of 1987 encouraged the Irish government to consider that the only apparent solution to the country's growing balance of payments deficit problem, which stemmed from extensive borrowing necessary to implement many infrastructural developments, was to prioritise introducing international 'financial services' industries to Ireland (as was also occurring in Britain) rather than attempting to boost regular industrial employment. This led to the initiation of plans to construct a new International Financial Services Centre (IFSC) on the Dublin docklands. This occured shortly before (on an American and British initiative) a Basel Accord was reached as a multilateral agreement between the central bankers of the ten 'group summit' nations to establish a common international standard to regulate capital risk management.[69] The IFSC was intended to serve as a flagship enterprise for attracting more multinational businesses (including financial services companies) to Ireland by offering a low corporation tax rate; the latter being an Irish proposal, suggested by Peter Sutherland, that the EEC agreed to partly because of Ireland's current financial difficulties.[70] More than anything else, this development would appear to have sparked the initiation of a positive impact of the EMS upon Ireland.

The nominal initiator of the IFSC was Charles Haughey, who would serve as Taoiseach for four years (1987–91) and used this opportunity to attempt to revive the 'social partnership' economic model that he had first championed during 1967. His Fianna Fáil party had been Ireland's largest political party ever since the 1930s, but had suffered greatly from embittered vanities of rival party leaders ever since its founders – de Valera, Aiken, O'Kelly and Lemass – began retiring from the political scene during the 1960s. Haughey was considered during the late 1960s as perhaps the most dynamic finance minister that Ireland had known. He resented deeply that his career was thereafter temporarily destroyed upon his being made the scapegoat of the very peculiar 'arms trial' controversy in 1970 by the (then) Irish justice minister Desmond O'Malley who, in failing to oust Haughey as party leader, would in 1985 create a short-lived party as a breakaway from Fianna Fáil, the Progressive Democrats, supposedly purely in opposition to Haughey's allegedly secretive and authoritarian approach to governance.[71] At a time when extensive foreign investment had also created a large foreign debt, the Progressive Democrats were generally seen to be a business-orientated party that were in favour of promoting more foreign direct investment in Ireland but were also calling for an emulation of Margaret Thatcher's programme of cutting back on social security expenditure.[72] This was not a popular policy. A de-prioritisation of purely national industries and even services (such as hospitals)[73] had resulted in many company closures, both private and semi-state, causing unemployment and emigration to rocket (boosted in part by extraordinarily high income taxes) while many staff of Córas Tráchtála, the old Irish export board, voluntarily retired in despair.[74] Reflecting this trend, efforts to revitalise Irish cities with anniversary events, such as Galway's 500th year in 1984, Cork's 800th year in 1986 and Dublin's 1,000th year in 1988, evidently focused more on promoting the operations of foreign multinationals, rather than national businesses, within Ireland.

Growing efforts to expand Irish trading operations through new multinational businesses sometimes created national controversies. For instance, Irish live animal exports to the Middle East, and in particular Iraq, became very large (£42 million). While this would not prevent Ireland from supporting the UN censor of Iraq for invading Kuwait in 1990,[75] it would lead to national accusations of undue favouritism being granted to a single Irish multinational businessman, just as the willingness of the Irish government (with some encouragement from the Irish embassy in Washington D.C.) to sell its share in the Irish sugar company to an American multinational was deemed controversial.[76] In general, however, the cessation of monopolies within state-owned Irish aviation and media industries, which had hitherto been a regular source of sinecures for retiring Irish diplomats and political leaders, helped to create some new thriving businesses, including a popular low-fares airline, Ryanair. Responding to Russia's new openness to extensive diplomacy and trade with the west around the same time that Mikhail Gorbachev made a brief diplomatic visit to Shannon Airport, Ireland's 'Aer Rianta' airport services company was able to launch Moscow Airport's first duty-free shopping centre with Haughey's encouragement.[77] Meanwhile, lest he be accused of not sharing the same clear vision as Fine Gael of the relevance of the European project, during 1989 Haughey would appoint to the European Commission Ray MacSharry. As commissioner for agriculture and rural development, MacSharry reorientated Europe's Common Agricultural Policy with a view to forthcoming European involvement with the United States and Australia in renegotiating the General Agreement on Tariffs and Trade (GATT) in multilateral trade talks that would be chaired by Peter Sutherland.[78]

Although Tip O'Neill retired from American politics in January 1987, the 'Congressional Friends of Ireland' movement that he had co-founded in 1981 continued to exist as a perpetual forum for annual American–Irish conferences. These were held in conjunction with a now-established tradition of Saint Patrick's Day visits to the White House by leaders of the Irish government.[79] By the late 1980s, however, Sean McManus' independent Irish National Caucus had been able to generate ever-growing public support in America for 'principles' that it had first drawn up during 1984 and to which it had succeeded in getting the elderly Irish figure of Sean MacBride (who died in 1988) to attach his well-known name.[80] Although this programme stated that American foreign investment and resulting employments within Northern Ireland must ensure that no discriminations should take place on religious grounds, the 'MacBride Principles' paradoxically demanded that, in the name of fair employment practices, a degree of positive discrimination should be taken in favour of the minority Catholic community in the light of the past discriminiations that they had suffered. Haughey and his foreign minister Brian Lenihan deemed the MacBride Principles to be unobjectionable and this placed Ireland's diplomatic corps in a difficult situation in implementing government policy, not least because Britain unsurprisingly declared that any outside attempts to influence employment legislation within Northern Ireland must be considered

illegal. As the US state department did not support it, the only potential
in the scheme essentially lay in its capacity to influence the operations
of the International Fund for Ireland at individual state level within the
United States.[81] John Hume actively opposed the whole scheme, judging
that their criteria had no intrinsic business logic and, therefore, would
actively create an incentive for non-investment, or even disinvestment,
in Northern Ireland.[82] Hume's stance was logical but, despite McManus'
well-known political ineptitude, the Catholic Church in Ulster and
America became inclined to throw its considerable weight behind the
'MacBride Principles'. This caused Hume to lose popularity within both
his own SDLP party and in Irish America, where a fresh wave of Irish
emigration had created a new Irish immigrant press in New York City
that, to Dublin's dismay, soon welcomed contributions from Sinn Féin
president Gerry Adams.[83]

On the question of Northern Ireland, Haughey had instated
as Fianna Fáil's permanent advisor Martin Mansergh, a son of the
former official historian of the British Commonwealth who had served
during the 1970s as an economic advisor to the Irish department of
foreign affairs before being appointed by Haughey as a secretary of the
department of the Taoiseach upon the launch of the tradition of British–
Irish intergovernmental conferences in 1980.[84] Both men desired to
revive, or sustain, an Irish political tradition that had been associated
with de Valera, whereby ecumenical movements and an Irish cultural
nationalism were to be considered as literally embodying 'the spirit
of the nation', for which Haughey was now to act as the spokesman.[85]
In practice, this meant that the consolidation, or representation, of
the wealth and interests of the churches, as well as their supporting
business networks, became a definite aspect of Fianna Fáil's approach
to Irish national politics. Although the relevance of this stance to the
international identity of the Irish state was perhaps limited, the potential
of Mansergh's vision to serve as a catch-all platform was enhanced by
the fact that it was in keeping with the Christian-democratic vision
of de Valera's extant Irish constitution, while it was also supported
by both T.K. Whitaker, a critic of the Anglo-Irish Agreement,[86] and
the established editorial policy of *The Irish Times* on both Northern
Ireland and British–Irish relations.[87] Haughey had initially indicated
a willingness to oppose the Anglo-Irish Agreement in the expectation

that it would prove unpopular with voters before a realisation that it had popular support led him to reverse this stance.[88]

In the interests of creating what he termed a peace process, Hume had recently initiated private talks with Gerry Adams, who had many IRA contacts. This development was purposively leaked to the press, however, not long after an Armistice Day commemoration (which had long been a practice of most western European governments) was bombed by the Provisional IRA in Enniskillen, County Fermanagh.[89] This led to Hume being condemned by Conor Cruise O'Brien, who now began defining himself in the British print media as a great moral defender of Ulster unionism against the evils represented by both the Irish government and John Hume.[90] At the time, the Irish government's Maryfield secretariat in Belfast was alive to reporting abuses of power by security forces within Northern Ireland, while high-profile legal cases were taking place in Britain of former miscarriages of justice against alleged IRA suspects. Be that as it may, O'Brien's lead articles in the London press actually set a tone for much writing on Ireland within the English print-media world thereafter, partly because he was widely considered to be a well-informed figure on international relations.[91] This may possibly explain why a recently appointed young official in Ireland's New York consular office would soon decide to retire and write a memoir that, while not denying its capacity for patriotism, essentially portrayed Iveagh House, the headquarters of Ireland's foreign service, as a refuge for men whose personal vanities and self-serving careerism was the only thing protecting them from realising that the rest of the world was simply not listening to them.[92] When Haughey assumed the six-month presidency of the European Council in January 1990, even the Irish national media was inclined to be highly sceptical about Irish pretensions to be significant figures on the international stage.[93] Be that as it may, in Europe itself, Haughey's presidency was generally regarded as extraordinarily efficient.[94]

Two European Council meetings were held in Dublin to facilitate the year-long process of German reunification initiated by the fall of the Berlin Wall in November 1989. This was predicated on creating a German monetary union that the EEC, excepting perhaps the UK, hoped would thereafter become an aspect of a greater plan for a European monetary and political union. To this end, Haughey set up an 'Intergovernmental Conference on European Political Union' with the support of Francois Mitterrand and Helmut Kohl with a view to creating a forthcoming European treaty. Meanwhile, Haughey's new foreign minister Gerry Collins chaired meetings at which plans were introduced to intergrate the European Free Trade Area states (Norway, Switzerland, Iceland and Liechtenstein) into a new European Economic Area. The process of German reunification naturally led to a dissolving of the eastern European security pact that had been drawn up in Warsaw over three decades previously. This led almost immediately to the re-emergence of new European states such as Poland and Czechoslovakia with which Ireland, in common with virtually all western countries, was now eager to establish diplomatic relations.[95] To the Poles, the USSR had always been considered to be a multi-ethnic and multi-resourced empire that had been held together not by ideology but by military force. The belief that this legacy was still intact, either economically or culturally,[96] would motivate its own desire to emerge as a significant military power itself. Russia had been suffering from deep imbalances in its state finances for some time. For many Russians, these difficulties (as well as the rise of a new criminal black market and political corruption within Russia itself) were considered to be longstanding issues that had predated Gorbachev's term of office. In the meantime, he had simply benefited from the fact that 'after Brezhnev, any leader of the USSR who could even speak normally was regarded as a hero'.[97]

Upon the replacement of the USSR by a new Russian Federation in December 1991, Ireland attempted to expand the parameters of pre-existing nuclear non-proliferation agreements and promote bans on both biological and chemical weapons through its permament representative at the UN, Mahon Hayes, who, for several years, had also been vice-president of the UN Commission on Human Rights. However, Hayes was soon encouraged to join Peter Sutherland's GATT negotiating team instead, perhaps reflecting the degree to which the globally orientated strategy of promoting intercontinental free trade agreements had become a priority at the UN.[98] To Haughey himself, his presidency of the European Council at such a momentuous time was the high point of his own career, although he would soon be forced to retire by his own finance minister Albert Reynolds, who succeeded him as Taoiseach. In a final note of controversy, Haughey would later become the subject of the most high-profile Irish tax avoidance scandal. The process of Ireland's adaption to an enlarging European community would have to be managed by other hands.

Once it was clear that Ireland was to vote on another major European treaty, university conferences were held on the question of Ireland and European integration. Unlike publications of the European Community's review *Libertas*, however, the resulting publications involved no international contributors, except for a couple of British authors,[99] perhaps indicating that Ireland's 'good citizen' approach to Europe did not really matter to its continental partners. The entry of the British pound into the European exchange rate mechanism during the autumn of 1990, aside from prompting Thatcher's retirement, led to a brief period when London economists, probably inspired by German reunification as much as the desire to limit fluctuations in the value of the British pound, celebrated the European project as an instrument for the 'rescue of the nation state' and, in particular, the ongoing development of the welfare state.[100] The Maastricht Treaty, signed by all European heads of government four days before Haughey's retirement in February 1992, was accepted by 70 per cent of Irish voters in a referendum. It planned to launch within two years both the European Union (EU) and a form of European citizenship by creating a legal suzerainty for European courts and a multinational policing system. Before this could happen, however, the British pound again dropped out of the European exchange rate mechanism (as did, temporarily, the Italian lira), reputedly due to damaging speculations on the value of sterling in foreign exchange markets by George Soros, a maverick Hungarian investor who favoured the creation of a European currency and the expansion of the EU into eastern Europe. Britain had consistently resisted efforts to create a European currency since 1978, but its subsequent claim that a European currency was an undemocratic idea because of the unaccountability of a proposed European central bank lacked credibility: the UK itself decided to make the Bank of England an entirely independent arbiter of British monetary policy shortly before the European Central Bank was created in 1998, while elective banking institutions were an unknown quantity everywhere.[101] Britain's argument did, however, reflect the fact that the status of the elective European Parliament was likely to be the subject of the next European treaty.

Despite the cessation of the Warsaw Pact, the replacement of the EPC with a new Common Foreign and Security Policy (CFSP) did not alter the European Community's ongoing acceptance of NATO, rather than the moribund Western European Union (WEU), as the essential basis for the operation of collective security in Europe. Seeing European unity as an economic and cultural matter, some Irish foreign ministers had expressed the idea that NATO was an outdated concept even prior to the fall of the Berlin Wall.[102] It survived because it enabled America, despite its engagements in Latin America, Asia and the Middle East, to retain its influence in Europe by subsidising states' defence budgets and, in the process, perhaps limit any potential revival of historic British-Franco-German rivalries. Be that as it may, Ireland was always inclined to question the wisdom of America's reliance on the operations of a military-industrial complex as a basis for sustaining its influence in the world. An alternative method was now developed, however, for dealing with potential issues in central and eastern Europe, which was the creation of European peacekeeping forces who would act as auxiliary police forces in support of UN-recognised treaties. Irish army personnel first joined one of these European peacekeeping missions as early as October 1991, in the former Yugoslavia.[103] UN-sanctioned missions were the extent to which Ireland was prepared to engage in collective security arrangements, although the post-Maastricht Irish referendum necessitated a revision of Ireland's constitutional article relating to international relations, which now emphasised that 'no provision of this constitution invalidates laws enacted, acts done or measures adopted by the state which are necessitated by the obligations of membership of the European Union'.[104] Although Europe involved no formal defence obligations, the development of new European security policies encouraged Ireland to develop a stronger sense of its role in an evolving new geopolitics. In particular, unlike states such as Finland, Ireland did not see its lack of neutrality in supporting European foreign policy and peacekeeping operations in the post-Cold War world as having served to undermine its policy of military neutrality.[105]

By 1991, 75 per cent of Irish exports went to the European community and the Irish government had willingly passed into Irish competition law a European law forbidding inter-state competition in a manner akin to inter-state, or federal, law in the United States. This reflected the extent to which the new European Union was intended from its inception to be a political federation that was designed to enable the emergence of Europe as a distinct regional trading bloc in intercontinental trading agreements across the globe. GATT agreements, rather than developmental aid schemes, were becoming the basis of a new 'globalisation' programme or debate. Reflecting this, the formation of the EU virtually coincided with the development of two American regional trading blocs. The North American Free Trade Agreement now encompassed Mexico as well as the US and Canada (which first came to a free trade agreement in 1988) and came into being around the same time as a new South American Common Market (Mercosur). This was followed by the creation of an Asia–Pacific Economic Cooperation Community and a significant enhancement of the increasingly powerful Association of Southeast Asia Nations. For Ireland, 'despite the obvious difficulties that the UK-opt out of the European Monetary Union poses' (Britain still accounted for one-third of Irish exports and was the home of a large amount of Irish investments), both the development of a European currency and Ireland's adoption of that currency would be essential if Ireland was to be able to adapt to, as well as benefit from, the existence of trading agreements between these regional institutions. Ireland's traditional food and drink industry now accounted for only 17 per cent of the country's gross domestic product because over 50 per cent of Ireland's industrial output and 70 per cent of its industrial exports were the result of the IDA and IFSC's success in attracting over 1,000 multinational firms to Ireland, operating under the country's attractive low corporation tax regime. For this reason, Peter Sutherland was totally convinced that 'Ireland's future lies clearly in an outward-looking Europe', making the regional identity of Europe as a solid trading bloc Ireland's outlet to the rest of the world.[106]

During 1993, Sutherland chaired the final session of talks, involving 123 countries, to initiate the General Agreement on Tariffs and Trade (GATT) that was first envisioned during 1986 and was effectively designed to create 'most-favoured nation' trading agreements that would operate on an inter-continental basis. This would lead to the creation of a World Trade Organisation at the outset of 1995, with Sutherland himself serving as its first director-general. Its primary responsibility was to arbitrate the operation of regional trade agreements to prevent the possibility of trade wars. As a former chairman of Allied Irish Banks, Sutherland did not ignore purely national Irish considerations. Echoing a founding premise of Dáil Éireann in 1919, he emphasised that the ongoing weakness of the Irish stock exchange and the Irish companies it represented was being sustained not least by an absurd practice whereby Irish shareholders, 'more than in any other EU state', were unnecessarily investing their money primarily in companies and, in particular, insurance and pension schemes that were managed outside the state (mostly in the UK). He was also a believer that the evolution of European law, with its preoccupation with issues of fundamental rights and combating corruption, was serving to make Ireland a more republican country than it had ever been in the past.[107] Be that as it may, his level of belief in the benevolence of international financial institutions was such that he believed that a growing trend of banks' international trading in personal bonds and property mortgages, not just in foreign exchange and multinational companies' goods or shares, should work for the benefit of all countries.[108]

While remaining an advisor to the Irish government, Sutherland would emerge from his WTO negotiations as a non-executive director of Goldman Sachs International, a London subsidiary of an American multinational bank, and a director of British Petroleum, which was perhaps the greatest success story in British multinational businesses over the previous decade. His role as an advisor on the dynamics of 'global' banking operations would later secure him many different employments abroad, especially within Europe or the UN,[109] but as was perhaps best reflected by the relatively unsuccessful political career of Sutherland's former close colleague Alan Dukes (a banker and FitzGerald's successor as leader of Fine Gael), the mere prevalence of prominent business figures in Irish politics was no guarantee that Ireland could adapt effectively to changes in the international order. As chairman of the Dáil's first foreign affairs committee, Dukes would give voice to the unpopular opinion within Ireland that so long as the country stayed outside NATO its moral credibility within Europe would be slight.[110]

In January 1993, Bill Clinton became the first Democratic Party president in America for over a decade and soon negotiated the North American Free Trade Agreement. In turn, this made him inclined to pay much attention to the development of the EU. Hitherto, the combination of American foreign direct investment and the influence of the Catholic Church reputedly made Ireland seem to the United States to be a political entity comparable to several Latin American countries.[111] Partly for this reason, John Hume considered Bill Clinton's appointment in March 1993 of Jean Kennedy Smith, a sister of Ted Kennedy and a sympathiser with Ireland, to be practically America's first 'real ambassador' to Ireland.[112] It was evidently an appointment that went against the grain of established thinking at the US state department,[113] although, as with all previous US ambassadors to Ireland, she was not a career diplomat.[114] Clinton would later claim that he was conscious of the fact that 'the conflict in Northern Ireland and the conflict in the Balkans … were the two things that were preventing Europe from becoming united', while Tom Foley, the Speaker of the US House of Representatives since 1989, was reputedly willing to encourage Clinton to take a greater interest in Ireland.[115]

John Hume's attempt to intiate a peace process with Gerry Adams had already failed in a blaze of bad publicity during 1988. However, Martin Mansergh of Fianna Fáil was secretly engaged in dialogue with both loyalist and nationalist paramilitaries in Ulster. In conjunction with the holding of more intergovernmental talks between the British and Irish governments, this effectively laid the groundwork for a declaration from Downing Street in December 1993 by both governments, announcing that they were open to the idea of constitutional change for Northern Ireland based on the principle of seeking the consent of all parties, even the representatives of paramilitary organisations.[116] Meanwhile, with some moral support from Irish president Mary Robinson, Hume encouraged the Americans to grant a visa to Gerry Adams. This helped to ensure that an IRA ceasefire was announced in August 1994, followed by a loyalist paramilitary ceasefire two months later.[117] That December, Bill Clinton appointed Senator George Mitchell as a 'Special Adviser for Economic Initiatives in Ireland', with a focus particularly upon Northern Ireland. Mitchell expected that this appointment would last only about six months, but it would take three and a half years before any kind of agreement between Northern Ireland's parties and, in turn, a potential role for America in this peace process would prove possible.[118]

In the twenty years since joining the EEC, Ireland's total diplomatic representation abroad had more than doubled to include about forty countries. Many ambassadors attempted to act as an accredited but non-resident representative to more than one country. Irish representation, however, was still less than half the size of that of other small European countries 'with a broadly comparable range of international interests and obligations'. Therefore, during 1994, Ireland's department of foreign affairs began preparing its first white paper that called for a dramatic increase in Ireland's future role in international affairs in the light of Ireland's membership of the EU.[119] Ireland would adapt to new regional trade policies quite quickly by means of the EU, in the process establishing profitable trading agreements with nations as distant as the Far East for the first time.[120] Traditional legacy issues, however, were still deemed to be central to the Irish state's foreign policy, such as the Northern question, the existence of an 'Irish diaspora' abroad, Ireland's development aid responsibilities towards the Third World and the resulting prioritisation of creating human rights policy documents at the UN. Conscious that the traditional role of the Irish president was essentially only to authorise the passing of legislation with a signature, since 1990 the new Irish president Mary Robinson had desired to enhance the profile of that office by means of greater diplomatic engagements. Instead, however, she would only find such an outlet by embarking on a new career as a senior legal advisor to the UN, with a focus not least upon human rights in Africa.[121]

In Ireland and elsewhere, sympathy had long existed for the Anti-Apartheid Movement in South Africa. The celebrated process of creating a new government, which was seemingly initiated with the release of imprisoned anti-apartheid leader Nelson Mandela in the wake of the fall of the Berlin Wall, actually began with a meeting of a new World Trade Centre.[122] This reflected the fact that a reorganisation of the South African Development Community, a purely economic body, had formed an essential context for this process, which would soon lead to the creation of not so radically (or racially) different a government. The eclipse of the Soviet bloc led to a very dramatic decline of interest from western multinationals in development aid programmes for either Third World countries or their populations. With regards to Africa, an alternative notion was now created of launching a continent-wide

African Union, which would aim to form a single market with a single currency that would operate as a regional trading bloc within thirty years.[123] Against this backdrop of a prioritisation of notions of a 'global economy' as a supposed panacea for all human ills, the humanist traditions of post-1945 bodies such as UNESCO were widely perceived to have declined. Reflecting this, the World Council of Churches began criticising UNESCO for evidently now viewing human culture to be entirely valueless if it could not be turned into an economic commodity to boost consumerism.[124]

Since 1989, some international commentators had typified the seeming reinvention of the European political order in a paradoxical fashion. The fall of the USSR was judged by some to have had brought an end to ideological wars in history, yet this process was also judged to have marked a worldwide triumph of an ideology of political and economic 'liberalism', represented by free-market capitalism.[125] Since 1968, the rhetoric of a global partnership essentially embodied within it the notion of a world order that would not be characterised by the hegemony of any one or more states. However, the new association of this idea with an ideology of liberalism, as opposed to either the Christian-democratic tradition in Europe of resisting totalitarian ideologies or else the American republican tradition of promoting patriotisms based upon values of anti-corruption and egalitarianism, effectively betrayed a mistaken linguistic tendency to equate contemporary circumstances with nineteenth-century British economic models.[126] It also essentially silenced a prevalent viewpoint within both central and eastern Europe. Here, the western cold war thesis of the 'social origins of dictatorship and democracy' and the idea that there had been some merits in the USSR's edition of national socialism (which had seen even Russian peasants acquire governmental office) were often considered to have the exact same premise: the modern world was still defined by the rise of the egalitarian republican idea of eliminating the distinction between 'lord and peasant' in society.[127] Reflecting this, virtually all new central and eastern European entries into the EU after 1994 were republics. Many were also developing Christian-democratic parties.[128] On this premise, the Poles and Czechs were already attempting to make an equal appreciation for the egalitarian ideology of the US declaration of independence and their own national traditions of belief in democracy a basis of their evolving political identities, including their willingness to embrace a pan-Europeanism through the medium of the EU.[129] In time, Ireland would frequently express its support for the enlargement of the EU as a matter 'of principle': 'we wish to see others benefit from the same opportunities that we have enjoyed'.[130] Meanwhile, in witnessing 'Irish foreign policy in transition', some students of internationalism would suggest that the Irish state after 1994 essentially became a combination of 'European republic' and 'global citizen' due to its broadening commitment to Europe.[131] In the face of these theoretical musings, however, naturally stood much more mundane realities. Indeed, particularly in the short term, a perpetual irony to Irish international relations after 1994 would be the seeming impossibility of the Irish state facing its 'challenges and opportunities abroad' until peace and stability could first be brought to Northern Ireland.[132]

Endnotes

1 *Foreign affairs*, vol. 53 no. 1 (Oct. 1974). This trend also led to a brief revival of the moribund International Labour Organisation (ILO). R.W. Cox, 'Labor and the multinationals', *Foreign affairs*, vol. 54 no. 2 (Jan. 1976), 344–65.

2 Noel Dorr, 'Ireland in an interdependent world: foreign policy since 1973', in B. Tonra, M. Kennedy, J. Doyle, N. Dorr (eds), *Irish foreign policy* (Dublin, 2012), 66, 68.

3 Michael Quinn, *Irish–Soviet diplomatic and friendship relations 1917–1991* (Maynooth, 2016), 145–6.

4 Noel Dorr, 'Ireland in an interdependent world', 54, 56, 69.

5 Mervyn O'Driscoll, Jamie Walsh, 'Ireland and the 1975 NPT Review Conference: norm building and small states', *Irish studies in international affairs*, vol. 25 (2014), 101–16.

6 During 1979, Michael O'Kennedy, as Ireland's foreign minister and president of the EEC Council of Ministers, made an address on behalf of the EEC to the UN that mentioned the Palestinian Liberation Organisation 'for the first time' and asserted 'that it would have to be a party to any Middle-East agreement'. J. Dooge, R. Barrington (eds), *A vital national interest*, 281.

7 B. Tonra, M. Kennedy, J. Doyle, N. Dorr (eds), *Irish foreign policy* (Dublin, 2012), 66–7.

8 Michael Kennedy, Deirdre McMahon (eds), *Obligations and responsibilities: Ireland and the United Nations 1955-2005* (Dublin, 2005), 70–3. In doing so, Ireland also sided with D.P. Moynihan.

9 Patrick Keatinge, *A singular stance: Irish neutrality in the 1980s* (Dublin, 1984), 29, 31, 58, 68–93.

10 Raymond Vernon, 'Apparatchiks and entrepreneurs: US–Soviet economic relations', *Foreign affairs*, vol. 52 no. 2 (Jan. 1974), 249–62; John Pinder, 'East–west trade and foreign policy: limits and potential', *Irish studies in international affairs*, vol. 1 no. 4

(1984), 41–8; Michael Quinn, *Irish–Soviet diplomatic and friendship relations 1917–1991* (Maynooth, 2016), chapter 8; Patrick Keatinge, *A singular stance: Irish neutrality in the 1980s* (Dublin, 1984), 28–9, 31, 86–93.

11 Michael Quinn, *Irish–Soviet diplomatic and friendship relations 1917–1991*, 86–96. In his involvement with the eastern Europe section of the EPC, Brennan had been most concerned with discouraging a trend whereby the Soviet press, essentially in a purely cynical effort to manipulate Russia's own relations with Britain, had given undue publicity to the existence of the secret 'IRA' conspiracy.

12 Patrick Keatinge, *A singular stance: Irish neutrality in the 1980s* (Dublin, 1984), 24, 25 (quote).

13 Ibid., 34–42.

14 The absence of a significant public role for the Irish army led to frequent reductions in its staff, equipment and pay, so that, by the late 1980s, spouses of Irish soldiers were led to create a union to advertise the demoralising fact of very low pay in its ranks, which led to many resignations. This union has continued to agitate to this day. Michael Martin, *Breaking ranks: the shaping of civil–military relations in Ireland* (Dublin, 2016).

15 Patrick Keatinge, *A singular stance: Irish neutrality in the 1980s* (Dublin, 1984), 29, 31, 58 (quote), 68–93.

16 Ibid., 110–11.

17 Michael D. Higgins, *Causes for concern* (Dublin, 2006), 201–5.

18 Michael Holmes, Nicholas Rees, Bernadette Whelan (eds), *The poor relation: Irish foreign policy and the Third World* (Trócaire, 1993).

19 John Hume, 'The Irish question: a British problem', *Foreign affairs*, vol. 58 (1979), quote p. 309.

20 Diarmaid Ferriter, *The transformation of Ireland* (London, 2005), 732–3. This was also in keeping with international Catholic trends, as was represented by Pope John Paul II's visits to South America, his expressed concern for workers in his native Poland and his issuing an encyclical Laborem Exercens (On Human Work). Michael Collins, *The fisherman's net: the influence of the papacy on history* (Dublin, 2003), 254–8.

21 Matthew Worley, 'Marx-Lenin-Rotten-Strummer: British Marxism and youth culture in the 1970s', *Contemporary British history*, vol. 30 no. 4 (2016), 505–21. During 1986, Ireland's smaller 'Self Aid' rock festival in Dublin to create work for the unemployed also bore no ideological slogans.

22 These 1980s essays have been reproduced as Michael D. Higgins, *Causes for concern* (Dublin, 2006).

23 William Crotty, D.E. Schmitt (eds), *Ireland on the world stage* (London, 2002), 32–3, 155–7.

24 Sean Farren (ed.), *John Hume: in his own words* (Dublin, 2018), 137–45; John Hume, 'The Irish question: a British problem', *Foreign affairs*, vol. 58 (1979), 301 (quote).

25 Sean Farren, Denis Haughey (eds), *John Hume: Irish peacemaker* (Dublin, 2015), 91–2.

26 Sean Farren (ed.), *John Hume*, 151–2; John Hume, 'The Irish question', 309–10 (quote).

27 John Hume, 'The Irish question: a British problem', *Foreign affairs*, vol. 58 (1979), 300–13, quotes pp. 304, 309, 310, 311, 313.

28 Michael Fitzpatrick, *John Hume in America* (Dublin, 2017), 118.

29 'Huge security operation for Reagan's visit', *Irish Independent*, 27 Dec. 2014.

30 The Reagan administration reputedly stepped up American legal proceedings against

organisations such as NORAID. Andrew Wilson, *Irish America and the Ulster conflict 1968–95* (Belfast, 1995), chapter 9.

31 'President Reagan in Ireland, 1 June 1984', https://www.c-span.org/. At Shannon, Patrick Hillery stated that this was Reagan's third visit to Ireland.

32 The 1960s figures are quoted in Robert McNamara, 'Irish perspectives on the Vietnam War', *Irish studies in international affairs*, vol. 14 (2003), 83. The 1984 figure was stated by the leader of the Irish Senate in response to Reagan's speech in the Dáil. 'President Reagan's speech to the Irish national parliament, Dublin, 4 June 1984' (shared by the Ronald Reagan Presidential Library and Museum on YouTube).

33 'President Reagan's speech to the Irish national parliament, Dublin, 4 June 1984' (video shared by the Ronald Reagan Presidential Library and Museum on YouTube).

34 Katherine Meehan, '1984: the end of Euro sclerosis', in J. Dooge, R. Barrington (eds), *A vital national interest: Ireland in Europe 1973–1998* (Dublin, 1999), 55–65.

35 Michael Quinn, *Irish–Soviet diplomatic and friendship relations 1917–1991*, 169.

36 Sean Farren, Denis Haughey (eds), *John Hume: Irish peacemaker* (Dublin, 2015), 92–3.

37 Michael Fitzpatrick, *John Hume in America* (Dublin, 2017), 116–19, 156 (quote p. 119).

38 John Dumbrell, 'The United States and the Northern Irish conflict 1969–94: from indifference to intervention', *Irish studies in international affairs*, vol. 6 (1995), 114–25.

39 Michael Fitzpatrick, *John Hume in America* (Dublin, 2017), 122–31; Ronan Fanning, 'The Anglo-American alliance and the Irish question in the twentieth century', 209–10.

40 Sean Cronin, *Washington's Irish policy 1916–1986* (Dublin, 1986).

41 G.T. Dempsey, review of 'Dublin's American policy', in *Irish historical studies*, vol. 31 no. 124 (Nov. 1999), 583–4. Dempsey served as political secretary of the American embassy in Dublin from 1988–92. Critical Irish attitudes towards US foreign policy in Latin America evidently influenced his perspective. G.T. Dempsey, 'Irish attitudes towards USA foreign policy', *Studies*, vol. 82 no. 327 (autumn 1993), 265–75.

42 Michael Lillis, 'Footnotes to the Anglo-Irish Agreement of 1985', in Jane Conroy (ed.) *Franco-Irish connections* (Dublin, 2009). In an extension of the tradition of British–Irish intergovernmental conferences since 1981, this Maryfield secretariat also included British personnel. In this way, it helped to create a better understanding in Anglo-Irish relations of each other's priorities. B. Tonra, M. Kennedy, J. Doyle, N. Dorr (eds), *Irish foreign policy* (Dublin, 2012), 64.

43 Particularly after 1985, Ireland Funds would be created in Britain, Australia, Canada, France, Germany, Japan and South Africa. Ivan Fallon, *The player: the life of Tony O'Reilly* (London, 1994), 309–312.

44 This was the DeLorean car company. Desmond O'Malley, *Conduct unbecoming*, 115–19.

45 Sean Farren (ed.), *John Hume: in his own words*, 195–6; Sean Farren, Denis Haughey (eds), *John Hume: Irish peacemaker* (Dublin, 2015), 93.

46 Michael Fitzpatrick, *John Hume in America*, 131.

47 K.A. Kennedy, T. Giblin, D. McHugh, *The economic development of Ireland in the twentieth century* (London, 1988), 183.

48 Dermot McAleese, 'Anglo-Irish economic interdependence: from excessive intimacy to a wider embrace', in P.J. Drudy (ed.), *Ireland and Britain since 1922* (Cambridge, 1986), 88–105.

49 Patrick Keatinge, 'Unequal sovereigns: the diplomatic dimension of Anglo-Irish relations', in P.J. Drudy (ed.), *Ireland and Britain since 1922* (Cambridge, 1986), 139–60; Geoffrey Cook, 'Britain's legacy to the Irish social security system', in P.J. Drudy (ed.), *Ireland and Britain since 1922* (Cambridge, 1986), 65–86. As the Anglo-Irish Agreement of 1985 coincided with the cessation of the sixty-year Irish contribution to the British national debt agreed in 1925, the management of An Post (the Irish post office) and its savings bank was regulated primarily from Dublin after 1984.

50 Gemma Hussey, *Ireland today: anatomy of a nation* (Dublin, 1993), 256–7.

51 Ibid., 224–5.

52 Otmar Franz (ed.), *European currency in the making* (Sindelfingen, 1988).

53 Russell King (ed.), *Ireland, Europe and the single market* (Dublin, 1992), chapter 1.

54 Frank Barry, 'Trade, investment, integration: the economics of Irish foreign policy', in B. Tonra, M. Kennedy, J. Doyle, N. Dorr (eds), *Irish foreign policy* (Dublin, 2012), 192–3.

55 Patrick Honohan, *Currency, credit and crisis: central banking in Ireland and Europe* (Cambridge, 2019), 12, 27.

56 John Bradley, 'The Irish economy in international perspective', in W. Crotty, D. Schmitt (eds), *Ireland on the world stage* (London, 2002), quote p. 60.

57 Patrick Honohan, 'Europe and the international monetary system', *Irish studies in international affairs*, vol. 1 no. 4 (1984), 49–62 (quote p. 52).

58 Paul Sharp, *Irish foreign policy and the European community* (Aldershot, 1990), quote p. 246.

59 Frank Casey, *Credit where credit is due: the evolution of business banking in Ireland* (Dublin, 2000). When Britain's percentage of Irish trade declined after 1973, it responded by increasing its level of investments in Ireland so that British investments constituted a sizeable percentage of all foreign direct investment in Ireland after 1978. Dermot McAleese, 'Anglo-Irish economic interdependence: from excessive intimacy to a wider embrace', in P.J. Drudy (ed.), *Ireland and Britain since 1922* (Cambridge, 1986), 96–7.

60 P.J. Drudy (ed.), *Ireland and Britain since 1922* (Cambridge, 1986), quoting Sir John Peck, p. 150.

61 Patrick Keatinge, 'Unequal sovereigns: the diplomatic dimension of Anglo-Irish relations', in P.J. Drudy (ed.), *Ireland and Britain since 1922* (Cambridge, 1986), 155–7.

62 R. O'Donnell, F. Keoghan, M. Quinn (eds), *A festschrift for Anthony Coughlan* (Dublin, 2017).

63 Michael Quinn, *Irish–Soviet diplomatic and friendship relations*, 170–3.

64 Dermot Keogh wrote two books on Ireland's relations with the Vatican: first *The Vatican, the bishops and Irish politics 1919–1939* (Cambridge, 1986), and then *Ireland and the Vatican 1922–1960* (Cork, 1995).

65 Dermot Keogh, *Ireland and Europe* (2nd ed., Dublin, 1990), 267.

66 Contemporary Irish debates on the SEA and the role of the EPC are covered in Dermot Keogh, *Ireland and Europe* (2nd ed., Dublin, 1990), chapter 8.

67 Diarmaid Ferriter, *The transformation of Ireland* (London, 2005), 681–5; Frank Barry, 'When histories collide', *History Ireland*, vol. 19 no. 3 (May/June 2011).

68 Government Information Services, *Ireland's neutrality: six key questions about the Single European Act* (Dublin, 1987), quote p. 1; Government Information Services, *Freer trade in the EEC: the benefits for Ireland* (Dublin, 1987).

69 E.B. Kapstein, 'Between power and purpose: central bankers and the politics of regulatory convergence', *International organization: knowledge, power and international policy coordination*, vol. 46 no. 1 (winter 1992), 265–87. Central bankers also met in Basel during the 1970s to deal with the oil crisis, leading to the first G7 summit in 1975. W.F. Mondale, 'Beyond détente: towards international economic security', *Foreign affairs*, vol. 53 no. 1 (Oct. 1974), 1–23.

70 Peter Sutherland, 'Completing the internal market and competition policy', in J. Dooge, R. Barrington (eds), *A vital national interest: Ireland in Europe 1973–1998* (Dublin, 1999), 291.

71 Desmond O'Malley, *Conduct unbecoming: a memoir* (Dublin, 2014).

72 Stephen Collins, *Breaking the mould* (Dublin, 2006).

73 In the past, an Irish Sweepstakes Lottery, which had operated internationally since 1930, had created funding for Irish hospitals, and its cessation in 1986 actually coincided with hospital closures. A new National Lottery was established the following year. Marie Coleman, *The Irish sweep: a history of the Irish hospitals sweepstake 1930–1987* (Dublin, 2009).

74 Frank Barry, John Bradley, 'On the causes of Ireland's unemployment', *The economic and social review*, vol. 22 no. 4 (July 1991), 253–86; Brian O'Doherty (ex-director of Córas Tráchtála) to author (phone interview Mar. 2018).

75 Michael Kennedy, Deirdre McMahon (eds), *Obligations and responsibilities: Ireland and the United Nations 1955–2005* (Dublin, 2005), 74–5. At the time, approximately 350 Irish citizens were living in either Iraq or Kuwait.

76 Albert Reynolds, *My autobiography* (London, 2009), 163–72, 223–4. Larry Goodman's beef-exporting firm was given the contract for exports to the Middle East.

77 Stephen Collins, 'US dismissive about summit between Haughey and Gorbachev', *The Irish Times*, 12 Aug. 2013.

78 Ray MacSharry, 'Reform of the CAP', in J. Dooge, R. Barrington (eds), *A vital national interest: Ireland in Europe 1973–1998* (Dublin, 1999), 293–311; Gemma Hussey, *Ireland today: anatomy of a nation* (Dublin, 1993), 225–8.

79 Andrew Wilson, *Irish America and the Ulster conflict 1968–95* (Belfast, 1995), chapter 9. In 1982, this congressional group, while also contacting the Northern Ireland Office, encouraged the formation of a sister 'Irish–US Parliamentary Group' in Dáil Éireann.

80 The role of the Irish National Caucus in promoting this programme is the principal theme of the otherwise highly personalised memoir, Sean McManus, *My American struggle for justice in Northern Ireland* (Cork, 2011). In his final days, MacBride actually opposed Ireland's acceptance of the SEA, although he had supported Irish entry into the EEC in 1972.

81 Kevin McNamara, *The MacBride principles: Irish America strikes back* (Liverpool, 2009), chapters 3–4.

82 Michael Fitzpatrick, *John Hume in America*, 162–6.

83 John Dumbrell, 'The United States and the Northern Irish conflict 1969–94', *Irish studies in international affairs*, vol. 6 (1995), 120–1. The new Irish immigrant paper was the *Irish Echo* (New York), founded by Niall O'Dowd, a recent arrival from Dublin.

84 On assuming office, Albert Reynolds recalled that, in speaking to Haughey, 'on the subject of Northern Ireland, all he had to say was "ask Mansergh"'. Albert Reynolds, *My autobiography* (London, 2009), 150.

85 Martin Mansergh (ed.), *The spirit of the nation: the speeches and statements of Charles J. Haughey 1957–1986* (Dublin, 1986).

86 Although nominally retired since 1976, Whitaker continued to advise the government in his capacity of chairman of various semi-state boards. He opposed the establishment of a Maryfield secretariat because he considered it to be deeply offensive to unionists. Anne Chambers, *T.K. Whitaker* (Dublin, 2014), 329.

87 Douglas Gageby, 'The North: ruminations', in Fionan O'Muircheartaigh (ed.), *Ireland in the coming times: essays to celebrate T.K. Whitaker's eighty years* (Dublin, 1997), 119–28. It was reputedly on Haughey's insistence that leaders of the Catholic Church were included in the New Ireland Forum during 1983–4.

88 B. Tonra, M. Kennedy, J. Doyle, N. Dorr (eds), *Irish foreign policy* (Dublin, 2012), 119. An additional factor that influenced Haughey was probably an expectation that Fianna Fáil should seek perpetually to win over supporters of Sinn Féin, who opposed the agreement. Ibid., 65.

89 Michael Fitzpatrick, *John Hume in America*, 143–54. The story of the Hume–Adams talks was leaked by Eamonn McCann, the author of polemical publications such as *War and an Irish town* (London, 1974).

90 Hume retorted to these personal criticisms by suggesting that O'Brien, being intensely eurosceptic, was evidently the very embodiment of the narrow nationalism that he professed to despise. Sean Farren (ed.), *John Hume in his own words* (Dublin, 2018), 252.

91 O'Brien did not write exclusively about Irish affairs but also about various international developments in the British press. This fact evidently helped to inspire publications such as Richard English, J.M. Skelly (eds), *Ideas matter: essays in honour of Conor Cruise O'Brien* (Dublin, 1998).

92 Eamon Delaney, *An accidental diplomat: my years in the Irish foreign service 1987–1995* (Dublin, 2001), 15, 20–8.

93 Gemma Hussey, *Ireland today: anatomy of a nation* (Dublin, 1993), 234, 517–18.

94 Fergal Lenehan, *Stereotypes, ideology and foreign correspondents: German media representations of Ireland 1946–2010* (London, 2016).

95 Ireland opened its Polish embassy in Warsaw in 1990 and a Polish embassy was established in Dublin one year later. Ireland had some slight diplomatic ties with Poland since 1976 through its embassy in Stockholm, Sweden. 'Irish embassy, Poland' (Irish department of foreign affairs and trade website).

96 Ryszard Kapuscinski, *Imperium* (London, 1994).

97 Boris Yeltsin, *Against the grain: an autobiography* (London, 1990), 114 (quote), 130, 182.

98 Turlough O'Riordan, 'Mahon Hayes (1930–2011)', *Dictionary of Irish biography* (online edition). Prior to becoming Ireland's permanent UN representative at Geneva (1981–7) and New York (1989–95), Hayes had represented Ireland at the 3rd UN Conference on the Law at Sea (1973–82).

99 Dermot Keogh (ed.), *Ireland: the challenge of European integration* (Dublin, 1991). Russell King (ed.), *Ireland, Europe and the Single Market* (Dublin, 1992).

100 Alan Milward, *The European rescue of the nation–state* (London, 1992). Milward was then professor of economic history at the London School of Economics.

101 David Sinclair, *The pound* (London, 2000), 264–6, 272–4.

102 John Cooney, Tony McGarry (eds), *Ireland and Europe in times of world change: Humbert International School chronicle and directory 1987–2002* (Ballina, 2002), 33, 51–3.

103   Colm Doyle, *Witness to war crimes: the memoirs of an Irish peacekeeper in Bosnia* (Dublin, 2018).

104   J.A. Foley, Stephen Lalor (eds), *Gill and Macmillan annotated constitution of Ireland, with commentary* (Dublin, 1995), 94.

105   Patrick Keatinge, *European security: Ireland's choices* (Dublin, 1996).

106   Peter Sutherland, 'Ireland and the challenge of globalisation', in Fionan O'Muircheartaigh (ed.), *Ireland in the coming times: essays to celebrate T.K. Whitaker's eighty years* (Dublin, 1997), 19–35 (quotes pp. 27, 35).

107   John Cooney, Tony McGarry (eds), *Ireland and Europe in times of world change: Humbert International School chronicle and directory 1987–2002* (Ballina, 2002), 18–19, 291.

108   Peter Sutherland, 'Ireland and the challenge of globalisation', 20, 30, 34.

109   Sean Whelan, 'Sutherland operated at the highest level of business and politics', RTÉ News (online), 7 Jan. 2018.

110   John Cooney, Tony McGarry (eds), *Ireland and Europe*, 142.

111   'Interview with Sean O'hUiginn', Edward Kennedy Oral History Project (PDF available online), 14.

112   'Interview with John Hume', Edward Kennedy Oral History Project (PDF available online), 9.

113   Ronan Fanning, 'The Anglo-American alliance and the Irish question in the twentieth century', in Judith Devlin, H.B. Clarke (eds), *European encounters* (Dublin, 2003), 210.

114   The first US envoy to the Irish Free State, Francis Sterling (who held office from 1927–34), was the only American representative to Ireland that was a career member of the US Foreign Office Service.

115   Michael Fitzpatrick, *John Hume in America* (Dublin, 2017), 156, 157 (quote from Clinton), 167–70.

116   Martin Mansergh, 'The background to the peace process', *Irish studies in international affairs*, vol. 6 (1995), 145–58.

117   Albert Reynolds left a lengthy account of these negotiations within *My autobiography* (London, 2009).

118   Senator George Mitchell, *Making peace: the inside story of the making of the Good Friday Agreement* (London, 1999).

119   Department of foreign affairs, *Challenges and opportunities abroad: white paper on foreign policy* (Dublin, 1996), quote 320–1.

120   Fan Hong, Jorn-Carsten Gottwald (eds), *The Irish Asia strategy and its China relations 1999–2009* (Amsterdam, 2010).

121   John Horgan, *Mary Robinson* (Dublin, 1997), 199.

122   Nelson Mandela, *Long walk to freedom* (London, 1994), 732.

123   Allister Sparks, *Beyond the miracle: inside the new South Africa* (London, 2003), chapter 10. Established in 2001, the African Union headquarters was based in Addis Ababa, in Ethopia, although South Africa, as the richest African country, was essentially its prime mover. Its envisioned date for the creation of the Afro currency was originally 2023.

124   M.P. Gallagher, *Clashing symbols: an introduction to faith and culture* (London, 1997), chapter 15.

125   The most notorious expression of this thesis at the time was Francis Fukuyama, *The end of history and the last man* (New York, 1992).

126 J.G. Ruggie, 'International regimes, transactions and change', *International organization*, vol. 36 no. 2 (spring 1982), 379–415; Kevin O'Rourke, Jeffrey Williamson, *Globalisation and history* (London and New York, 1999).

127 Barrington Moore Jr., *Social origins of dictatorship and democracy: lord and peasant in the making of the modern world* (Washington and London, 1966).

128 Adrian Karatnycky, 'Christian democracy resurgent – raising the banner of faith in Eastern Europe', *Foreign affairs*, vol. 77 (1998), 13–18.

129 Teresa Walas (ed.), *Stereotypes and nations* (Cracow, 1995); Jacek Purchla (ed.), *The historical metropolis: a hidden potential* (Cracow, 1996). Vaclav Havel, the first president of the Czech republic, made recitations of the US declaration of independence compulsory in Czech schools.

130 Department of foreign affairs and trade, *The global island: Ireland's foreign policy for a changing world* (Dublin, 2015), 69.

131 Ben Tonra, *Global citizen and European republic: Irish foreign policy in transition* (Manchester, 2006).

132 Department of foreign affairs, *Challenges and opportunities abroad: white paper on foreign policy* (Dublin, 1996).

8

Beyond Hegemonies:
Ireland in the EU and on
the World Stage since 1994

During the mid-1990s, the creation of new regional trading blocs and the World Trade Organisation (WTO) was essentially an end result of joint work by the UN and the World Bank dating back to 1960. Individual Europeans continued to play a significant diplomatic role within all interrelated UN and World Bank initiatives. As Peter Sutherland discovered, however, the United States was hesitant about abiding by the new 'rules-based' economic system that it had largely inspired if it potentially had to curtail its own freedom of action, a development that was equated with a theoretical loss of sovereignty.[1] In addition, London economists expected that America would have little sympathy for the idea of a new European currency that could potentially compete with the US dollar on foreign exchange markets.[2] Nevertheless, the new European Union (EU) was welcomed because it had the diplomatic potential to deal effectively with the Middle Eastern, African and former Soviet blocs through a practical 'good neighbour' policy. Like all EU member states, Ireland signed up to the essentially French-inspired (but often Spanish-led) 'Barcelona Process' that envisioned the development of a 'Union for the Mediterranean' that would promote free trade between the EU and the Arab League's 'Council of Arab Economic Unity', which had existed since the 1960s with a headquarters in Cairo, Egypt. Combined with €6 billion in developmental aid to the Third World and over a billion euros a year in development aid to the Middle East, this action by the EU was designed to encourage a new spirit of political cooperation between Israel and its Arab neighbours, while also laying a basis for the future African Union project.[3] Although it was not widely perceived in such terms in Ireland, the Northern Ireland peace process was often considered internationally to be a comparable development in terms of the operations of the global economy and the resulting cessation of the Cold War. After a 'last remaining NATO military installation in Northern Ireland' closed during 1990, European and American support for the Ulster-focused 'International Fund for Ireland' had the potential to undo some of the legacies of the Northern Troubles, which had been caused and perpetuated not least by a prioritisation of military solutions to political problems. The prospect of greater free movement of labour within the EU also had the potential to undo the 'cold war' in relations between Northern Ireland and the Republic of Ireland.[4]

On a political level, the reunification of Germany initially bred much uncertainty. This was appeased in the wake of Haughey's 1990 European Council meetings in Dublin, when German chancellor Helmut Kohl emphasised that a common foreign and security policy for Europe must rest upon a purely economic, rather than military, basis. This reflected the degree to which NATO remained a basis whereby America could provide Europe with a defence capability without necessarily either imposing strategic directives or creating a basis for the rise of European militarism.[5] To many, however, Europe's relative difficulty in solving the crisis in the former Yugoslavia substantiated the longstanding belief held by British international relations theorists: any claim that militarism was not inherently the key factor in international relations was both naïve and unrealistic.[6] By contrast, just prior to serving a rare term on the UN Security Council (2001), Ireland would term Europe's new approach to international affairs as a non-hegemonic one that was marking the birth of a new 'era of enlightened multilateralism', characterised by an astute anti-militarism.[7] In this sense, Ireland's intended identity in the post-1994 international order was to support the idea of rules-based international order that would operate beyond the great powers' perpetual preoccupation with the notion of rising and falling hegemonies.

A growing trend in European cultural diplomacy was to emphasise that, in the past, 'national, ideological, religious and ethnic stereotypes', as well as a fear of migrants, had been propagated for purely ulterior motives by totalitarian regimes who saw cultural diplomacy as 'an instrument of psychological warfare—for them foreign policy was warfare' as well as a bid for 'cultural predominance'. As 'cultural diplomacy is part and parcel of a nation's foreign policy', it was argued that there was a need for 'a joint European approach based on agreed principles', such as the creation of 'a European Cultural Charter for the promotion and protection of fundamental cultural rights of European citizens'. As was the case with the EU Charter of Fundamental Rights, it was argued that such a cultural charter should 'define fundamental cultural rights as individual rights'.[8] Closer European cooperation at the UN encouraged the development of new human rights initiatives, as well as the creation of a Human Rights Unit within the Irish department of foreign affairs. This trend also provided a basis for extensive eastern European involvement, on a supposedly equal basis, in a new 'Organisation for Security and Cooperation in Europe' (OSCE), which was chaired by neutral Austria, included Irish political representation and was sustained in part by German economic support for the redevelopment of many central and eastern European cities.[9] The political impact that this trend had upon Ireland was to stimulate the growth of an almost aggressive individualism within the Irish media and a clear political prioritisation by Irish, as much as central European, governments of urban over rural development.[10] Meanwhile, a perceived positive impact upon Irish educational and social policies made by European legislation saw an almost immediate cessation of the traditional euroscepticism of the Irish Labour Party.[11] This helped to make the 1990s a rather transitional decade in Irish life. A growth in Spanish–Irish relations, reflected by the launch of *Estudios Irlandeses* by the University of Salamanca in 1994, also led to a deepening of Irish relations with Latin America.[12]

Significant efforts were made to expand Ireland's international trading links as soon as EU participation in the latest GATT agreements became operational. Efforts to expand the export operations of Irish food or drink companies to countries like Japan, although ultimately fairly successfully, initially faltered because of the priorities of the foreign exchange markets of what were termed the 'Asian Tiger' economies, namely the former British colonies of Singapore and Hong Kong, and the American-influenced countries of South Korea and Taiwan.[13] As a result, Ireland's 'Asia strategy' thereafter focused on promoting the exports of American firms within Ireland in the same technological and pharmaceutical industries that had become the basis of a rapid growth in the Chinese economy.[14] This led many to speak of the existence of a new 'Celtic Tiger' economy.[15] Some interpreted this development as evidence that Ireland's role in the Atlantic economy had shifted from being a satellite economy of Britain to being a satellite economy of the United States,[16] although the flaw in this perspective was that it did not take into account how Ireland's access to these global trading markets was dependent on its membership of the EU. Within Ireland itself, a reason for this political oversight was that the department of the Taoiseach took a directing role in Irish foreign affairs without necessarily prioritising deepening Ireland's relationship with Europe. This created a situation whereby Ireland's staff at Brussels 'frequently had to rely on their personal judgment in the absence of instructions from Dublin'.[17]

Despite this hesitancy, Ireland was evidently more inclined to identify with the EU's efforts to promote a common political and cultural identity for Europe than its nearest neighbour. No political party within the Irish state joined the British Conservative Party (which also represented the Ulster Unionist Party) in the small European Conservative group within the European Parliament. Fine Gael allied itself with the Republican Party of France and the German Christian Democrat and Christian Socialist parties in the European People's Party, which was the largest, as well as most federalist, party within the European Parliament. Within the medium-sized Party of European Socialists, the Irish Labour Party joined the British Labour Party, which also practically abandoned its former euroscepticism. The Irish Labour Party had recently taken a lead in forming a non-governmental 'Institute of International and European Affairs' in Dublin. During 1994, Dick Spring became the first Irish Labour Party leader to serve as an Irish foreign minister in a Fine Gael-led coalition which also featured a strongly pro-European Labour minister for finance.[18] Fianna Fáil, a nominally republican party that was eager to disassociate itself from what it saw as its more conservative past, was allied to the smaller Liberal Democrat group within the European Parliament,[19] as were the Progressive Democrats, a small breakaway party from Fianna Fáil that, up until its demise in the mid-2000s, sat in a few Fianna Fáil-led coalition governments and encouraged the pro-business trend of favouring foreign direct investment, low corporation tax rates and privatisation of former semi-state companies.[20] One of its founders, Pat Cox, who had been a member of the European Parliament since 1989, would serve as president of the European Parliament from 2002 to 2004, a president of the European Movement International and later, after joining Fine Gael, president of the Jean Monnet Foundation for Europe. John Bruton, who was Taoiseach of the Fine Gael-led coalition government between 1994 and 1997, would later serve as a vice-president of the European People's Party and, in the post-Amsterdam Treaty era, an EU ambassador to the United States, in the process becoming one of the first Irish leaders to essentially transfer entirely to the EU political arena, which he identified with not least because of his Christian-democratic values.[21]

Ireland's national development plans were sustained by the EU's regional development, or 'cohesion policy', funds up until 2007. This shaped Ireland's longstanding desire to secure equality of representation for both small and large states at meetings of the European Council of foreign ministers.[22] The UK was inclined to judge that this preoccupation, combined with Ireland's lack of 'great power status', was the only logical explanation for the seeming inclination of the Irish to ally themselves with both the Mediterranean entrants into the EC during the 1980s as well as the new central and eastern European entrants to the EU after 1995.[23] However, there were also some ideological reasons for Ireland's identification with the experimental nature of the European project, including its piecemeal and sequential approach to attaining an effective monetary union.[24] In particular, Pádraig MacKernan, Ireland's former chief representative at Brussels who succeeded to the position of general secretary of Ireland's department of foreign affairs in 1995, particularly admired how Europe's approach to security considerations was based upon 'a political commitment, as distinct from a legal obligation.'[25] Under MacKernan's six-year tenure, over twenty new Irish embassies were established in Europe, Latin America and Asia, while there would be an ever-growing tendency to view Anglo-Irish relations as only one aspect of Ireland's European identity.[26] However, in common with his predecessor Noel Dorr, he believed that although Ireland's prosperity depended on Europe, the level of Irish intellectual engagement with Europe was slight, not least because Ireland's business, academic and media communities were focused largely upon the UK.[27] The recent suggestion by Anne Anderson, as Irish ambassador to America, that 'we may appeal to hearts and minds, but it is those who control the purse strings that can wield the greatest influence'[28] perhaps also reflected a belief that Ireland's diplomatic and cultural identities were frequently out of sync.

Ever since 1952, a civil service tradition had existed whereby the leader of the Anglo-Irish division of Ireland's foreign service usually succeeded to the key position of general secretary of the Irish department of foreign affairs. Sean O'hUiginn, who performed diplomatic roles for Ireland in London, Washington and Maryfield during the 1990s, later recalled that this administrative tradition had become so deeply rooted and was considered to be such a natural situation that 'nobody objects to it'.[29] The Irish department of foreign affairs was actually inclined to see 'the origins of our special relationship with the United States' as being rooted in the exact same dynamic as Ireland's relationship with the United Kingdom, as well as the British Commonwealth, because 'the long and complex history of our relationship with Great Britain has influenced many key aspects of our foreign policy', and, therefore, 'an awareness of its impact is crucial to an understanding of Ireland's foreign policy and the concerns which underlie it'. Therefore, 'a number of extremely important bilateral relationships – for example with Britain and the US – will remain critical to Irish foreign policy priorities' notwithstanding the fact that, 'through our membership of the European Union, Ireland is now in the mainstream of European decision making' and that 72 per cent of Irish exports now went to the EU (one-third of which went to the United Kingdom). The 1996 Irish foreign policy white paper also noted that 'the still unresolved question of Northern Ireland' ensured that 'building and sustaining the peace process on this island will continue to be the key priority around which other priorities are ranked'.[30]

Brigid Laffan, a prevalent Irish scholar of European integration, judged that Irish government officials tended to rely upon a process of social interaction between a small number of department heads in order to create some 'common understandings and norms' without necessarily formulating any clear strategic interests or approaches towards Europe.[31] This absence of strategic thinking may explain why Sean O'hUiginn deemed John Hume to be 'probably the most significant character in Irish politics in the second half of the twentieth century' and to be a quite exceptional figure primarily because 'his strategic insights were paramount.'[32] By 1994, Hume was convinced that Ireland should be concentrating almost entirely on promoting closer US–EU relations.[33] As it was 'the biggest single market in the world', Hume realised that the EU could make anywhere on the island of Ireland a basis for European headquarters of American firms. Meanwhile, on the understanding that the EU was the greatest 'peace process' anywhere on the globe since 1945, Hume would invite UN secretary-general Kofi Annan and future EU president Romano Prodi to speak before a new American-inspired Tip O'Neill Centre for Peace Studies in Derry.[34]

The Irish department of foreign affairs certainly agreed with Hume that the EU was a model of attaining 'unity in diversity'. It noted that 'Europe is not a melting pot in which national identities are destined to be submerged or lost. On the contrary, it is intended to be a place where variety is a strength rather than an encumbrance, where differences are not denied but understood and accommodated.'[35] On the other hand, the Irish government was acutely conscious that accommodating the British government's perspective and priorities regarding Northern Ireland was always a diplomatic necessity. In the short term, this would be reflected by the transfer during 1997 of Dermot Gallagher, formerly Irish ambassador at Washington D.C., to the position of secretary-general of the department of the Taoiseach and the Irish government's chief administrator in the peace process. He would prioritise such responsibilities until such time as he ultimately replaced MacKernan as secretary-general of the department of foreign affairs in 2001.[36] Dublin also had every reason to take into account that the europhilia of John Hume as the leader of the SDLP was very atypical within Northern Ireland. Both the main unionist parties and Gerry Adams' Northern edition of a Sinn Féin party were very eurosceptic. Ian Paisley's DUP actually prioritised European Parliament representation only as a means of finding an additional means of protesting against any outside interference in Northern Ireland's affairs.[37] London fully supported this stance. Reflecting this, a reference to the need for 'new approaches' in the light of the European political context within the British and Irish government's joint declaration on Northern Ireland in December 1993 had almost been excised at Britain's request.[38] This was despite the fact that the EU, which had been both monitoring and contributing to the International Fund for Ireland since 1989, was in the process of creating a perpetual peace task force to ensure that as much as 80 per cent of its financial support would reach disadvantaged communities in the border counties.[39] Between 1995 and 1997, the EU would provide £350 million for the economic development of Ulster and its border regions by means of its Special Support Programme for Peace and Reconciliation.[40] This was done on the understanding that the border counties of Northern Ireland and the Republic of Ireland were the areas which had been most badly affected economically by the Troubles and, some would argue, by the very partition of Ireland itself.[41]

By 1994, the Irish government's secretariat in Belfast was led by David Donoghue, a former Irish ambassador to the Holy See. After diplomatic postings in central Europe and Russia, Donoghue would later succeed (as Ireland's representative at the UN) in co-drafting a UN declaration on human rights that won almost universal approval. However, during the 1990s he was not entitled to play any direct role in the Northern Ireland peace process. This was because the Maryfield secretariat could only act in an advisory capacity to the Irish and British governments.[42] In this capacity, the Maryfield team occasionally attempted to co-draft reports on the Northern situation to assist Senator George Mitchell's four-man American team who first arrived in Belfast in February 1995 to promote America's involvement in the International Fund for Ireland, but Mitchell's team would actually be subject to character assassinations by the Belfast press whenever it was suspected that they may possibly be listening to Irish nationalists. This essentially highlighted to Mitchell why the Irish government had always exhibited a tendency to walk on eggshells in its dealings with London or Belfast regarding Northern Ireland circumstances.[43]

An early peak in American involvement in the peace process was Bill Clinton's decision to make the first-ever visit of an American president to Northern Ireland at the end of November 1995. By this time, soldiers were off the streets, police searches of civilians had ceased and new businesses and employments were being created in Ulster.[44] Remarkably, Clinton chose to address the general public at open-air events,[45] while he gave the keynote speech of his visit on a factory floor in west Belfast. On this occasion, he was accompanied by members of the 'Friends of Ireland' US Congressional Group, US Secretary of Commerce Ron Brown and Admiral William Crowe, the US ambassador to Britain and the former chairman of the US armed forces' joint chiefs of staff under Reagan and Bush's Republican administrations of the 1980s. Emphasising that his government was the first US administration to give the International Fund for Ireland (first anticipated in 1977 and nominally established in 1986) its 'official support', Clinton noted that it was going to promote not only job-training and job creation but also women's groups and cross-community sporting events. He cited the civil war history of his home state of Arkansas as proof that Hume's favourite American expression – the possibility of attaining 'unity in diversity' – was always possible, as if America and Europe had managed to achieve this, so too could Northern Ireland, provided it had 'the courage of an open mind' to forgive, transcend differences and engage in honest dialogue with a desire to ensure that 'everybody can win'.[46] The positivity surrounding Clinton's visit, however, would prove to be shortlived.

David Trimble, the new leader of the Ulster Unionist Party and a former law lecturer in Queen's University Belfast, viewed any American involvement in Northern Ireland, as well as Clinton's visit, 'with great reserve'.[47] John Hume was hoping that 'a new Ireland will evolve' through an all-island 'vote for an agreed Ireland' that was based on an understanding that 'their common interests are economic development' and that, within the orbit of the EU, 'it is the people of Ireland who are divided, not the territory'.[48] By contrast, Trimble believed that the only purpose of the peace process must be the restoration of the historic Stormont assembly that had been disbanded in 1972. If there was to be any American involvement, it must be directed solely towards that end: 'the only thing which I cared about was getting Clinton into Stormont'.[49] Trimble was not happy that Clinton had celebrated the fact that the British and Irish governments had decided on a 'twin track approach' to solve the Northern peace process between them. This was because he considered it very damaging to give any credence to the idea that Northern Ireland needed outside assistance, because this might be seen to support the southern Irish idea that it was a flawed political entity. In support of Trimble's stance, the Northern Ireland secretary of state had already told the US state department at Washington D.C. that the holding of all-party talks within Northern Ireland must be the sole focus of the peace process. He also argued that the decommissioning of all paramilitary weapons must be a prerequisite to the holding of such talks. This practically gave the secret paramilitary organisations (the membership of which sometimes overlapped with security forces) a veto over the whole process. John de Chastelain, a former head of the Canadian Defence Forces, was employed alongside George Mitchell and the Irish government's suggested peace envoy, Harri Holkeri, a former Finnish prime minister and future UN general assembly chairman, to oversee a decommissioning process. However, to the dismay of Sinn Féin leaders Gerry Adams and Martin McGuinness, the IRA broke its ceasefire in February 1996 for an undisclosed reason.[50]

The Royal Ulster Constabulary (RUC) had given assurances to Senator Mitchell that figures like Gerry Adams had no authority over secret paramilitary organisations like the Provisional IRA. However, unionists were thereafter able to make the complete exclusion of Sinn Féin from party talks a requisite for their own willingness to participate on the grounds that Sinn Féin and the IRA were one and the same thing.[51] Dublin had often championed this same perspective on the basis of police intelligence. On this occasion, however, Dublin and London responded by suggesting that Sinn Féin could be allowed back into negotiations if the IRA reinstated its ceasefire. This would not occur for another sixteen months, not least because loyalist paramilitaries had also broken their ceasefire. In the meantime, Mitchell faced frequent demands from many unionists that he cease all involvement in Northern Irish affairs on the grounds that only de Chastelain, being a fellow British citizen, could be entitled to interest himself in the UK's internal affairs. David Trimble risked not giving his formal approval to this stance, however, as he had to counterbalance Ulster unionists' desire to remove American influence from the peace process with his ultimate end objective of securing American support for his envisioned restoration of Stormont.[52] Meanwhile, the peak of Taoiseach John Bruton's involvement in the peace process came in March 1996 when he gave a speech at the White House that echoed John Hume's ongoing call for a tripartite approach to the negotiations that involved both the British and Irish governments, not just all the Northern Ireland parties.[53] No further negotiations were possible, however, until the return of new British and Irish governments in the summer of 1997 because of Ulster unionist opposition.

Bruton had actually preferred that his foreign minister Dick Spring would take responsibility for the Irish government's necessary involvement in the peace process,[54] not least so that he could concentrate on assuming the role as Ireland's president of the European Council (July–December 1996). In this capacity, Bruton helped to arrange an Amsterdam Treaty (1997) that saw the creation of an EU foreign policy representative to the rest of the world and a simultaneous introduction of a common visa policy, leading to the abolition of purely national passports for citizens of all EU member states. Be that as it may, the Irish government felt it necessary to join the British government in not giving its full assent to this EU common visa policy, prompting Brussels to allow for a unique opt-out arrangement for both countries. A 'common travel area' arrangement had existed that was unilaterally governed by Britain's Ireland Act (1949), which stated that Ireland was not to be regarded in the UK as a foreign country for legal purposes. Combined with the UK's Immigration Act of 1971, this was the basis for Britain's claim to common citizenship rights to vote, work and receive social security payments to all residents within the two states, notwithstanding their differing electoral systems, constitutions, labour laws and social security systems. The Irish government gave its consent to this principle under the Anglo-Irish Agreement of 1985, but it had effectively always been encouraged to abide by this situation, particularly in the post-1969 period, because it made security operations along the Irish border, which cut across almost two hundred roads, sufficiently inexpensive that the Irish government could handle this challenge.[55] This 'common travel area' arrangement was now also postulated by Britain, however, as a potential solution to the seemingly perpetual divide within Northern Ireland. This was because it could potentially form a legal basis for people in Northern Ireland to identify themselves as Irish, British or both without interfering in any way with the existing law of the United Kingdom.[56] As Pat Cox would point out, however, the common travel area was 'not specifically provided for in legislation' within Ireland. Instead, its first formal 'legal recognition' in Ireland would actually be the EU's Amsterdam Treaty of 1997, which had provided for it as a special provision *within* the overall operations of the EU's 'Schengen Area' common visa policy.[57] EU treaties were not only the basis of European law but had also been binding on Irish law ever since Ireland's Maastricht Treaty referendum of 1992. Therefore, in Irish law, the Amsterdam Treaty was the sole legal basis of the operations of Ireland's common travel area with the United Kingdom.[58]

By the time of the Amsterdam Treaty, a new Fianna Fáil–Progessive Democrats coalition, led by Taoiseach Bertie Ahern, had been elected as an Irish government. Acting on the advice of Martin Mansergh, a new peace process team led by foreign minister David Andrews decided to emphasise the potential role of the churches in promoting peace and reconciliation within Northern Ireland. Mansergh's Northern clerical and lay intermediaries had recently introduced him to Mary MacAleese, a Catholic vice-chancellor and director of legal studies at Queen's University Belfast. John Hume declined, with regret, an invitation to stand for election as president of Ireland,[59] but MacAleese was chosen as the Fianna Fáil candidate for Ireland's 1997 presidential election. On her nomination and return, she adopted a rhetoric of 'building bridges' as a theme of her presidency. This was essentially a euphemism for her personal longstanding interest in religious ecumenism, partly as a means of dealing with both the internal divide within Northern Ireland and the North's poor relations with the Republic of Ireland.[60] This was a significantly different approach to the post-1994 idea that vocal American support for the International Fund for Ireland could help to persuade Northerners to reach a political agreement. With regards to Ireland, US President Bill Clinton acted at all times on the understanding that he could do no more than speak occasionally on the advice of George Mitchell. Reflecting the Irish government's current approach, Mitchell would suggest to Clinton during 1997 and again in 1998 that he speak to all Irish church leaders. Therefore, although Clinton personally identified with and admired John Hume's political vision, on the few occasions that the US president did speak on Northern Ireland thereafter, he would emphasise the churches' capacity to promote peace and reconciliation rather than his initial emphasis upon either the role of the International Fund for Ireland or changes in the political landscape of Europe.[61]

During 1997, a new British Labour government under Tony Blair implemented a policy of making the Bank of England an independent arbiter of British monetary policy. This was done while introducing a devolution programme for Scotland, Wales and Northern Ireland so that English representation in the Westminster parliament could work in conjunction with the Bank of England in influencing British monetary policy without undue Scottish, Welsh or Northern Irish influence. This was also done to assist the Bank of England in its preparations for maintaining the existing competitive advantage of sterling as the principal currency traded in foreign exchange markets worldwide, alongside the US dollar and the Japanese yen, before the European Central Bank and its envisioned Euro could be formed as a rival currency in June 1998.[62] This was why Blair was adamant that May 1998 must be made the absolute deadline for reaching a political agreement in Northern Ireland. On this understanding, the British and Irish governments rushed through a compromise solution during the spring of 1998.[63]

For Ireland, *The Agreement* of the spring of 1998 was significant for two reasons. First, it was put successfully to an all-Ireland referendum vote that May. Second, it was an international agreement, signed by both the British and Irish governments (in addition to Northern Irish representatives), that was subsequently registered at the UN as an aspect of international law. At the risk of being blasphemous, Irish nationalists often mistakenly referred to it as the 'Good Friday Agreement', nominally because it was signed on a day of significance to all Christians, while Irish and British unionists often mistakenly referred to it as the 'Belfast Agreement' to denote their belief that it did not involve the Republic of Ireland and that the all-Ireland vote on the matter was a legal irrelevance. The UN chose an alternative title: the Northern Ireland Peace Agreement.[64] Although it technically repealed the Government of Ireland Act of 1920,[65] the most controversial aspect of *The Agreement* within Northern Ireland was that, in dealing with the issue of paramilitaries, it was decided to allow an amnesty for all alleged political prisoners in return for the continued operations of de Chastelain's decommissioning body for as long as was deemed necessary. This was a messy compromise that would give birth to a healthy, if very native, brand of Ulster political satirism.[66] For Ireland as a whole, the most significant aspect of *The Agreement* was the creation of several cross-border institutions. A north–south ministerial council without executive powers was established for the purposes of economic consultation, but its existence was made entirely co-dependent with that of the Northern Ireland Assembly as a devolved British parliamentary assembly. Therefore, the north–south ministerial council would be disbanded in the event of a restoration of direct rule by London. As a concession to unionists, a British–Irish Council, without executive powers and with its secretariat based in Edinburgh, was created to include Irish and British government representatives, and this replaced the secretariat in Maryfield, Belfast, which was disbanded. Finally, the Northern Ireland Assembly itself was to embody a power-sharing arrangement whereby a ministry could only be established if it had the consent and support of both the largest unionist and nationalist party within Northern Ireland. On this level, *The Agreement* was partly a modification of the 'three-strands solution' that George Mitchell, acting not least on the advice of Hume, had first suggested during October 1996.[67] However, it also enhanced the tradition, first established in 1981, of regular British–Irish intergovernmental conferences without necessarily involving any direct Northern Ireland representation beyond its secretary of state, a British cabinet position first established in 1972 and which continued to exist.

As he desired nothing more than the restoration of Stormont, David Trimble was so opposed to the north–south strand of *The Agreement* that Hume was uncomfortable about the idea of serving in the proposed Northern Ireland Assembly as a deputy leader to Trimble. Therefore, Hume chose Seamus Mallon to take his place as the SDLP's leading representative, or Trimble's deputy first minister, in the new Northern Ireland Assembly. Mallon was a tough negotiator and a much greater sympathiser than Hume with the notion of the MacBride Principles, which were popular among Ulster Catholics and had begun to influence but never came to formally define the legal operations in America of the International Fund for Ireland.[68] In deference to Trimble, Tony Blair invited US President Bill Clinton but no Irish government personnel to the initial meeting of the Northern Ireland Assembly at

Stormont that September. On this occasion, Mallon emphasised simply that 'we are of the people of Ireland'. Meanwhile, Clinton emphasised his belief that all the specifics of *The Agreement* must not be ignored, such as the establishment of a new and more widely acceptable policing system to what had existed in the past; the promotion of cross-border community projects with the Irish government; the promotion of small businesses within Northern Ireland; and the creation of grassroots non-governmental organisations to heal community divisions.[69] By contrast, David Trimble emphasised simply that 'Northern Ireland is back in business'. Having succeeded in getting Clinton to attend an assembly at Stormont, he told the US president directly, before occupying Clinton's chair on the platform, that 'I will hold you to your claim to support peace' by scrutinising the extent to which the American government proved itself capable of being a champion of democracy in the future. To Trimble's mind, America's capacity to be democratic was dependent upon its willingness to support the UUP in ensuring that Northern Ireland henceforth became the island of Ireland's sole 'gateway to Europe' on behalf of the United Kingdom.[70] In this way, Trimble effectively spoke for traditional Ulster unionist culture, which had been defined since the days of James Craig by an almost religious belief that maintaining a competitive advantage for British business interests on the island of Ireland, via Belfast, was essential to the preservation of democracy, the Union and a civilised international order. On Trimble's advice, British state subsidies for Northern Ireland would continue to focus largely on the Lagan Valley area and Belfast, which received a massive budget covering both the extensive redevelopment of its quays and the building of new Northern Ireland Assembly buildings. By contrast, as soon as Clinton returned to the United States, the factory in the disadvantaged area of west Belfast that had hosted President Clinton's keynote speech during his 1995 visit was shut down.[71]

In October 1998, John Hume was awarded a Nobel Peace Prize in Oslo in recognition of his status as 'the clearest and most consistent of Northern Ireland political leaders'. For having 'showed great political courage' in defying accepted notions of unionist majority rule within Northern Ireland, David Trimble was awarded a prize as well, although this reputation was sufficient to ensure that, henceforth, both Trimble's London Tory biographers and the Ulster unionist community itself began to turn against him, as if he was a cowardly compromiser with an enemy.[72] The DUP actively opposed *The Agreement*. The Nobel Committee also recognised the part played by the Irish, British and American governments in creating peace in Northern Ireland after three decades of disturbances that had tragically cost over three thousand lives. In the process, it was argued, they had provided hope 'to inspire peaceful solutions to other religious, ethnic and national conflicts around the world'.[73] On accepting his prize two months later, Hume chose to welcome the fact that the European Convention of Human Rights was 'to be incorporated into the domestic law of our land [Northern Ireland] as an element of the Good Friday Agreement' before delivering an effective eulogy about the relevance of the EU to the future of Ireland:

> We in Ireland appreciate this solidarity and support, from the United States, from the European Union, from friends around the world ... Peace could not have been won without this good will and generosity of spirit ... The European [Union] visionaries decided that difference is not a threat ... Difference is the essence of humanity ... therein lies a most fundamental principle of peace: respect for diversity ... Two major political traditions share the island of Ireland. We are destined by history to live side by side ... No-one is asked to yield their cherished convictions or beliefs. All of us are asked to respect the views and rights of others as equal to our own ... That is what a new, agreed Ireland will involve ... I want to see Ireland, North and South, the wounds of violence healed, play its rightful role in a Europe that will, for all Irish people, be a shared bond of patriotism and new endeavour.[74]

Ireland continued to differ, however, from certain EU legal norms. An unprecedented rise in the number of asylum seekers from outside the EU (almost 10,000 a year) encouraged the Irish state to pass a number of immigration laws after 1998. While Ireland was expected to harmonise its practices with the Common European Asylum System, it could only comply with this system 'to the maximum extent compatible with the maintenance of its Common Travel Area with the United Kingdom'.[75] Prior to *The Agreement*, Articles Two and Three of the Irish constitution had referred to 'the whole island of Ireland' as a 'national territory' but also stated that this assertion had no direct legal implications 'pending the re-integration of the national territory'.[76] During 1999, these were replaced by referendum with new articles that referred exclusively to the concept of citizenship, while also noting that 'a united Ireland shall be brought about only by peaceful means with the consent of a majority of the people, democratically expressed, in both jurisdictions in the island'. This was considered necessary in light of the fact that the original terminology, which had always been deemed unnecessary by many sympathisers with the idea of a united Ireland (including John Hume, who would retire due to ill health in 2004), had been cited by some Northern Ireland paramilitaries as an alleged cause of their conflict. With regards to the Irish state's international identity, both Articles Three and Twenty-Nine of the Irish constitution, which covered the state's international relations, were modified to recognise that new cross-border bodies without executive functions now had an authority to act. In Article Three, however, it was stated that, in theory, 'institutions with executive powers and functions that are shared between those jurisdictions may be established'.[77] Reflecting this, historians of Ulster politics tended to view *The Agreement* as evidence that both the British and Irish governments desired 'that any settlement – whatever its form – is publicly seen to reflect their planning and their wishes'. London was particularly concerned that 'any final deal over British Ireland will be offered to world opinion as a reflection of the strategies and dignity of the imperial government', even if 'the most convincing recent prospect for a settlement reflects a European model of consociationalism', whereby power-sharing was to be established by means of reaching agreement upon some overarching common standards.[78] In so far as this was true, the existence of the EU and its emerging traditions of cultural diplomacy was a significant inspiration for the existence of *The Agreement*.

By 1998, a ten-year programme of trade diversification had led to Ireland enhancing its trade with every European state, while also maintaining, on an ever-rising scale, a positive balance of total trade. By the mid-to-late 1990s, total Irish exports to the EU had risen to 18,880 million pounds, compared to 2,500 million pounds to the United States. To many observers, this was a revolutionary change because just twenty years previously total Irish exports had amounted to just £400 million. Membership of the European Single Market had also facilitated a rise in Irish exports specifically to the United Kingdom (6,000 million pounds to Britain and 750 million pounds to Northern Ireland), while there was also a rise in exports to countries like Japan (800 million pounds).[79] Although the Irish currency had nominally been independent ever since 1979, by the mid-1980s Ireland's membership of the European Monetary System had been expected to lead to its eventual acceptance of a European Monetary Union.[80] Ireland's adoption of the euro currency as soon as it went into circulation in 2002 saw the volume of annual trade between Ireland and China grow rapidly to $6.4 billion,[81] while shortly thereafter new Irish export markets developed in countries such as Russia (€600 million).[82] In the realm of financial services, new Irish links with Latin America and the Middle East would reach billions of euros' worth of trade over the next decade because of Ireland's membership of the Eurozone, reflecting the principal advantage of the euro over the Irish pound: the direct access it provided to global financial markets.[83]

These sudden advantages acquired by Ireland led to something of a counter-reaction in Belfast. In particular, Ireland's adoption of the euro in 2002 coincided with an alleged bank raid by nationalist revolutionaries within Northern Ireland that saw the Northern Irish Assembly collapse for five years. The fact that a former Northern Ireland secretary of state served as the European commissioner for trade during much of this period does not appear to have helped significantly in remedying this dispute.[84] The decision to restore power-sharing to Northern Ireland was ultimately made possible by means of a Saint Andrews Agreement (2007). This was signed in Edinburgh, the home of the standing secretariat of the (non-executive) British–Irish Council which met biannually and also included representation from the devolved UK assemblies of Scotland and Wales (as well as the Crown dependences of Jersey, the Isle of Man and Guernsey). The existence of this assembly and London's insistence upon Irish governmental participation *if* it wanted to have a voice regarding Northern Ireland was essentially a reflection of the ongoing British Commonwealth desire to keep Ireland as closely tied to its orbit as was possible. To most observers, the chief significance of the Saint Andrews Agreement was that it led to the creation of a new Northern Irish Assembly in which the longstanding majority parties, the UUP and the SDLP, were now reduced to being a minority voice. The new first minister was DUP leader Ian Paisley, who retired in 2008 and was replaced by his understudy Peter Robinson, while Martin McGuinness of Sinn Féin served as deputy first minister.

By 2008, €849 million had been provided in economic assistance to Northern Ireland by means of the International Fund for Ireland.[85] Some considered that it was this development, rather than the attitudes of local politicians, that was the essential reason why the peace process had evidently reached a fairly successful conclusion. If so, credit for creating this situation rested largely with international supporters of the Irish government in institutionalising this fund. Up until 2007, Ireland had used some of its EU regional development or 'cohesion policy' funds to promote plans for common tourism, electricity and agricultural production plans by means of the North–South Ministerial Council. Non-partisan Ulster businessmen had been inclined for some time to consider that an all-island economy actually made a great deal of sense, although the east–west divide within Northern Ireland, both in terms of British state subsidies and voting patterns, evidently continued.[86] A traditional belief in Dublin was that all-Ireland economic and political cooperation could operate harmoniously so long as Belfast recognised the extent to which its economy and, in turn, that of Ulster as a whole would naturally benefit from integrating with that of the island as a whole rather than attempting to enforce an opposite trend.[87] In 2009, David Cooney, a London-born official with Ireland's London embassy, succeeded Dermot Gallagher as secretary-general of the Irish department of foreign affairs, technically making him the first non-Irish born holder of that office. He had played a quite pivotal role in the Anglo-Irish negotiations during the late 1990s due to his popularity with all sides,[88] and this might explain why he was chosen to become the administrative head of foreign affairs in the wake of the Saint Andrews Agreement.

The admission of nine central and eastern European republics (Czech Republic, Slovakia, Poland, Hungary, Estonia, Latvia, Lithunia, Malta, Slovenia) into the EU during Ireland's 2004 presidency of the European Council was widely considered to have elevated Ireland's standing in international relations to that of a more 'middle-sized' power because of the extent to which its European performance was deemed worthy of emulation by the EU's newest member states.[89] By 2000, the department of the Taoiseach was the only Irish government department that did not also have staff working in Brussels, as both the office of the attorney general and the department of defence had just appointed delegates for the first time. The latter development led the department of defence to issue its first official white paper. This drew attention to the fact that Irish army troops were embarking on (EU-supported) UN peacekeeping operations in Kosovo, East Timor and Bosnia, but there was also a need for the development of Ireland's naval and air corps to support such troops. Ever since the 1980s, even the Irish state's minimal defence budget for its own coastguard services was sustained mostly due to European structural funding.[90] With EU support, after 2000, seven fully up-to-date Irish patrol ships were commissioned. In addition to continuing to assist in EU fisheries protection and anti-smuggling work, they occasionally provided supplies to Irish troops on UN missions abroad.[91] However, when Irish troops joined the peacekeeping mission in Chad in central Africa (where many Irish non-governmental organisations were already active), it would be necessary to hire Russian helicopters to transport Irish troops because the Irish air corps was forbidden to take part in overseas operations and kept entirely unarmed at the insistence of the government. This fact had already limited the relevance of the development of the Irish navy for national defence purposes because it meant that it was not allowed to develop aircraft carrier functions.[92] The latter decision was taken despite a recent upgrading of Ireland's air defence capabilities (as represented by the army's purchase of surface-to-air missiles and anti-aircraft guns), evidently because it was decided to minimise Ireland's overall defence spending (0.6 per cent of the country's gross domestic product), which was kept at the lowest rate in all of Europe.[93] The Irish government may have feared that increases in defence spending would serve only to put diplomatic pressure on the country to join NATO.

Despite this deliberate under prioritising of defence budgets, Irish voters, albeit on a very low turnout, surprised the Irish government in June 2001 by rejecting the EU's Nice Treaty, nominally due to a fear of militarism. The Nice Treaty was intended to grant each EU state a number of seats on the European Council to match the size of a country's population. Irish voters feared that this could result in a compromising of Irish military neutrality through the country being perpetually outvoted under the European Council's proposed 'qualified majority voting' scheme. This led the Irish government to secure from the EU a 'Seville Declaration' that recognised the perpetual applicability of the Irish 'triple lock' procedure, whereby the sending of Irish troops abroad had to be approved not just by the UN (whose Security Council had the authority to validate a war)[94] but also by a vote of the Irish cabinet and the entire Dáil. This being secured, Ireland became the last European country to accept the Nice Treaty in October 2002. By that time, the Irish army had begun to benefit slightly from the launch of the first-ever strategic studies programme in an Irish university as well as an associated *Defence Forces Review*.[95]

Popular fears of the outbreak of major international wars grew considerably after the United States made an essentially unilateral decision to occupy Iraq in the wake of the destruction of the World Trade Center in New York in September 2001 by a terrorist group that evidently stemmed from somewhere in the Middle East. As a member of the UN Security Council at the time, Ireland had expressed support for the idea of weapons inspections of Iraq only, rather than an invasion, but this advice was ignored.[96] In February 2003, simultaneous protests against the invasion of Iraq were held in many European capitals, with the greatest of these being held in London (about one million people) as a result of Britain's support for the invasion. An anti-war demonstration in Dublin attracted about 100,000 people and led to public debates as to whether or not Ireland should continue to offer landing rights to American military aircraft at Shannon.[97] While a prominent French government official cited these trends as evidence that a 'new European nation' was manifesting itself on the streets,[98] academics in Britain and elsewhere generally voiced their support for those Americans who claimed that a new era in history had begun in the wake of the attack upon the World Trade Center whereby 'the implications of international migration for security' must henceforth be treated as the predominant security concern of all countries, in both their national and international relations, as part of a greater 'war against terror'.[99] The reputed role of Islamic religious fundamentalists in inspiring conflict was also sufficient to persuade some prominent British academics to expand upon Anthony Giddens' initial thesis of a supposed divide between cosmopolitans and religious fundamentalists within Europe by suggesting that religion had now actually become an enemy of the entire civilised world.[100] This trend of thought certainly served to lessen the influence of the hitherto strong Christian-democratic tradition within Europe.

This emphasis on migration as a security threat was actually quite polemical in a European context because nine central and eastern European republics (Czech Republic, Slovakia, Poland, Hungary, Estonia, Latvia, Lithunia, Malta, Slovenia) were just about to join the EU after they accepted the common visa policy of the Schengen Area, as had the non-EU European Free Trade Association (Switzerland, Norway, Liechtenstein and Iceland).[101] Sean O'hUiginn, then Ireland's ambassador to America (and subsequently Germany), told a recent American National Security advisor that he considered the military occupation of Iraq to be a very irresponsible policy, not least because the United States had recently spent billions of dollars on developing more sophisticated surveillance tools for intelligence purposes supposedly to avoid precisely such situations.[102] Meanwhile, some Irish army officers pondered whether or not the invasion of Iraq had made the UN more irrelevant than ever as a forum for regulating the implementation of international law.[103] Nevertheless, in public, the Irish government was far less inclined to criticise the Anglo-American alliance regarding the Iraq war. Perhaps reflecting this, a professor of government at University College Cork wrote a study on European security challenges that emphasised the supposed new threats of 'migration' and 'weapons of mass destruction'.[104] Likewise, a study of the degree to which 'changes in the Republic of Ireland's international role' were taking place judged that the country evidently accepted the emerging 'Anglo-American narrative' of international relations more so than the vantage point of a 'European republic'.[105]

Just as the Russian Federation had done, along with the neutral European powers of Austria, Finland, Sweden, Switzerland and Malta, Ireland had joined the NATO-sponsored 'partnership for peace' programme during the 1990s to indicate its willingness to support all non-military peacekeeping operations.[106] However, both this development and the principle of 'permanent structured cooperation' (PESCO) introduced into the EU's defence and security policy by the

December 2007 Lisbon Treaty would be questioned in some Irish circles.[107] Not least to satisfy Britain, the EU's Lisbon Treaty made the European Parliament a bicameral institution with the European Council of Ministers and also provided a legal mechanism for any member state to leave the Union. An Irish referendum on the treaty was due to be held in June 2008, just a month after Bertie Ahern, an increasingly unpopular Taoiseach, resigned from office to face a corruption charge. Voting against his government (which had been in power for over a decade), only 47 per cent of Irish voters agreed to the Lisbon Treaty in June 2008, but in the face of a growing economic recession – stemming from the virtually simultaneous announcement of a crisis in American and Irish banks in Stepember 2008 – 67 per cent of Irish voters chose to accept the Lisbon Treaty in October 2009.[108] Despite the pre-existing Seville Declaration, the issue of Irish neutrality was made the central issue in both these referenda. NATO's criticisms of the EU's lack of a defence policy in the wake of its failure to support Britain and America's 2003 invasion of Iraq created fears of rising militarism. Britain, France and Germany did create a 'European Union Military Staff' that tested the possibility of creating EU 'battle groups', but there was subsequently little or no will to either fund or deploy such forces.[109] Reflecting this, when the EU did actually draft a new security strategy it emphasised simply that 'the fundamental framework for international relations is the UN Charter' and that 'strengthening the UN is a European priority'.[110] If a change took place in the Irish government's attitude at this time, it was that it became increasingly inclined to define Irish military neutrality as being the same as that of all other small neutral European states: the country would always remain neutral, unless attacked, but it would always be prepared to consider supporting any peacekeeping missions that were sponsored by the UN and the EU. For the Irish army, both the NATO-affiliated, yet independent, 'partnership for peace' programme and the EU's PESCO programme enhanced its capabilities to engage in such missions by increasing its level of access to the latest technical developments and training programmes.[111] Crucially, unlike NATO states, Ireland retained the unilateral right to determine the extent to which it cooperated with such bodies.

Some Irish opponents of the Lisbon Treaty deemed that the essential issue at stake was whether or not the country should be 'joining EU collective defence in order to improve the Union's capacity to shape globalisation'.[112] Monnet professors of European studies now existed in most Irish universities,[113] but some Irish academics had actively campaigned against the Lisbon Treaty on the grounds of their resentment of the growing pro-European tenor of Irish academic institutions.[114] Within some all-island academic forums, schools of literary scholarships actually deemed Ireland to be a postcolonial society, akin to the Third World countries within the Non-Aligned Movement at the UN,[115] rather than the pro-European state actor in international relations that the Irish state had both defined itself as and was generally recognised to be ever since the mid-1970s. This evidently reflected a lack of engagement by Irish academics with intellectual trends on the continent. By contrast, Ireland's Austrian embassy served as Dublin's permament liaison with all those international organisations based in Vienna that were focused primarily on the closer integration of central and eastern Europe into EU structures and this campaign was focused upon the role of universities. In this context, Irish foreign ministers' typification of Europe as 'a marketplace of ideas' meant that it was generally seen to be a benevolent, if not a powerful, ally of central and eastern European nations at various intergovernmental conferences.[116] Since 1991, Vienna had promoted a federation of central and eastern European universities to dwell on the potential role of all European metropolises on both a national and an international level.[117] The central experience of the former eastern bloc was judged to be that its cities' wealth had been used not for their own development but instead had been used to bolster 'inert economies in the Soviet Union', with the end result that central and eastern European cities had suffered unnecessarily from the same inertia as Russia's great cities.[118] A prioritisation of urban development and a desire to undo through international dialogue (not least with Scandinavia) all 'stereotypes' regarding east–west relations that had been established at the time of the Helsinki Act of 1975 was the essential goal of this university campaign, but most Irish minds evidently had little time for the new pan-Europeanism espoused by writers such as Norman Davies.[119]

In the wake of neutral Austria's entry into the EU during 1995, the 'Committee of Security and Cooperation in Europe', first established in 1975, became known as the 'Organisation for Security and Cooperation in Europe' (OSCE). Its strongly academic vision of Europe was soon challenged by NATO powers who, upon joining the OSCE (in the process expanding its membership to over fifty nations), asked it to adopt a rather different approach. It was now called upon to focus exclusively upon assessing, or even policing, the degree to which central and eastern European commercial media were equally as 'free' as the western European media was supposed to be. Unsurprisingly, Irish army and foreign affairs staff who liaised with the Austrian embassy and the OSCE became conscious of the challenges that this peculiar mandate involved.[120] The Defence (Amendment) Act formally authorised Defence Forces personnel to take part in OSCE operations during 2006. The Russian Federation's principal forum for interacting with the EU had always been the CSCE/OSCE, through which its rather unique cultural status as both a European and extra-European nation could sometimes find a voice. Nevertheless, its relations with that body were often strained because the Russian leader Vladimir Putin believed that the economic challenge of maintaining internal security within a multi-ethnic Russian Federation was either being downplayed or deliberately ignored by a Western media that attributed an undue significance to his former status as a USSR intelligence officer.[121] Noting rising trading relations between Russia and Ireland, as well as with Europe as a whole, during 2007 Ireland's ambassador to the Russian Federation welcomed the fact that Putin favoured Russia's entry into the World Trade Organisation to prevent future trade wars and also expressed support for the work of the European Court of Human Rights. Russia supplied the EU with a high percentage of its oil and gas and had become a stable economy by 2007, a decade after suffering a financial crash under Boris Yeltsin. Meanwhile, the EU provided 70 per cent of all foreign direct investment within Russia.[122] Partly as a result, European perspectives of Russia sometimes differed from those of America or even Britain, although an aggressive foreign policy rivalry, arising from an expansionist impulse, could also shape European attitudes towards Russia because of the legacy of central European fears of Russian militarism.[123]

During 2008, Padraig Murphy, a former Irish ambassador to the USSR, was given an EU monitoring mission in Georgia, while during 2012 an OSCE conference on peacekeeping would be held in Dublin, to which spokesmen from the Northern Ireland Assembly were also invited.[124] Eamon Gilmore, an Irish foreign minister who was later made an EU special envoy to the Colombia peace process, would be given the responsibility of supervising the situation in Moldova (bordering Romania and Ukraine) in his capacity as OSCE chairman. At the same time, Pat Cox, an Irish veteran of European projects, was given the responsibility of monitoring allegations of corruption within the Ukraine,[125] which would experience an upheaval two years later in the wake of a Russian incursion into the Crimea. In its performance of these responsibilities, Ireland adopted EU policy but also expressed a closer sense of identification with the 'group summit' tradition of joint meetings of the political leaders and central bankers of the world's wealthiest nations as a basis of the international order. This system was first launched by the G7 summits in the wake of the Helsinki Act of 1975 and it was a forum to which Russia was later added. The UK, which hosted six such summits, invited an Irish Taoiseach to attend one such forum, purely as an observer, when it was held in Northern Ireland during 2013. This was the only time that an Irish representative had ever been able to attend a group summit conference.[126]

Within Ireland, it was often assumed that multinationals operating in the country from the 1960s until the 1990s were primarily American and thereafter became mostly European. As late as the 2010s, however, as much as 70 per cent of all foreign direct investments in Ireland came from the United States (over $200,000 million), which constituted about 10 per cent of all American investments in Europe or roughly 5 per cent of all American foreign direct investments in the world.[127] Total annual Irish exports to America would be valued at over €200,000 million (about 15 per cent of total Irish exports), while the process of American firms establishing themselves in Ireland also played a part in encouraging more Irish firms to establish themselves in America. During 2009, of international companies operating on the Nasdaq stock exchange in New York, only the countries of Israel, Canada and Japan had more companies than either Ireland or the United Kingdom, which each had five.[128] Be that as it may, the staffing of Ireland's diplomatic representation in America remained much lower than the European average.[129] Meanwhile, Ireland had not necessarily lost its reputation as a satellite economy. Mostly foreign-owned pharmaceutical companies in Ireland accounted for 48 per cent of all Irish exports and stimulated 12 per cent of the country's gross domestic product, but provided only 2 per cent of the country's employment. This was an imbalanced situation.[130]

A new tradition of G20 summits was first launched in Washington D.C. in November 2008 in response to an American fiscal crisis that was reputedly caused by a prolongment of its occupation of Iraq. Subgroups adopted by the G20 for deciding the rotating chair at its regular summits would appear to have reflected a shifting international balance. For instance, Russia was now grouped with India and Turkey to reflect its role as an intermediary between Asia and Europe. Reflecting its desire to exercise a strong economic influence over both the British Commonwealth and the Middle East, the US was grouped with Canada, Australia and Saudi Arabia. This formed a significant contrast to the far more geographically homogenous Far Eastern, Latin American and European groupings within the G20, with the UK being included exclusively within the European group. As such, these groups practically reflected the prioritisation of new regional trading blocs as a fixed entity. By 2010, the Euro had become the world's second-most traded currency after the US dollar. However, the top five individual countries in the world in terms of the highest volume of trade – China, the United States, Germany, Japan and Britain – were no doubt still conscious of their 'great power' status, with the perhaps notable exception of Germany because of its status as the monetary centre of EU. Due to the EU's status as 'an important global actor, supported by its size and diversity, its economy and its experience of promoting common approaches over five decades of integration', Ireland now decided to make it 'the primary framework through which we pursue many of our foreign policy goals', including Ireland's own commitment to encouraging a fuller integration of the European continent into the Eurozone as a matter 'of principle'.[131] Meanwhile, an Irish army officer judged that Russia had no intrinsic problem with the integration of eastern European countries into the EU: it simply felt that the formal incorporation of many of these countries into the NATO collective security arrangement was essentially an unfriendly act.[132]

A former Finnish president, who was awarded a Nobel Peace Prize for his role in mediating past conflicts in Kosovo and Iraq, emphasised on a visit to Dublin that reports of the Global Peace Index indicated that 'Europe remains the most peaceful region in the world', not least because of the successful operations of the EU as a proven forum for multilateral negotiations between member states based on effective foreign policy consultations.[133] Like most EU countries, Ireland generally supported all member states' right to continue to prioritise their own purely national diplomatic priorities at the UN.[134] Be that as it may, by 2010 Ireland was evidently a strong believer that the EU, as much as the UN, had a key diplomatic role to play in bringing peace to the Middle East and Africa, albeit by relying on purely economic, rather than military, channels.[135] A period of instability in the pivotal state of Egypt and the emergence of civil war in Syria after it was suspended from the Arab League (and suspended itself from the Mediterranean union) in 2011 weakened but did not halt the 'Union for the Mediterranean' project, while the EU also assisted refugees fleeing from Syria. During 2015, the Irish navy provided assistance to over ten thousand such refugees as part of the EU's strategy of promoting mutually beneficial economic cooperation between the Islamic and non-Islamic worlds, respecting but transcending their differences by means of finding common grounds of economic interest.[136] Meanwhile, as president of the Jean Monnet Institute, Ireland's former EU president Pat Cox worked as the coordinator of an intended new EU 'transport corridor' to improve links between Scandinavia and the Mediterranean region.[137] This effectively laid a basis for the EU's Polish-led Three Seas Initiative, which was intended to create a common market linking the Baltic, Adriatic and Black Seas.

During 2010, a shocking bailout programme for most Irish banks necessitated the intervention of both the European Central Bank and the IMF. It also saw anti-European, as well as anti-American, sentiment seemingly reaching a peak during a subsequent period of austerity. Evident failures of party politics, as well as a seeming disconnection between the operations of the so-called 'global economy' and humanitarian notions of social justice, became a common subject of Irish debate both before and after the first-ever state visit to Ireland by a British monarch.[138] Internationally, the US Federal Reserve, the Bank of England, the Bank of Canada and the Bank of Japan had all played a major role in dealing with the international financial crisis of

2008. In Ireland, the Central Bank of Ireland's direct affiliation with the European Central Bank ensured that a European stability mechanism was utilised. This meant that the Irish state, in intervening to prevent a crash of the Irish banking system, could remain secure in the knowledge that the resulting long-term debts would be made manageable under an EU-supported national recovery plan. Although this Irish banking crisis essentially originated in the United States, two-thirds of the assistance that Ireland received to help it manage its banking problems came directly from the European stability mechanism.[139]

If such debts cast a shadow upon the Irish state's performance throughout the 2010s, Ireland's role in international relations was widely perceived to have become proactive rather than reactive, certainly when compared to the situation as late as the 1980s. It was not until 2011 that the Irish government finally decided to fully integrate the state's trading priorities into its foreign policy formation. While this did not result in major changes to the parameters of the Irish department of foreign affairs' operations,[140] it reflected a trend whereby thirty-two offices of Enterprise Ireland, which was established purely to assist Irish rather than international companies (unlike the IDA), were now directly affiliated with Irish embassies abroad.[141] This integrated approach to international trade could be interpreted as a sign that Irish foreign policy was truly coming of age by actively promoting rather than merely representing Irish interests abroad. Irish government policy regarding the IFSC and Ireland's corporate tax rate remained the prerogative of the department of the Taoiseach, however, whose role in acting as a pillar of the state's foreign policy formation, particularly in terms of determining a unitary stance, remained very strong,[142] partly because of an established political tradition in Ireland of the Taoiseach, rather than the foreign minister, representing the country at European Council meetings.

Not long after the Irish department of foreign affairs was renamed the 'Department of Foreign Affairs and Trade', a new foreign policy white paper was created. This effectively committed Ireland to a strategy of acting as a European hub within the global economy. This was done in recognition of the fact that Ireland's status as 'a longstanding and fully engaged member of the European Union' was the most 'significant factor in the stabilisation of our national finances' and, in turn, 'in our bourgeoning economic recovery'. Since the turn of the twenty-first century, Ireland's representation abroad had almost doubled in size to over sixty diplomatic and twenty consular offices, which was roughly in keeping with the European norm for small states. In addition to the operations of sixteen other state agencies and the activities of approximately eighty honorary consuls, these were practically managing Irish relations with 178 different countries, albeit in many cases with the most minimal of staffing.[143] In the belief that 'our security, our prosperity and the well being of our own people are connected to the wider world as never before', it was decided 'to coordinate across all government departments and state agencies' a foreign policy based on the relevance of the 'global economy' to Irish trade, tourism and investment. On the premise that 'nothing is entirely foreign or wholly domestic', it was also judged that 'foreign policy is more important to us now than at any time in our history'.[144] Nevertheless, Ireland's foreign ministers also maintained that the 'same principles' and 'enduring values' were 'a common thread which runs through our foreign policy from the foundation of the state' a century previously.[145] The relative significance, or applicability, of these claims shall now be assessed to form this book's conclusion.

Endnotes

1   Peter Sutherland, 'Interview as ex-director general of the World Trade Organisation (9 Feb. 2011)', accessible through https://www.wto.org

2   D.R. Wightman, 'Europe and the dollar', *Irish studies in international affairs*, vol. 4 (1993), 13–18.

3   John Pinder, *The European Union* (Oxford, 2001), 150–3.

4   Ronan Fanning, 'The Anglo-American alliance and the Irish question in the twentieth century', in Judith Devlin, H.B. Clarke (eds), *European encounters* (Dublin, 2003), quote p. 211.

5   Valur Ingimundarson, 'The American dimension: Britain, Germany and the reinforcement of US hegemony in Europe in the 1990s', in Klaus Larres (ed.), *Uneasy allies: British–German relations and European integration since 1945* (Oxford, 2000), 165–83.

6   Chris Brown, Kirsten Ainley, *Understanding international relations* (3rd ed., London, 2015).

7   Brian Cowen, 'Challenges to liberal internationalism', *Irish studies in international affairs*, vol. 12 (2001), 1–5.

8   Frans Alting von Geusau, 'Cultural diplomacy and national stereotypes: for official use only?', in Teresa Walas (ed.), *Stereotypes and nations* (Cracow, 1995), 247–51.

9   Jacek Purchla (ed.) *The historical metropolis: a hidden potential* (Cracow, 1996); Judith Devlin, 'The city as symbol: architecture and ideology in post-Soviet Moscow', in J. Devlin, H.B. Clarke (eds), *European encounters* (Dublin, 2003), 363–404.

10   Jacek Purchla (ed.) *The historical metropolis: a hidden potential* (Cracow, 1996). In Ireland, Mary Harney, as deputy Irish prime minister (Tánaiste) and leader of the short-lived but influential Irish 'Progressive Democrats' party (1993–2005), argued that not to have faith in politics was not to have faith in civilisation, and the essence of civilisation was to prioritise urban rather than rural development. Joe Mulholland (ed.), *Why not? Building a better Ireland* (Dublin, 2003), 34–8.

11   Fintan O'Toole, *The ex-isle of Erin: images of a global Ireland* (Dublin, 1997), 11–12; Mairéad Considine, Fiona Dukelow, *Irish social policy* (Dublin, 2009), 161, 166, 203, 217.

12   Department of foreign affairs and trade, *The Irish in Latin America* (Dublin, 2016).

13   Department of foreign affairs and trade, *Celebrating sixty years: Ireland–Japan diplomatic relations* (Dublin, 2017). Among the Irish companies who attempted to break into the Japanese market after 1993 were Bewleys and Guinness (which was merged with British firm Diageo in 1997).

14   Fan Hong, Jorn-Carsten Gottwald (eds), *The Irish Asia strategy and its China relations 1999–2009* (Amsterdam, 2010).

15   Stephen Loyal, *Understanding immigration in Ireland: state, capital and labour in a global age* (Manchester, 2011), 154–9.

16   Denis O'Hearn, *The Atlantic economy: Britain, the US and Ireland* (Manchester, 2001).

17   Brigid Laffan, 'Managing European dossiers in the Irish civil service', in Mark Callanan (ed.), *Foundations of an ever closer union: an Irish perspective on the fifty years since the Treaty of Rome* (Dublin, 2007), 190–3 (quote p. 193).

18   Ruairi Quinn, *Straight left: a journey in politics* (London, 2005), chapters 13–14.

19   Patrick Keatinge, Brigid Laffan, 'Ireland in international affairs', in John Coakley, Michael Gallagher (eds), *Politics in the republic of Ireland* (2nd ed., Dublin, 1993), 227–49, especially p. 238.

20   Stephen Collins, *Breaking the mould* (Dublin, 2006), 230–40.

21   John Bruton, *Faith in politics: a collection of essays on politics, economics, history and religion* (Dublin, 2015).

22   Mark Callanan (ed.), *Foundations of an ever closer union: an Irish perspective on the fifty years since the Treaty of Rome* (Dublin, 2007), 83, 85–6, 94–5,187–8, 232–3.

23   J.W. Young, *Britain and European unity 1945–1999* (London, 2000), 188; D. Naurin, H. Wallace (eds), *Unveiling the council of the EU: games governments play in Brussels* (London, 2010), 33–4.

24   Brigid Laffan, *The finances of the European Union* (London, 1997).

25   Dermot Keogh, *Ireland and Europe* (2nd ed., Dublin, 1990), 265 (quote), 267.

26   Patrick Keatinge, Brigid Laffan, 'Ireland in international affairs', in John Coakley, Michael Gallagher (eds), *Politics in the republic of Ireland* (2nd ed., Dublin, 1993), 227–49.

27   John Cooney, Tony McGarry (eds.), *Ireland and Europe*, 141, 216 (reported speeches of Padraic MacKernan and Noel Dorr).

28   Paul McArthur, *The MacBride principles* (Liverpool, 2002), 156 (quoting Anne Anderson).

29   'Interview with Sean O'hUiginn', Edward Kennedy Oral History Project (PDF available online), 3.

30 Department of foreign affairs, *Challenges and opportunities abroad: white paper on foreign policy* (Dublin, 1996), 52–3, 64–5, 321.

31 Brigid Laffan, 'Managing European dossiers in the Irish civil service', in Mark Callanan (ed.), *Foundations of an ever-closer union* (Dublin, 2007), 189, 191.

32 'Interview with Sean O'hUiginn', Edward Kennedy Oral History Project (PDF available online), 8–9.

33 John Hume, 'A personal view', in J. Dooge, R. Barrington (eds), *A vital national interest: Ireland in Europe 1973–1998* (Dublin, 1999), 327–33.

34 'Interview with John Hume', Edward Kennedy Oral History Project (PDF available online), 5–13.

35 Department of foreign affairs, *Challenges and opportunities abroad: white paper on foreign policy* (Dublin, 1996), 58.

36 Senator George Mitchell, *Making peace: the inside story of the making of the Good Friday Agreement* (London, 1999), 105–6, 149.

37 Although then a minority unionist party within Northern Ireland, the DUP had consistently won the majority of unionist votes for representation in the European Parliament ever since Northern Ireland representatives were first admitted to that assembly in 1979. Brendan O'Leary, John McGarry, *Explaining Northern Ireland* (Oxford, 1995), 201.

38 Brendan O'Leary, John McGarry, *Explaining Northern Ireland* (Oxford, 1995), 416, 409.

39 Gerard Collins, 'The European Union and the peace process in Northern Ireland', *Études Irlandaises*, vol. 22 no. 2 (1997), 149–59.

40 Colonel Michael Beary, 'Peace dividends and statecraft instruments: United States and EU economic intervention facilitating peace in Northern Ireland', *Defence Forces Review* (2010), 91.

41 C. O'Grada, B.M. Walsh, *Did (and does) the border matter?* (Institute for British–Irish Studies, University College Dublin, 2006).

42 David Donoghue, plenary speech at 'Multilateralism and interdependence: prospects and challenges' conference, Royal Irish Academy, 2 May 2018.

43 Senator George Mitchell, *Making peace: the inside story of the making of the Good Friday Agreement* (London, 1999), 20, 90–5, 105–6, 149.

44 'President Clinton's remarks at Londonderry 1995' (courtesy of the William J. Clinton Presidential Library, on YouTube). It was on welcoming Clinton to Derry that John Hume announced the formation of a Tip O'Neill Chair of Peace Studies at the University of Ulster.

45 He would do the same on a brief visit to Dublin to receive the freedom of the city. This took place on 1 December 1995, a day after his visit to Northern Ireland. 'President Clinton's remarks in Dublin, Ireland, 1995' (courtesy of the William J. Clinton Presidential Library, on YouTube).

46 Quote from 'President Clinton's remarks at the Mackie Plant 1995' (courtesy of the William J. Clinton Presidential Library, on YouTube).

47 Michael Fitzpatrick, *John Hume in America* (Dublin, 2017), quoting Trimble, p. 178.

48 'Interview with John Hume', Edward Kennedy Oral History Project (PDF available online), 5–13.

49 Dean Godson, *Himself alone: David Trimble and the ordeal of unionism* (London, 2004), quote 392.

50　Adams gives his own account of the situation surrounding the IRA breaking its ceasefire in Gerry Adams, *An Irish voice* (Dingle, 1997), 201–7.

51　Senator George Mitchell, *Making peace: the inside story of the making of the Good Friday Agreement* (London, 1999), 24–32.

52　Senator George Mitchell, *Making peace*, 40–2, 47–63.

53　Michael Fitzpatrick, *John Hume in America* (Dublin, 2017), 177–8.

54　Nora Owen and Hugh Coveney of Fine Gael would assist Dick Spring. Senator George Mitchell, *Making peace*, 105.

55　Stephen Loyal, *Understanding immigration in Ireland: state, capital and labour in a global age* (Manchester, 2011), 66–8.

56　Imelda Maher, *The common travel area: more than just travel* (Royal Irish Academy and British Academy, 2018), 3–4.

57　Pat Cox, *Europe after Brexit* (Lausanne, 2016), 17–18.

58　Brian Doolan, *Principles of Irish law* (6th edition, Dublin, 2003), 82.

59　Sean Farren (ed.), *John Hume in his own words* (Dublin, 2018), 291–2.

60　Justine McCarthy, *Mary McAleese: the outsider* (Dublin, 1999), 148, 155, 158, 169–71.

61　Senator George Mitchell, *Making peace*, 105–6, 149; 'President Clinton's address to the Northern Ireland Assembly, 3 September 1998' and 'President Clinton's address to the people of Armagh, 3 September 1998' (courtesy of the William J. Clinton Presidential Library, on YouTube).

62　David Sinclair, *The pound* (London, 2000), 271–2.

63　Senator George Mitchell, *Making peace*, 103.

64　Northern Ireland Peace Agreement, https://peacemaker.un.org/sites/peacemaker. un.org/files/IE%20GB_980410_Northern%20Ireland%20Agreement.pdf.

65　Ibid., 4.

66　Newton Emerson, *The last of the Portadown News* (Dublin, 2006). The author later became an *Irish Times* columnist.

67　Senator George Mitchell, *Making peace*, 85.

68　The Irish National Caucus was keen to claim that the MacBride Principles were the essential basis of the peace settlement on the grounds that individual American state assemblies, as opposed to the federal government, passed resolutions expressing sympathy with them. Sean McManus, *My American struggle for justice in Northern Ireland* (Cork, 2011), 187–8, 247–51.

69　Clinton's speech was partly a reaction to the fact that a recent bombing in Omagh by a supposed IRA splinter group was being used by some as a justification for demanding the immediate cessation of all cross-border schemes. Both the US president and Mallon's speech can be seen in the video 'President Clinton's address to the Northern Ireland Assembly, 3 September 1998' (courtesy of the William J. Clinton Presidential Library, on YouTube).

70　David Trimble's speech can be seen in the video 'President Clinton's address to the Northern Ireland Assembly, 3 September 1998' (courtesy of the William J. Clinton Presidential Library, on YouTube).

71　This was Mackie International, a textile-machinery and engineering plant, which had existed since the 1840s but ceased operations in 1999. For the state of the company during 1995, see 'President Clinton's remarks at the Mackie Plant 1995' (courtesy of the William J. Clinton Presidential Library, on YouTube).

72　Dean Godson, *Himself alone: David Trimble and the ordeal of unionism* (London, 2004), 841.

73   https://www.nobelprize.org/prizes/peace/1998/press-release/.

74   https://www.nobelprize.org/prizes/peace/1998/hume/lecture/.

75   Ursula Fraser, Colin Harvey (eds), *Sanctuary in Ireland: perspectives on asylum law and policy* (Dublin, 2003), quote p. 28.

76   *Bunreacht na hÉireann* (Dublin, 1937), 4.

77   *Bunreacht na hÉireann* (Dublin, 2004), 6 (quote), 116.

78   Alvin Jackson, 'Ireland, the Union and the Empire', in Kevin Kenny (ed.), *Ireland and the British Empire* (Oxford, 2004), 152.

79   Fionan O'Muircheartaigh (ed.), *Ireland in the coming times*, 38–40.

80   W.F. Duisenberg, 'EMU and Ireland: happy together?', in Fionan O'Muircheartaigh (ed.) *Ireland in the coming times: essays to celebrate T.K. Whitaker's eighty years* (Dublin, 1997), 55–67. Duisenberg was then president of the European Monetary Institute in Frankfurt.

81   Fan Hong, Jorn-Carsten Gottwald (eds), *The Irish Asia strategy and its China relations 1999-2009* (Amsterdam, 2010), 99.

82   Justin Harman, Dermot Ahern, 'Russia's global perspective: defining a new relationship with Europe and America', *Irish studies in international affairs*, vol. 19 (2008), 3–8.

83   Government of Ireland, *Global Ireland: Ireland's global footprint to 2025* (Dublin, 2018), 33, 36, 39.

84   This was Peter Mandelson of the British Labour Party who, along with Chris Patten and Catherine Ashton, was a major British player in the EU at the time.

85   Colonel Michael Beary, 'Peace dividends and statecraft instruments: United States and EU economic intervention facilitating peace in Northern Ireland', *Defence Forces review* (2010), 91.

86   Michael D'Arcy, Tim Dickson (eds), *Border crossings: developing Ireland's island economy* (Dublin, 1995). Ulster businessmen, as well as Peter Sutherland, Tony O'Reilly and a number of academics from across the island, contributed to this publication.

87   Sean Milroy, *The case of Ulster* (2nd ed., Dublin, 1922); Michael Kennedy, *Division and consensus: the politics of cross-border relations 1925-69* (Dublin, 2000).

88   Senator George Mitchell, *Making peace*, 105–6, 149.

89   B. Tonra, M. Kennedy, J. Doyle, N. Dorr (eds), *Irish foreign policy* (Dublin, 2012), 9–12, 60, 131; Ben Tonra, *Global citizen and European republic: Irish foreign policy in transition* (Manchester, 2006). Bertie Ahern, a Fianna Fáil Taoiseach, served as Ireland's EU president during 2004.

90   Tom MacGinty, *The Irish navy: golden jubilee* (Tralee, 1995), 190.

91   Aidan McIvor, *A history of the Irish naval service* (Dublin, 2006), 217–21.

92   Joe Maxwell, P.J. Cummins, *The Irish air corps: an illustrated guide* (Antrim, 2009), 218–20.

93   Ben Tonra, 'Security, defence and neutrality: the Irish dilemma', in B. Tonra, M. Kennedy, J. Doyle, N. Dorr (eds), *Irish foreign policy* (Dublin, 2012), 235.

94   Ibid., 222–4.

95   Mark Callanan (ed.), *Foundations of an ever closer union* (Dublin, 2007), 182. The contents of the *Defence Forces review* are freely available online.

96   B. Tonra, M. Kennedy, J. Doyle, N. Dorr (eds), *Irish foreign policy* (Dublin, 2012), 67.

97   Ibid., 110.

98   Timothy Garton Ash, *Free world* (London, 2004), quote p. 54.

99   S. Castles, M.J. Miller, *The age of migration* (4th edition, London, 2009), chapter 9 (quote p. 207).

100 Michael Burleigh, *Sacred causes: religion and politics from the European dictators to Al Qaeda* (London, 2006).

101 Along with two more entrants into the EU during 2007 (the republics of Bulgaria and Romania), four significant powers – Sweden, Poland, Hungary and the Czech Republic – were not due to enter the Eurozone until the values of their currencies converged.

102 'Interview with Sean O'hUiginn', Edward Kennedy Oral History Project (PDF available online), 30.

103 Ben Lindsay, 'Unauthorised and pre-emptive use of force: is the authority of the UN irrelevant?', *Defence Forces review* (2011), 99–104; Jean-Marc Coicaud, 'The future of peacekeeping', *Defence Forces review* (2008), 151–5.

104 Andrew Cottey, *Security in twenty-first century Europe* (2007, 2nd ed., London, 2013).

105 Ben Tonra, *Global citizen and European republic: Irish foreign policy in transition* (Manchester, 2006), 2, 83, 195.

106 Ray Murphy, 'Europe's return to UN peacekeeping? Opportunities, challenges and ways ahead – Ireland', *International peacekeeping*, vol. 23 no. 5 (2016), 721–40. Although with other European neutrals (and non-NATO member states of the EU) such as Austria, Denmark, Sweden and Finland, Ireland had 'observer status' in the old Western European Union (WEU) defence arrangement (established in 1954 as part of a modification of the Brussels Treaty of 1948) from 1992 until its disbandment in 2011.

107 Karen Devine, 'The ethos and elements of Irish neutrality', in I.S. Novakovic, *Neutrality in the 21st century: lessons for Serbia* (Belgrade, 2013), 67–78. This book was published with the support of the Swedish Armed Forces.

108 Karen Devine, 'Irish political parties' attitudes towards neutrality and the evolution of the EU's foreign, security and defence policies', *Irish political studies*, vol. 24 no. 4 (2009), 467–90.

109 Commandant Ian Byrne, 'Clearing the EU "fog of war": ends, ways and means', *Defence Forces review* (2012), 15–25; Ronan Corcoran, 'Ready for battle?: the EU battle group as EU force projection', *Defence Forces review* (2013), 63.

110 Tony Cudmore, 'Ireland's presidency of the Council of the EU and the development of the CSDP in 2013', *Defence Forces review* (2013), 53–60, quote p. 55.

111 John Doyle, 'Defence, security and the Irish EU presidency', *Defence Forces review* (2013), 7–14.

112 Karen Devine, 'The ethos and elements of Irish neutrality', in I.S. Novakovic, *Neutrality in the 21st century: lessons for Serbia* (Belgrade, 2013), 67–78 (quotes p. 77).

113 This included the independent National College of Ireland that had initially been founded by the Jesuits purely as a business school. Nicholas Rees, a former author for Trócaire, assumed the position of its Monnet professor. Brigid Laffan, another former author for Trócaire, was a Monnet professor at University College Dublin (a college of the National University of Ireland) and the European University in Florence. She then became director of the latter body's director of the Robert Schuman Centre for Advanced Studies as well as director of its Global Governance Programme.

114 Ruan O'Donnell, F. Keoghan, M. Quinn (eds), *A festschrift for Anthony Coughlan: essays on sovereignty and democracy* (Dublin, 2017). This publication was designed to celebrate the tenth anniversary of the campaign against the Lisbon Treaty.

115 Declan Kiberd, *Inventing Ireland* (Dublin, 1996).

116 Mark Callanan (ed.), *Foundations of an ever closer union* (Dublin, 2007), 77, 113, 239–40 (quote from Irish foreign minister Brian Cowen, p. 239).

117 Jacek Purchla (ed.), *The historical metropolis: a hidden potential* (Cracow, 1996).

118 Ibid., 131, 132 (quote), 179, 249 (quote), 254; Judith Devlin, 'The city as symbol: architecture and ideology in post-Soviet Moscow', in J. Devlin, H.B. Clarke (eds), *European encounters* (Dublin, 2003), 363–404.

119 Teresa Walas (ed.), *Stereotypes and nations* (Cracow, 1995), 13, 21; Jacek Purchla (ed.), *The historical metropolis*, 254.

120 Commandant Mark Hearns, 'From Vancouver to Vladivostok with Valentia in between: Ireland's chairmanship of the OSCE', *Defence Forces review* (2011), 123–32.

121 Ibid.

122 Justin Harman, Dermot Ahern, 'Russia's global perspective: defining a new relationship with Europe and America', *Irish studies in international affairs*, vol. 19 (2008), 3–8.

123 Amy Verdun, G.E. Chira, 'The Eastern partnership: the burial ground of enlargement hopes?', *Comparative European politics*, vol. 9 (2011), 448–66.

124 J.C. O'Shea, 'The Irish OSCE chairmanship and the aftermath of the 2008 war in Georgia', *Defence Forces review* (2013), 48–50. The Northern Ireland speakers at the OSCE conference in Dublin on 28 April 2012 were Peter Robinson (first minister) and Martin McGuinness (deputy first minister), while former American envoy George Mitchell also attended, as did British, Russian and European representatives.

125 J.C. O'Shea, 'The Irish OSCE chairmanship and the Transdniestrian Settlement Process', *Defence Forces review* (2012), 1–6.

126 Department of foreign affairs and trade, *The global island: Ireland's foreign policy for a changing world* (Dublin, 2015), 7. Perhaps reflecting this growing dispensation, Dan O'Brien, an Irish-born journalist with *The Economist* who later became an economist for Dublin's Institute for International and European Affairs, effectively wrote a panegyric about the G20 summits within his collection of essays, *Ireland, Europe and the world: writings on a new century* (Dublin, 2009).

127 Department of foreign affairs and trade, *A focused policy review of Ireland's bilateral diplomatic mission network in the United States of America* (Dublin, 2017), 11, 19–20.

128 Dan Senor, Saul Singer, *Start-up nation: the story of Israel's economic miracle* (New York, 2009), 12–13.

129 Department of foreign affairs and trade, *A focused policy review of Ireland's bilateral diplomatic mission network in the United States of America* (Dublin, 2017), 11, 19–20.

130 John O'Hagan, 'The Irish economy 1973–2016', in T. Bartlett (ed.), *Cambridge history of Ireland* (Cambridge, 2017), 518.

131 Department of foreign affairs and trade, *The global island*, 69.

132 Commandant Mark Hearns, 'From Vancouver to Vladivostok with Valentia in between: Ireland's chairmanship of the OSCE', *Defence Forces review* (2011), 123–32.

133 Martti Ahtisaari, 'The role of the European Union in conflict resolution', *Irish studies in international affairs*, vol. 18 (2017), 195–99.

134 It had been suggested that there should be a permanent EU representative on the UN Security Council, but there was little or no support for this idea. R. Wong, C. Hill (eds), *National and European foreign policies* (London, 2011), 79, 85, 90–1.

135 Department of foreign affairs and trade, *The global island: Ireland's foreign policy for a changing world* (Dublin, 2015), 71.

136 Pat Burke, 'Troubled waters', *Defence Forces review* (2016), 177–87; Brian Fitzgerald, 'Ireland – an islander's perspective', *Defence Forces review* (2016), 192–6.

137 Pat Cox, *Europe after Brexit* (Lausanne, 2016).

138 Conor McCabe, *Sins of the father: tracing the decisions that shaped the Irish economy* (Dublin, 2011). Michael D. Higgins, *Causes for concern* (Dublin, 2006), 305–20.

139 Of the €67.5 million provided in support, the European stability mechanism provided €45 million and the IMF provided the remainder. The UK, Sweden and Denmark also provided bilateral loans of nearly €5 million. Diarmuid Smyth, 'The recovery in the public finances in Ireland following the financial crisis', *Journal of the statistical and social inquiry society of Ireland* (vol. 156, 2017), 150–73; Central Bank of Ireland, *A chronology of main developments 1943-2013* (Dublin, 2013), 34–5, 48–54.

140 B. Tonra, M. Kennedy, J. Doyle, N. Dorr (eds), *Irish foreign policy* (Dublin, 2012), xviii, 88.

141 Ibid., 188–90, 200–1. In 2012, Enterprise Ireland's thirty-two overseas offices included fourteen in Europe, ten in Asia, three in North America, three in South America and two in the Middle East. In 2010, the IDA had six offices in America, nine in Asia and four in Europe (London, Paris, Frankfurt and Moscow).

142 B. Tonra, M. Kennedy, J. Doyle, N. Dorr (eds), *Irish foreign policy* (Dublin, 2012), chapter 6.

143 Department of foreign affairs and trade, *The global island: Ireland's foreign policy for a changing world* (Dublin, 2015), 7, 77.

144 Ibid., introduction.

145 Charles Flanagan, 'Identity and values in Irish foreign policy', *Irish studies in international affairs* (2016), 1–5.

Conclusion

The Evolution of Ireland's Role in International Relations, Past and Present

It has been suggested that, in Ireland, 'national sovereignty today has less the absolute and infeasible character claimed for it in the [1916] Proclamation and is more about, in [Robert] Emmet's words, taking our place amongst the nations of the world'.[1] The original Sinn Féin policy called simply upon Ireland to assert its distinct existence on the world stage. By contrast, Dáil Eireann's claim in 1919 that an independent Ireland should serve as a benefit and safeguard to Europe and America demonstrated a greater awareness that states in international relations do not exist in isolation. Therefore, they must both define and defend their interests accordingly. There was some truth to the claim of the First Dáil that Britain's colossal First World War debts to the United States had altered greatly the international context in which Ireland operated, although the significance of this development did not become more apparent until 1932 when Britain defaulted on these debt payments at the same time as its Commonwealth uniformly imposed tariffs against the United States. America's central role in shaping the international economic order in the wake of the Bretton Woods conference of 1944 was both intended and effectively insured that such tactics could not be used against America again. While the US considered that 'the most important relations of Americans to Ireland always have been informal, spontaneous and familial',[2] Ireland was likely to respond to shifts in Anglo-American relations in its own way. During the 1930s, this was witnessed by the revival of post-1918 calls for Irish banking reform and for Ireland's relations with Britain to be fundamentally reassessed. By the 1950s, America's leadership of international financial markets had created a process of parallel evolution for Ireland and Europe. US involvement in European security allowed states to concentrate on undertaking programmes of economic development without a commensurate reliance on defence spending, while US support for European integration helped to enhance the diplomatic voice of small states, as was reflected by the maximising of a Belgian role in debates on European security and a Dutch role in debates on international law. The context of Ireland's role in international relations, however, was not always as clearly defined, particularly prior to its entry into the EEC.

As was reflected by the collapse of the Fine Gaedhael initiative in 1922 and the Anglo-Irish financial settlement of 1926, the necessary imposition of London's foreign trade priorities stemming from Irish membership of the British Commonwealth limited Irish options for development. British compendiums of significant speeches in twentieth-century international relations cited de Valera's assertion that Ireland aspired to be 'the home of a people who valued material wealth only as the basis for right living' as the most significant Irish contribution,[3] although so long as Ireland remained part of the commonwealth its voice was essentially muted. As late as 1960, Ireland was generally mentioned in international newsreels only when British media outlets chose to do so and then usually just to provide Ireland with a bad press.[4] Nationally, a discrediting of Arthur Griffith's Sinn Féin policy and an almost exaggerated acclaim during this period for T.K. Whitaker's 'trade-restrictive and capital-immobile' ideas (which were abandoned on his retirement in 1976) was justified by economic commentators who argued that 'independence had done nothing for Irish economic development' while inexplicably not acknowledging that Ireland's ongoing membership of the sterling area ever since 1922 still practically governed its diplomatic and trading choices and effectively constituted a lack of independence.[5] Notwithstanding a brief interlude during the mid-1960s, it was not essentially until Ireland's entry into the European Monetary System in 1978 that the country began to adapt strategically to changes in the international economic order. Therefore, Garret FitzGerald judged that, 'however paradoxical it may at first sight appear, the ultimate justification for Irish independence will, I believe, eventually be seen to lie in Ireland's accession in 1972 to the European Union.[6] Implicit in this perspective was the existence of a restrictive set of choices hitherto and a resulting unfulfilled potential, even if many commentators chose instead to focus on the idea that European social policy was serving to alter Ireland's sense of national identity.

Many pre-independence Irish nationalist thinkers, as well as some later scholars on Ireland's relations with Europe, tended to see a tradition of Christian humanism, reputedly disavowed by many British imperial journalists, as a potential bridge between Ireland and the European continent, perhaps particularly Belgium and the Netherlands.[7] Indeed, in common with the Netherlands and future European republics with Christian-democratic governments, to guarantee freedom of will and conscience, there was purposively no state religion, nor a state church, within Éire/Ireland after 1937, as is the case within the United States but not within either the United Kingdom or the British Commonwealth. Be that as it may, interest in the European Christian-democratic tradition within Ireland would appear to have been relatively slight in the post-1945 period. Aside from the fact that the ecclesiastical capitals of Ireland were in Northern Ireland, an explanation for this development could be found in a contemporary Irish tendency to equate internationalism with a decline in the influence of religion on social policy.[8] The European Christian-democratic tradition was focused less on social policy, however, than seeking to influence the formulation of international law and evolving theories of human rights.[9] An Irish parallel with this process could be found in its own efforts to promote anti-belligerent attitudes in international relations, such as in its implicit or direct criticisms of the operations of a military-industrial complex and, in particular, the affect of an international arms trade on the Middle East and Africa. If a tradition existed of Irish diplomats making rather bald statements of Irish national identity on the international stage (a criticism sometimes levelled against de Valera, Sean MacBride and Frank Aiken as well as many other small-state actors at the UN), Ireland's record in attempting to develop actual legislation relating to international disarmament and human rights has been a fairly consistent one, as well as a common bond between the avowedly Christian moral standpoint of early Irish diplomats and more recent Irish diplomatic activity, including the emergence of Irish legal figures like Mahon Hayes and Mary Robinson as leaders of UN commissions on human rights.[10]

Debates on international relations can witness the existence of conflicting undercurrents of opinion even among nominal allies. For instance, American distaste for the role of the London School of Economics (LSE) in schooling Marxist critics of US foreign policy throughout the developing world, a trend made particularly evident during the 1970s,[11] evidently influenced even the most Anglophile of American scholars, who suggested that the influence of the LSE in shaping discourse on international history may not have been an entirely positive one.[12] There was evidently an Irish parallel in this process,[13] even if the primary feature of the critiques of the international order by Michael D. Higgins, Trócaire and others focused instead on the role of the international banking in shaping the operations of developmental aid. Indeed, if reactions to the 'global partnership' system launched in 1968 can serve as a useful barometer of states' opinions, Ireland's self-image in this regard would appear to have governed by two distinct beliefs: first, 'in the case of small donors like Ireland, [self-interested strategic] power does not figure in its relations with developing countries', and second, significant Irish contributions to non-governmental aid organisations have been the aspect of foreign policy in which the Irish public was 'most personally and actively involved'.[14] Indeed, the Irish army, which consistently made one of the highest contributions in Europe to UN peacekeeping,[15] and Irish non-governmental organisations alike have taken up the cause of protesting about the lack of 'specific humanitarian guidelines' for all UN-sponsored developmental aid programmes to follow.[16]

As UN Secretary General, Kofi Annan was awarded a Nobel Peace Prize for launching a 'Global Compact' to promote a greater sense of corporate social responsibility among multinational companies in promoting 'sustainable development goals', but as it deals with little or no human factors (other than financial management) the idea would be criticised widely, with even leaders of the World Trade Organisation (WTO) suggesting that the only real difference between the WTO and the Global Compact programme was that the former was not pretending to be fulfilling a humanitarian function.[17] As someone who worked closely with both Annan (in her capacity as a UN High Commissioner) and Ireland's army and voluntary organisations, Mary Robinson found from experience that the most effective suggestions for dealing with humanitarian crises invariably came from amateur activists in various non-governmental organisations who, unlike the legions of highly-paid professional diplomats, academics, bankers and lawyers who theorised about matters from their ivory towers, were dealing directly with victims and so actually understood their concerns.[18] More recently, studies of African trade have found that, echoing past colonialism, European and British free trade agreements have always prioritised their own economic interests over that of their nominal African partners.[19] Ireland's response to these trends has evidently been to focus on developing international law to compensate for the fact that, since the 1990s, the creation of both a UN High Commission for Human Rights and the Global Compact programme has operated on the basis seeking political mandates without possessing the legal authority to enforce compliance. Therefore, David Donoghue, a recent Irish representative to the UN who succeeded in getting over one hundred 'developing countries' to accept a declaration in favour of the Global Compact programme, suggested that the possibility of 'heading in the direction of codified [human] rights', with a degree of national freedom for each country in implementing such a legal code, was actually 'the only way forward' in creating a more just international order.[20] Some European professors of international law have echoed this belief,[21] while the fact that the United Nations Development Programme negotiated by Donoghue also involved a clear commitment to environmentalism as part of a broader programme of health promotion may potentially serve to enhance its overall relevance.[22]

In support of such initiatives, longstanding UN agencies such as UNESCO and the UN's migration agency have argued that 'globalisation' (or the 'global partnership' system launched in 1968) is actually a social and educational issue of responsibility, not just an economic trend.[23] Irish foreign ministers have been keen to suggest that 'central to Irish foreign policy...since the foundation of the state' has been a promotion of humanitarian principles because 'as a small state, we are instinctively sympathetic to the problems faced by those whose size, situation or history leaves them relatively powerless' or are 'afflicted by poverty and prone to natural disasters'.[24] Irish governments have also argued that 'because it affects poorest communities most, climate change is a priority in our international development policy', primarily through supporting the EU's 'Framework on Climate and Energy', while Irish ex-president Mary Robinson has served as the UN Special Envoy for Climate Change.[25] The interconnection between the environmental movement and pre-existing UN developmental aid policies can be witnessed in EU policy documents, such as those that have drawn a direct connection between energy issues, including solar power, and the idea of sustainable economic development in Africa.[26] There is certainly logic to such policies, although environmental debates have also witnessed a degree of polemical attitudes. For instance, while the Holy See has championed the idea of the interrelationship between promoting universal human rights and protecting the environment,[27] international relations theorists within the British Commonwealth have argued that 'immorality pretending to virtue' and false ideas of a 'one world religion' have become an ever-growing feature of UN environmental debates and associated financial projects, leading in turn to a potentially dangerous subversion of national economic interests in favour of promoting false ideas of universality.[28] This belief may also have affected attitudes within the United States, while some Dutch scholars have suggested that philosophical opposition to ideas of universal values may be partly rooted in the fact that, in medieval times, Roman Catholic thinkers were essentially the first to express such supranational ideas as a legal concept in order to encourage a greater separation between church and state or between what were considered to be either the educated or the warrior classes.[29] As environmental scientists have pointed out, however, a much more relevant question was a purely logistical one; namely, the potentially great difference between the theory and practice of all climate change programmes.[30]

Perhaps the best illustration of the viability of the Global Compact has been that, rather than rejecting the idea of a global economy, growing non-governmental organisations, in Ireland and elsewhere, have called for the *reform* of the operations of the global economy so that each state can better meet the set UN recommendation whereby each member state should (but rarely do) provide 0.7 per cent of their gross national income to the World Bank for the sake of developmental aid programmes, including those affecting the environment.[31] Reflecting the priorities of bodies such as Médicins sans Frontières, since the 1960s there has been a tradition of direct Irish medical assistance in Sub-Saharan Africa,[32] while a degree of sincerity to Irish attitudes may perhaps be witnessed by a recently declared willingness of the Irish government not to pursue oil exploration options (the Irish navy had suggested that there could be €850 billion worth of unmined oil directly off Ireland's coastline)[33] purely for the sake of protecting the environment.

A very influential alternative viewpoint to the idea that 'globalisation' is a social and educational issue of responsibility can be found in the argument of British commentators on international relations (Marxist and non-Marxist alike) who have equated 'globalisation' purely with an economic trend of enforced urbanisation and have typified all 'terrorism' as an inevitable violent and direct reaction to this trend by poor and disaffected migrants from rural areas.[34] This question of urban or rural development has undoubtedly been a major factor governing the history of modern Ireland, from the great crises that the country faced during the seventeenth and nineteenth centuries through to the operations of European regional development funds from the 1970s until the 2000s. However, it is perhaps on this very question of urban or rural development and its impact on migration that an Irish philosophy of international relations has been developing that mirrors mainland European and American philosophies of international relations far more so than those of the United Kingdom.

The origins of Irish nationalism in the nineteenth century could well be understood in terms of popular opposition to the role of state centralisation within the United Kingdom in deprioritising Irish urban development and, in turn, forcing both Irish urban and rural migrants to enter the English, rather than the Irish, urban labour market.[35] The relative popularity of successive Irish governments from the 1920s until the 1960s with the general Irish public often hinged on the government's capacity to reverse this trend, while a Charles Haughey-inspired notion of a 'social partnership' between government and urban trade unions essentially became the keynote of a limited programme of Irish national economic planning from the late 1960s up until the 1990s. Peter Sutherland judged that the principal reason why Ireland and other small nations were able to capitalise upon opportunities presented by the growth of multinational businesses was that, in contrast to the experience of Europe's industrial giants of yesteryear, 'we did not have to dismantle shipbuilding, steel, coal—all of the industries that really crippled and paralysed the economies during the "eurosclerosis" of the 1970s and 1980s' in order to create sufficient market space for the development of 'new' industries, be they pharmaceuticals, information and communications technology or digital media. At the same time, however, his advice to the Irish government and the UN Secretary General on migration and development was that it was not correct to link rural–urban migrations with security issues, even if a 'switch from extreme tolerance to extreme intolerance' of migrants was temporarily made evident in cities such as London and Amsterdam after it was announced that nearly half their populations were born outside their host countries.[36] The claim that 'terrorism' is a reaction against urbanisation has also been rejected by many in central Europe and America, where scholars have equated politicians' call for a 'war against terror' with a rhetoric that was invented by sections of Anglophone academia in the wake of the financial reforms of 1968.[37]

Neither an Irish nor an evolving European role in shaping international relations theory has yet to become a very recognisable feature of most British or American studies of international relations, which have tended to emphasise that efforts 'to monopolise the means of legitimate violence' are always necessary before any international arrangement can begin to be considered as 'viable'.[38] Upon this basis, there has been a British tendency, rooted not least in centuries of its own efforts to define and maintain a balance of power within Europe,[39] to view the EU purely as a creation of the Cold War and to assert that the post-1945 'bi-polar' European order, as well as the balance of power that it implied, should remain a permanent fixture.[40] A very remarkable continuity in British political thought has been the belief that the state of nature is a state of anarchy and, therefore, only the will of the nation-state to exercise an unnatural supremacy and dominance over the natural world and the creation of an appropriate balance of power between states creates orderly government, both nationally and internationally, as opposed to a natural and barbaric state of human anarchy.[41] This philosophy, which is essentially rooted in the early-modern political philosophy of Thomas Hobbes (1588–1679) and, to a lesser extent, the idea of the national sovereignty associated with the Westphalia settlement of 1648, has been termed as the 'English School' of international relations as well as a 'realist' school of thought. It has formed an essential theoretical framework for most modern British textbooks on international relations theory, which have suggested that this 'realist' school of thought should also be seen as the perpetual antidote to unrealistic or 'neo-liberal' schools of thought, associated with the EU, that are based on the idea that militarism is not inherently the key factor in international relations.[42] Irish foreign ministers have referred directly to this British debate only on a few occasions, but whenever they did it was generally to question its fundamental assumptions.[43]

Although notions of an Anglo-American worldview have been prevalent within Britain since at least the days of James Bryce and Winston Churchill, the United States' own academic debate regarding the competing roles of liberalism and republicanism in shaping perceptions of the modern world have never actually found an audience within the United Kingdom because of its inherent political antipathy to republicanism.[44] As a republic, America was always particularly conscious that 'crusades, even crusades conducted in the name of freedom, threaten freedom at home' since 'the history of republican experiments across history show that foreign entanglements and adventures created dangerous concentrations of political power within and undermined the very civic virtues on which the survival of any republic depended'. On this basis, fearing corruption, Americans were still on their guard against the notion of exercising unnatural hegemonies in international affairs and perpetually inclined to question 'to what end' such ideas of hegemony had ever been entertained in the first place.[45] Ireland's self-identification as a republic has never been as strong as in the case of the United States, as has been reflected by the fact that Irish studies of republicanism have tended to focus exclusively on purely domestic civics in the south rather than international relations.[46] Meanwhile, connections have been drawn between republicanism and 'terror' within both the United Kingdom and the British Commonwealth,[47] while the tenor of Belfast commentaries on the theme may also have persuaded Irish government ministers to couch their thought in 'liberal internationalist' terms without ever referring to republicanism in the context of either humanitarian or internationalist values.[48] However, a clear continuity in the history of Irish involvement in international diplomacy since 1919 was a belief in the need to assert the equal right of small nations to have their liberties recognised internationally while also maintaining the integrity of the nation at home. On this basis, during the era of the League of Nations (1919–45), Ireland strove to be 'recognised at Geneva as one of the main upholders of the complete independence of the smaller states' as much as it was a nominal supporter of collective security,[49] while Ireland's policy at the UN was defined largely by a search for the development of effective platforms to protect the rights of small nations while balancing this ambition with its desire to be seen as a strong supporter of the principle of collective security *if* it was based upon recognised principles of international law as opposed to selective military alliances based upon aspirations for imperial hegemony.[50]

Long before the development of environmentalism, American philosophical debates on what constituted 'natural', or 'republican', 'virtue' were focused on the relationship between the urban and rural worlds. In this debate, American geography may explain why it tended to see virtue as most likely to stem from rural societies, just as English geography (particularly since the nineteenth century) may have led British commentators to adopt an opposing viewpoint.[51] Although the US was essentially a champion of the EEC from its inception, levels of appreciation in America for the EU would appear to have been shaped far more by the potential of its economy (including its prospects for a more effective banking union) than either its evolving tradition of cultural diplomacy or the operation of European law.[52] By contrast, membership of the EU has made Ireland a dedicated supporter of 'maximising the EU's voice and influence on human rights issues', including codifying actual human rights legislation. Both the well-established European Court of Human Rights (based in Strasbourg, France) and the more recent International Criminal Court (based in the Hague, Netherlands) have encompassed human rights legislation that may influence future UN policy formation, but the United Kingdom has always expressed serious reservations about the former court and the United States refused to join the latter. By contrast, Ireland has declared its full support for the operations of both these courts,[53] even though the potential relevance of such European human rights legislation to Ireland was limited by the fact that they 'cannot be enforced and a breach cannot be remedied in our courts'.[54] Indeed, like the United States and the United Kingdom but unlike most of Europe, Ireland has always had a common law, rather than a codified, legal system. Aside from issues of language, this legal issue could be a logical reason for greater Irish susceptibility to British or American intellectual influences. Be that as it may, in suggesting that the Irish government did not share the belief of 'many in the world of foreign policy who see a fundamental tension between the pursuit of interests and the promotion of values', Irish foreign ministers have been keen to emphasise their identification with both the supranational legal dimension and traditions of foreign policy consultation that have defined the EU. This has been done because of a belief that 'multilateralism strengthens our independence, self-confidence and security rather than diminishes it' and that the EU tradition of multilateral diplomacy can fully encompass the Irish state's geopolitical outlook.[55]

From its inception, the European project was designed to encompass the concerns of militarily neutral states, which naturally suited Ireland, while in recent times Irish diplomats have expressed appreciation for the fact that the EU is 'perhaps best thought of as a wholly new kind of polity—most aptly described as "a Union of States and of Peoples"'.[56] Indeed, a strength of the European project and a merit in its evolving tradition of cultural diplomacy as far as Ireland was concerned was that, unlike the traditional British Commonwealth (which attempted after the 1960s to redefine itself according to UN principles), it was not based on the priorities, ideological traditions or political self-image of any single founding state.[57] Irish participation in cultural projects such as Europeana, designed to promote and protect all European cultures according to a single humanitarian standard, increased the international audience for the Irish language (Gaeilge),[58] while, more recently, the development of the EU's Horizons digital education programme and Galileo satellite system promised to strengthen the connection between Ireland's digital technology industries and the European continent.

The Irish desire to avoid military alliances, such as NATO, has probably been rooted primarily in a national anti-militarist tradition rather than the former British Commonwealth tradition of keeping

Ireland as a neutralised state. For instance, the Irish anti-enlistment movement during the First World War clearly influenced the formative years of Dáil Éireann. Arthur Griffith had justified non-enlistment on the grounds that Britain's imperial wars had never been a direct concern of Ireland, but nevertheless the country was forced to contribute many millions of pounds to these war efforts despite the fact that 'every pound of that Irish gold could have been better spent in Ireland'.[59] The creation of several international pacifist organisations during the First World War encouraged an Irish expression of belief in the potential of these movements to create a new international order and evidently enhanced the Irish desire to de-emphasise military spending as much as a deep-seated Irish abhorrence of carnage. In this context, Ireland's mere signing of the Kellogg–Briand Pact of 1928 probably reflected national opinion less than either the ethos of the post-1920 Irish White Cross movement or de Valera's later assertion, meant for mainland European as much as Irish ears, that 'the chief significance of the new [Éire/Ireland] constitution' was 'that it bears upon its face, from the first words of its preamble to the dedication at its close, the character of the public law of a great Christian democracy'.[60]

If a recent decline in the notion of a European Christian-democratic tradition has also found reflections in Ireland,[61] its core philosophical belief that a literary trend of encouraging a societal acceptance of political ideologies was a tool of the totalitarian state (a reason for the great popularity of the Christian-democratic school of thought in post-1989 central and eastern European republics) nevertheless played a significant role in Irish intellectual life. It essentially motivated the Éire constitution's purposeful distinction between human liberty (including the liberty to be entirely non-political) and political liberty on the grounds that recognition of the inherent primacy of the former is necessary if basic cultural freedoms and individuals' rights and liberties are to be protected under all circumstances.[62] The role of Christian-democratic ideas and politics after 1945 in countering ideological polemics, as well as potentially totalitarian ideas, in Europe has been recognised widely because it shaped founders of the European project, such as Robert Schuman and Konrad Adenaeur (also founder of Germany's Christian Democratic Union), and it also inspired individuals like Jacques Maritain, a creator of the UN's Universal Declaration of

Human Rights; a document that attempted to make the American and French republican legal principle of the inherent equality of all human beings a universal value.[63] After 1989, however, both Western media and diplomats generally associated this question of equality with notions of a liberal individualism, based upon the rhetoric of promoting non-discriminatory values, rather than either a republican patriotism or legal internationalism. Reputedly, this made the west of Europe largely deaf to central European calls for Europe to unite behind 'the spirit of 1989'; a trend that, it has even been suggested, could potentially lead the EU to become divorced intellectually from the founding fathers of the EEC itself.[64]

Ireland's second foreign policy white paper, *The Global Island: Ireland's foreign policy for a changing world* (2015), essentially invited the country to reflect on its state within the global economy more so than its status as a European nation. In this context, a perceived weakness of Ireland abroad compared to other 'small nation' success stories, such as that of Israel, had been its economic dependence upon foreign direct investment without necessarily boosting either its national labour market or productivity in essential resources.[65] However, efforts have evidently been made in recent years to compensate for this fact and to increase the number of Irish businesses that also operated abroad, with as many as 500 Irish companies reportedly operating in the United States.[66] In terms of trade in goods, a perpetual limitation to Ireland's capacity to be a significant export-orientated nation was underdeveloped Irish shipping. The fact that 'sea based transport accounts for 99 per cent of Ireland's trade [in goods]' had always been seen by the Irish navy as a reason to expand the operations of Irish mercantile fleets.[67] Instead, however, there was a consistent reliance upon employing British transport firms, so much so that the latter have been described as practically serving as Ireland's 'land bridge' to both the United Kingdom and, in turn, the European continent.[68] Multinational companies who exported actual goods (as opposed to banking assets) from Ireland did so primarily to the same countries as did traditional Irish food exporters: namely, the United Kingdom and, to a lesser extent, 'northern Europe' rather than other regions.[69] If the use of British shipping seemed more cost effective than creating an Irish mercantile marine, the fact remained that if Britain opted out of a free trade agreement with Europe at any time after 1973 Ireland would not have been able to rely on British shipping without facing customs in transporting its goods to other European countries despite its own continued European membership. Nevertheless, the potential availability of European shipping services as an alternative may explain the Irish government's willingness to allow for the disbandment of Irish Shipping Limited as early as 1984.[70]

Ever since 1968, in Ireland as elsewhere, over 70 per cent of banks' savings have tended to be invested in international 'financial services' schemes, rather than in national goods-based industries, simply because banks can earn much greater returns from such investments.[71] If international criticisms of growing disparities of wealth across the world and the evident supremacy of bankers' and economists' market forecasts over parliaments in determining government policies, both nationally and internationally, have also found echoes in Ireland, the most critical issue in terms of the country's potential economic vulnerability was perhaps imbalances in terms of its trade in goods and services. In recent times, however, a balance of sorts has evidently existed in various aspects of Ireland's trade in goods within Europe. For instance, the reported total of exported Irish goods to Germany (€10 billion) has operated according to a positive balance of trade of roughly €2 billion and this has been on an equal scale to Ireland's reported total export of 'services' to Germany (€10.5 billion),[72] which evidently relates to banking transactions exclusively. Perhaps surprisingly, a similar balance has reportedly existed in Irish trade in goods and services with the United States.[73] By contrast, total trade in goods between Canada and Ireland (€2.75 billion) has only been a fifth of the amount of banking investments between the two countries.[74] A similar imbalance probably accounts for a very high percentage of (a recently claimed) €16 billion worth of Irish exports of 'goods and services' to both India and China,[75] just as an EU–Singapore trade deal reportedly saw a very sudden emergence of Irish 'investments' in Singapore of €5 billion.[76] Countries like Canada, India and Singapore either are or have been pivots of traditional British imperial banking markets, with the latter two being closely related to banking developments in the Far East as well as Australia and New Zealand. With these same countries in mind, Northern Ireland has expressed a desire to compete with the Republic's 'unfair' advantage of having a low corporate tax rate for attracting internationally focused investment firms.[77] This may indicate that many banks or companies that utilised Dublin's IFSC were British ones,[78] with the principal difference between such companies and those operating within either Northern Ireland or on the island of Britain being that their Dublin offices traded exclusively in euros. By contrast, a claim that as much as $2 billion worth of trade occurred between America and Ireland every week would point to an evident supremacy of American business or banking interests among international investment firms operating within Ireland.[79]

The contemporary European context of such developments are less in evidence in the activites of the European Central Bank, which manages the European currency, than in the operations of the European Development Bank and the London-based European Bank for Reconstruction and Development, which have been the basis for EU investments across the continent of Europe as well as into Central Asia and the Middle East.[80] The impact of this trend on Ireland can be witnessed in the fact that while sizeable Irish food exports to the Middle East have evidently continued since the 1980s, only €400 million of nearly €4 billion worth of reported Irish exports to the Middle East evidently constituted traditional Irish food exports,[81] which may well indicate that most 'exports' are simply banking investments made to enhance the diplomatic soft power of the EU. Participation in EU trading agreements also saw the development of new Irish trading links with Latin America (€3 billion total trade), whose Mercosur trading bloc has been holding economic summits with the EU since 1998,[82] and a professed likelihood of Ireland entering into significant future African trading markets, presumably as soon as the African Union project grows stronger.[83] If this has been what Ireland's acceptance of the role of being a European hub within a 'global economy' has meant in practice, it is possible that its impact on Ireland's diplomatic stance may be to make economics, rather than humanitarianism, the practical basis of its engagement with the developing world as far as the international community at large was concerned, irrespective of the specific moral postures adopted by Irish foreign ministers, the UN or non-government organisations. However, in contrast to Karen Devine's suggestion that Ireland's membership of the Eurozone was leading the country into being exclusively preoccupied with improving the EU's capacity to shape globalisation, the increase in the number of multilateral and bilateral forums available to Ireland through Europe has undoubtedly served to enhance its own diplomatic voice. In particular, a direct historical correlation has existed between an expansion in Ireland's role in foreign trade and the increase in size of Ireland's diplomatic service. Indeed, the recent suggestion that the very status of Ireland as a small open economy is precisely 'why a strong international presence matters', rather than the reverse, might be said to betray a normalisation of Irish state's approach to international relations.[84]

In British debates on Europe, there was an acknowledgement that if Britain were not in the EU 'it will be hard for the UK to maintain its influence in areas where access to EU markets and, in some cases, the prospect of EU membership is a powerful policy lever' as well as for it to sustain 'its role as a diplomatic "bridge" between the US and Europe'.[85] The centrality of naval considerations to America's overall approach to diplomacy worldwide can certainly explain the comparative limit of Ireland's appeal as a bridge between America and Europe when compared to other European states. If Germany was the economic heart of Europe, the French were more inclined to offer a naval conception of the potential evolution of EU–American relations,[86] while the British were keen to advertise the greater extra-European significance of their own navy.[87] The American preoccupation with international defence spending, as well as a strong tradition of naval intelligence-sharing with the British Commonwealth,[88] was evidently self-interested rather than governed by national biases. The inclusion of Canada and Australia, but not Britain, within the same group as the United States in G20 summits and Australia's concentration since the 1980s upon developing its own trading relations with Asia and Latin America (not least by means of its own novel initiative of the Cairns Group)[89] partly reflected America's priorities in this regard, just as the likelihood of fresh EU trade agreements with Australia and India, in addition to Canada (which evidently encouraged the Irish government to view its own North American strategy as applying equally to the United States and Canada),[90] pointed to the fact that although the British Commonwealth could still act as a united front at the UN and in times of war it was no longer a means specifically for the United Kingdom to exercise an economic leverage internationally. Against this backdrop, Ireland's 'cold war era' notion of the existence of an 'Anglo-American protectorate'[91] may have been of far less relevance than the question of how EU–American relations could work to the strategic interests of both.

Historically, the question of Britain's 'western approaches' practically served to make Ireland 'a neutralised state', dependent on the UK for national defence, during the era of naval armament races between 1922 and 1945. Notwithstanding the Cold War, Ireland's disinclination to revise such geopolitical considerations after it left the British Commonwealth or, indeed, at any time before 1991 was perhaps a curious oversight of government.[92] A peculiar origin of the Irish culture of anti-militarism can be seen in the fact that a future general secretary of the Irish department of foreign affairs found it 'deeply disturbing' during 1970 to learn that a close departmental colleague thought that the Irish state and its army should concentrate on developing a better national security strategy, immediately denouncing this suggestion as being equivalent to an irrational advocacy of political violence.[93] The origins of this way of thought within the Irish civil service was a belief that 'the peace of our own state' was dependent largely on a purely internal security consensus, whereby, aside from the activity of the police force and the churches, politicians were expected to keep an ever-watchful eye on the Irish public to stem the rise of military sentiments of any kind, thereby sustaining the idea that the army must act only as an aid to the civil power of the police and not develop a comprehensive national and international defence policy.[94] The Irish government believed not only that the Irish public would always oppose any extension in the Irish army's responsibilities in national or international affairs but also that the Irish army could never cope with assuming a defence responsibility for the whole island, should this theoretical situation ever arise, and therefore partition should be welcomed as a guarantor of both peace and security for the whole island.[95] This perhaps raises questions regarding the practicality of Ireland's longstanding professed desire to see an eventual political reunification of the island by a process of consent. For instance, it would appear that the confinement of the activities of the Irish navy and air corps to purely coast guard services from 1945 onwards was an almost incomprehensible sense of patriotism to those educated under the UK's

system of state education within Northern Ireland.[96] Both Ulster and
Scotland retained an almost inherent geopolitical significance to the
policing of the sea lanes of the North Atlantic.

International regard for the Irish army's service in forty-two UN
sponsored international peacekeeping missions after 1958 (in the
process, suffering eighty-six casualties) did not prevent many Irish
policy makers from expressing a deep fear of the Irish army being
expected to partake in any future military, as opposed to purely
policing, UN operations abroad.[97] After the establishment of the EU,
Irish governments were occasionally more willing to accede to the Irish
military's requests to purchase supplies for the Irish army from many
different countries,[98] but there was still an unwillingness to consider
financing a more comprehensive Irish national defence programme.
In a sense, this was unavoidable: the geopolitics of partition effectively
negated the possibility of conceiving of the island of Ireland as a
geopolitical entity with the need for a comprehensive military, naval
and air defence policy. Notwithstanding its own brand of localism, this
perspective was probably understood better in Belfast than in Dublin
due to the extent to which politics within the former city were also
shaped by broader British international debates.

European and 'Anglo-American' worldviews reputedly played a
competing role in shaping the evolution of Ireland's diplomatic identity
ever since Ireland's adoption of the Euro currency in 2002. Potentially
the greatest disruption to Europe and Ireland's role within it, however,
arose from Britain's evident interest in leaving the EU. As only seventeen
of the twenty-seven EU states were, as yet, members of the Eurozone,
in the wake of the post-2008 financial crisis the notion of a two-tier
Europe became more prevalent, with the Eurozone countries, including
Ireland, supposedly receiving preferential treatment through occupying
the 'top' tier. Against this backdrop, Pat Cox predicted during 2015
that Britain would soon leave the EU because of a combination of two
factors: first, it was being relegated to the second-tier of Europe due
to its non-membership of the Eurozone; and second, historic British
desires to be a direct economic rival, rather than ally, of Germany were
still strong.[99] Hitherto Britain had considered that it could better match
American power within the EU than without, but British historians had
long pointed out that the UK had never identified with the notion of a

regional identity for Europe and so exhibited no genuine desire to be a part of any commonwealth that it could not lead or use purely for its own national advantage.[100] The most critical issue, however, was evidently the differing priorities of the sterling area and eurozone, with a former Irish ambassador to Britain noting that, although Ireland desired close relations on all sides, there was a seemingly unavoidable reality that 'if the UK stays in the EU, the gap between British preferences and Eurozone realities will widen', potentially to the disadvantage of both.[101]

A significant difference between the WTO and the GATT arrangements that preceded it was that, aside from trade in goods, the WTO rules also covered issues of intellectual property and the operations of financial services. The latter issue was potentially very important to Britain because even in the event that it arranged, as a non-member state, a new free trade deal with the EU, this deal could not have covered financial services, which was a key British strategic interest globally in terms of using sterling to leverage the international system.[102] If British voters were concerned about migration, Britain's non-membership of the Schengen Area effectively made this a non-issue, which indicated that the essential context of the British government's decision to hold a referendum to leave the EU was not a concern about migration or even trade in goods but rather a purely foreign policy desire to enable Britain to better deal with America's desire to reform the World Bank system that underpinned both the WTO and the financing of NATO. Ideas about reforming the WTO were coloured by rival American and Chinese efforts to utilise alternative banking alliances for the sake of maintaining their competitive economic advantages, just as providing or denying access to international banks' payment systems had long been used as a political leverage tool by the United States, particularly in the Middle East. In terms of central banks' reserves, the Euro had rapidly outgrown the British pound and Japanese yen to become the world's second most traded currency after the US dollar. However, the EU declared itself unwilling to use its own currency as a leverage tool in international relations in a manner comparable to the US dollar or, in yesteryear, the pound sterling.[103]

The expressed desire of the Westminster parliament (which is sovereign under the UK's unwritten constitution) to unilaterally determine the terms of Britain's departure pointed to the possibility of WTO arbitration being necessary in the event that Britain refused to come to a new trading agreement with the EU but as WTO arbitrations had hitherto involved trade relations between 'developed' and 'developing' countries only, the idea of Britain attempting to act exclusively under WTO trading rules only was widely deemed to be both imbalanced and counterproductive. The WTO itself estimated that if Britain traded only under WTO rules it could result in a loss to Britain's gross domestic product of up to 90 trillion dollars (or nearly thirty times the size of the gross domestic product of the entire African continent) within fifteen years, and, therefore, Britain should recognise the folly of this idea.[104] The Irish government's response to this development was essentially to re-emphasise its belief in the central significance of the EU to contemporary international relations. For instance, a surprising initiation within Britain of an inverted rhetoric on the theme of an alleged European belligerence prompted an Irish Taoiseach to re-emphasise Ireland's sense of identification with the EU on the grounds that 'the EU is not just an entity of a single market and customs unions; it is the longest lasting peace process on the planet'.[105] Meanwhile, Ireland responded to Britain's vote to leave the EU by stating that Ireland's future relations specifically with Britain 'will be underpinned by the Common Travel Area and the Good Friday Agreement'.[106]

Ever since the cessation of the occupation of Iraq (2003–11), Britain had claimed that there was a need for what it termed as 'hard borders' for a new 'fortress Europe' to protect it against the terrorist threat of migration from the Islamic world. This was a claim that the subsequent civil war and refugee crisis in Syria was supposed to validate,[107] although Mediterranean EU countries (perhaps most notably Greece) with a first-hand experience of both the Syrian refugee situation and the Mediterranean Union project generally deemed migration to be a purely humanitarian question, as did Turkey. However, EU summit declarations upon such matters often did not reflect a united foreign policy stance in practice,[108] while a specific problem for Ireland arising from Britain's vote to leave the EU was that Britain's own professed readiness to erect a 'hard border' for the United Kingdom threatened to undo the operations of the free movement of labour between Northern Ireland and the Republic of Ireland ever since *The Agreement*, endangering an on-going peace process by returning matters to a pre-1994 situation. A complicating factor in this situation was that were it not for a belief that the legal loophole of a 'common travel area' was a means to maintain peace in Northern Ireland,[109] Ireland would probably never have requested, alongside Britain, a special exemption provision with regards to the operations of the EU's Schengen Area and, in turn, continued to seek to accommodate Irish social security programmes with British as much as European standards.[110] While the Irish government evidently viewed this question primarily in terms of the peace process, the UK government viewed the 'common travel area' primarily as a means of strengthening its links with Ireland irrespective of the operations of the EU,[111] leading it to increase greatly (almost triple) its volume of trade with Ireland after it voted to leave the EU in 2016.[112] The Irish business community's facilitation of this process may have indicated to Britain that its power to influence the future of Ireland remained strong and perhaps even stronger than the EU,[113] although the Irish government, if seemingly willing to promote an interdependence with Britain,[114] accepted that the future status of the Irish border must be determined between Britain and Europe alone as part of an overall agreement regarding the future of UK–EU diplomatic and trade relations.[115]

A majority of the residents of Northern Ireland voted to remain in the EU during the UK's successful June 2016 referendum to leave, partly because, by 2011, the economic reasoning of the Northern Ireland Assembly had pointed to a process of parallel economic evolution with the Republic. Domestic Ulster businesses, like those in the Republic, were mostly small-to-medium sized firms that needed access to the largest possible markets, while there was also a growing desire in Ulster to attract more multinational businesses in a fashion akin to the system operating in the Republic. This pointed to the relative significance of the Euro zone and the sterling area in determining long-term developments both within the operations of the global economy and as a practical basis of Ireland's peace process ever since the banking reforms of the late 1990s had underpinned *The Agreement*. Some deemed this as evidence that a choice was now being presented to Northern Ireland whether or not it wished to act purely as a peripheral and regional economy of the UK, sustained by British state subsidies, or embrace more fully the notion of an all-island economy within a Europe free trade zone in an effort to meet its economic need to promote local businesses, attract more foreign direct investments and reach the largest possible export markets.[116] Implicit in this idea was that the prospect of the UK leaving the EU was raising as many questions, or choices, for Ulster as the formation of the EU itself had done for Éire.

Ever since the registration of *The Agreement* with the UN in 1998, the situation in Northern Ireland was considered by the Irish government to be a significant factor in shaping 'our international reputation' primarily because 'sharing our experience of peace and reconciliation on the island of Ireland' was practically an international expectation.[117] As Britain's 'common travel area agreement' with Ireland related to the movement of labour rather than goods, an all-island Irish economy was practically dependent on the existence of free trade between the UK and the EU. InterTrade Ireland, established as a result of *The Agreement*, would note that cross-border trade amounted to only 5 per cent of the total value of the trade of each (if financial services were included), but this cross-border trade was nevertheless critical in assisting those border regions that had suffered the most economically from the Troubles,[118] as was partly reflected by the fact that if cross-boder exports from the North amounted to only a small percentage of Northern trade in terms of value, it nevertheless amounted to over 35 per cent of Northern trade specifically in terms of volume of goods, while half of all cross-border trade constituted agri-food exports.[119] One of the chief significances of *The Agreement* was that, in the name of sustaining interlocking relationships, it was designed to maintain a perpetual all-island dialogue to ensure that developments in either part of Ireland should not be allowed to adversely affect the other. If the mass exoduses of the 1920s, 1950s and 1980s and the resulting rise in political extremism pointed to a downside of Ireland's common labour market with Britain, the declared interest of both the EU and the United States not to allow any future trading agreement with Britain unduly undermine the Irish economy was evidently governed by an awareness that any renegotiation of a UK–EU, or indeed a UK–US, trade agreement was likely to take much longer than an exiting process under article 50 of the Lisbon Treaty. If this necessitated the maintenance of a united EU stance in the matter, it also meant that the factors governing the peace that had been established as a result of *The Agreement* had become more internationalised, reflecting the long-term operations of the global economy as much as political or community relations within the North itself. Furthermore, the fact that Britain's trade with its Commonwealth had declined from over half of British exports in the wake of the Second World War to under 10 per cent indicated the importance of very harmonious relations with Europe if it was to deal effectively with its internal economic challenges.[120]

Against this backdrop, Jennifer Todd suggested that the political attitudes of Northern Irish citizens may be developing in a fashion more akin to 'liberal nationalist' than 'realist' (militarist) attitudes towards international relations.[121] This may point to a cultural impact having been made by either the EU or the continued existence of all-Ireland civic dialogues. For much of the twentieth century, however, Northern Ireland's influence over media attitudes towards international affairs in the Republic was evidently much stronger than the other way around.[122] This reflected the legacy of Belfast's practical status as a banking capital of Ireland during Ireland's membership of the sterling area, making Northern Ireland a means for London to exercise a British political leverage over the island as a whole. This leverage practically ceased, however, upon the establishment of the independence of the Bank of England in 1997 and the Central Bank of Ireland's federation with the European Central Bank in 1998, both of which coincided with a rapid growth in the Irish economy (which took veteran economists and tenured academics in Ireland completely by surprise)[123] and also facilitated *The Agreement*. One testament to the success of *The Agreement* was that trends in international migration had not resulted in greater emigration from either part of Ireland from the 1990s onwards. Indeed, by the 2010s, for the first time since the era of the Great Famine of 1845–51, the all-island population of Ireland had risen to about 6.5 million people, with as little as 6 per cent of labour within the Republic now employed within agriculture.[124] The latter statistic, as well as patterns of migration (both to and from the country),[125] pointed to an evident transformation of modern Ireland. However, the Irish department of foreign affairs still found it necessary to offer €3 million annually to approximately 150 'community, voluntary and civil society organisations' within Northern Ireland through the operations of a 'Reconciliation Fund' in order to help Northern Ireland deal with the fact that it 'remains a very deeply divided society' where a 'fault line runs through education, housing and many other aspects of daily life'.[126]

By the twenty-first century, Ireland's diplomatic corps had risen to over eighty representatives or about a third of the size of the foreign office of the United Kingdom,[127] although its profile in Northern Ireland remained low during decades of shared EU membership. Indeed, the ongoing reality of a divergent educational, commercial and political system in Northern Ireland made the development of an all-island sense of patriotism unlikely, even if there were perhaps greater economic reasons than in the past, both nationally and internationally, for many to potentially welcome the idea of an all-Ireland state. Critically, if the removal of a NATO presence within Northern Ireland reflected a decline in Ulster's geopolitical significance, this did not mean that Northern Ireland had ceased to be a party to the British Commonwealth's overall defence arrangements or that its citizens necessarily came to identify with the Irish national tradition of anti-belligerence, the most practical manifestation of which has been Ireland's role in developing multilateral diplomatic alliances in support of the non-proliferation of weapons of mass destruction, including a desire to actually ban all nuclear weapons. Although no major military power (including the United Kingdom) has supported Ireland's efforts in this regard, during 2008 Ireland persuaded almost a hundred countries and many more non-governmental organisations to sign a treaty that attempted to ban cluster-bomb munitions and thereafter also found new allies on the issue of nuclear weapons.[128] Meanwhile, although Britain expressed a definite resolve to leave the EU it exhibited no desire to leave NATO, a body in which it has remained a senior partner. Therefore, the UK was bound to continue to play a critical role in European defence. An unanswered question, however, was how it could play such a role effectively when withdrawing from the EU inherently meant that Britain could no longer take a direct part in the EU's common foreign and security policy or have direct access to European markets.[129] If the British military tradition were to play a major role in determining the nature of the UK's future relations with European countries, this could well affect educational and political attitudes within Northern Ireland, although (in keeping with Todd's theory) it would appear that Britain's preference has been to maintain as close an economic relationship with the EU as can fit its envisioned role of working with the United States to reform the WTO with an eye to the situation in the Far East. In such an event, this may result in an enhanced role for the EU in shaping diplomatic relations with the Middle East and Eurasia and a decline in the relative importance of NATO.

A likely challenge for Ireland resulting from Britain's resolve to leave the EU will be how to define its own place in Europe now that the chief anti-federalist voice (Britain) is liable to be silenced. The prevalence of graduates of the College of Europe, which has its headquarters in Bruges and Warsaw, specifically among younger Irish diplomatic staff may make it seem likely that the country's sense of European identity will grow stronger. However, a combination of longstanding educational and geopolitical factors might also serve to limit such a trend. Considerable 'soft power' has been inherent in British initiatives such as the Association of Commonwealth Universities, which was based on a sense of the global reach of both the English language and English publishing companies with a shared world view,[130] while the UK itself has been rated as the most influential 'soft power' in the world, meaning that its capacity to shape international discourse for its own ends is virtually unparalleled.[131] If such factors naturally shaped the evolution of Irish academia during the early years of the state, more recently a growing business model for university education, in Ireland and elsewhere, has encouraged bodies such as Science Foundation Ireland to argue that collaboration with British universities was still essential for Ireland, both to access research funding schemes and to convince international stakeholders of the quality of Irish research. This business model for higher education in Ireland can explain why a recent report has shown that three-quarters of Irish academics have deemed the existence of very close links specifically between Irish and British universities to be 'very important' to their career prospects, as well as their scholarly priorities or interests.[132] Those willing to consider the possibility of a different model for higher education in Ireland nevertheless also desired that the UK remain a part of the European Research Area so that the priorities of Irish universities would not have to be reinvented,[133] while public 'think-tanks' on international relations within Ireland have continued to invite participation primarily from British lecturers.[134] In this sense, if (as one Irish diplomat unflatteringly described the situation) Ireland was not 'psychologically ready' to 'stand up for ourselves diplomatically' because 'we've been hiding behind British skirts institutionally for donkey's years',[135] the ethos of the Irish university system may actually be the most logical cause of this situation. If this situation continues, the suggestion of David O'Sullivan, a former Irish diplomat and an EU ambassador to the United States, that 'the role of academic, cultural and scientific bodies in fostering a greater sense of shared interests will be key' in terms of the future diplomatic relations of all European nations (including Ireland) with the United States,[136] is perhaps unlikely to elicit an efficient Irish response.

The fact that American and European journals of Irish studies such as *Éire-Ireland* (Minnesota, established 1966), *Études Irlandaises* (Rennes, established 1976), *Estudios Irlandeses* (Salamanca, established 1994) and *Studi Irlandesi* (Florence, established 2011) have evidently inspired studies of Irish literature exclusively, rather than studies of either the international profile of the Irish state or the respective bilateral relations between Ireland and their host countries, may be something of an inevitable consequence of Irish academics' lack of intellectual engagement with the world of American or European interests and ideas. In such matters, like all states, Ireland would appear to have a quite strong sense of its own national traditions. One aspect of this has been an almost purely diaspora-conscious programme of Irish cultural diplomacy. However, both during and after Ireland's initial struggle for independence, perceptions of Ireland within the English-speaking world were coloured by the fact that the British and, in turn, American governments were inclined to equate the Irish diaspora purely with internal questions of ethnic relations, or labour politics, within their own jurisdictions rather than a manifestation of the emergence of Ireland as a distinct nation on the international stage.[137] As such, a reliance upon a diaspora policy could potentially backfire upon Irish governments, even if a greater Irish concentration upon dealing directly with the US government from the time of the Kennedy presidency onwards evidently helped to create a stronger Irish diplomatic relationship with the United States without necessarily lessening the significance of the diaspora concept as an aspect of the Irish state's limited soft power.

As neighbouring islands, shared geopolitical considerations between Britain and Ireland may have been inevitable throughout much of history: technological advances as well as globalised communications, or business, networks have not altered how nature inherently makes all states 'prisoners of geography' and climate,[138] while even in the world of high finance it has been suggested that the significant role played by Irish figures such as Peter Sutherland, be it in Europe, the WTO or even Ireland's peace process, would have been lessened were it not for their close business and social ties with significant British influencers.[139] The most significant geopolitical fact regarding Ireland, however, may actually be that 'the country's physical geography is deceptively cruel', as 'the country is shaped like a saucer, the coastal areas tending to be higher than the interior', which consequently has short rivers and frequently poor land.[140] As an island, Ireland's coastline is not only its greatest attraction spot for tourism, travel and urban development but it also remains its essential connection to the wider world. Irish governments have recently suggested that 'although geographically a small island on the periphery of Europe, Ireland's people and our outlook are [now] global, influenced by and connecting with people and events around the world',[141] but, if this has been the case, then the world of international trade and commerce has been the essential source of that connection, as well as perhaps the greatest potential resident in the country's diaspora concept, as reflected by the recent creation of 'a global Irish network' of Irish businesses abroad.[142]

As a European state, in the light of the fact that new EU entrants have tended to look upon Ireland as a potential role model despite its lack of involvement with NATO, Ireland could conceivably play a more significant role in the future in European integration plans, should the country become more involved in a process of European cultural diplomacy. In practice, however, while the department of the Taoiseach has pronounced that 'Ireland will always be at the heart of the common Europe we have helped to build',[143] Ireland's European policy would appear to have always been governed by more traditional 'western European' factors, such as differing attitudes of EU leaders towards the role of the Atlanticist financial world in governing the operations of bodies such as NATO. In this context, if France has always remained sympathetic to the idea of lessening European dependence on America, Ireland and several small states (perhaps most notably the Netherlands) tended to support Germany in defending the status quo,[144] just as extant fears of Russian militarism have evidently ensured that countries like Poland have been very eager to see the perpetuation of collective security arrangements that had formerly been championed by both Britain and the United States.[145] As NATO and EU have remained 'essential partners',[146] this may inherently limit the relevance of Ireland to countries like Poland and its neighbours because of the absence of direct Irish involvement in the military aspects of European security. In itself, this may also explain why Ireland's level of engagement with European cultural diplomacy has hitherto remained comparatively low.[147]

Perhaps most of all, the evolution of Irish international relations, past and present, points to a state whose most enduring values and principles have been based on its declared constitutional goal since 1937 of seeking purely 'pacific settlement of international disputes' according to 'generally recognised principles of international law'. Since the mid twentieth century, this anti-belligerent stance was championed by a combination of promoting disarmament talks in forums of multilateral diplomacy, engaging in UN peacekeeping, promoting the development of humanitarian law and avoiding military alliances. It has been suggested that Ireland's non-membership of NATO in its performance of these tasks may actually have served to better advertise the distinctiveness of its own diplomatic voice.[148] It might be more accurate to argue that Ireland has attempted to present an example to the world of attempting to support international alliances politically whilst simultaneously emphasising that such alliances do not have to be based upon military power. This can explain its consistent commitment to multilateralism, whereby 'the principal normative objective from a multilateralist perspective is contribution to the creation of universal rules'.[149] Whether or not such 'rules' can encompass moral as much as economic standards may become the key issue in determining if the future will be governed as much as the past by the exercise of military hegemonies.[150]

American theorists who have drawn a contrast between 'hard' (military) and 'soft' (cultural) power have always emphasised that these concepts are not mutually exclusive.[151] In fact, their necessary combination has been described as the exercise of 'smart power'.[152] An alternative idea of 'smart power', however, may lie in the claim that battles are frequently won or lost purely in the world of ideas. In particular, for any state's diplomatic relations to prove effective they generally need to be based upon ideas and interests that are as relevant and applicable to their audience as much as they are to their authors. By the turn of the twenty-first century, Ireland's embrace of the EU was evidently governed less by ideology than a purely practical consideration that it was a comparable forum to the UN for economic, cultural and humanitarian diplomacy, as well as non-belligerent peacekeeping. The EU's potential capacity to make this strategy effective stemmed not least from its growing status as the world's largest trading bloc with a tradition of close foreign policy consultation. In effect, within the combination of these two forums of the UN and EU, the Irish state professed to have found a means to discover a fully aligned place within the world of international relations that could match the historic, political and cultural traditions of the Irish nation itself, including with regards to its (perhaps evolving) attitudes towards both geopolitics and questions of security. There would appear to be little reason to doubt the accuracy of this claim. In addition, if Ireland's 'messages to the free nations of the world' have begun to find a more receptive audience this could well be said to have also vindicated many of the visions of the founding fathers and authors of the Irish state itself. Should such a trend continue, there would seem to be little reason to doubt that Ireland will have a significant international story to tell as a small European nation. In addition, should Ireland develop a deeper interest in European traditions of cultural diplomacy this process may end up being reciprocated, thereby potentially enhancing the security of Ireland on the world stage through a process of mutual understanding, political cooperation and intellectual engagement. To a significant degree, this would be in keeping with the professed aspiration of a former Irish foreign minister who suggested that Europe should be seen neither as an economic nor a cultural construct but instead as a genuine leader in promoting world peace and, last but not least, a perpetual, vibrant and viable 'marketplace for ideas'.[153]

Endnotes

1 Martin Mansergh, 'Creating a new state', address at La Touche Legacy Weekend, 30 Sep. 2017.

2   D.H. Akenson, *The United States and Ireland* (Harvard, 1973), ix.

3   Brian MacArthur (ed.), *The Penguin book of twentieth-century speeches* (London, 1999), 218–21.

4   Ciara Chambers, *Ireland in the newsreels* (Dublin, 2012).

5   Michael Mulreany (ed.), *Economic Development fifty years on* (Dublin, 2009), quote p. 75.

6   Garret FitzGerald, *Ireland in the world: further reflections* (Dublin, 2005), 23. FitzGerald was given a state funeral when he died in 2011.

7   J.M. Morton, *The new Ireland* (London, 1938). Irish-Belgian parallels were the themes of John O'Leary, 'Some guarantees for the protestant and unionist minority', *Dublin University Review*, vol. 2, no. 12 (Dec. 1886), 959–65; Eugene Davis, *Souvenirs of Irish footprints over Europe* (Dublin, 1889) and Erskine Childers, 'Christian democracy in Belgium', *Studies*, vol. 2 (1913). For Dutch parallels, see Owen McGee, *Arthur Griffith* (Dublin, 2015), 64–6, 90–5.

8   Fintan O'Toole, *The ex-isle of Erin: images of a global Ireland* (Dublin, 1997); Tom Garvin, *Preventing the future* (Dublin, 2005).

9   Frans Alting von Geusau, *European unification into the twenty-first century* (Tilburg, 2012); *Neither justice nor order: reflections on the state of the law of nations* (Tilburg, 2014).

10 Robinson drew a good deal of her inspiration as a human rights activist from religion as much as from legal developments. See Mary Robinson, *Everybody matters: a memoir* (London, 2013).

11 Michael Franczak, 'Losing the battle, winning the war: neo-conservatives versus the new international order 1974–82', *Diplomatic history*, vol. 43, no. 5 (2019), 867–89.

12 Zara Steiner, 'On writing international history', *International affairs*, vol. 73 no. 3 (Jul. 1997), 531.

13 This was witnessed principally in the Irish media. G.T. Dempsey, *From the embassy* (Dublin, 2003), 52, 189. See also Michael Cox, 'Bringing in the "International": the IRA ceasefire and the end of the cold war', *International affairs*, vol. 73, no. 4 (1997).

14 Helen O'Neill, 'The evolution of Ireland's foreign aid over the past twenty years', *Irish studies in international affairs*, vol. 24 (2013), 193.

15 M. Kennedy, D. McMahon (eds) *Obligations and responsibilities: Ireland and the United Nations* (Dublin, 2005), 362–83. The Irish police force also participated in many UN missions. Ibid., 343–61.

16 Kevin McCarthy, 'Irish Aid and the Defence Forces: a synthesis of humanitarian forces or an incompatible union', *Defence Forces review* (2009), 33–43 (quote p. 35). Cooperation by NATO forces with non-governmental humanitarian organisations in Kosovo and Chad was also very rare. Graham Heaslip, 'Challenges of civil military cooperation and the coordination of humanitarian relief', *Defence Forces review* (2010), 49–62.

17 Philippe Legrain, *Open World: the truth about globalisation* (London, 2002), 183 (quote), 205, 264.

18 Interview with Mary Robinson, *International Review of the Red Cross*, vol. 92, no. 877 (Apr. 2010).

19 Chinedum Muotto, 'Re-imagining the African Continental Free Trade Area and the future of the EU–African partnership', Institute of international and European affairs, *Emerging voices* (Dublin, 2019), 129–45. Belgium and, to a lesser extent, Holland have

been to the fore in influencing European attitudes towards Africa, as is witnessed by the European Centre for Development Policy Management (ECDPM). Meanwhile, Irish developmental aid to Tanzania has resulted in trade agreements, leading to approximately €1 million of imports from Tanzania, one of the world's poorest countries, but as much as €6 million worth of Irish exports to Tanzania. B. Tonra, M. Kennedy, J. Doyle, N. Dorr (eds), *Irish foreign policy* (Dublin, 2012), 157–61.

20 David Donoghue, plenary speech at Royal Irish Academy conference on Multilateralism and Interdependence, 2 May 2018. In the 2015 negotiations, Donoghue was given the job of representing 'the global north' and worked with a Kenyan as the representative of 'the global south' in negotiating with the G77, which really involved 134 countries or two-thirds of the entire membership of the UN.

21 Frans Alting von Geusau, *Neither justice nor order: reflections on the state of the law of nations* (Tilburg, 2014). See also Paul Craig, Gráinne de Burca, *EU Law* (3rd ed., Oxford, 2003), 317–40.

22 United Nations Development Programme, *Sustainable development goals in short* (New York and Geneva, 2016).

23 See, for example, United Nations Educational, Scientific and Cultural Organization, *Global citizenship education: preparing learners for the challenges of the twenty-first century* (Paris, 2014).

24 Charles Flanagan, 'Identity and values in Irish foreign policy', *Irish studies in international affairs* (2016), 1–5.

25 Department of Foreign Affairs and Trade, *The Global Island: Ireland's foreign policy for a changing world* (Dublin, 2015), 42–3 (quote p. 42).

26 European Political Strategy Centre, *Ten trends reshaping climate and energy* (Brussels, 2018).

27 See, for instance, http://web.unep.org/environmentassembly/holy-see.

28 Michael Hart, *Hubris: the troubling science, economics and politics of climate change* (Ottawa, 2015), 450–518, 559–72 (quotes pp. 451, 559).

29 Frans Alting von Geusau, *European unification into the twenty-first century* (Tilburg, 2012), chapter 2. A Masonic tradition of 'Christian-Zionism' that Noam Chomsky (a Jewish agnostic) claimed to have exerted a very significant influence upon the historical evolution of British Commonwealth and American foreign policy may well have inspired the expression of such anti-Catholic attitudes, based on a literal and Arian (or non-Trinitarian) idea of Christianity whereby, as in Judaism, no mediator (such as the paraclete of the 'Holy Spirit') can exist between the individual and God. David V. Barrett, *A brief history of secret societies* (London, 2007).

30 Bjorn Lomborg, *The sceptical environmentalist: measuring the real state of the world* (Cambridge, 2001).

31 See, for instance, the latest development of *Coalition 2030 For Sustainable Development*. In common with most other countries, Ireland has never actually succeeded in meeting this target. Helen O'Neill, 'The evolution of Ireland's foreign aid'.

32 Sinead Walsh, Oliver Johnson, *Getting to zero: a doctor and a diplomat on the Ebola frontline* (London, 2018). Irish missionaries were formerly prevalent in such activities, as was partly documented by Werner Herzog's 1969 documentary *The flying doctors of East Africa* and *Radharc*.

33 Valerie Cummins, 'Opportunity in the face of adversity: the potential role of the military in contributing to Ireland's economic recovery with a focus on the Irish naval service', *Defence Forces review* (2011), 7–12.

34 Paul Collier, *Wars, guns and votes: democracy in dangerous places* (London, 2005); Eric Hobsbawm, *Globalisation, democracy and terrorism* (London, 2007), 32–4, 64–71, 155–67; Anthony Giddens, *Europe in the global age* (London, 2007).

35 This is a central theme to Owen McGee, *Arthur Griffith* (Dublin, 2015).

36 Peter Sutherland, 'Lessons and reasons', in Paul Sweeney (ed.), *Ireland's economic success: reasons and lessons* (Dublin, 2008), 14–25 (quotes pp. 21, 24).

37 Lisa Stampnitzky, *Disciplining terror: how experts invented "terrorism"* (Cambridge, 2013).

38 Andrew Heywood, *Political theory* (3rd ed., London, 2004), 116–19 (quote p. 117). American expressions of this viewpoint can be witnessed in journals such as *Survival* and the *Naval War College review*. For a fresh debate on this theme, see *Global Society*, vol. 34, no. 1 (2020).

39 Brendan Simms, *Britain's Europe: a thousand years of conflict and cooperation* (London, 2016).

40 J.W. Young, *Britain and European unity 1945–99* (2nd ed. London, 2000), 143–8, 160–4; Anthony Giddens, *Europe in the global age* (London, 2007), 199–230; Tim Marshall, *Prisoners of geography* (London, 2015).

41 F.H. Hinsley, *Power and the pursuit of peace: theory and practice in the history of relations between states* (Cambridge, 1963). Quentin Skinner has recently given international lectures on this theme that can be seen on YouTube.

42 Chris Brown, Kirsten Ainley, *Understanding international relations* (3rd ed., London, 2015). For a fresh debate on this theme, see *Global Society*, vol. 34, no. 1 (2020). The premise of European thought in such matters was not actually political liberalism but rather the interrelationship between natural law theory and codified human rights. Von Geusau, *European unification*, 243–59.

43 Brian Cowen, 'Challenges to liberal internationalism', *Irish studies in international affairs*, vol. 12 (2001), 1–5.

44 Joyce Appleby, Margaret Jacob, Lynn Hunt, *Telling the truth about history* (New York, 1994).

45 Michael H. Hunt, *The American ascendancy* (North Carolina, 2007), 322–4.

46 Garret FitzGerald, 'Civic and Irish republicanism', in *Ireland in the world: further reflections* (Dublin, 2005); Mary Jones (ed.), *The Republic* (Cork, 2005); Iseult Honohan (ed.), *Republicanism in Ireland: confronting theories and traditions* (Manchester, 2008); Michael D. Higgins, *Renewing the republic* (Dublin, 2011).

47 Norman Porter (ed.), *The republican ideal* (Belfast, 1998); Fearghal McGarry (ed.), *Republicanism in modern Ireland* (Dublin, 2003); Brian Jenkins, *The Fenian problem: insurgency and terrorism in a liberal state 1858–1874* (Liverpool, 2008); Fearghal McGarry, James McConnel (ed.), *The black hand of republicanism* (Dublin, 2009); David Fitzpatrick (ed.), *Terror in Ireland* (Dublin, 2012). The Oxford Concise English Dictionary introduced 'an advocate of a united Ireland' into its definition of the noun 'republican' in 1995. Della Thompson (ed.), *The Concise Oxford Dictionary* (9th ed., Oxford, 1995), p. 1168.

48 Brian Cowen, 'Challenges to liberal internationalism', *Irish studies in international affairs*, vol. 12 (2001), 1–5.

49 Michael Kennedy, 'The Irish Free State and the League of Nations, 1922–32: the wider implications', *Irish studies in international affairs* (1992), 15, 22.

50 M. Kennedy, D. McMahon (eds), *Obligations and responsibilities: Ireland and the United Nations* (Dublin, 2005).

51 Eric Hobsbawm, *Globalisation, democracy and terrorism* (London, 2007), 32–4, 64–71, 155–67.

52 Roger Altman, 'The fall and rise of the west: why America and Europe will emerge stronger from the financial crisis', *Foreign affairs*, vol. 92 (2013), 8–13.

53 M. Kennedy, D. McMahon (eds), *Obligations and responsibilities*, 362–83; Department of Foreign Affairs and Trade, *The Global Island* (Dublin, 2015), 36.

54 Brian Doolan, *Principles of Irish law* (6th edition, Dublin, 2003), 63–5 (quote p. 64), 78–85.

55 Charles Flanagan, 'Identity and values in Irish foreign policy', *Irish studies in international affairs* (2016), 1–5 (quote); Simon Coveney, 'Address to UN General Assembly, 28 Sep. 2018', at www.twitter.com/dfatirl (quote).

56 Noel Dorr, 'Ireland in an interdependent world: foreign policy since 1973', in B. Tonra, M. Kennedy, J. Doyle, N. Dorr (eds), *Irish foreign policy* (Dublin, 2012), quote p. 56.

57 J.T. Checkel, 'International institutions and socialisation in Europe', *International Organization*, vol. 59, no. 4 (autumn 2005), 801–26; John Hume, 'A personal view', in J. Dooge, R. Barrington (eds), *A vital national interest: Ireland in Europe 1973–1998* (Dublin, 1999), 327–33.

58 Since 1937, the Gaelic language has been the official 'first language' of Ireland. Fearing absorption into an Anglo-American world, de Valera judged occasionally that, in the future, 'our national distinctiveness will depend on the [Gaelic] language more than on any other factor for its continued assertion'. *Documents on Irish foreign policy*, vol. 6, no. 78. Gaelic language media in Ireland was both commercialised and internationalised for the first time during the 1990s but it did not have a large audience, evoking only a small and passive interest in countries like Scotland and the United States. More recently, efforts have been made to promote the teaching of the Irish language in north American and European universities 'to provide a platform on which the Irish language can be accessed and showcased as an international language'. Government of Ireland, *Global Ireland: Ireland's global footprint to 2025* (Dublin, 2018), 42.

59 Owen McGee, *Arthur Griffith* (Dublin, 2015), quote p. 104.

60 J.B. Morton, *The New Ireland* (London, 1938), quote p. 97.

61 Michael D. Higgins has cited appreciatively the crusade of American ideologue Noam Chomsky against the depoliticising influence of religion by arguing that to separate notions of personal liberties from political liberties is a 'profoundly reactionary' idea that must be counteracted at all sections of society. Michael D. Higgins, 'The personal is political and the political is personal', in M.D. Higgins, *Causes for concern* (Dublin, 2007), quote p. 58.

62 Dermot Keogh, Andrew McCarthy, *The making of the Irish constitution 1937* (Cork, 2007).

63 F.A. von Geusau, *European unification into the twenty-first century* (Tilburg, 2012), 243–59.

64 Ibid., chapter 3.

65 Dan Senor, Saul Singer, *Start-up nation: the story of Israel's economic miracle* (New York, 2009), 170, 229–30. Funding for research and development purposes in Ireland was carried out almost exclusively by multinational rather than national businesses.

66 Interview with Taoiseach Leo Varadkar, Bloomberg Politics Online, 16 Mar. 2018; IDA Ireland, *Local impact: how foreign direct investment is shaping Ireland* (Dublin, 2018), 26–7.

67 Brian Fitzgerald, 'Ireland – an islander's perspective', *Defence Forces review* (2016), 196.

68 Government of Ireland, *Global Ireland: Ireland's global footprint to 2025* (Dublin, 2018), 65–6.

69 Ibid., 48–9.

70 Tom MacGinty, *The Irish navy* (Tralee, 1995). A couple of small Irish shipping companies, such as Arklow Shipping (established 1966), have established business links with the Netherlands.

71 E.B. Kapstein, 'Between power and purpose: central bankers and the politics of regulatory convergence', *International organization*, vol. 46, no. 1 (winter 1992), 265–87, especially p. 274.

72 Department of Foreign Affairs and Trade, *Ireland in Germany: a wider and deeper footprint* (Berlin, 2018), 12. Imports of 'services' from Germany was quite probably larger, but no figure was given.

73 In 2018, Ireland reportedly enjoyed a positive balance of trade in goods with the United States that effectively balanced out America's positive balance of trade in services with Ireland. Interview with Taoiseach Leo Varadkar, Bloomberg Politics Online, 16 Mar. 2018.

74 Canadian banking investments in Ireland have been estimated at 9 billion euros, while Irish banking investments in Canada have been approximately half this figure. Government of Ireland, *Global Ireland: Ireland's global footprint to 2025* (Dublin, 2018), 32.

75 Government of Ireland, *Global Ireland: Ireland's global footprint to 2025* (Dublin, 2018), 34; Interview with Tánaiste Simon Coveney, Bloomberg Markets and Finance Online, 11 Mar. 2018.

76 Sean Kelly, *Fine Gael/European People's Party 2017 Summer Newsletter*, p. 11.

77 John Bradley, 'The Irish-Northern Irish economic relationship, the Belfast Agreement, UK devolution and the EU', *Ethnopolitics*, vol. 17, no. 3 (2018), 268–72.

78 Dáithí O'Ceallaigh, Paul Gillespie (eds), *Britain and Europe: the endgame – an Irish perspective* (Dublin, 2015), chapter 11.

79 Interview with Taoiseach Leo Varadkar, Bloomberg Politics Online, 16 Mar. 2018.

80 Details of such schemes can be found in *Info*, the quarterly magazine of CEB (the Council of the European Development Bank), and *Horizons* of the European Bank for Reconstruction and Development. For their political significance, see Mark Leonard, J. Pisani-Ferry, E. Ribokova, J. Sharipo, G. Wolff, 'Security Europe's economic sovereignty', *Survival*, vol .61, no. 5 (2019), 75–98.

81 Government of Ireland, *Global Ireland: Ireland's global footprint to 2025* (Dublin, 2018), 36, 38.

82 J. Dooge, R. Barrington (eds), *A vital national interest* (Dublin, 1999), 260.

83 Government of Ireland, *Global Ireland*, 33, 36, 39.

84 Ibid., 11, 17 (quote), 24–7.

85 Malcolm Chalmers, *UK foreign and security relations after Brexit* (London, 2017), 1.

86 Benoit Silve, 'From leadership to partnership: a new American security strategy for Europe', *Naval War College review*, vol. 50, no. 1 (winter 1997), 88–103. Silve was a commander in the French Navy.

87 Martin Murphy, 'Sea power: does Europe still get it?', *Naval War College review*, vol. 72, no. 1 (winter 2019), 157–9.

88 Angus Ross, Review of 'A tale of two navies', *Naval War College review*, vol. 71, no. 1 (winter 2018), 168–9.

89 This had paralleled the strategy of Europe's common agricultural policy in creating an international free market in agricultural produce to assist in the future development of WTO rules for food.

90 Government of Ireland, *Global Ireland: Ireland's strategy for the US and Canada 2019-2025* (Dublin, 2019).

91 G.T. Dempsey, 'Review of Eunan O'Halpin *Defending Ireland*', *Irish Historical Studies*, vol. 32, no. 126 (Nov. 2000), 296 (quote); Ronan Fanning, 'Small states, large neighbours: Ireland and the United Kingdom', *Irish studies in international affairs*, vol. 9 (1998), 127–9.

92 J.P. Duggan, *A history of the Irish army* (Dublin, 1991).

93 Noel Dorr, *Sunningdale: the search for peace in Northern Ireland* (Dublin, 2017), chapter 9: 'How policy is formed'.

94 Garret FitzGerald, *All in a life: an autobiography* (Dublin, 1991), quote p. 224.

95 Garret FitzGerald, 'The 1974-5 threat of a British withdrawal from Northern Ireland', *Irish studies in international affairs*, vol. 17 (2006), 141–50.

96 Joe Maxwell, P.J. Cummins, *The Irish air corps: an illustrated guide* (Antrim, 2009).

97 B. Tonra, M. Kennedy, J. Doyle, N. Dorr (eds), *Irish foreign policy* (Dublin, 2012), 182–3, 227–34.

98 http://web.archive.org/web/20101126082516/http://military.ie/army/equipment/weapons/weapons.htm.

99 Pat Cox, *From economic crisis to political crisis in the European Union?* (Lausanne, 2015), 10–11, 16–17, 26, 39–43, 50.

100 J.W. Young, *Britain and European unity 1945-1999* (2nd ed., London, 2000), 196–9; Brendan Simms, *Britain's Europe* (London, 2016).

101 Dáithí O'Ceallaigh, Paul Gillespie (eds), *Britain and Europe: the endgame - an Irish perspective* (Dublin, 2015), 13.

102 Kevin O'Rourke, *A short history of Brexit* (London, 2019), 185–6, 188, 214–15, 222.

103 Mark Leonard, J. Pisani-Ferry, E. Ribokova, J. Sharipo, G. Wolff, 'Security Europe's economic sovereignty', *Survival*, vol. 61, no. 5 (2019), 75–98.

104 https://www.wto.org/english/news_e/news18_e/ddgra_18dec18_e.htm.

105 Interview with Taoiseach Enda Kenny by Bloomberg Markets and Finance, 18 Oct. 2017 (available on YouTube).

106 Government of Ireland, *Global Ireland: Ireland's global footprint to 2025* (Dublin, 2018), 4.

107 Matthew Carr, *Fortress Europe: inside the war against immigration* (London, 2012), part one: 'Hard borders'. Since 2015 the Syrian conflict has grown even more controversial due to Russian military intervention.

108 Practical sources of division were very differing attitudes towards Turkey as well the possibility of the EU Council of Ministers assuming a more authoritarian approach, akin to what was originally envisioned by deGaulle. Von Geusau, *European unification*, 197–200, 272–7, 283–8.

109 Imelda Maher, *The common travel area: more than just travel* (Royal Irish Academy and British Academy, 2018), 3–4.

110 Pat Cox, *Europe after Brexit* (Lausanne, 2016), 9–11, 17–18.

111 Her Majesty's Government, *Northern Ireland and Ireland: position paper* (London, 2016), 21, 27.

112 In the year after its 'Brexit' vote, Britain concentrated on strengthen its trading links with Ireland and this saw total trade between the two countries rise from £22.7 billion (Her Majesty's Government, *Northern Ireland and Ireland: position paper* (London, 2016), 13) to £55.8 billion (What trade deals has Britain done so far?', bbc.com/news/uk-47213842), making Ireland Britain's sixth-biggest trading partner and a country

with which it has maintained a very positive balance of trade. Within a year, this rose from an advantage of £4 billion to over £12 billion. This may be due primarily to British firms relocating to Ireland in order to have better access to the European market. Frank Barry, 'Ireland and the changing global FDI landscape', *Administration*, vol. 69, no. 3 (2019), 104–107. Ireland has since decided to appoint a former UK treasury official to the position of the next governor of the Central Bank of Ireland while total trade between the two countries has reportedly risen as high as 70 billion euro (£61 billion), indicating an active promotion of interdependence between the two countries.

113　Dáithí O'Ceallaigh, Paul Gillespie (eds), *Britain and Europe: the endgame – an Irish perspective* (Dublin, 2015), chapter 11.

114　Department of Foreign Affairs and Trade, *Statement of strategy 2017–2020* (Dublin, 2017), 4; Tony Connelly, *Brexit and Ireland* (2nd ed., London, 2018), 70, 82, 343. Ireland has also declared a willingness to make the 'common travel area' a purely bilateral agreement with Britain in Irish law for the first time. https://www.diplomat. ie/tanaiste-signs-agreement-with-uk-on-common-travel-area/.

115　Pat Cox, *Europe after Brexit* (Lausanne, 2016), 17–18.

116　John Bradley, 'The Irish-Northern Irish economic relationship, the Belfast Agreement, UK devolution and the EU', *Ethnopolitics*, vol. 17, no. 3 (2018), 263–75; Katy Hayward, M.C. Murphy, 'The EU's influence in the peace process and agreement in Northern Ireland in the light of Brexit', *Ethnopolitics*, vol. 17, no. 3 (2018), 276–91.

117　Department of Foreign Affairs and Trade, *The Global Island*, 13, 27 (quotes); B. Tonra, M. Kennedy, J. Doyle, N. Dorr (eds), *Irish foreign policy* (Dublin, 2012), 115.

118　John Bradley, 'The Irish-Northern Irish economic relationship, the Belfast Agreement, UK devolution and the EU', *Ethnopolitics*, vol. 17, no. 3 (2018), 268–72.

119　Her Majesty's Government, *Northern Ireland and Ireland: position paper* (London, 2016), 13.

120　D. Hearne, A. De Ruyter, H. Davies, 'The Commonwealth', *Contemporary Social Science*, vol. 14, no. 2 (2019), 342; Brendan Simms, *Britain's Europe* (London, 2016), 148, 177, 184, 186.

121　Jennifer Todd, 'From identity politics to identity change: exogenous shocks, constitutional moments and the impact of Brexit on the island of Ireland', *Irish studies in international affairs*, vol. 28 (2017), 57–72.

122　Although *The Irish Times* was always the Dublin journal with the highest percentage of foreign correspondents, most of these writers actually came from Northern Ireland. Terence Brown, *The Irish Times: 150 years of influence* (London, 2015).

123　J.W. O'Hagan (ed.), *The economy of Ireland: policy and performance of a European region* (8th ed., Dublin, 2000), 43–4.

124　John O'Hagan, 'The Irish economy 1973–2016', in T. Bartlett (ed.), *Cambridge history of Ireland* (Cambridge, 2017), 508, 512–15, 522. The principal employers in Ireland were in construction, retail, accommodation services, public administration, health, education, transport and financial services.

125　Institute of International and European Affairs, *Emerging voices: a future of Europe anthology* (Dublin, 2019), 95–112. In recent times, it has been estimated that about one-seventh of Ireland's workforce were born outside the country while 70 per cent of the 250,000 Irish who emigrated after 2008 were in their twenties.

126　Department of Foreign Affairs and Trade, *The Global Island*, 13.

127 In 2011, the United Kingdom had 260 posts abroad in 145 countries while Ireland had 80 posts abroad, which attempted to represent Ireland in 178 countries. R. Wong, C. Hill (eds), *National and European foreign policies* (London, 2011), 85; Department of Foreign Affairs and Trade, *The Global Island*.

128 B. Tonra, M. Kennedy, J. Doyle, N. Dorr (eds), *Irish foreign policy* (Dublin, 2012), 221–2, 238–40. Since 1981 Ireland has been involved in the 'Vienna Group of Ten' for the non-proliferation of nuclear weapons and since 1998 in a 'New Agenda Coalition' for the same purpose.

129 Sarah Lain, *The future of post-Brexit Germany-UK security relations* (London, 2016); Malcolm Chalmers, *UK foreign and security relations after Brexit* (London, 2017).

130 Brendan Simms, *Britain's Europe* (London, 2016), 215–18.

131 Richard Higgott, Elke Boers, 'Rhythms of soft power influence and transatlantic higher education relations', *European Foreign Affairs Review*, vol. 24 (2019), 119–36, especially pp. 126, 135. The next two most influential powers in terms of higher education have been rated as America and France.

132 Imelda Maher, *The common travel area: more than just travel* (Royal Irish Academy and British Academy, 2018), 3–4; Royal Irish Academy, *Research and higher education on the island of Ireland after Brexit* (Dublin, 2017).

133 Dublin City University, *Brexit report* (Dublin, 2018), 42–3.

134 See, for instance, the list of speakers at the IIEA between 2010 and 2015 in D. O Ceallaigh, P. Gillespie (eds), *Britain and Europe: an endgame* (Dublin, 2015), appendix.

135 Tony Connelly, *Brexit and Ireland* (2nd ed., London, 2018), quoted p. 343.

136 David O'Sullivan, 'Foreword', *European Foreign Affairs Review*, vol. 24 (special issue 2019), 1.

137 Elizabeth McKillen, 'Ethnicity, class and Wilsonian internationalism reconsidered: the Mexican-American and Irish-American left and US foreign relations 1914-1922', *Diplomatic history*, vol. 25 (fall 2001), 553–87.

138 Tim Marshall, *Prisoners of geography* (London, 2015).

139 John Walsh, *The globalist* (London, 2019).

140 D.H. Akenson, *The United States and Ireland* (Harvard, 1973), 4.

141 Government of Ireland, *Global Ireland: Ireland's global footprint to 2025* (Dublin, 2018), 5.

142 Department of Foreign Affairs and Trade, *Global Irish: Ireland's diaspora policy* (Dublin, 2015), 43–4.

143 Government of Ireland, *Global Ireland: Ireland's global footprint to 2025* (Dublin, 2018), 4.

144 Institute of International and European Affairs, *Emerging voices: a future of Europe anthology* (Dublin, 2019), 51–63.

145 Daniel Keohane, *EU military cooperation and national defence* (Washington, 2018).

146 Thierry Tardy, Gustav Lindstrom (eds), *The EU and NATO: the essential partners* (Luxembourg, 2019).

147 F.A. Von Geusau, *Cultural diplomacy: waging war by other means?* (Tilburg, 2009).

148 Ben Tonra, 'Security, defence and neutrality: the Irish dilemma', in B. Tonra, M. Kennedy, J. Doyle, N. Dorr (eds) *Irish foreign policy* (Dublin, 2012).

149 R.P. Barton, *Modern diplomacy* (London, 2013), 3.

150 Frans Alting von Geusau, *Neither justice nor order: reflections on the state of the law of nations* (Tilburg, 2014).

151 Joseph Nye, 'Soft power', *Foreign policy*, no. 80 (autumn 1990); Joseph Nye, Robert Keohane, 'Transnational relations and world politics', *International organization*, vol. 25, no. 3 (1971), 721–48.

152 Joseph Nye, 'The information revolution and soft power', *Current history*, vol. 113 (2014), 19–22.

153 Brian Cowen, 'Annual John Hume lecture: Clarity, Courage, Change', in Joe Mulholland (ed.), *Why not? Building a better Ireland* (Dublin, 2003), 25–32; Brian Cowen, 'New world order?', *Irish studies in international affairs*, vol. 15 (2004), 3–12; Mark Callanan (ed.), *Foundations of an ever closer union*, 239 (quoting Irish foreign minister Brian Cowen).

Select Bibliography

Manuscript Sources and Government Publications

Dáil Éireann, *Miontuaric an chead Dala 1919–1921* (1922, 2nd ed., Dublin, 1994).

Dáil Éireann, *Debate on the treaty between Great Britain and Ireland* (Dublin, 1922).

Dáil Éireann, *Select constitutions of the world, prepared for presentation to Dáil Éireann* (Dublin, 1922).

Department of Foreign Affairs, *Challenges and opportunities abroad: white paper on foreign policy* (Dublin, 1996).

Department of Foreign Affairs and Trade, *The global island: Ireland's foreign policy for a changing world* (Dublin, 2015).

Department of Foreign Affairs and Trade, *Global Irish: Ireland's diaspora policy* (Dublin, 2015).

Department of Foreign Affairs and Trade, *A focused policy review of Ireland's bilateral diplomatic mission networks in the United States of America* (Dublin, 2017).

Department of Foreign Affairs and Trade, *Celebrating 60 years: Ireland–Japan diplomatic relations* (Dublin, 2017).

Department of Foreign Affairs and Trade, *Ireland in Germany: a wider and deeper footprint* (Berlin, 2018).

Éamon de Valera papers (University College Dublin Archives).

Government of Ireland, *Global Ireland: Ireland's global footprint to 2025* (Dublin, 2018).

Government of Ireland, *Global Ireland: Ireland's strategy for the US and Canada 2019–2025* (Dublin, 2019).

Kennedy, Michael et al. (eds), *Documents on Irish Foreign Policy*, vols 1–10 (1919–57).

Lloyd George papers (Parliamentary Archives, Westminster).

Art Ó Briain papers (National Library of Ireland).

Tierney, Mark (ed.), 'Calendar of Irlande, Collection Europe, 1918–1940 in the Archives Diplomatiques, Paris', *Collectanea Hibernica*, 21–6 (1979–83).

Winston Churchill papers (Churchill Archives, Cambridge).

Online Resources

Bureau of Military History, http://www.militaryarchives.ie
Dáil Éireann Debates, https://www.oireachtas.ie/en/debates/find/
Department of Foreign Affairs, https://www.dfa.ie/
Defence Forces Review, https://www.military.ie/en/public-information/publications/
defence-forces-review/
Dictionary of Irish Biography, https://dib.cambridge.org/
Documents on Irish Foreign Policy, https://www.difp.ie/
Edward M. Kennedy Oral History Project https://www.emkinstitute.org/resources/
oral-history-miller-center
European Council on Foreign Relations, https://www.ecfr.eu/
European Political Strategy Centre, https://ec.europa.eu/epsc/home_en
European Union Institute of Security Studies, https://www.iss.europa.eu/
Institute of International and European Affairs, https://www.iiea.com/
Journal of the Statistical and Social Inquiry Society of Ireland, http://ssisi.ie/
journals.php
Northern Ireland Peace Agreement, https://peacemaker.un.org/uk-ireland-good-
friday98
World Trade Organisation, https://www.wto.org

Newspapers and Magazines

Foreign Affairs
Irish Examiner
Irish Independent
The Irish Times
Nationality
The World Today
Young Ireland

Books, Articles and Pamphlets

Aan de Wiel, Jerome, *The Irish factor 1899–1919: Ireland's strategic and diplomatic importance for foreign powers* (Dublin, 2008).

Ahtisaari, Martti, 'The role of the European Union in conflict resolution', *Irish studies in international affairs*, vol. 28 (2017), 195–9.

Akenson, D.H., *The United States and Ireland: vol. 20 of American foreign policy library* (Harvard, 1973).

Appleby, J.C., O'Dowd, Mary, 'The Irish Admiralty: its organisation and development c. 1570–1640', *Irish historical studies*, vol. 24 no. 95 (May 1985), 299–326.

Barry, Frank, Ó Fathartaigh, Mícheál, 'The industrial development authority 1949–59', *I.I.I.S. discussion paper no. 407* (Sep. 2012).

—, 'Ireland and the changing global FDI landscape', *Administration*, vol.69, no.3 (2019).

Barry, Gearoid, *The disarmament of hatred: Marc Sangnier, French Catholicism and the legacy of the First World War 1914–1945* (London, 2012).

Beary, Michael, 'Peace dividends and statecraft instruments: United States and EU economic intervention facilitating peace in Northern Ireland', *Defence Forces review* (2010).

Bonney, Norman, *Monarchy, religion and the state: civil religion in the United Kingdom, Canada, Australia and the commonwealth* (Manchester, 2013).

Boyd, Ernest, 'Ireland: resurgent and insurgent', *Foreign Affairs*, vol. 1 no. 15 (1922).

Bradley, John, 'The Irish–Northern Irish economic relationship, the Belfast Agreement, UK devolution and the EU', *Ethnopolitics*, vol. 17 no. 3 (2018).

Brown, Terence, *The Irish Times: 150 years of influence* (London, 2015).

Brown, Tony, *The first presidency: Ireland's presidency of the council* (Dublin, 2013).

Browne, E.M., 'Ireland in the EEC', *The world today*, vol. 31 no. 10 (Oct. 1975), 424–32.

Butler, H.D., *The Irish Free State: an economic survey* (Washington D.C., 1928).

Callanan, Mark (ed.), *Foundations of an ever closer union: an Irish perspective on the fifty years since the Treaty of Rome* (Dublin, 2007).

Carroll, Francis, 'Official visits: President Cosgrave comes to Ottawa', *Canadian journal of Irish studies*, vol. 36 no. 2 (fall 2010), 174–90.

Casement, Roger, *Ireland, Germany and the freedom of the seas* (Philadelphia, 1914).

Castles, S., Miller, M.J., *The age of migration* (4th edition, London, 2009).

Chambers, Anne, *T.K. Whitaker* (Dublin, 2014).

Chambers, Ciara, *Ireland in the newsreels* (Dublin, 2012).

Checkel, J.T., 'International institutions and socialisation in Europe', *International organization*, vol. 59 no. 4 (autumn 2005), 801–26.

Childers, Erskine, *The framework of home rule* (London, 1911).

Clark, Ian, *Globalization and international relations theory* (Oxford, 1999).

Cohen, B.J., 'Balance of payments financing: evolution of a regime', *International organization*, vol. 36 no. 2 (spring 1982), 457–78.

Collier, Paul, *Wars, guns and votes: democracy in dangerous places* (London, 2005).

Collins, Gerard, 'The European Union and the peace process in Northern Ireland', *Études Irlandaises*, vol. 22 no. 2 (1997), 149–59.

Connolly, Sean, *Contested island: Ireland 1460–1630* (Oxford, 2007).

— (ed.), *Belfast 400* (Liverpool, 2012).

Conroy, Jane (ed.), *Franco-Irish connections: essays, memoirs and poems in honour of Pierre Joannon* (Dublin, 2009).

Considine, Mairéad, Dukelow, Fiona, *Irish social policy* (Dublin, 2009).

Cooney, John, McGarry, Tony, *Ireland and Europe in times of world change: Humbert International School chronicle and directory 1987–2002* (Ballina, 2002).

Corcoran, D.P., *Freedom to achieve freedom* (Dublin, 2013).

Cottey, Andrew, *Security in twenty-first century Europe* (2007, 2nd ed., London, 2013).

Cowen, Brian, 'Challenges to liberal internationalism', *Irish studies in international affairs*, vol. 12 (2001), 1–5.

Cox, Pat, *From economic crisis to political crisis in the European Union?* (Lausanne, 2015).

—, *Europe after Brexit* (Lausanne, 2016).

Craig, Gordon, 'The United States and the European balance', *Foreign affairs*, vol. 55 no. 1 (Oct. 1976), 187–98.

Cronin, Sean, *Washington's Irish policy 1916–1986* (Dublin, 1986).

Crooks, Peter (ed.), *Government, war and society in medieval Ireland* (Dublin, 2008).

Crotty, William, Schmitt, D.E. (eds), *Ireland on the world stage* (London, 2002).

Crowley, J., O'Driscoll, D., Murphy, M. (eds), *Atlas of the Irish revolution* (Cork, 2017).

D'Arcy, Michael, Dickson, Tim (eds), *Border crossings: developing Ireland's island economy* (Dublin, 1995).

DeCourcy Ireland, J., Sheehy, D.C. (eds), *Atlantic visions* (Dún Laoghaire, 1989).

Delaney, Eamon, *An accidental diplomat* (Dublin, 2001).

Dempsey, G.T., *From the embassy: a US foreign policy primer* (Dublin, 2004).

De Valera, Éamon (Moynihan, Maurice ed.), *Speeches and statements of Éamon de Valera 1917–1973* (Dublin, 1980).

Devine, Karen, 'The ethos and elements of Irish neutrality', in I.S. Novakovic, *Neutrality in the 21st century: lessons for Serbia* (Belgrade, 2013), 67–78.

—, 'Irish political parties' attitudes towards neutrality and the evolution of the EU's foreign, security and defence policies', *Irish political studies*, vol. 24 no. 4 (2009).

Devlin, J., Clarke, H. B. (eds), *European encounters* (Dublin, 2003).

Devoy, Luke, 'The British response to American interest in Northern Ireland 1976–1979', *Irish studies in international affairs*, vol. 25 (2014), 221–38.

Dickson, D., Pyz, J., Shepard, C. (eds), *Irish classrooms and British Empire* (Dublin, 2012).

Dickson, David, *Dublin* (London, 2014).

Donaghy, Greg, Carroll, M.K. (eds), *In the national interest: Canadian foreign policy, the department of foreign affairs and international trade 1909–2009* (Calgary, 2011).

Donnelly, James, *The great Irish potato famine* (Gloucester, 2002).

Dooge, J., Barrington, R. (eds), *A vital national interest: Ireland in Europe 1973–1998* (Dublin, 1999).

Doorley, Michael, *Irish-American diaspora nationalism: the Friends of Irish Freedom, 1916-1935* (Dublin, 2005).

Dorr, Noel, *Sunningdale: the search for peace in Northern Ireland* (Dublin, 2017).

—, 'A year in the life: behind the scenes in Irish foreign affairs in 1972', *Irish studies in international affairs*, vol. 28 (2017).

Downey, D.M., MacLennan, J.C. (eds), *Spanish–Irish relations through the ages* (Dublin, 2008).

Doyle, David, *Irish Americans, native rights and national empires* (Dublin, 1976).

—, Edwards, O.D. (eds), *America and Ireland 1776–1976: the American identity and the Irish connection* (Connecticut, 1980).

Doyle, John, 'Defence, security and the Irish EU presidency', *Defence Forces review* (2013), 7–14.

Drea, Eoin, 'The Bank of England, Montagu Norman and the internationalisation of Anglo-Irish monetary relations 1922–1943', *Financial history review*, vol. 21 no. 1 (2013), 59–76.

—, 'The role of T.A. Smiddy in Fianna Fáil economic policy-making 1932–45', *Irish studies review*, vol. 24 no. 2 (2016), 175–90.

Drudy, P.J. (ed.), *Ireland and Britain since 1922* (Cambridge, 1986).

Duff, J.B., 'The Versailles Treaty and the Irish Americans', *Journal of American history*, vol. 55 (Dec. 1968), 582–98.

Duggan, John, *A history of the Irish army* (Dublin, 1991).

Dumbrell, John, 'The United States and the Northern Irish conflict 1969–94: from indifference to intervention', *Irish studies in international affairs*, vol. 6 (1995), 107–25.

Dunn, Seamus, Fraser, T.G. (eds), *Europe and ethnicity: World War I and contemporary ethnic conflict* (London, 1996).

Duverger, Maurice, *Political parties: their organisation and activity in the modern state, with a foreword by Denis Brogan* (2nd ed. English language translation, London, 1959).

Edel, Doris, *The Celtic West and Europe* (Dublin, 2001).

Edwards, O.D. (ed.), *Conor Cruise O'Brien introduces Ireland* (London, 1969).

Edwards, R.D. (ed.), *Ireland and the Italian Risorgimento* (Dublin, 1960).

Elliott, Marianne, *Partners in revolution: the United Irishmen and France* (Yale, 1982).

Evans, Bryce, 'A semi-state archipelago without ships: Sean Lemass, economic policy and the absence of an Irish mercantile marine', *UCD working papers in history and policy no. 6* (2012).

—, Kelly, Stephen (eds), *Frank Aiken: nationalist and internationalist* (Dublin, 2014).

Fanning, Ronan, 'Playing it cool: the response of the British and Irish governments to the crisis in Northern Ireland 1968–9', *Irish studies in international affairs*, vol. 12 (2001), 57–85.

—, *A will to power: Éamon de Valera* (London, 2015).

Farren, Sean (ed.), *John Hume in his own words* (Dublin, 2018).

Farren, Sean, Haughey, Denis (eds), *John Hume: Irish peacemaker* (Dublin, 2015).

Ferriter, Diarmaid, *The transformation of Ireland* (London, 2005).

FitzGerald, Garret, *Towards a new Ireland* (Dublin, 1972).

—, *All in a life* (Dublin, 1991).

—, *Ireland in the world: further reflections* (Dublin, 2005).

—, 'The 1974–5 threat of a British withdrawal from Northern Ireland', *Irish studies in international affairs*, vol. 17 (2006), 141–50.

Fitzpatrick, Michael, *John Hume in America* (Dublin, 2017).

Flanagan, Charles, 'Identity and values in Irish foreign policy', *Irish studies in international affairs*, vol. 27 no. 1 (2016), 1–5.

Franz, Otmar (ed.), *European currency in the making* (Sindelfingen, 1988).

Fraser, Ursula, Harvey, Colin (eds), *Sanctuary in Ireland: perspectives on asylum law and policy* (Dublin, 2003).

Funchion, Michael (ed.), *Irish American voluntary organisations* (Connecticut, 1983).

Geiger, Till, 'Why Ireland needed the Marshall Plan but did not want it: Ireland, the sterling area and the European Recovery Program 1947–8', *Irish studies in international affairs*, vol. 11 (2000), 193–215.

—, Kennedy, Michael (eds), *Ireland, Europe and the Marshall Plan* (Dublin, 2004).

German, Tracey, 'Re-visioning war and the state in the twenty-first century', *International affairs*, vol. 95 no. 4 (2019), 759–63.

Giddens, Anthony, *Europe in the global age* (London, 2007).

Gillespie, Paul, 'Optimism of the intellect, pessimism of the will: Ireland, Europe and 1989', *Irish studies in international affairs*, vol. 11 (2000), 163–78.

Gillespie, Raymond, *Seventeenth-century Ireland* (Dublin, 2006).

Girvin, Brian, *The emergency: neutral Ireland 1939–45* (London, 2006).

—, Murphy, Gary, (eds), *The Lemass era* (Dublin, 2005).

Godson, Dean, *Himself alone: David Trimble and the ordeal of unionism* (London, 2004).

Griffith, Arthur, *The resurrection of Hungary: a parallel for Ireland with appendices on Pitt's Policy and Sinn Féin* (3rd ed., Dublin, 1918).

—, *Arguments for the treaty* (Dublin, 1922).

Groutel, Anne, 'American Janus-faced economic diplomacy towards Ireland in the mid-1950s', *Irish economic and social history*, vol. 43 no. 1 (2016), 3–20.

Guelke, Adrian, 'The American connection to the Northern Ireland conflict', *Irish studies in international affairs*, vol. 1 no. 4 (1984), 27–39.

Gwynn, Stephen, 'Ireland: one and divisible', *Foreign affairs*, vol. 3 (1924), 183–98.

—, 'Ireland since the treaty', *Foreign affairs*, vol. 12 (1934).

—, 'Ireland and the War', *Foreign affairs*, vol. 18 (1940), 305–13.

Harkness, David, *The restless dominion: the Irish Free State and the British Commonwealth of Nations 1921–1931* (London, 1969).

Harland-Jacobs, Jessica, *Builders of Empire: freemasons and British imperialism 1717–1927* (North Carolina, 2007).

Harman, Justin, Ahern, Dermot, 'Russia's global perspective: defining a new relationship with Europe and America', *Irish studies in international affairs*, vol. 19 (2008), 3–8.

Hart, Michael, *Hubris: the troubling science, economics and politics of climate change* (Ottawa, 2015).

Hayward, Katy, Murphy, M.C., 'The EU's influence in the peace process and agreement in Northern Ireland in the light of Brexit', *Ethnopolitics*, vol. 17 no. 3 (2018), 276–91.

Healy, Róisín, *Poland in the Irish nationalist imagination 1772–1922: anti-colonialism within Europe* (London, 2017).

Hearns, Mark, 'From Vancouver to Vladivostok with Valentia in between: Ireland's chairmanship of the OSCE', *Defence Forces review* (2011), 123–32.

Herring, G.C., *From colony to superpower: US foreign relations since 1776* (Oxford, 2008).

Higgins, Michael D., *Causes for concern* (Dublin, 2007).

—, *Renewing the Republic* (Dublin, 2011).

Higgott, Richard, Boers, Elke, 'Rhythms of soft power influence and transatlantic higher education relations', *European foreign affairs review*, vol. 24 (2019), 119–36.

Hinsley, F.H., *Power and the pursuit of peace: theory and practice in the history of relations between states* (Cambridge, 1963).

Hobsbawm, Eric, *Globalisation, democracy and terrorism* (London, 2007).

Holmes, Michael, Rees, Nicholas, Whelan, Bernadette (eds), *The poor relation: Irish foreign policy and the Third World* (Blackrock, 1993).

Hong, Fan, Gottwald, Jorn-Carsten (eds), *The Irish Asia strategy and its China relations 1999–2009* (Amsterdam, 2010).

Honohan, Patrick, 'Europe and the international monetary system', *Irish studies in international affairs*, vol. 1 no. 4 (1984), 49–62.

—, *Currency, credit and crisis: central banking in Ireland and Europe* (Cambridge, 2019).

Horgan, J.J., 'Ireland and world contact', *Studies*, vol. 8 no. 29 (Mar. 1919), 35–45.

Horgan, John, *Mary Robinson: an independent voice* (Dublin, 1997).

House, Edward, 'The running sands', *Foreign Affairs*, vol. 1 no. 15 (1922).

Hume, John, 'The Irish question: a British problem', *Foreign Affairs*, vol. 58 (1979).

Hunt, Michael, *The American ascendancy* (North Carolina, 2007).

Hussey, Gemma, *Ireland today: anatomy of a nation* (Dublin, 1993).

Institute of Bankers in Ireland, *Economic planning and the banking system* (Dublin, 1968).

Institute of International and European Affairs, *Emerging voices: a future of Europe anthology* (Dublin, 2019).

Irish Banks Standing Committee, *The control of banking in the Republic of Ireland* (Dublin, 1984).

Kapstein, E.B., 'Between power and purpose: central bankers and the politics of regulatory convergence', *International organization*, vol. 46 no. 1 (winter 1992), 265–87.

Kavanagh, Martha, 'The Irish Free State and collective security 1930–1936', *Irish studies in international affairs*, vol. 15 (2004), 103–22.

Keane, Elizabeth, 'Coming out of the cave: the first inter-party government, the Council of Europe and NATO', *Irish studies in international affairs*, vol. 15 (2004).

Keatinge, Patrick, *The formulation of Irish foreign policy* (Dublin, 1973).

—, *A singular stance: Irish neutrality in the 1980s* (Dublin, 1984).

—, *European security: Ireland's choices* (Dublin, 1996).

Kelly, Stephen, 'A policy of futility: Éamon de Valera's anti-partition campaign 1948–51', *Études Irlandaises*, vol. 36 no. 2 (2012), 1–13.

—, 'The totality of relationships: the Haughey–Thatcher relationship and the Anglo-Irish Summit, 8 December 1980', *Éire-Ireland*, vol. 51 nos 3–4 (fall/winter 2016).

Kennan, George, 'The United States and the Soviet Union 1917–1976', *Foreign affairs*, vol. 54 no. 4 (July 1976), 670–90.

Kennedy, Edward, 'The Persian Gulf: arms race or arms control?', *Foreign affairs*, vol. 54 no. 1 (Oct. 1975), 14–35.

Kennedy, K.A., Giblin, T., McHugh, D., *The economic development of Ireland in the twentieth century* (London, 1988).

Kennedy, Michael, *Ireland and the League of Nations 1919–1946* (Dublin, 1996).

—, *Division and consensus: the politics of cross-border relations in Ireland 1925–1969* (Dublin, 2000).

—, 'Joseph Walshe, Éamon de Valera and the execution of Irish foreign policy 1932–8', *Irish studies in international affairs*, vol. 14 (2003).

—, O'Halpin, Eunan, *Ireland and the Council of Europe* (Strasbourg, 2000).

—, Skelly, J. (eds), *Irish foreign policy 1919–1966* (Dublin, 2000).

—, McMahon, Deirdre (eds), *Obligations and responsibilities: Ireland and the United Nations 1955–2005* (Dublin, 2005).

Kennedy, Paul, *The rise and fall of the great powers: economic change and military conflict from 1500 to 2000* (London, 1988).

Kenny, Kevin (ed.), *Ireland and the British Empire* (Oxford, 2004).

King, Russell (ed.), *Ireland, Europe and the single market* (Dublin, 1992).

Keogh, Dermot, *The Vatican, the bishops and Irish politics 1919–1939* (Cambridge, 1986).

Keogh, Dermot, *Ireland and Europe* (2nd ed., Dublin, 1990).

— (ed.), *Ireland: the challenge of European integration* (Dublin, 1991).

—, O'Driscoll, Mervyn (eds), *Ireland in World War Two: neutrality and survival* (Cork, 2004).

—, O'Shea, F., Quinlan, C. (eds), *Ireland in the 1950s: the lost decade* (Cork, 2001).

Keogh, Niall, *Con Cremin: Ireland's wartime diplomat* (Cork, 2006).

Keohane, Daniel, *EU military cooperation and national defence* (Washington, 2018).

Keohane, Robert, Nye, Joseph, 'Transnational relations and world politics', *International organization*, vol. 25 no. 3 (1971), 721–48.

Keown, Gerard, 'Sean Lester: journalist, revolutionary, diplomat, statesman', *Irish studies in international affairs*, vol. 23 (2012), 143–54.

—, *First of the small nations: the beginnings of Irish foreign policy in the interwar years 1919–1932* (Oxford, 2015).

Laffan, Brigid, *The finances of the European Union* (London, 1997).

Laing, Victor, Kennedy, Michael (eds), *The Irish Defence Forces 1940–1949: the chief of staff reports* (Dublin, 2011).

Lake, David, 'The state and American trade strategy in the pre-hegemonic era', *International organization*, vol. 42 no. 1 (winter 1988).

Lambert, J.R., 'Enlargement of the common market: Denmark, Norway and Ireland', *The world today*, vol. 18 no. 8 (Aug. 1962), 350–60.

Larres, Klaus (ed.), *Uneasy allies: British–German relations and European integration since 1945* (Oxford, 2000).

Legrain, Philippe, *Open World: the truth about globalisation* (London, 2002).

Lenehan, Fergal, *Stereotypes, ideology and foreign correspondents: German media representations of Ireland 1946–2010* (London, 2016).

Lennon, Colm, *Sixteenth-century Ireland* (Dublin 1994).

Leonard, Mark, Pisani-Ferry, J., Ribokova, E., Sharipo, J., Wolff, G., 'Security Europe's economic sovereignty', *Survival*, vol. 61 no. 5 (2019), 75–98.

Lomborg, Bjorn, *The sceptical environmentalist: measuring the real state of the world* (Cambridge, 2001).

Lowry, Donal, 'The captive dominion: imperial realities behind Irish diplomacy 1922–49', *Irish historical studies*, vol. 36 no. 142 (Nov. 2008).

Loyal, Stephen, *Understanding immigration in Ireland: state, capital and labour in a global age* (Manchester, 2011).

Lynch, John, 'The Anglo-Irish problem', *Foreign affairs*, vol. 50 no. 4 (Jul. 1972), 601–17.

Lyons, M.A., O'Connor, T., *Strangers to citizens: the Irish in Europe 1600–1800* (Dublin, 2008).

McBride, Ian, *Eighteenth-century Ireland* (Dublin, 2009).

MacBride, Sean, *That day's struggle: a memoir 1904–1951* (Dublin, 2005).

McCarthy, Mick, *International affairs at home: the story of the Irish Institute of International Affairs* (Dublin, 2006).

McCracken, Donal (ed.), *Ireland and South Africa in modern times* (Durban, 1996).

McCullagh, David, *De Valera: rule 1932–1975* (Dublin, 2018).

McGee, Owen (ed.), *Eugene Davis' Souvenirs of Irish footprints over Europe* (1889, 2nd ed., Dublin, 2006).

—, *Arthur Griffith* (Dublin, 2015).

MacGinty, Tom, *The Irish navy: golden jubilee of the Irish naval service* (Tralee, 1995).

McGowan, Padraig, *Money and banking in Ireland* (Dublin, 1990).

McIvor, Aidan, *A history of the Irish naval service* (Dublin, 2006).

MacKernan, Padraic, 'Ireland and European political cooperation', *Irish studies in international affairs*, vol. 1 no. 4 (1984), 15–26.

McKenzie, B.A., 'The European youth campaign in Ireland: neutrality, Americanisation and the Cold War 1950 to 1959', *Diplomatic history*, vol. 40 no. 3 (2016), 421–44.

McKenzie, Francine, 'Renegotiating a special relationship: the Commonwealth and Anglo-American economic discussions, September–December 1945', *The Journal of Imperial and Commonwealth history*, vol. 26 no. 3 (1998), 71–93.

McKillen, Elizabeth, 'Ethnicity, class and Wilsonian internationalism reconsidered: the Mexican–American and Irish–American left and US foreign relations 1914–1922', *Diplomatic history*, vol. 25 (fall 2001), 553–87.

McLaughlin, E., Fisher, N.F., 'State dissolution, sovereign debt and default: lessons from the UK and Ireland 1920–1938', *European historical economics working paper no. 61* (August 2014).

McLaughlin, Robert, *Irish Canadian conflict and the struggle for Irish independence* (Toronto, 2011).

McLoughlin, P.J., Meagher, Alison, 'The 1977 "Carter Initiative" on Northern Ireland', *Diplomatic history*, vol. 43 no. 4 (2019).

McMahon, Deirdre, *Republicans and imperialists: Anglo-Irish relations during the 1930s* (Yale, 1984).

McManus, Sean, *My American struggle for justice in Northern Ireland* (Cork, 2011).

McNamara, Kevin, *The MacBride principles* (Liverpool, 2009).

McNamara, Robert, 'Irish perspectives on the Vietnam war', *Irish studies in international affairs*, vol. 14 (2003).

Maher, D.J., *The tortuous path: the course of Ireland's entry into the EEC 1948–73* (Dublin, 1986).

Maier, Charles, 'The politics of productivity: the foundation of American international economic policy after World War II', *International organization*, vol. 31 no. 4 (autumn 1977), 607–33.

Mansergh, Martin, 'The background to the peace process', *Irish studies in international affairs*, vol. 6 (1995).

Mansergh, Nicholas, 'Ireland: the republic outside the commonwealth', *International affairs*, vol. 28 no. 3 (Jul. 1952), 277–91.

Maye, Brian, *The search for justice: Trócaire: a history* (Dublin, 2010).

Midleton, Lord, *Ireland: dupe or heroine* (London, 1932).

Millikan, M.F., 'An introductory essay: the global partnership', *International organization*, vol. 22 no. 1 (winter 1968), 1–15.

Mitchell, George, *Making peace: the inside story of the making of the Good Friday Agreement* (London, 1999).

Mondale, W.F., 'Beyond détente: towards international economic security', *Foreign Affairs*, vol. 53 no. 1 (Oct. 1974).

Moodie, Graeme, *The government of Great Britain* (London, 1964).

Morton, J.B., *The new Ireland* (London, 1938).

Mulreany, Michael (ed.), *Economic development fifty years on* (Dublin, 2009).

Murphy, Anna, 'Turn and face the change: Ireland and enlargement of the European Union', *Irish studies in international affairs*, vol. 10 (1999), 167–83.

Murphy, Martin, 'Sea power: does Europe still get it?', *Naval War College review*, vol. 72 no. 1 (winter 2019), 157–9.

Murphy, Ray, 'Europe's return to UN peacekeeping? Opportunities, challenges and ways ahead – Ireland', *International peacekeeping*, vol. 23 no. 5 (2016), 721–40.

Murray, Peter, *Facilitating the future? US aid, European integration and Irish industrial viability 1948–73* (Dublin, 2009).

Naurin, D., Wallace, H. (eds), *Unveiling the council of the EU: games governments play in Brussels* (London, 2010).

Nolan, Aengus, *Joseph Walshe: Irish foreign policy 1922–46* (Cork, 1996).

Nye, Joseph, 'Multinational corporations in world politics', *Foreign affairs*, vol. 53 no. 1 (Oct. 1974), 153–75.

O'Brien, C.C., *Writers and politics* (London, 1965).

—, *Neighbours* (London, 1980).

O'Brien, Dan, *Ireland, Europe and the world: writings on a new century* (Dublin, 2009).

O'Connell, J.J., 'The vulnerability of Ireland in war', *Studies*, vol. 27 no. 125 (Mar. 1938), 125–35.

—, 'Can Ireland remain neutral in war?', *Studies*, vol. 27 no. 108 (Dec. 1938), 647–55.

Ó Cróinín, Dáibhí, *A new history of Ireland*, vol. 1 (Oxford, 2005).

O'Donnell, Liz, Norrback, Ole, 'Small states and European security', *Irish studies in international affairs*, vol. 9 (1998), 1–9.

O'Driscoll, Mervyn, *Ireland, Germany and the Nazis: politics and diplomacy, 1919–1939* (Dublin, 2004).

—, Keogh, D., Aan de Wiel, J. (eds), *Ireland through European eyes: Western Europe, the EEC and Ireland 1945–1973* (Cork, 2013).

—, Walsh, Jamie, 'Ireland and the 1975 NPT Review Conference: norm building and small states', *Irish studies in international affairs*, vol. 25 (2014), 101–16.

O'Farrell, Patrick, *The Irish in Australia* (Kensington, 1987).

O'Hagan, J.W. (ed.), *The economy of Ireland: policy and performance of a European region* (8th ed., Dublin, 2000).

O'Halpin, Eunan, 'Irish–Allied security relations and the American note crisis: new evidence from British records', *Irish studies in international affairs*, vol. 11 (2000), 71–83.

—, *Defending Ireland* (Oxford, 1999).

O'Hearn, Denis, *The Atlantic economy: Britain, the US and Ireland* (Manchester, 2001).

O'Leary, Brendan, McGarry, John, *Explaining Northern Ireland* (Oxford, 1995).

O'Muircheartaigh, Fionan (ed.), *Ireland in the coming times* (Dublin, 1997)

O'Neill, Helen, 'The evolution of Ireland's foreign aid over the past twenty years', *Irish studies in international affairs*, vol. 24 (2013), 179–236.

Ó Nualláin, Labhrás, 'A comparison of the economic position and trend in Éire and Northern Ireland', *Journal of the statistical and social inquiry society of Ireland*, vol. XVII (1945–46).

—, 'A comparison of the external trade of the twenty-six and six counties of Ireland', *Studies*, vol. 41 no. 161 (Mar. 1952).

O'Rourke, Kevin, 'Burn everything British but their coal: the Anglo-Irish economic war of the 1930s', *Journal of economic history*, vol. 51 no. 2 (June 1991), 357–66.

—, Williamson, Jeffrey, *Globalisation and history* (London and New York, 1999).

—, *A short history of Brexit* (London, 2019).

O'Sullivan, Kevin, 'Biafra to Lomé: the evolution of Irish government policy on official development assistance 1969–1975', *Irish studies in international affairs*, vol. 18 (2007), 91–107.

—, 'Between internationalism and empire: Ireland, the like-minded group and the search for a new international order 1974–1982', *The international history review*, vol. 37 no. 5 (2015), 1083–101.

Phelan, Edward Joseph, 'Ireland and the International Labour Organisation', *Studies*, vol. 15 nos. 57–9 (1926).

Piers, L.N., 'Transatlantic relations in the Johnson and Nixon eras', *London school of economics research online* (2010).

Pinder, John, 'East–west trade and foreign policy: limits and potential', *Irish studies in international affairs*, vol. 1 no. 4 (1984), 41–8.

—, *The European Union* (Oxford, 2001).

Purchla, Jacek (ed.), *The historical metropolis: a hidden potential* (Cracow, 1996).

Quinn, Michael, *Irish–Soviet diplomatic and friendship relations 1917–1991* (Maynooth, 2016).

Ranger, Pierre, 'The world in Paris and Ireland too: the French diplomacy of Sinn Féin 1919–1921', *Études Irlandaises*, vol. 36 no. 2 (2011).

Richter, Michael, *Medieval Ireland* (2nd ed., Dublin, 2005).

Robinson, Mary, *Everybody matters: a memoir* (London, 2013).

Ruggie, J.G., 'International regimes, transactions and change', *International organization*, vol. 36 no. 2 (spring 1982), 379–415.

Sachs, Jeffrey, *To move the world: JFK's quest for peace* (London, 2013).

Sagarra, Eda, *Kevin O'Shiel: Tyrone nationalist and Irish state builder* (Dublin, 2013).

Sanders, Andrew, 'Landing rights in Dublin: relations between Ireland and the United States 1945–72', *Irish studies in international affairs*, vol. 28 (2017), 147–71.

Schifrin, Andre (ed.), *The cold war and the university: towards an intellectual history of the post-war years* (New York, 1997).

Senor, Dan, Singer, Saul, *Start-up nation: the story of Israel's economic miracle* (New York, 2009).

Servan-Schreiber, Jean-Jacques, *The American challenge* (London, 1968).

Shannon, Catherine B., *Arthur J. Balfour and Ireland 1874–1922* (Washington D.C., 1988).

Sharp, Paul, *Irish foreign policy and the European community* (Aldershot, 1990).

Silve, Benoit, 'From leadership to partnership: a new American security strategy for Europe', *Naval War College review*, vol. 50 no. 1 (winter 1997), 88–103.

Sim, David, *A union forever: the Irish question and US foreign relations in the Victorian age* (New York, 2013).

Simms, Brendan, *Britain's Europe: a thousand years of conflict and cooperation* (London, 2016).

Sinclair, David, *The pound* (London, 2000).

Skelly, J.M., 'Ireland, the department of external affairs and the United Nations 1946–55', *Irish studies in international affairs*, vol. 7 (1996).

Sloan, Geoffrey, 'Ireland and the geopolitics of Anglo-Irish relations', *Irish studies review*, vol. 15 no. 2 (2007), 163–79.

Smith, B., Ohlmeyer, J., Kelly, J., Bartlett, T. (eds), *Cambridge history of Ireland*, 4 vols (Cambridge, 2018).

Smith-Gordon, Lionel, *The place of banking in the national programme* (Dublin, 1921).

Smyllie, R.M., 'Un-neutral Neutral Éire', *Foreign affairs*, vol. 24 (1946), 317–26.

Smyth, Diarmuid, 'The recovery in the public finances in Ireland following the financial crisis', *Journal of the statistical and social inquiry society of Ireland* (vol. 156, 2017).

Sparks, Allister, *Beyond the miracle: inside the new South Africa* (London, 2003).

Stafford, David, *Roosevelt and Churchill: men of secrets* (London, 1999).

Stampnitzky, Lisa, *Disciplining terror: how experts invented 'terrorism'* (Cambridge, 2013).

Steiner, Zara, 'On writing international history', *International affairs, vol. 73 no. 3: globalisation and international relations* (Jul. 1997), 531–46.

Suri, Jeremi, *Power and protest: global revolution and the use of détente* (Harvard, 2003).

Sweeney, Paul (ed.), *Ireland's economic success: reasons and lessons* (Dublin, 2008).

Tardy, Thierry, Lindstrom, Gustav (eds) *The EU and NATO: the essential partners* (Luxembourg, 2019).

Tonra, B., Kennedy, M., Doyle, J., Dorr, N. (eds), *Irish foreign policy* (Dublin, 2012).

—, *Global citizen and European republic: Irish foreign policy in transition* (Manchester, 2006).

—, 'Irish diplomacy in a time of crisis and the evolution of a "European" diplomatic service', *Irish studies in international affairs*, vol. 28 (2017), 117–31.

Vaughan, W.E. (ed.), *A new history of Ireland*, vols 5 & 6 (Oxford, 1996).

Verdun, Amy, Chira, G.E., 'The Eastern partnership: the burial ground of enlargement hopes?', *Comparative European politics*, vol. 9 (2011), 448–66.

Vinen, Richard, *A history in fragments: Europe in the twentieth century* (London, 2000).

Von Geusau, Frans Alting, *Cultural diplomacy: waging war by other means?* (Tilburg, 2009).

—, *European unification into the twenty-first century* (Tilburg, 2012).

—, *Neither justice nor order: reflections on the state of the law of nations* (Tilburg, 2014).

Walas, Teresa (ed.), *Stereotypes and nations* (Cracow, 1995).

Walsh, Maurice, *G2 in defence of Ireland: Irish military intelligence 1918–45* (Cork, 2010).

Whelan, Bernadette, *US foreign policy and Ireland: from empire to independence 1913–1929* (Dublin, 2006).

—, *American government in Ireland, 1790–1913: a history of the US consular service* (Manchester, 2010).

Wightman, D.R., 'Europe and the dollar', *Irish studies in international affairs*, vol. 4 (1993).

Wilson, Andrew, *Irish America and the Ulster conflict 1968–95* (Belfast, 1995).

Wong, Rueben, Hill, Christopher (eds), *National and European foreign policies* (London, 2011).

Wylie, Paula, *Ireland and the Cold War* (Dublin, 2006).

Young, J.W., *Britain and European unity 1945–1999* (2nd ed., London, 2000).

Young, Peter, 'Defence and the new Irish state 1919–1939', *Irish sword*, vol. 19 (1995), 1–10.

Index